MW01194769

PSYCHOANALYTIC CONVERSATIONS

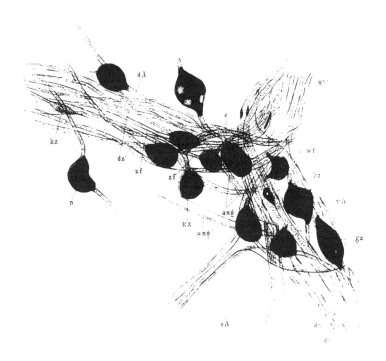

Was Freud's core identity that of a natural scientist? Freud's drawing of the spinal ganglia of *Ammocoetes (Petromyzon planeri)*, a primitive form of fish, for his 1878 monograph on the subject is adduced in support of this thesis by Frank J. Sulloway during his conversation with Peter L. Rudnytsky.

PSYCHOANALYTIC CONVERSATIONS

Interviews with Clinicians,
Commentators, and Critics

Peter L. Rudnytsky

THE ANALYTIC PRESS

2000   Hillsdale, NJ   London

Published by The Analytic Press, Inc.
Editorial Offices: 101 West Street, Hillsdale, NJ 07642

Library of Congress Cataloging-in-Publication Data

Rudnytsky, Peter L.
    Psychoanalytic conversations : interviews with clinicians, commentators, and critics / Peter L. Rudnytsky.
        p. ; cm.
    Includes index.
    ISBN 0-88163-328-3
    1. Psychoanalytic interpretation—Case studies.   2. Psychoanalysts—Interviews.   3. Psychoanalysts—Psychology.   I. Title.
    [DNLM: 1. Psychoanalytic Therapy—Interview.   2. Psychoanalytic Theory—Interview.
    WM 460.6 R916p 2000]
    RC506 .R835 2000
    616.89'17—dc21   00-063985

Printed in the United States of America
10 9 8 7 6 5 4 3 2 1

To Peter Greenleaf

"Each man I meet is my superior in some way. In that I learn from him."

—Emerson

Biographical Notes

The late MARY SALTER AINSWORTH taught psychology at The Johns Hopkins University and the University of Virginia. She was the author of *Infancy in Uganda* (1967) and *Patterns of Attachment* (1978), and contributed two chapters to the revised edition of John Bowlby's *Child Care and the Growth of Love* (1965). Professor Ainsworth introduced the concept of the secure base and developed the Strange Situation Procedure, an experimental method to test the strength and style of infants' attachments to their primary caregiver.

The late ENID BALINT was a training and supervising analyst in the British Psycho-Analytical Society. Her papers are collected in *Before I Was I* (1993).

JESSICA BENJAMIN is an analyst in private practice in New York City. She is on the faculties of the New York University Postdoctoral Program in Psychotherapy and Psychoanalysis and the New School of Social Research. She is the author of *The Bonds of Love* (1988), *Like Subjects, Love Objects* (1995), and *Shadow of the Other* (1998).

PETER D. KRAMER is associate clinical professor of psychiatry at Brown University and has a private practice in Providence. He is the author of *Moments of Engagement* (1989), *Listening to Prozac* (1993), and *Should You Leave?* (1997). Dr. Kramer writes a monthly column for *Psychiatric Times*.

PETER LOMAS worked in general medicine and psychiatry before training at the Institute of Psychoanalysis in London. He practices in Cambridge, England, and now prefers to call himself a psychotherapist. He is the author of *True and False Experience* (1973), *The Limits of Interpretation* (1987), *Cultivating Intuition* (1993), *Personal Disorder and the Family* (1998), and *The Psychotherapy of Everyday Life* (1993), a revised edition of *The Case for a Personal Psychotherapy* (1981).

STEPHEN A. MITCHELL is founding editor of *Psychoanalytic Dialogues*, a training and supervising analyst at the William Alanson White

Institute, and on the faculty of the New York University Postdoctoral Program in Psychotherapy and Psychoanalysis. He is the author of *Object Relations in Psychoanalytic Theory* (1983, with Jay Greenberg), *Relational Concepts in Psychoanalysis* (1988), *Hope and Dread in Psychoanalysis* (1993), *Psychoanalysis and Beyond* (1995, with Margaret J. Black), *Influence and Autonomy in Psychoanalysis* (1997), *Relationality: From Attachment to Intersubjectivity*.

The late CHARLES RYCROFT, a Fellow of the Royal College of Psychiatrists, practiced psychoanalysis in London. His books include *Imagination and Reality* (1968), *The Innocence of Dreams* (1979), *Psychoanalysis and Beyond* (1985), *Viewpoints* (1991), and *A Critical Dictionary of Psychoanalysis* (1968), a revised edition of which appeared in 1995.

ROY SCHAFER is a training and supervising analyst at the Columbia University Center for Psychoanalytic Training and Research and was the first Freud Memorial Professor at University College, London. His books include *Aspects of Internalization* (1968), *A New Language for Psychoanalysis* (1976), *The Analytic Attitude* (1983), *Retelling a Life* (1992), and *Tradition and Change in Psychoanalysis* (1997).

FRANK J. SULLOWAY is a research scholar at the Massachusetts Institute of Technology and a former MacArthur Fellow. He is the author of *Freud, Biologist of the Mind* (1979) and *Born to Rebel* (1996).

PETER J. SWALES, an erstwhile associate of the Rolling Stones, is an independent scholar living in New York City. He is the author of influential essays reappraising Freud's relationships with his wife, sister-in-law, and Wilhelm Fliess, tracing the sources of Freud's ideas, and identifying several of his early patients.

Contents

Preface

This book is a contribution to what has become a distinctive genre of psychoanalytic literature. Although several other interview collections have been published in recent years, my own project, which dates back to 1991, was conceived and undertaken independently of any of its predecessors.[1] As a scholar of psychoanalysis and the humanities keenly interested in the subjective roots of creativity, I hope this book justifies its existence both by the intimacy of its personal revelations and by the daring of its intellectual leaps.

Psychoanalysis is a discipline in which the evanescent medium of speech has always enjoyed a privileged position alongside more permanent written texts. Not only is psychoanalytic therapy notoriously a talking cure, but psychoanalytic education in large measure takes place orally. The interview, as the transcribed record of an oral encounter, is thus an ideal mode of psychoanalytic discourse.

I have sought to make these conversations psychoanalytic in form as well as in content. My interlocutors have reflected with exceptional honesty on the events and forces that shaped their lives (including, where appropriate, their experiences as patients in analysis) even as we explored issues of theory and practice. At their best, the exchanges take on a genuinely free-associative quality and capture unconscious processes on the wing. There are also moments of comedy sprinkled throughout. In all but two instances, I had not previously met the person to whom I was speaking, and perhaps my comparative anonymity facilitated the process of self-disclosure. The

---

1. The works known to me are Elaine Hoffman Baruch and Lucienne J. Serrano (1988), *Women Analyze Women in France, England, and the United States*. New York: New York University Press; Virginia Hunter (1994), *Psychoanalysts Talk*. New York: Guilford; Laurie W. Raymond and Susan Rosbrow-Reich, eds. (1997), *The Inward Eye: Psychoanalysts Reflect on Their Life and Work*. Hillsdale, NJ: The Analytic Press; and Anthony Molino, ed. (1997), *Freely Associated: Encounters in Psychoanalysis with Christopher Bollas, Joyce McDougall, Michael Eigen, Adam Phillips, Nina Coltart*. London: Free Association Books.

xi

sessions sometimes ended abruptly either because the tape ran out or because of time constraints. No attempt has been made to smooth over the resulting inconsistencies among the texts.

Inevitably, there is something aleatory in my choice of interview subjects. My peregrinations (both literal and figurative) have not taken me to the four corners of even the Anglo-American psychoanalytic world, but this microcosm nonetheless boasts Freud's plenty. I spoke to two members of the International Psychoanalytic Association, two people who had resigned from the same body, two analysts unaffiliated with the I.P.A., a nonanalytic psychiatrist, a developmental psychologist, and two of Freud's most stringent critics. As one who occupies a potential space neither inside nor outside psychoanalysis, I take pride in this diversity; for I am convinced that, if psychoanalysis is to survive in the new century, it can only be by expanding its horizons and learning from those who have taken it to task.

Although I have tried to place myself in the background when eliciting the autobiographical narratives of my subjects, I have not concealed my intellectual allegiance to the Independent tradition of object relations theory or my admiration for attachment theory. If I have allowed myself to press a line of questioning on occasion, I hope the resulting sparks shed light as well as heat. Stephen Mitchell, for example, accepted my analogy between drive theory and creationism, on one hand, and relational theory and evolution, on the other, but would not agree that science provides a means of choosing between these alternative epistemologies. Frank Sulloway, conversely, an ardent defender of science, disputed my insistence that Darwin's inability to recognize the word "mother" in a Scrabble-like word game provides evidence for the workings of unconscious repression. In many interviews, I invoke the name of John Bowlby as someone who sought to provide a scientific grounding for psychoanalysis while showing how this can be integrated with its hermeneutic dimension.

The interviews are arranged in chronological order. Those with Enid Balint and Mary Salter Ainsworth took place in 1991. My meetings with Peter Lomas and Charles Rycroft did not follow until 1997. I saw Peter Kramer, Stephen Mitchell, Frank Sulloway, and Roy Schafer in 1998, and Jessica Benjamin and Peter Swales in 1999. (I met Jessica Benjamin at a conference on "Psychoanalyses/Feminisms" I organized in 1994 at the University of Florida; Peter Swales has been a comrade-in-arms of long standing.) Mary Ainsworth, Enid Balint, and Charles Rycroft have, I regret to say, died since I had the privilege of meeting them. My dialogue with Frank Sulloway continued in writing through several rounds of give-and-take on both sides that added many pages to the original transcript. For the rest, the emendations proposed by my subjects have been quite modest, and all such requests have been silently honored. Comprehensive bibliographical documentation has been provided for the benefit of the interested reader.

Acknowledgments

My greatest obligation is to the ten people who graciously allowed me to probe their lives and work for the public record. The transcripts of our conversations were submitted for their approval and are published here with their permission, with the exception of that of Enid Balint, which appears by permission of her daughter, Mrs. Barbara Clark. An abridged version of my interview with Mary Salter Ainsworth was published in *The Psychoanalytic Study of the Child* (1997, 52:386–405); the other nine interviews appear for the first time in this book. The photographs were provided by the individuals themselves or by their families, except that of Mary Salter Ainsworth, which was taken by Robert S. Marvin; of Peter Kramer, which was taken by John Foraste of Brown University; and of Peter Swales, which was taken by Joe Masters of Haverfordwest. The cover photograph of Freud in the garden of 20 Maresfield Gardens taken in 1939 by Omri David Marlé was kindly provided by Michael Molnar of the Freud Museum in London. The frontispiece of Freud's 1878 drawing of the spinal ganglia of *Petromyzon* was furnished by Frank Sulloway.

Like all authors published by The Analytic Press, I owe an incalculable debt to Paul Stepansky, who preceded me as a Kanzer Fellow at Yale. Eleanor Starke Kobrin expertly shepherded the book from manuscript to print. My wife, Cheryl, has allowed me to bring these psychoanalytic interlopers into our home. My friendship with Peter Greenleaf, like that with Paul Stepansky, dates back to our graduate school days at Yale. I have not been able to locate the epigraph in Emerson. *Se non è ben trovato, almen' è vero.*

Enid Balint

The Broken Couch

Peter L. Rudnytsky: I thought I would begin by asking how you got interested in psychoanalysis, what sort of work you were doing before you trained, and how you came into it.

Enid Balint: I came into it by discovering that I understood nothing about human relationships during the war. I had young children, and I started a school for German refugees. I was also mainly concerned with running Citizens' Advice Bureaus. They were ad hoc bodies set up during the war to help people who had difficulties of one kind or another, which one would expect during a war, but they continued and are now quite valuable in peacetime. I was responsible for setting up and starting the Bureaus in the metropolitan London area. I had about 20 or 30 of them. I knew nothing about it. I had a degree or two but was totally untrained, and somebody had to do it.

PLR: What field were your degrees in?

EB: Economics and sociology. Well, public administration. I was at the London School of Economics. It was just a question of seeing what one could do. In working with people who had serious problems—relatives being killed, losing their limbs and their children, and one thing or another—I discovered that they were much more interested in talking to me about some trivial thing like their neighbor's unpleasant smell or their gas cooker was leaking, that kind of thing. I was all prepared to tell them about the War Damage Act. They didn't want to know.

PLR: You had also worked with German refugees?

EB: Yes. Before the war, I started a school for German refugee children.

PLR: How did you come to do that?

EB: Coincidence. My then husband, Robert Eichholz, had a German cousin who came to visit us about 1934. We had a house in Sussex. He told us what was going on in Germany. He was a very cultured man, and he said, please do something. He told us what was going to happen. We didn't know about it then. Of course, we were terribly shocked. So I, being very young and omnipotent, decided we must get a school. One school is a bit absurd, when you look back on the scale of the problem, but one had no conception of it then. So I got hold of a friend of mine whose father was influential. Between us, we raised enough money and bought a house. I was in my 20s.

PLR: You said you already had a family?

EB: I had two young children.

PLR: And when the war came along, you shifted to work with English people?

EB: Yes. I was also on committees of various kinds in London and Tumbridge Wells that got help for adult refugees as they arrived.

PLR: Was this part of any religious organization?

EB: No. It was just Jews getting together. They knew I was interested because I had started a school, so I was put on these committees. I also knew quite a lot of people in one way or another. But once the war started, that was over. I then had a lot of children—other people's children—living with me in my house. I was terribly active, as one is, and worried. And so I did go to London, which I guess was wrong, because I had children of my own and shouldn't have left. But I went to Oxford with the children to get them out of the house where we were, which was in a dangerous location. I started working in a Citizens' Advice Bureau there because I wanted to do something moderately useful. Then, when I went back to where we lived, which was not far from London, I started these Bureaus in London. It was there that I learned about my lack of knowledge about human relations and how people wanted to talk. At the end of the war, when I was working with the Family Welfare Association and these Citizens' Advice Bureaus, I met a marvelous man, Dr. Tommy Wilson. During the war he had been in the officer selection committees, where he worked with Bion and Rickman. He also worked in a hospital for officers with nervous difficulties.

PLR: Was he an analyst?

EB: They all were. Wilson was in training. Rickman was already an analyst. He became my analyst.

PLR: But you also had analysis with Winnicott?

EB: Yes. Rickman died after two years.

PLR: Then you switched over to Winnicott?

EB: Whom I stayed with for a number of years.

PLR: We can get to that later.

EB: Anyway, I was very lucky to meet Tommy Wilson and the others. He was starting the Tavistock Institute of Human Relations and asked if I would like to work with him, which was wonderful. I never had met anybody who talked the language of these analysts. I had read Freud during the war. My then husband had his books in the house—people like us would have Freud—so I started reading them.

PLR: What did your husband do?

EB: My first husband? I've had three husbands.

PLR: Yes, your first husband.

EB: He was a lawyer. His father, Alfred, was the head of what was then the Board of Education. He was a physician and a civil servant. He was a marvellous man and interested in human problems. He really did a lot of good. He was a very special man. My first husband was his eldest son. He also was a civil servant to begin with but switched over and became a lawyer and remained a lawyer till he died. We were together about 15 or 16 years before we separated. He died fairly soon after I married Michael.

PLR: And you had two children with your first husband?

EB: I had two daughters, yes. Seven grandchildren since.

PLR: Were those your only children?

EB: Yes. By the time I married Michael, he had a grown son. We wondered whether to have a child, but he didn't really want another one. It was probably unsuitable, so we didn't. Anyway, I started with this group of people and eventually began what I called the Family Discussion Bureau, which is now called the Institute of Marital

Studies. Before we started working with patients, or clients, or whatever you call them, I went around London and got to know what people thought about relationships. I went into schools, and different fire stations, and so on.

PLR: Did you interview them on their views?

EB: We had groups. It was all groups in those days. I worked with Bion to begin with.

PLR: Tell me about your work with Bion. He's legendary.

EB: He was a marvellous man and absolutely unique. He *thought* about things. Nothing was cut-and-dry. He also supervised me during my analytic training. Soon after I went to the Tavvy, I started analysis with Rickman. Then I was accepted and started my training in 1949–50. These were all marvellous people. Rickman was, too, but as he was my analyst, I've got a special feeling for him. He was quiet.

PLR: I know he was a Quaker. He did so much work during the war to bring people out.

EB: Absolutely. And before the war. Do you know the book he wrote with Geoffrey Gorer about the Russians?[1] It's a marvellous book. He went as a Quaker doctor to Russia. He wrote about the poverty of their lives and about women having babies. He was a doctor who went into people's homes.

PLR: The history of the British Society during this period is very turbulent. As I remember, Rickman stayed in the Klein group, or did he become an Independent?

EB: He was never a real Kleinian. He wasn't a member of the Klein group. I was analyzed by him, so I wasn't a member of the Klein group either.

PLR: So he was an Independent?

EB: We didn't call them that at that stage. There were Klein and B groups, and if you weren't Klein or B, you were just nothing. He wouldn't call himself a Kleinian. After I qualified, I went for supervision with Melanie Klein, who wanted me to have a Klein analysis because I couldn't be a Kleinian if I didn't. I had had Winnicott and Rickman, and that wasn't Klein.

---

1. Geoffrey Gorer & John Rickman (1962), *People of Great Russia: A Psychological Study.* New York: Norton.

PLR: Did you want a Kleinian analysis?

EB: No. I wanted supervision from Mrs. Klein to see how she worked.

PLR: With whom else did you have supervision?

EB: I had supervisions with Marion Milner and Sylvia Payne before I was qualified. I was terribly lucky. Then I went to Mrs. Klein, who wanted me to have a Klein analysis, and I didn't want to. I was already married to Michael. I was still in analysis with Winnicott. The whole thing was too difficult.

PLR: What did she have in mind?

EB: She wanted me to go to Hanna Segal. I didn't want it anyway. She never pressed me. She was terribly well mannered with me. There were no problems at all. She just thought it was a pity that I hadn't seen one of her people. Anyway, I didn't, and that was that. I spent a very long time working with Michael on *his* ideas more than on my own, which took me a long time to overcome. He's been dead now for over 20 years, and it's only really in the last five or 10 years that I've begun to write my own ideas.

PLR: You gave up a lot to work with him, I imagine.

EB: Well, it was a privilege. He was a marvellous thinker. We used to talk all the time. He always wanted to talk about analysis and about work. He used my clinical material. I think that basically I'm a clinician. I love working with patients. Only recently have I begun to write about what I think, which I enjoy doing now.

PLR: What was the age difference between you and Michael?

EB: The age difference wasn't all that much. It was only nine years. But Michael was a training analyst in Budapest when he was 27.

PLR: They had their own way of doing things. [laughs]

EB: He had analysis for about six or seven years, first from Sachs in Berlin and then, of course, from Ferenczi. It was mad, if you like, but he wrote some wonderful papers.

PLR: Yes, indeed. But we were speaking before about Bion and the Tavistock.

EB: Let's go there again.

PLR: Did you also have supervision with him?

EB: I could have. It was very silly that I didn't have a supervision with him. No, he did clinical seminars at the Institute. I've done that for years and years and years. I was made a training analyst in the 60s. He was a training analyst, of course. He, and all training analysts, do clinical seminars for candidates. And so I went to two, even three of his clinical seminars. He was wonderful. He saw things and thought things out and never jumped to conclusions, never had any pat answers. He was absolutely honest in his thinking. I found him quite a marvellous man.

PLR: When I read his work, I find it to be somewhat dry and abstract. Somehow the human dimension doesn't come through for me very clearly.

EB: I don't know how to describe it. Because what you say is right. But he really wanted to get inside people; he wanted to understand people. He worked mostly with severely ill people, which I do too. He really wanted to understand their language. Can I give you two examples?

PLR: Please.

EB: The first example comes from a clinical seminar. My second patient under supervision when I was a student was extremely ill. In fact, she had been with another candidate, who had found her impossible. And so she was handed on to me. I was rather older than the other people. I didn't train until I was 44 or 45. So I had this very sick girl who was diagnosed with cancer of the breast but wouldn't go to a doctor. The bit I want to tell you about is talking about her to Bion. I remember once I said, "Well, she can't really talk. She starts talking but doesn't form words." I've gotten used to this behavior now, but I wasn't used to it then. And Bion said, "She babbles, doesn't she?" which was the most useful bit of help I think I've ever had as long as I've worked. Because that was what she did: she babbled. And he was perfectly delighted if one talked about patients who didn't talk sensibly, for whom one could make no interpretations but just had to accept that they were really badly regressed. Anyway, that was a bit I always remember. The other bit that comes to mind has to do with something called the 1952 Club. I don't know if you know what that was.

PLR: I've had it described to me as a group of senior British analysts. I've also heard it described as a group of Independents in the Society. So I'm not clear exactly what it is.

EB: Well, I was qualified in 1952. It started being a group of analysts—just us—who had all qualified in 1952. That's why it's called the 1952 Club.

PLR: I see. Who were the other founding members?

EB: Pearl King and Masud Khan are the ones I remember. Actually, when it came to it, it wasn't all of us; it was those of us who were Independent. The Kleinians didn't come for long. Then it became people who qualified in 1953 and 1954. We took in other people.

PLR: But the name continues?

EB: The name continues. Now it is a group of Independents, though I think there are some Kleinians who are members.

PLR: Did Masud Khan qualify that early?

EB: Yes, he did.

PLR: He must have been quite young when he qualified.

EB: He was the youngest. He was only in his 20s. He didn't have to work. He was a rich young man. He was with Rickman, too, and went on to Winnicott.

PLR: So there's a twinship there.

EB: Yes, there was. We had a very odd relationship. By the end, it was very difficult.

PLR: His end is known.

EB: For a long time, I had quite a few problems with Masud. We were very fond of each other. And I knew his wives, Jane and Svetlana. I went to his wedding to Svetlana. For a long time we worked in the same kind of way. But he and Michael had a kind of sparring relationship.

PLR: So he was part of the 1952 Club.

EB: He was very much a part of it. Isobel Menges qualified the year afterward, but she was a Kleinian and didn't join in. It really was almost entirely Independents, and not Kleinians or B Group people. Michael and I got married just after I qualified. I was terribly taken up with my children, a new marriage, a new house, a new way of living, and writing. I mixed mostly with Michael's lot, who were senior analysts. So I was taken out of the world of the people with whom I trained and saw a lot of Anna Freud and Melanie Klein—the older people.

PLR: Whereas the 1952 Club was newly qualified people.

EB: They were all newly qualified. Quite often, we gave our own papers. But we asked distinguished people—like Bion and Michael—

to give us papers every now and again. I was chairman for a long time. For about 10 years, it always met at our house. I think they were monthly meetings. I'm talking now about the 50s. By the mid-60s, I was still going to meetings, but not so much, because Michael and I went to every scientific meeting at the Society, which was once a fortnight. I became a member of the Council; then I became a member of the Education Committee; and later I became chairman of the Admissions Committee. I did an awful lot of work at the Institute for about 15 or 20 years. That took over, and I went on doing that until I married Robin, to whom I am now married.

PLR: What does he do?

EB: He writes history. When I first married him, he was a diplomat, but he retired early. I went to Washington with him once, but we couldn't afford to live abroad. He has four sons. I couldn't work while he was a diplomat, so he retired from the diplomatic service when he was about 57. One has to retire when one is 60, anyway.

PLR: So he was posted in different parts of the world?

EB: I went only to Washington. We then were assigned to Mexico, where he would have been ambassador, but we didn't do that. He retired, and I resumed my practice, and we went on from there. Then he started writing history. He's just finished a book,[2] which got a very good review yesterday in *The New York Times.*

PLR: That's very gratifying.

EB: It's had very good reviews here, but the important ones are the American ones. Anyway, I went on working tremendously hard at the Institute. I was chairman of the Admissions Committee for years, which is a lot of work—more than working with a patient—about seven or eight hours a week. I did a lot of interviewing. But I enjoyed that, actually.

PLR: That's a terribly important position in the Society.

EB: I wasn't ever President. But I think it's perhaps the most important committee. People are always trying different methods for selecting candidates, but none of those methods are very good. Turning down people is awful. Accepting people who are unsuitable is awful. It's terribly difficult to get it right. But I had a very nice group of people to work with. On the committees, there is a Gentleman's

---

2. Robin Edmonds (1991), *The Big Three: Churchill, Roosevelt and Stalin in Peace and War.* New York: Norton.

Agreement that we have an equal number of each group. So you're working with Kleinians, Bs, and Independents. At the time, I had as my Hon. Sec. Eric Brenman, and we worked very well together. It was quite a good period. But let's get back to the Tavvy.

PLR: Yes.

EB: Bion was different from the others. I was talking about the 1952 Club. He came and gave a paper. It was one of the ones about Alpha and Beta elements, and I couldn't understand a word. I was the hostess, and at the end I said I enjoyed it very much, that I was very moved by it, but that I really didn't understand a thing. And he said, in a smiling way, "I don't think I understand it either." I don't think he did. As you know, he moved to America.

PLR: To Los Angeles.

EB: He had to get out of the Society, I think.

PLR: Why?

EB: Too much pressure. A terrible amount of pressure.

PLR: On him particularly?

EB: From the Kleinians, yes. He was analyzed by Melanie Klein. He had to do his own thinking. It was terribly difficult.

PLR: You mean he found it difficult to pursue his own development within the Kleinian camp?

EB: That's my view. And I think it's the view of other people. He came back to England just before he died, but from the time he left in the mid-60s I didn't see him again. I knew him only as a student, really. But over and over again I read what he wrote. I go back to it all the time.

PLR: What do you find most inspiring about his work?

EB: His emphasis on not intruding on patients, which is very important to me. It's the earlier books I like—the 60s work.

PLR: There's a certain similarity between Bion's interests and those of Michael Balint in regressed patients.

EB: But their attitudes are entirely different.

PLR: Is that something you could talk about?

EB: Michael had this idea of primary love and that patients want to make new beginnings, which are benign and not terrifying, from which they can emerge. I think his ideas of life are not so much of horror and strife and alienation and feeling a stranger in the world, though he wrote about that. But he wrote about regression—we talked about this for 20 years, I suppose—in a way that made primary love, and the ability to get back to it, the most important things.

PLR: That goes back to his 1937 paper.[3]

EB: Yes, and to the work he did with Alice Balint. I think her paper on mother love is one of her best.[4] But when Bion talked about regression, he was concerned with psychotic patients for whom there was no reality and so for whom there was no thought. They couldn't think, because to think you have to suffer. They couldn't bear the suffering that they had had, so they were shutting out thought. This is a kind of madness state, because, if you can't suffer pain, you can't suffer pleasure. It's an absolutely different world from Michael's because it's a world of pain where there isn't anything good. Michael's idea of being able to make a patient feel accepted wouldn't be part of Bion's equipment. It would be much more tolerant of a patient's *inability* to feel accepted. And that's where I am in my thinking. Primary love means nothing to me at all. But panic states and chaos and an infant's losing touch with reality—or one who has had reality, had something that was okay, and then lost it—are the kinds of experience that I have with patients. Whereas Michael had an ability to make patients feel loved, I don't find that relevant to my way of thinking. To me it's much more a matter of helping them to feel that they exist. They are in the world, and the world is an alien. I get a lot of that from Bion. When I am in trouble about my work and I read Bion, I feel nearer to my patients than when I don't read Bion. He's the only writer on these very primitive states who makes me feel that way. Winnicott also wrote about all of this in the early papers, and his thinking would have been nearer to Bion's than to Michael's. Again, I like the 60s papers. Marvellous papers.

PLR: But Winnicott started writing in the 1930s.

EB: Yes, quite true. His 30s papers mostly were pediatrician's papers, weren't they?

---

3. Michael Balint (1952), "Early Developmental States of the Ego: Primary Object Love." In *Primary Love and Psycho-Analytic Technique.* London: Maresfield Library, 1985, pp. 90–108.

4. Alice Balint (1939), "Love for the Mother and Mother Love." In *Primary Love and Psycho-Analytic Technique,* pp. 109–127.

PLR: I think he wrote "The Manic Defence" for his qualifying paper in 1935.[5]

EB: Yes, I think he did. Whatever he wrote was absolutely okay with me.

PLR: It's interesting to think about how Bion, Winnicott, and Balint line up on these questions.

EB: They would disown each other. Michael thought he was very near Winnicott; he loved Winnicott's work. Winnicott didn't like Michael's at all.

PLR: How do you know that?

EB: We spoke about it. After Michael and I had been married for a couple of years, I stopped analysis with Winnicott. It just wasn't going to work. Winnicott wanted me to go on, but I couldn't have.

PLR: What year did you end the analysis?

EB: I think I ended about 1955. I started analysis with Rickman in 1949. Six years altogether. Then, after about six or seven years, I went back and had once-a-week with Winnicott again for about a year, which was quite strange. And then after that I saw him quite a lot. We did some work together with children. Even when I was working with him as a patient, he would make it perfectly clear that he had no use for Balint's ideas. He was a terribly honest man. He just said what he thought. Bion, Winnicott, and Michael were totally different kinds of people. Do you know what kind of people they were?

PLR: I never knew any of them personally.

EB: No, naturally.

PLR: I have read the work of all three to a greater or lesser extent and formed an impression of them that way. Winnicott has been at the center of my work; Balint has also been very important; Bion is the least accessible to me of the three.

EB: That's what was so wonderful about him. He really got inside. I think one just has to read it and read it and read it. The first reading, you get nothing. He was really precise in his thinking.

PLR: It's a question of how one conceives of infancy and the relationship of the infant to the mother. If there is a psychotic patient,

---

5. D. W. Winnicott (1935), "The Manic Defence." In *Through Paediatrics to Psycho-Analysis*. New York: Basic Books, 1958, pp. 129–144.

how does one reconstruct the evolution of that person's psychosis? Is it the result of a breakdown in a relationship, or does it come in the first instance from the inner world of the patient? Is communication possible in a normal relationship, or is the world alien under the best of circumstances? These are philosophical problems.

EB: Yes, those are the root questions one has to ask oneself. One can answer them for oneself at one particular moment with one particular patient. I've got two patients I'm working with at the moment for whom those questions are very important. One of them I don't think ever had a relationship that made him feel he was a person. That is, I can't find that he did. The other patient is a woman who, in my view, started with something quite good for perhaps three days.

PLR: It's extraordinary to be able to say something like that.

EB: Winnicott once said to me it's all right if they have half an hour. In a way, it was a joke. In a way, it wasn't. It's enough if there was something.

PLR: I've been reading Bowlby, who shows through observational studies that mothers who have women who support them during delivery are more likely to be awake after the baby is born and therefore more likely to have contact with the baby in that first hour or so.[6]

EB: That's terribly important.

PLR: They're therefore likely to have more contact with the baby in the next month and year and so on. So the first half hour could be considered to be extremely important.

EB: I think that's absolutely right.

PLR: You said your patient had something good for three days, and then in the analysis you arrived at the sense that something went wrong.

EB: Well, I know what went wrong with this particular patient. I didn't know for the first two or three years. It emerged that it wasn't just the mother's mood—though it can be—but in this case the patient's father had a serious illness and almost died. So the mother, although she went on feeding her baby once she returned from the hospital, was obviously distracted and the baby was no longer *there* for her. And the baby herself felt that she wasn't there. She lost that

---

6. John Bowlby (1980), "Caring for Children." In *A Secure Base: Clinical Applications of Attachment Theory*. London: Tavistock, 1988, pp. 13–15.

feeling of belonging. When she first came to see me, she was a beautiful, wealthy girl living in an extremely well-adapted family circle from which she felt totally alien. I've had her now for a long time, and she's doing quite well, but she can go still into sudden panic states, where she feels that she's no longer there. She says, "You're speaking through a tunnel." I suddenly disappear, totally disappear. And if I were to touch her or approach her physically at that moment, it would be catastrophic. I have to remain very, very still, which I do. So my view is that she must have had something, because I can get back to it. She can't say what it is in words, but she can feel . . . bliss.

PLR: This is a fascinating clinical case.

EB: With the other patient—the man—there's nothing there at all. He once showed me photographs, but he's not really there. I hardly exist for him even now, but I just barely do. In fact, yesterday, at our most recent session, he read me a love poem, which was for somebody else, because he can't even allow that it's for me. The transference is a true transference; it isn't to the mother. It couldn't possibly be.

PLR: In other words, it's for you and not for the mother?

EB: No, therefore it's not really for me; it has to be displaced onto somebody else.

PLR: So it's not true transference, or it is true transference?

EB: Well, it is true transference, in the sense that the mother never had it. So I can't have it.

PLR: In other words, that it's not for you *is* a true transference.

EB: But I had to hear that he could read the poem. He couldn't express any emotion until now. So that's something.

PLR: I was curious how you were able to date when the father of your female patient became ill.

EB: It's very difficult, because I could ask her to ask her mother, but I haven't.

PLR: I was struck by the fact that you said three days, which was such a precise length of time.

EB: It's what I picked up. I've had her for about five or six years, and I've tried to get some feeling from things she's said, but not by direct questions. I've stuck to three days in my mind. I don't know.

PLR: It's metaphorical.

EB: Yes, it is.

PLR: I was also very struck by your saying that you didn't have much use for the idea of primary love. Was that something you ever told Michael, or have your views changed?

EB: He and I fought about that. We discussed things. We wrote *The Basic Fault* together, but I didn't sign it. He wanted me to. Just before he died, I promised him that if there were a second edition, I would say Michael and Enid Balint. I never did, and I couldn't after he died. And I don't agree with all of it, though in fact I wrote quite a lot of it. All the bits about the malignant and benign forms of regression were mine, not his. That was my idea. But I disagreed—as he disagreed with a lot of what I said—with the idea that if a patient regressed, he would find bliss, because I've never come across a patient who did. Even this patient, who I think had the three good days, when she gets her moments of bliss, I couldn't possibly connect them either with me or with her mother, though I've tried.

PLR: Don't they come from having experienced a bit of a good relationship or a capacity for illusion at some point? Or do you think they're simply innate states that she has managed to retain?

EB: There is a capacity for illusion, but it has to remain intact.

PLR: I'm more of the attachment school. I think primary love is a good concept, because it is a relational theory. In other words, it implies that the basic human need is for a relationship, and a baby is predisposed to form this attachment. If there is a failure on the part of the mother or the environment to meet this need, of course the consequences will be catastrophic. If a patient has a malignant regression or is unable to recapture that experience, it's because he or she was deprived of it, as of oxygen, for example, which is an analogy that Michael Balint often used. So I have a hard time understanding Bion's theory, or the one you are in a sense presenting, which doesn't seem to me to be one that takes the environment fully into account. But maybe I don't understand.

EB: Bion wrote about patients for whom there isn't an environment. Michael wrote about patients, and you're talking about the same patients, who have an environment. I totally agree with you that before birth, right from the beginning, there is not just one person; there are two. The baby has sounds and smells, and all sorts of things.

PLR: A whole milieu.

EB: Yes. Daniel Stern's work is quite relevant.[7]

PLR: Precisely.

EB: In fact, I've been told by people who work with Daniel Stern that what I wrote in the 60s was what Daniel Stern has proved in the last decade. I just did it from analysis; he's done it from observation.

PLR: But that's why I'm surprised by your questioning the idea of . . .

EB: Well, primary *love* seems wrong. It's primary . . .

PLR: Attachment?

EB: No, it isn't attachment. That's the wrong word. I'm sorry, this is a word thing, not a concept thing. A child is conceived with the opportunity of living in a world, if things go well, where there are other people. If he's not living in a world where there are other people, he's not alive. He's not really human.

PLR: Right. I would accept all of that.

EB: But in a vast number of cases, people have very limited opportunity for using the world, because, unless the world can see what they're like, they can't begin. There has to be a reflection of them. I wouldn't call it primary love. It's primary . . .

PLR: It's not narcissism, that's for sure. [laughs]

EB: No, not narcissism. Absolutely no.

PLR: For me, whether we call it dependence, as Winnicott does; or attachment, as Bowlby would call it; or love, as Balint would call it, isn't so important.

EB: I've got it—recognition!

PLR: And now you say recognition. These are fine distinctions, but to me they are talking about much the same thing.

EB: Yes, but the word you use is important.

PLR: I agree. Therefore Bowlby criticizes "dependence," because for him the word has a negative connotation.[8]

---

7. Daniel N. Stern (1985), *The Interpersonal World of the Infant: A View from Psychoanalysis and Developmental Psychology.* New York: Basic Books.

8. John Bowlby (1977), "The Making and Breaking of Affectional Bonds." In *The Making and Breaking of Affectional Bonds.* London: Tavistock, 1989, p. 132.

EB: It conveys a certain world, doesn't it?

PLR: I like "recognition."

EB: I suppose we used it in *The Basic Fault.*[9]

PLR: It implies a mirroring capacity.

EB: Yes, which I've written about. And I think one of my better papers is about the metaphor of the mirror.[10] I talk about it too in "On Being Empty of Oneself."[11] It's the ability of a child—a child who is recognized or can accept the way he is seen—to begin to live. Then things begin to be mutual. But there are no *words* to that. Of course, this is all preverbal. There has to be a feeling of being alive, of being somebody, which the baby can recognize.

PLR: Exactly.

EB: I used to work with babies at one time, but I've also had children. I had a houseful of children during the war. I had to look after one psychotic baby. I don't think observations are any good, in fact. Analysis is much better. But the observations can back up what one sees in analysis. Primary love seems to be much too *sticky,* much too loaded. It's not love. One wants to be recognized, wants to be *seen.* So this is really where I come in.

PLR: Right.

EB: Michael agreed. At the end of his life, we wrote *The Basic Fault,* and the last chapter I wrote was the one on malignant and benign forms of regression. I remember one night when we were discussing it—it was in bed, actually—I said the malignant form of regression is for satisfaction, and the benign is for recognition. He liked that very much, and we wrote that in. He *terribly* needed love. He was a very loving man. He needed an immense amount of it. His mother was a very loving woman. He needed me full-time—100%. And that was fine for me, except the times when he almost couldn't see, as you probably know, in the last few years.

---

9. Michael Balint (1968), *The Basic Fault: Therapeutic Aspects of Regression.* New York: Brunner/Mazel, 1979, p. 144.

10. Enid Balint (1968), "The Mirror and the Receiver." In *Before I Was I: Psychoanalysis and the Imagination,* eds. Juliet Mitchell & Michael Parsons. London: Free Association Books, 1993, pp. 57–62.

11. E. Balint (1963),"On Being Empty of Oneself." In *Before I Was I,* pp. 37–55.

PLR: No, I didn't know about that.

EB: He pretty well had no sight. It was my job to hide it from the world. He didn't want anybody to know. But I had to read everything to him. He was very dependent. And so not only did he need me all the time because he needed me all the time, but he also needed me because he couldn't see. And this became absolutely awful for him.

PLR: What was the problem?

EB: Glaucoma. It was a time when they didn't know what to do about it. But he had lots of operations. Finally, luckily, we found a man in Berne, to whom we went every second month for about two years, and he saved a little bit of sight, but in the end it went almost completely.

PLR: I don't think that's a well-known fact.

EB: No. It's not important, actually. It was important for us. It was important for him. He couldn't have lived without any sight at all. He had a little. Very, very little. But he had to read everything. So I read the *BMJ* and *The Lancet* to him. Every week. Always. He had to know everything.

PLR: That must have been a full-time job.

EB: It was.

PLR: For me, just to close this up, the main question is the relative importance of the environment versus the inner world of fantasy. And the Kleinian view is one that concentrates so much on the role of fantasy . . .

EB: Well, there aren't two people. There's just somebody projecting into somebody.

PLR: Exactly. And so my question is whether Bion doesn't tend to fall into that extreme Kleinian view.

EB: Yes, I see your point. I don't think he does. When you talked to him—I can only tell you what it was like talking to him—he was really with the patient, just as much as he was with himself. I think there probably is something in what you say. But he was totally different from the *present* Kleinians; Mrs. Klein wasn't like a Kleinian. She really wasn't. She helped me enormously with the case I discussed with her.

PLR: Let's come back to something you said before, which is that Michael admired Winnicott's work greatly, but Winnicott made clear that he had little use for Michael's work. That's surprising to me. Was that because Winnicott didn't agree with Michael's work or because he simply didn't want to have to take it into account in developing his own thinking?

EB: I saw an enormous difference in their outlook. Winnicott really identified with babies. I worked with him with children.

PLR: But wouldn't someone like Michael, who needed so much love himself, also have identified with the baby?

EB: He didn't see the complexity of the baby. Winnicott saw the complexity much more, I think.

PLR: In terms of ruthlessness . . .

EB: In terms of what the baby would choose, what he'd pick up off the ground, what he was willing to accept.

PLR: The spatula game, and so forth?[12]

EB: Yes. Of course, Winnicott never had a child. Michael had one. Winnicott was very much in touch with the need to separate and the need to be together. I don't know whether you know that book by Alice Balint about education, do you?[13]

PLR: I don't.

EB: Actually, it's a book I can't bear. It's all about what children need, and I don't believe in it at all. I don't think Alice and Michael at that stage knew anything about child upbringing or the subtleties of a child's thinking.

PLR: What was it that Winnicott did not have use for in Michael's work?

EB: I think he just felt that Michael knew nothing about the mother–baby relationship. I don't think he was right. But he felt that Michael just didn't understand it at all.

PLR: Did Michael know that this was Winnicott's view?

EB: No, I never told him. It would have hurt him greatly. It would have been terribly painful. They hardly met. We hardly met socially.

---

12. D. W. Winnicott (1941), "The Observation of Infants in a Set Situation." In *Through Paediatrics to Psycho-Analysis,* pp. 52–69.

13. Alice Balint (1931), *The Psycho-Analysis of the Nursery,* ed. Michael Balint. London: Routledge & Kegan Paul, 1953.

I saw Winnicott by myself. Michael was very generous about that. When I wanted to go back and have another short treatment in about 1961 or 1962, all I did was sit on the floor and sob. Winnicott didn't try to make interpretations. I found the conflict between Winnicott and Michael terribly painful. It was almost too much. I don't think I've ever said this before.

PLR: And Michael was not aware of this conflict?

EB: Michael had to be protected. He was very fragile, though he didn't look it.

PLR: He could be very assertive.

EB: Terribly assertive. He was very cruel to his analytic students. Wonderful to his G.P.s, who adored him. Michael was a leader of G.P. groups. I've done that.

PLR: Yes, that's very well known.

EB: He was quite different with the G.P.s, but with the analytic students, he was terribly hard. And also with analysts. He was always provoking people to fight with him because he defended Ferenczi. You were quite right in what you said. Winnicott openly said that he didn't want to read Ferenczi, for instance, because he wanted to think it out for himself. So he didn't read. He'd read Freud when he was a student, I suppose. He knew Freud absolutely. I didn't know Winnicott until 1950. But he mightn't have liked anybody who was anywhere near to himself and his ideas. He was not ashamed to say that. He wanted to do it on his own. He didn't want interference from reading Ferenczi.

PLR: In my view, the review of Fairbairn, which Winnicott wrote with Masud Khan in 1953, was so critical precisely because Fairbairn was thinking along lines that Winnicott later agreed were valid in many respects.[14] He was comfortable seeing his views as evolving from Freud's views, without recognizing the degree to which he was shifting theory and working along lines that were similar to those of other people.

EB: Yes, he would absolutely have denied that they were similar to other people's. And so the split with Michael was the same as it would have been with anybody else working on the same idea. I can

---

14. D. W. Winncott & M. Masud R. Khan (1953), Review of W. R. D. Fairbairn, *Psychoanalytic Studies of the Personality*. In D. W. Winnicott, *Psycho-Analytic Explorations*. Cambridge, MA: Harvard University Press, 1989, pp. 413–422.

understand that. When I'm working on some idea, I don't mind when people say it's in a footnote in Freud—everything is in a footnote in Freud, so it doesn't matter—but if I'm told somebody else is doing it, I find myself with a twinge of anxiety.

PLR: Yes, most people do. You seem to be saying that Winnicott, on one hand, felt that Michael didn't understand the complexity of the baby's experience; and, on the other hand, he felt threatened to some degree that Michael's work was parallel to his own, and he didn't want to try to work through the connections that existed between them. Is that right?

EB: Yes, it could well have been that. I tried to work on this when I first married Michael. I remember I got this huge piece of paper and had different topics along one side and Michael Balint, Winnicott, and Melanie Klein on another one, and I wanted to find out how the three of them thought about the same things.

PLR: Have you saved those notes you made?

EB: No, it's a pity. I had great difficulty with it, because I wanted to see the differences, not the similarities.

PLR: You had analysis with Winnicott for several years before you married?

EB: Yes, I did. What happened was I started this unit at the Tavvy— the Family Discussion Bureau—and I looked around for people who might be of use to us clinically. We had seminars from Henry Dixon, Jock Sutherland, the lot, and they didn't seem any good. We had case conferences twice a week, and one day there was a new man there with a funny accent. I remember going to my analytic session afterward, which was with Rickman, and saying there was a very strange chap there who seemed to know what he was talking about, and I thought I'd ask him to come and work with our group. I was very arrogant in those days; I thought I could do anything. And Rickman said, "Do you mean Michael Balint?" He'd been to Hungary and knew Michael. I said, "I don't know his name," but it was Michael Balint. Rickman said I should keep clear of him. But I didn't keep clear of him. In fact, I married him later. I got him into the Family Discussion Bureau. And when Rickman died suddenly—I was rung up on Sunday by his G.P. and told that he was dead and there wouldn't be any session on Monday—Michael came to see me and was extremely supportive and helpful. I suppose my close relationship with Michael started when Rickman died. At the same time, I started my analysis with Winnicott.

PLR: Had you already been separated from your husband?

EB: Yes, I had been separated from him for about five years. We hadn't been divorced; we hadn't bothered.

PLR: When you went back to Winnicott for the sessions when you were crying, you connected that to the conflict between him and Michael. You seem to have been the person who lived through this most deeply, because you felt very close to both men.

EB: Yes. At the end, what happened was I dished it for myself. They both died within a month of one another. Michael died; Winnicott came to his funeral. He said, "Would you like to come and see me?" I said, "In a bit, but not straightaway." And I didn't go and see him. Then Winnicott died. Clare, his wife, told me that Winnicott expected me every day. He always said, "Enid will come today," but I never went. So I let Winnicott down. I didn't go and see him. So I lost both of them. Then I was asked by the Institute, because I was teaching a lot, to talk about Michael's work and about Winnicott's work.

PLR: Immediately afterward?

EB: Quite soon after.

PLR: That must have been devastating.

EB: Absolutely awful. And all I could do was run them both down. I remember going on and, instead of saying how wonderful they were, saying how awful they were. I mean, not quite so crudely as that, but more or less, until I decided I must stop. I used to go home in a terrible state.

PLR: And you were alone?

EB: I was alone. My daughters were grown up. I was alone, which was a good thing. But Michael then was ringing me up all about coming around. I was alone.

PLR: Michael?

EB: Yes. No. I'm sorry, that was after Rickman died. After Michael and then Winnicott died, I was totally alone for about three or four years. I kept myself alone. I was very busy. It was awful. And everybody thought I was just being bloody about Winnicott and about Michael. I can still do that. When I talk about Winnicott publicly, people hate it because I don't convey the Winnicott they want me to. So I've stopped doing that. I was too ambivalent.

PLR: I'd like to come back to those once-a-week sessions with

Winnicott. You were working out the problem of their relationship in some way.

EB: I became unhappy, and Michael knew I was. He thought I had been awful to Winnicott because I hadn't been back to see him, and he had always been ill.

PLR: Constant coronaries.

EB: Yes. Rickman had died of a coronary. Winnicott asked if I would like to go to him for analysis. I said, "Not at once," but I did go within two or three months. For six months, I couldn't lie on his couch, because I thought I'd break it. Why did I have to go to a second person who had coronaries? It was pretty daft, wasn't it? But anyway, I did. Later, I was quite unhappy because I had neglected him. I hardly saw him. I didn't want to see him. And when I spoke about him, it wasn't at all like the other Winnicott adorers. I didn't *adore* him like that. He had a marvellous brain and mind. He had a superb intelligence. People all talk about him as if he were a kind of . . .

PLR: Transitional object. Something soft.

EB: Yes. He wasn't. Absolutely not. He was not a transitional object. He was hard and straight and firm and really there. Except when he didn't want to be, and then he just went to sleep. I don't like the way people talk about him, on the whole. Nothing soft and loving. He was very firm. He wouldn't stand rubbish. But when Masud talked about him or wrote about him, I couldn't recognize Winnicott at all. In the last book, he gave examples of what Winnicott said to him, and he claims that Winnicott said "Mr. Khan."[15] Winnicott would never have said Mr. Khan. He called him Masud. The whole thing was phony and unpleasant. People make him much cuddlier than he was, much too transitional. He was not. He was tough, very hard. Absolutely trustworthy. When I speak about him in public, people usually get cross.

PLR: People should be very interested to hear how differently he struck different people and shouldn't be surprised at that.

EB: Margaret Little and I know each other.

PLR: I was just thinking about Margaret Little.

---

15. M. Masud R. Khan (1988), *When Spring Comes: Awakenings in Clinical Psychoanalysis.* London: Chatto & Windus, pp. 26–51. In fact, Khan reports Winnicott's addressing him simply as Khan.

EB: She really knew him. We had a very different experience, but I should think we agree about the kind of person he was.

PLR: But she says that the Winnicott she knew was different from everybody else's, and so part of his ability in analysis was to become the object that that person needed.[16]

EB: Yes, if he wanted to. If he didn't, he just didn't do it.

PLR: With you, do you think he wanted to and did it, or not?

EB: I think he wanted to do it for me, yes, and for Margaret. That didn't mean that he liked me. But he knew I needed something that he could give me, which I did.

PLR: What was it you needed that he could give you?

EB: I'm associating. What my mind goes to is he joined me up.

PLR: You were in pieces?

EB: There was a particular bit of the analysis. We all think everybody's the same as we are. I thought that everybody had an ache in their bodies and in their back. I mean, that there was a division between the top and the bottom of everyone.

PLR: That's the way you felt?

EB: That's the way I felt. I thought everyone must feel this way. And then the most painful bit of my analysis—absolutely dreadful—was when I was joined up. And he did that for me, which was quite remarkable. What I relived presumably was the moment when I was broken. I don't know what it was about.

PLR: You might have some idea.

EB: It was almost certainly prenatal. My mother wanted to get rid of me, and she didn't know what she could do to get rid of me.

PLR: Did she try to induce a miscarriage?

EB: Yes. She even made herself fall down the stairs just before I was born. That must have some effect on the fetus, I would think.

PLR: So how did Winnicott join you up? You must have had to relive the breaking.

---

16. Margaret I. Little (1990), *Psychotic Anxieties and Containment: A Personal Record of an Analysis with Winnicott*. Northvale, NJ: Aronson, pp. 64–65.

EB: Well, it was just terrible. It was not a verbal thing, obviously. It was just a terrible agony. A period of enormous pain. I don't really know how to describe it.

PLR: You said when you first saw him, for six months you wouldn't lie on the couch?

EB: No. I was afraid of breaking it. I thought I was too heavy.

PLR: With Rickman, you didn't have any problem? You could lie down from the beginning.

EB: No, I *could* lie down. But I didn't actually. I sat on the floor. But that was the kind of thing one could do with Winnicott.

PLR: That was when you went back to Winnicott?

EB: Yes.

PLR: I meant with Rickman. The first analysis.

EB: I had no trouble about that.

PLR: You would lie down.

EB: I hadn't killed anybody then. The point was that I had killed Rickman, hadn't I? Rickman died. So I didn't want to kill another one.

PLR: I see.

EB: If I lay on the couch, it would break. Anyway, I got over that. So I was on his couch for a number of years.

PLR: That's extraordinary.

EB: It's extraordinary how strong these things are, isn't it? I was so terribly lucky that these people were around.

PLR: Absolutely. If Winnicott had these competitive feelings with Michael . . .

EB: He didn't want me to marry Michael.

PLR: He felt Michael didn't understand the important things, in some way.

EB: That's my fantasy. It's what I think. He told me Michael would never marry me, that I'd better look out, because Michael was a well-known lady-killer. He wouldn't marry me. He would just have an affair with me, and I should keep away from him.

PLR: Did he give you this advice during the analysis?

EB: Rickman had already told me to keep away from Michael. Then I had various dreams. Winnicott interpreted them in terms of how I saw Michael. He thought I should keep away from Michael. Michael was seen as a very dangerous chap. In fact, he was totally faithful to me. One of the last things he told me was, "You ruined my life because you stopped me having other people."

PLR: [laughs] It sounds as though Winnicott gave you something that was absolutely essential by allowing you to get back to this feeling of not being a whole person, and yet he was doing something extremely unconventional in a negative sense in that he was trying to tell you what you should and should not do in your life.

EB: Well, he was very clever. He never said, "You mustn't." He could have. It would have been well within his technique to say "Don't." But he never did. He thought I never would.

PLR: Did you have an engagement? Or did you suddenly go off and get married one day? How did it happen?

EB: We started living together in a kind of fitful way. I kept my own house. But we did sleep together. And then we both decided to get divorced and get married. I think we did it during a holiday.

PLR: I'm wondering whether Winnicott wasn't somehow competing with Michael for you.

EB: He didn't bring pressure. I think he almost brought less than Rickman had. I wouldn't have minded if he had. I remember when I came and said I had gotten married, he was terribly nice. He thought, "My goodness, she's done it." He felt it was quite an achievement. And then we just got on with the work. I think the sobbing year was very much about my first husband. By then, I was quite old, after all. I saw how much suffering there is. How many awful things I had done.

Mary Salter Ainsworth

The Personal Origins of Attachment Theory

Mary Salter Ainsworth: When asked what's the best introductory article to read on attachment theory, I have recommended Robert Karen's article in the *Atlantic Monthly*.[1] I don't know of any better introduction, really. It's hard to do in a small space, and I think he did a wonderful job.

Peter L. Rudnytsky: He introduces us to many of the people and summarizes the ideas quite well.

MSA: Yes.

PLR: I know we'll be going over some of the ground that Karen already covered in that article, but I was struck by the fact that you met Bowlby through a want ad in *The London Times*.

---

1. Robert Karen (1990), "Becoming Attached," *Atlantic Monthly,* February, pp. 35–70. See also Robert Karen (1998), *Becoming Attached: First Relationships and How They Shape Our Capacity to Love.* New York: Oxford University Press. For further salient discussion, see Mary D. S. Ainsworth & Robert S. Marvin (1995), "On the Shaping of Attachment Theory and Research: An Interview with Mary D. S. Ainsworth." In *Caregiving, Cultural, and Cognitive Perspectives on Secure-Base Behavior and Working Models: New Growing Points of Observation Theory and Research,* ed. Everett Waters et al., *Monographs of the Society for Research in Child Development,* 60:3–21; Inge Bretherton (1995), "The Origins of Attachment Theory: John Bowlby & Mary Ainsworth." In *Attachment Theory*, ed. Susan Goldberg, Roy Muir, & John Kerr. Hillsdale, NJ: The Analytic Press, pp. 45–84; Jeremy Holmes (1993), *John Bowlby and Attachment Theory.* London: Routledge, pp. 13–36; and Suzan van Dijken (1998), *John Bowlby: His Early Life: A Biographical Journey into the Roots of Attachment Theory.* London: Free Association Books.

MSA: [laughs] Yes, I did. It was advertising a position for a senior research psychologist to work on a project on the effects on personality development of early separation from the mother, and they wanted someone who had had experience in research in child development and was expert in projective techniques.

PLR: That was made to order for you!

MSA: I made friends with a woman in the British Army during World War II when I was on a tour with the Canadian Army in England. Edith Mercer her name was. She wound up in the Civil Service Selection Board, and she phoned me and said, "You know, there's an advertisment in the *Times Educational Supplement* that I think is right down your alley." So I applied and got it! [laughs]

PLR: That's amazing!

MSA: It was even after the deadline. I think the magic word was "Bill Goldfarb," because I had read an article in *The Rorschach Review* by Bill Goldfarb on projectives he used in a study on institutionally reared children, and Bowlby thought this was the best research he had seen. Not so much the projective part of it, but the study as a whole. In the course of the interview, I mentioned Bill Goldfarb as my entry to maternal deprivation work. I think that was almost more than anything else the thing that made Bowlby and me feel that we were going to work congenially.

PLR: Had you already published on Rorschach tests yourself before that time?

MSA: No. I had collaborated with Bruno Klopfer on a book called *Developments in the Rorschach Technique* and brought that work with me to England. It was published four years after I encountered Bowlby.[2]

PLR: And were you in England because of your husband at that time?

MSA: Yes. This was in 1950. That's also how I happened to go to Uganda three years later, because my husband had come to London to get his Ph.D. at the University of London. And when Len looked for a first post-Ph.D. job, he had the notion that he wanted to go to Africa. It's not the easiest thing in the world to get a job in Africa! And Edith phoned and said, "You know, there's an ad in *The London*

---

2. Bruno Klopfer, Mary D. Ainsworth, Walter G. Klopfer & Robert R. Holt (1954), *Developments in the Rorschach Technique,* Vol. 1. Yonkers, NY: World Book.

Times that sounds as though it would suit Len." [laughing] And I went along.

PLR: What was he doing?

MSA: He was a psychologist. I think he labeled himself as a social psychologist at that point, which is how he got into social psychology research there.

PLR: Since we've mentioned the Rorschach tests, I wonder what you see to be the similarities or divergences between Rorschach tests and the kind of research that you have concentrated on involving attachment.

MSA: I think the only real link is my interest in personality organization and development. As it turns out, Bowlby had thought that in one of the research projects his team was doing in London he would like to use the Rorschach test. And when I got there I thought that this was simply not a feasible thing to do. As a clinical psychologist I kept using the Rorschach for diagnostic work for some years after I left London and Africa, but I have never really settled down to make a new system of analysis that would fit the attachment theory. I just dubbed it in, as it were. [laughs]

PLR: Dubbed it in! But do you feel that the Rorschach is valuable?

MSA: Yes I do. It's a good diagnostic procedure. But I think that it's only as good as the person using it. It has been automated in terms of computer scoring, and I've never been into that myself. I'm very leery.

PLR: I can understand that. Let's talk now about your period in London beginning in 1950.

MSA: I had tried to get a position by correspondence before I got there, but I was quite unsuccessful. I even wrote to a friend at the Tavistock Clinic, and he said sorry, they had nothing. I had lined up an appointment with Hans Eysenck at the Maudsley. This was about the same time that I applied for an interview at the Tavvy with Bowlby. I heard rather quickly that I had the job at the Tavvy, and so I canceled off with Eysenck. Even though I often think, gee, my life would have been different! [laughs]

PLR: He's been one of the severest critics of psychoanalysis altogether, hasn't he? What can you tell me about Bowlby's relationship to psychoanalysis during the time that you worked with him? Were there analysts whom you also knew personally, or was it very separate from the analytic community?

MSA: No. The Tavistock Clinic is essentially a psychoanalytically oriented clinic. I think there was only one other person there beside me who had not either been through analysis or was currently in analysis. [laughs]

PLR: Who was the other person?

MSA: Hana Popper her name was. She was a Czechoslovakian refugee and a psychologist. So I knew quite a number of the analysts at the Clinic and in the department. They were, on the whole, object relations oriented, not Freudian. Jock Sutherland was the head of the Tavistock at that point. His favorite was Fairbairn. And, of course, Melanie Klein counts as object relations, too.

PLR: Did you know Sutherland had written an intellectual biography of Fairbairn?[3]

MSA: No, but I'm not surprised. Jock and John Bowlby were very close. They didn't find any particular things to quarrel about. But most of the people in the Department for Children and Their Parents, of which Bowlby was the director, were Kleinians. Bowlby and Melanie Klein just did not get on at all. She had supervised him when he qualified as an analyst, but then he went on to child analysis, and he just couldn't agree with the way she looked at things.

PLR: There's the bit in Karen's article about his first case, where she wouldn't allow him to see the mother of a disturbed boy, and so forth.

MSA: That's right. And whenever Bowlby was asked to talk about how he came to do what he did, that was almost always a part of the story he told. [laughs] And so, because he didn't find the work of the people in the department he was directing congenial in terms of the clinical data they collected that might have been used for research, he established a separate research unit and got funding for it, and that's the one I joined.

PLR: How was that funded?

MSA: Private grants. The first grant he got was from the International Children's Center in Paris.

PLR: Not the W.H.O.? Was this after that?

MSA: No, I think he actually got the first grant from the

---

3. John D. Sutherland (1989), *Fairbairn's Journey into the Interior.* London: Free Association Books.

International Children's Center before the W.H.O. asked him to do that *Maternal Care and Mental Health* study.

PLR: You must have known a number of the analysts at the Tavistock personally.

MSA: Yes.

PLR: Do any of them stand out in your mind?

MSA: I wish to goodness I could remember all their names! There was a pair of Hungarians. They put a lot of stress on close bodily contact, and their name has just gone out of my head.

PLR: Michael and Enid Balint?

MSA: Yes.

PLR: She is English, though, his second wife.

MSA: Well, it was Michael I knew really well, but I had read some of his earlier writings.

PLR: With his first wife, Alice?

MSA: Yes, it was Alice Balint's work that I knew.

PLR: Did you have any sense of Bowlby's relation to Balint?

MSA: They got along fine. But Balint was in the Adult Department, so they didn't have much direct contact. Bion was the family therapy man.

PLR: Did you know him, as well?

MSA: No, I didn't, for some reason or other.

PLR: Do you know how Bowlby felt about Bion?

MSA: Bowlby thought that the way to go was family therapy. And as far as he knew, he wrote the first paper on family therapy, which I have somewhere in the welter on my desk. Did you read the paper that Bowlby and I did in *The American Psychologist*?[4]

PLR: No, I haven't seen it.

MSA: We were given a joint award by the American Psychological Association.

---

4. Mary D. Salter Ainsworth & John Bowlby (1991), "An Ethological Approach to Personality Development." *American Psychologist,* 46:331–341.

PLR: That's great! When was that?

MSA: The award was given in 1989. The pattern they have for these Distinguished Scientific Contribution awards is that you're given the award one year, the next year you turn up at the annual meeting and give a talk, and then the year after that the talk is prepared for publication and published in *The American Psychologist.*

PLR: So your paper came out in 1991 for the award in 1989?

MSA: That's right. John was working on Darwin and didn't want to break to come either to accept the award in 1989 or to join in the address, but he did contribute to the reading paper that I gave, and then we prepared it for publication. He was still working on Darwin until May of 1990, I think. I had hoped that he might undertake the first draft of the paper, but no, as soon as he got the Darwin book out he had surgery and so he couldn't do very much with it. And after he recovered from surgery, he had an advanced draft of the paper that I had prepared to put the finishing touches on it, and he didn't quite get it done before he died. But his wife sent me the notes of the revisions he was going to bring in.

PLR: Did you incorporate them?

MSA: Yes, I did.

MSA: Anyhow, this is a twin interwoven autobiographical kind of thing, and it cites that first family therapy paper.[5]

PLR: Marvelous! That's the connection. I think Bion would have worked in a very different way; he was much more Kleinian, so I don't know how Bowlby and he would have gotten along. What I'm really interested in is what you can tell me about Bowlby's relations to the psychoanalytic community, if that is something you have first-hand knowledge about. Did he have an analytic practice all the way through?

MSA: Yes. I'm not sure how much of it was classical analysis, but he certainly worked with patients throughout his whole career. It was on a very part-time basis, but he put a lot of stock in what he learned from his clinical practice. He played quite an active role in the British Psycho-Analytical Society. He was Treasurer for some time; he was also, I think, Director of Training. And throughout the period when both Melanie Klein and Anna Freud were so very critical, he was still

5. John Bowlby (1949), "The Study and Reduction of Group Tensions in the Family." *Human Relations,* 2:123–128.

a respected member of the Society as an administrator and that kind of thing.

PLR: Were their criticisms published in any one place that would be the most important source?

MSA: The main lot of critical papers were in *The Psychoanalytic Study of the Child* in the early 1960s some time.

PLR: And Bowlby responded to these criticisms, of course?

MSA: No, he didn't! He published one paper in *The Psychoanalytic Study of the Child*.[6] I think it was called "Grief and Mourning in Childhood." One of the things that I always greatly admired about Bowlby was that he just let this criticism roll off his back. He was disappointed that his ideas weren't more acceptable to his colleagues, but he didn't fight back, and there are very few places in his writing that he criticizes other psychoanalytic approaches. I know that in "Pathways for the Growth of Personality,"[7] he refers to Anna Freud's *Normality and Pathology in Childhood*. He says her ideas are more elaborate than Karl Abraham's, but then compares her view and his own [reads]: "These two alternative theoretical models can be likened to two types of railway system. The traditional model resembles a single main line on which there are set a series of stations; at any one of them, we may imagine, a train can be halted, either temporarily or permanently; and the longer it halts the more prone it becomes to return to that station when it meets with difficulty further down that line."

PLR: That's funny!

MSA: [reads]: "The alternative model resembles a system that starts as a single main route which leaves a central metropolis in a certain direction but soon forks into a range of distinct routes. Although each of these routes diverges in some degree, initially most of them continue in a direction not very different from the original one. The further each route goes from the metropolis, however, the more branches it throws off and the greater the degree of divergence of direction that can occur." And so on.

---

6. See John Bowlby (1960), "Grief and Mourning in Infancy and Early Childhood." *The Psychoanalytic Study of the Child,* 15:9–52. New York: International Universities Press.

7. Bowlby (1973), *Separation: Anxiety and Anger.* London: Hogarth Press, 1985, pp. 364–365.

PLR: This is his view?

MSA: Yes. [reads]: "The implications of the different models for research and practice are far-reaching." And the tone of it is, well, there are two ways of looking at it, and I think the second way has merit and let's talk about *it*.

PLR: But you're saying he didn't waste a lot of time on polemics or on letting things get to him. He just continued to pursue his own development.

MSA: That's right.

PLR: He had independence enough. And a group of researchers, too.

MSA: Then he does have an appendix here reviewing the literature on separation, and he gives six different views. Also, at the end of the first volume on *Attachment*, I think he gives five views of the origins of attachment. And so he does refer to these others, but, again, he doesn't have to knock down other people in order to present his own stuff.

PLR: Did you have any contact with Joan Riviere?

MSA: No, not directly.

PLR: Did Bowlby talk about her at all?

MSA: She was his analyst.

PLR: Right. That's why I'm asking! [both laugh]

MSA: No, he didn't talk much about her, and I felt that he found her much easier to take than Melanie Klein.

PLR: Really? My impression from reading her writings is that she could be rather acerbic.

MSA: Yes. You know, I think there was an awful lot about analysis that he took with a grain of salt as he went through the process of training—both personal training analysis and the actual training— because before he had ever actually engaged in this training, he had come to the conclusion that real-life experiences, not fantasy, were the origins of pathology.

PLR: Do you know how he arrived at that conclusion?

MSA: Well, that's referred to in the *Atlantic Monthly* article.[8] He

---

8. See Footnote 1.

spent a year after obtaining his undergraduate degree at Cambridge in a residential institution for maladjusted children.

PLR: What field was his degree in at Cambridge?

MSA: It was premed, essentially. Natural science.

PLR: Do you know what college he attended?

MSA: Trinity. And his mentor, his tutor, was Lord Adrian, the famous neurologist. In any event, natural science was what you might call his major, but he also read psychology. I don't know how he got into this postbachelor job, but nevertheless he did spend a year in this institution, I think it would have been the late 30s.

PLR: I know he spent quite a bit of time in the Army as well.

MSA: Yes. I think it was 1940 when he was commissioned. He had finished his psychiatric training when he went into the Army, and I think he was also a qualified analyst. Anyhow, there were two boys in this institution whom he particularly recalled. One of them had had a very disturbed background of separations; he was quite affectionless and had a character disorder. Bowlby didn't say anything about the background of the other child, who latched onto Bowlby and followed him everywhere. [laughs] He shadowed him for the year. In a sense, here are the two kinds of major outcomes of early disturbed separations from attachment figures. One, the inability to manifest an attachment; and the other, a very insecure kind of intense manifestation of attachment.

PLR: That's nice!

MSA: And so he was quite convinced that these traumatic experiences in real life were the answer, rather than an autonomous fantasy. Obviously, coming in with this kind of conviction, he couldn't accept everything that he was taught in his training. And now, you know, the way things are emerging with evidence of sexual abuse, which was just pushed aside as fantasy for so long, one thinks that Freud made a mistake when he changed his mind. [laughs]

PLR: In *A Secure Base*, Bowlby says that this was a disastrous abandonment of his earlier view.[9] Of course, Jeffrey Masson has made a great deal out of this change of heart in Freud's thinking. I remember that Charles Rycroft published a very critical review of Masson

---

9. John Bowlby (1988), "Violence in the Family." In *A Secure Base: Clinical Applications of Attachment Theory.* London: Tavistock, 1989, p. 78.

in which he said, in essence, "If you want to go back to the trauma theory, you should use Bowlby."[10] So there's a close connection here. I was wondering whether Bowlby ever discussed Masson's work or whether the controversy over the so-called seduction theory in the popular press was something that he got involved in.

MSA: No, I don't think he took up arms there, but it's clear what he thought.[11]

PLR: I'm curious in a general way about the influence of his experiences in the war on his work and what you could tell me about that.

MSA: He was involved in officer selection. He was asked by the authorities to undertake a study of the success of the selections made by the War Office Selection Boards (WOSBs) versus the ones that used to be made simply through an interview by a retired colonel. I think that he got a significance level of about .09, which is not considered really significant, but he said it was pretty good considering the very complex nature of the thing he was doing. And I think that two important things came out of Bowlby's war experience. One was a circle of colleagues and friends that continued their association after the war, and nearly all the new Tavistock Clinic—new in 1946—came from among that circle.

PLR: Who were some of the people?

MSA: Well, Sutherland for one, and Eric Trist.

PLR: Did you know William Gillespie?

MSA: No. I attended a lot of meetings of the Adult Department, but I didn't work closely with anybody but John and Eric and also a psychologist by the name of Herbert Phillipson.

PLR: So there were two things about the war experience. One was the group of people . . .

---

10. Charles Rycroft (1984), "A Case of Hysteria." *The New York Review of Books,* April 12, p. 6.

11. See Christopher Fortune (1991), "Psychoanalytic Champion of 'Real-Life Experience': An Interview with John Bowlby." *Melanie Klein and Object Relations,* 9, December. Bowlby says that he is "exasperated" by Masson's *The Assault on Truth* because, while he is in "total agreement" with Masson's emphasis on actual experiences, Masson "seems to be totally unaware" of the recent research that corroborates his thesis and "his grandiose claims and hypotheses about why Freud abandoned the seduction theory overshadowed" the valuable aspects of his book (pp. 77–78).

MSA: And the other was that he was very much more knowledge-able about research, and how to go about it, than most psychiatrists. He wasn't a super statistician, but at least he knew somthing about it. [laughs] The notion of control groups and controled variables, testing for significance, and things like that.

PLR: Right. He understood principles of that kind.

MSA: And so his theory itself is very much more conducive to research than most psychoanalytic theories. You could get a handle on it. I think a lot of the research that attempted to test Freudian hypotheses just didn't know how to get at it. The kind of thing that Bob Sears wrote up back in the 40s on psychoanalytic research.[12]

PLR: That was not as successful a way of testing. I wanted to ask you on a somewhat different but yet related theme, you yourself had some analysis?

MSA: Yes, I've had a personal analysis.

PLR: In Baltimore?

MSA: Yes.

PLR: And so you went in the opposite direction from Bowlby, in the sense that your background was more in the developmental and research fields, and then you had a personal experience of analysis.

MSA: Yes. Well, I was interested in personality theory and also personality assessment, but that was mostly after the war. Before that I was working with another developmental theory that turned out in many ways to be very, very congenial and something I took with me to attachment theory—William Blatz's security theory.

PLR: This was from your Toronto days?

MSA: Yes, this was from my Toronto days. And I know there are a lot of things that Blatz believed that I didn't believe, but the whole notion of a secure base was Blatz's. At least I got it from Blatz.

PLR: What were the things that he believed that you didn't believe?

MSA: He had absolutely no use for the notion of an unconscious, which is ridiculous. [laughs]

PLR: So it was more something you believed that he didn't believe, rather than the other way around.

---

12. Robert R. Sears (1943), *Survey of Objective Studies of Psychoanalytic Concepts*. New York: Social Sciences Research Council.

MSA: Yes. [laughs]

PLR: Did you keep in contact with him? Since he was your professor, I assume he was somewhat older.

MSA: Well, he died. I did keep in touch with him more or less. I was Blatz's choice for his successor, and the position was offered to me three times—Director of the Institute of Child Study in Toronto.

PLR: That would have been great.

MSA: By this time I had started my own research, and I was in analysis.

PLR: This is when you were in Baltimore?

MSA: Yes.

PLR: So quite a bit of time had passed?

MSA: Yes.

PLR: That was a tempting offer, I'm sure.

MSA: Well, it was. I had a great deal of difficulty turning it down, but I think I made the right choice.

PLR: Yes. Did you have a full-time position at Johns Hopkins?

MSA: Yes.

PLR: Professor?

MSA: Yes, by this time I think it was Professor.

PLR: In psychology?

MSA: Yes. But my Ph.D. dissertation was based on Blatz's theory, and it's had a lot of influence on my emphasis on *patterns* rather than discrete variables, and that, I must say, is my own.

PLR: The patterns?

MSA: Yes. Blatz thought there were three major bases of security. One he called "immature dependent security," and this is character- istic of the infant and young child whose security really rests on a base of parental responsiveness. But gradually, through the learn- ing of skills and knowledge, one's security can rest *more* on inde- pendent security. But no one can be totally independent, and so there's what he called "mature dependent security." In a sense, you can think of this as patterning. I devised some tests—paper-and-pen- cil things—that suggest whether someone is mainly a mature dependent secure person, although there has to be some independence to go with that, or is insecure. Then he talked about "deputy agents," which was his term for defense mechanisms. And you can't make sense of defense mechanisms without believing in the unconscious. These are unconscious processes! So that's where one of our difficulties came in. The other one was that he thought, quite in line with psychoanalytic thinking at the time, that one cannot remain immaturely dependent on parents and be healthy. If you like, the attachment figure has to shift, or the attachment would have to shift, to some age peer or some age peers, with emancipation from the parents altogether. Of course, Bowlby doesen't believe that at all. You never really lose the bond with parents. You may not have them as your principal attachment figures any more, but you still need them.

PLR: How long were you in analysis?

MSA: I was in for seven years and took a year off and then went back. It was the best thing I ever did.

PLR: Was this with the same analyst?

MSA: Yes, it was somebody whom I had had some professional contact with before. He had also been the analyst of several friends, and they spoke very well of him. One thing that was terribly important to me was that I not have someone who was doctrinaire. He was a training analyst in the Baltimore Institute, which meant a Freudian background, but there was never anything in the interpretations that you could say was doctrinaire.

PLR: I'd like to hear more about whether you feel there is a compatibility between analysis and attachment theory. What has to be thrown out?

MSA: Well, I think metapsychology. I think Bowlby felt that that was very outmoded. He was a great admirer of Freud's, in many ways. Freud's metapsychology really was an attempt to make a science of psychoanalysis, and Bowlby thought it was just too bad that he picked a Helmholtzian model rather than an evolutionary model.

PLR: Right.

MSA: And Bowlby's critique was terribly interesting to me, because I was in London working on the research that his team was doing at the time he first discovered ethology. As a matter of fact, I was ahead of him, in a way [laughs], because I had read *King Solomon's Ring* before he had ever heard of Konrad Lorenz, but it was just like the flash that pulled everything together.

PLR: This was through Julian Huxley?

MSA: I think it was Julian Huxley that he consulted.

PLR: Who told him to read this stuff?

MSA: Yes, but it was somebody else he didn't know terribly well and met at a meeting somewhere who originally mentioned ethology and thought he might be interested, and then he consulted Julian. And there's absolutely no doubt that ethological concepts are at the basis of Bowlby's science of psychoanalysis.

PLR: Yes, indeed. Of course, people raise the question of the extent to which animal research can be extrapolated to apply to human experience.

MSA: Well, he was most interested in the primate stuff, of course, and he touched that interest off in me, and I read an awful lot of studies about it.

PLR: I was interested to learn from Karen's *Atlantic Monthly* piece that Harry Harlow had himself been influenced by René Spitz, so that there is a kind of continuous cross-fertilization between ethology and psychoanalysis.

MSA: Yes, and Bowlby and Harlow influenced each other because Harlow's work just fit with many of Bowlby's notions.

PLR: Where was Harlow teaching?

MSA: Wisconsin. I think it was in 1959 that Bowlby organized a Tavistock Mother–Infant Interaction study group, and this was international and interdisciplinary. And it was modeled on the Macy Foundation study groups that he had attended. Harlow was a charter member of the Tavistock group. I was not. I think Bowlby thought I had gone off in other directions, and it wasn't until we met in the summer of 1960 and I had gotten around to analyzing the data I had collected in Africa that it became obvious that this was pertinent.

PLR: You had been a junior person in the London situation, and then you left his immediate orbit?

MSA: I wasn't all that junior!

PLR: Well, I was trying to gather why he didn't invite you in on the study group.

MSA: We had sort of lost touch. I went off to Africa and collected this data, and then my first post-African job was at Johns Hopkins, and it was perforce clinical. I was to teach the courses on personality and personality assessment and cognitive assessment.

PLR: Did your husband have an appointment as well?

MSA: Not at Hopkins.

PLR: Where was he?

MSA: Medical Services of the Supreme Bench of the City of Baltimore. He turned into a forensic psychologist, as a matter of fact. [laughs] And what with getting even older stuff published and starting a new career that involved both clinical work and teaching, it took me some time to pick up the threads. It wasn't until 1962 or 1963, when I got a grant and also could change my job at Hopkins, that I could pursue something similar to the research I had done in Africa. And there was that period in there when I was not very active.

PLR: And then you set up research projects in the Baltimore area?

MSA: Yes. But in any event, I attended all the rest of this Mother–Infant Interaction series.

PLR: Were these annual conferences?

MSA: Biennial. I was a frequent guest and got an awful lot out of those discussions.

PLR: Since you've had the experience of analysis and this very deep involvement with the attachment work, I'd like to ask you about the question of fantasy. What do you feel is the place of fantasy in attachment theory?

MSA: I think it's been neglected. Quite deliberately! [laughs]

PLR: Can one work it back in? Because there's always a dialectic between the inner world and the environment.

MSA: I think Bowlby handled the inner world in terms of working models. And now that attachment research has gotten beyond infancy [laughs] with Mary Main's work on the Adult Attachment Interview, I'm quite convinced that, whereas behavioral observation is the only way you can get at what goes on in infancy, increasingly with development an interview method is probably the way to go.

PLR: She was your student?

MSA: Yes.

PLR: At Hopkins?

MSA: Yes.

PLR: In the Adult Attachment Interview parents or adults recollect their own childhood experiences, and there is some correlation between how they describe their experiences and . . .

MSA: Well, that's part of it. But she insists that her method of analyzing the Adult Attachment Interview material reveals the current state of mind regarding attachments. The way the past attachments are described throws light on present attachment relationships, and one makes an inference from all that material about the current state of mind about attachments. So it's by no means the *content* that's reported of childhood experiences that leads to the assessment, but the *way* it's reported—the form. It's like good old Rorschach! And an awful lot of emphasis is put on the language used and the consistency and coherence of the thought that's reflected in the language.

PLR: This falls into the general category of transference between past and present relationships.

MSA: Yes. You were asking some time ago about what Bowlby kept and what he threw out, and I said I thought he threw out the metapsychology. I think he kept a lot of the process, and I think that's the thing he admired most about Freud. Certainly, he didn't actually use the term transference, but it's implicit. He didn't talk about projection either, but obviously the concept is there. In any event, when a patient evaluates his experience with an analyst or a therapist, he does so in the light of the working models that he formed with his primary attachment figure long ago. At least sometimes, if a patient is having difficulties, the chances are that it is old working models that have been preserved rather than modified with growth and development and experience and are being projected onto the analyst. And the notion, as you know from *A Secure Base*, is to build up enough trust so that these working models can be explored without too much anxiety.

PLR: Exactly. Is there any sense in which your view and Bowlby's diverge at all, or is there a complete meeting of the minds?

MSA: Well, I think there's more to the oedipal situation than he does. Bowlby just doesn't talk about it. And having had quite an oedipal situation myself, it became the focus of my analysis. Not that the word was ever used. [laughs]

PLR: Well, it might have been. In seven years, it would be hard to avoid it completely. [laughs]

MSA: Well, the situation was discussed. But I think Bowlby tends to interpret this very much in attachment terms rather than in more literally sexual terms. This is probably another place where he departs from analytic theory. He certainly thinks of sexuality as being one of the major behavioral systems in reproduction, but that in infancy the pertinent behaviors are fragmented, and the more important system is attachment. I think that you can reinterpret an awful lot of the oedipal stuff in early childhood in attachment terms, and that would be congenial to him.

PLR: Has that been done?

MSA: I'm sure he does it in different cases, but he doesn't mention oedipal matters in all his writings. It just isn't there.

PLR: Do you have any explanation for that? Was he avoiding something, or was he just trying to build up his own ideas?

MSA: I think that he was just building up his own ideas.

PLR: You're saying that sexuality has a greater autonomy. That is, Bowlby wanted to say that feeding behavior and sexuality were subsystems of attachment behavior.

MSA: Not subsystems! They were independent systems, but the sexual system doesn't get organized until later on.

PLR: So he would not have agreed with the concept of infantile sexuality?

MSA: No, he would not.

PLR: And you?

MSA: I'm not impressed with it.

PLR: But isn't the oedipal already sexual?

MSA: I am not aware, even after years of analysis, of the sexual implications of my view of my father, but I am of the love implications in terms of attachment. I wanted to be with him. He was the person who was my secure base.

PLR: Did you want to have a baby with him?

MSA: No!

PLR: You just wanted to be with him?

MSA: Yes. I wanted to be close to him. Father was the one who put me to bed every night, singing and with a pat, pat, pat, pat.

PLR: That's nice.

MSA: And all the feelings of warmth, love, and security were invested in him.

PLR: Yes.

MSA: My mother didn't like it.

PLR: Do you have brothers and sisters?

MSA: Yes. He went through the same thing with two younger sisters.

PLR: You were the eldest of three girls?

MSA: Yes. And each one of us was given a great deal of paternal attention. Well, I'll tell you one of my favorite stories about this. When I was three years old we lived near Cincinnati. Father had to go on a business trip to Indianapolis, and he took me along. We might have stayed over two nights in Indianapolis, and this is one of my fond early memories. I can remember a lot of things that went on in those two or three days. And I was so pleased to have father to myself, you know. [laughs]

PLR: Yes.

MSA: I recalled this in one of my analytic sessions, and my analyst asked a very obvious question: "How did he happen to take you?" I had no idea why. Currently my analyst was trying, I think, to get me to think about how my parents were feeling and what kind of experiences they were having at various times as a background to my recollections of myself and my feelings. So I began to wonder, was there any family reason? My younger sister was about a year old. Was there any illness, or a reason to get me out of the way because of a crisis of some sort? My mother was about the same age as I am now. She was visiting me one day, and I said, "Mother, do you happen to remember that business trip to Indianapolis that father took me on?" She said, "I certainly do!" And I said, "Well, why did he take me?" She said in a very angry voice, "Because he thought you were old enough, that's why! And, moreover, he was so much more interested in anything that you said than anything I said!" [laughs] So that answered that question. And this was the kernel of my difficulties, I think.

PLR: Did your parents remain together?

MSA: Yes.

PLR: And your own divorce, was this your initiative or your husband's?

MSA: No, it was my husband's initiative. He found somebody else he wanted to marry. I felt absolutely, utterly, totally betrayed, and a failure. So I decided I needed psychotherapy just to get me over the hump. And after two sessions of psychotherapy, it became psychoanalysis. One thing that my mother taught me was that anger is very wicked. And after a great deal of struggling, I got to the point of not ever being able to feel angry. I would just feel hurt. And at the beginning of the second therapeutic session, my analyst said, "I don't know whether you realize how angry you were last week." All of sudden I realized I was *furious* with this man! I wasn't hurt; I was furious. But it was something I had just been repressing all along.

PLR: Yes. The incident you described about your mother sounds as though she was angry too.

MSA: Yes.

PLR: Even though she was, in a sense, teaching you not to be angry, she herself had a lot of anger.

MSA: I think so.

PLR: We were talking about infantile sexuality and the significance of the oedipal situation and whether Bowlby slighted that side of development.

MSA: Yes.

PLR: You seem to be equivocating on this. You're giving material that shows a dynamic of father–daughter relationship, but you're explaining it in terms of needing an attachment and a closeness rather than giving a sexual meaning to it.

MSA: I mean, the analyst *could* say, of course, that all this is just a coverup for sexuality.

PLR: Well, I'm asking you.

MSA: No, I don't feel that way. I think that the whole thing can be talked of in attachment terms, at least my end of it. I have gone on to think about attachments beyond infancy, and I believe attachment can be a very important component of relationships that are not based solely on the attachment system. And certainly, from adolescence on, there are sexual relationships—bonds—in which the reproductive system is inconsequential. But these relationships also involve attachment and caregiving. And so, in an important attachment with a sexual partner, each serves as a secure base for the other and each takes care of the other, sexually and otherwise.

PLR: Sure.

MSA: There's no question in my mind that, in the oedipal situation, there is a lot of sexuality in the parents' dynamics. Not necessarily in the parent–child relationship. But there must have been sexual dynamics in my parents' relationship to each other, and I played a role in that.

PLR: Exactly. I'm just asking about the role of fantasy and the inner world because Freud's shift in point of view had do with his emphasis on infantile sexuality. It doesn't have to mean that the external world is excluded or that the role of actual experience isn't terribly important. But if one then goes to the extreme of denying what's called infantile sexuality or the role of infantile fantasy, then one has moved very far away from a psychoanalytic point of view to a more pre-Freudian view.

MSA: Yes. But anyhow, just to finish up, when it comes to all the writing that I have done about attachments across the life span, John Bowlby certainly had no word of criticism.

PLR: There's nothing in your work that he dissented from?

MSA: No.

PLR: I am struck by how generous he was in citing others. I don't know if this conforms with your impression, but when I read his work I see that a great many people played a part in his thinking.

MSA: Yes. And he was ready to credit them. We did a videotape here at the University of Virginia. He came to give a David C. Wilson lecture in psychiatry, and, while he was here, I asked him whether he'd speak to the Psychology Department. And there was no point really in replicating the kind of thing he was going to say to the Psychiatry Department. We could all go to that lecture too. So I suggested that he just very informally talk about himself and how he got onto the trail of attachment. One of the things that was so outstanding on this particular occasion was the way he talked about where he got his ideas from.

PLR: I'd love to have seen it. I was curious also about Jimmy Robertson's *A Two-Year-Old Goes to Hospital*.

MSA: The New York University film library has it to rent. They also have a collection at Penn State that includes it along with his other films. He has five other films.

PLR: Do you feel that there is an innate aggression, or do you feel that aggression is the response to an environmental deprivation?

MSA: I've always gone along with the idea of frustration. There has to be a situation that sets it off. I'm inclined to think that Bowlby felt the same way. There's a system there, but it is brought into action only under certain circumstances.

PLR: That makes a lot of sense. What do you think about Jerome Kagan and his criticisms of attachment theory?

MSA: The thing I object to is his claim that nothing in the experience of the infant has any permanent effect on behavior. He based this claim on a study he did in Guatemala in which he found that all the infants were deprived, whereas at age six the siblings of the infants seemed to be perfectly normal. He based his conclusion on the fact that, when he or someone visited the homes of these babies, they found the babies with a blanket or whatever—a covering—over their eyes, and he called that deprivation. But that is not the same thing as deprivation of maternal care because these babies were held in arms, they were responded to immediately when they cried, and they had a lot of close bodily contact. So it wasn't deprivation in anything but a visual sense.

PLR: Right.

MSA: And the test that he did was based on surprise, where you show infants a ball rolling down an incline and it comes out at the bottom. Then, if for some reason or other you stop it midway, they register surprise. Apparently, these Guatemalan babies didn't show this surprise, and therefore he said they weren't developing normally intellectually.

PLR: I see.

MSA: The definition of intellectual development was very narrow, and he quite overlooked that probably the reason the babies had their eyes covered was to protect them from the evil eye when a stranger came in.

PLR: Good point! So you believe he overgeneralized from a sample.

MSA: Yes.

PLR: That's what he said about your work. [laughs] It's a curious reversal. What about Piaget? Was he important in your thinking?

---

13. Jean Piaget (1936), *The Origins of Intelligence in Children*, trans. Margaret Cook. New York: International Universities Press, 1952.

MSA: Yes. Mainly *The Origins of Intelligence in Children.*[13] I was interested in the sensorimotor period, and that is very compatible.

PLR: Did Bowlby share your admiration for Piaget?

MSA: Oh, yes. The main thing he mentioned is Piaget's notion of egocentrism and the infant's gradually overcoming it in the sense of being able to take the perspective of another person.

PLR: So you deliberately tried to integrate that with attachment theory?

MSA: Yes. Piaget was a member of the Macy Foundation series of conferences, along with John Bowlby, Margaret Mead, and all sorts of people. And I think it was very important to Bowlby.

PLR: Did you know Piaget?

MSA: I met him once. He refused to speak English, and my French is very limited. He was at Hopkins, and we were having dinner in a group. I told him that I was very interested in tracing the similarities and the incompatibilities between his theory and Bowlby's, and he said, "*C'est facile!*" [laughs] That was the extent of our conversation, pretty much!

PLR: But he liked the idea.

MSA: Yes.

PLR: And did you know Margaret Mahler at all?

MSA: No. I never met her. I've read mostly her early work, as a matter of fact. Everything's in reverse! [laughs] Instead of attachments being formed, they're in a sense broken. Separation and individuation. It's the growing apart that's important for her rather than growing together.

PLR: Interesting point!

MSA: The early reports of her research that got into actual behavior made me think that we had something in common. It was the theoretical interpretation we placed on what's happening that differed.

PLR: Yes. Do you admire Daniel Stern's work?

MSA: Yes, I do very much. I consider his work very compatible with attachment theory. I think he feels the same way, but he certainly has gone his own way rather than following Bowlby, as it were.

PLR: Right, but, again, it's a very impressive synthesis of experimental and theoretical work. I'm glad we talked about Kagan, because when I read the *Atlantic Monthly* article, it was hard for me to make much sense of what he was saying, but it's considered an important critique.

MSA: He places all this emphasis on temperament. I think that some of the research he has done on termperament is good, but it's very limited. The fussy baby that he assumes is temperamentally and genetically scared and shy and insecure represents a very small percentage of the population.

PLR: Yes. And, of course, even a newborn baby has had a lot of experiences, so, if the mother is in some way depriving the baby in the womb, there's already an environment there.

MSA: Yes. I don't think for a minute that there's a gene or a combination of genes that makes for secure versus insecure attachment. You can have infants that really are very badly put together to start with—very fussy, whiny, difficult—but, if the mother is able to be responsive to the behavior anyhow, despite the difficulties, they can wind up being securely attached. But when you get a mother who finds it difficult to be responsive because of her own personality and a baby that is badly put together, then you have trouble.

PLR: So you are leaving some room for the role of temperament?

MSA: Yes. But a mother can be appropriately responsive to a given baby even if she's had several babies who may differ quite a lot in their characteristics to start off, and she can be sensitive to each one in terms of his or her own leads.

PLR: So you're saying that there is something innate that each child brings?

MSA: Yes. Everybody knows that.

PLR: But it wouldn't be something as simple as a gene for security.

MSA: No.

PLR: The personality of the child is just there.

MSA: And I do put an awful lot of emphasis on the experiences of the infant.

Peter Lomas

An Independent Streak

Peter L. Rudnytsky: What I would most like to hear about is what led you to psychoanalysis in the first place and your experiences in the British Society. What was it like to be a candidate and an analyst? Who were the people you knew in the Society? Finally, what were the reasons you resigned from the Society and what are the directions you have taken since then?

Peter Lomas: Well, I'll tell you, and you butt in if you want to ask me something.

PLR: Fine.

PL: I was drawn to the idea of helping people because I come from a long line of clergy. The idea that one should help people was in my religious upbringing. I first became a doctor, and then I realized I was not much good as a doctor and that I was much more interested in what was going on in people's lives. Quite apart from that—no direct connection—I myself went for psychoanalysis because I was suffering from anxiety. And I had an ordinary analysis, as it were, from a Freudian in Manchester.

PLR: Was that with anyone whose name I would know?

PL: Hilde Lewinski, who subsequently went to America. In fact, that's why the analysis was stopped. But I'd already decided that I would like to do this work, so I moved to London. With a view to continuing personal therapy, I found an analyst, but with the hope that I would be able to do this work myself. In a stroke of good fortune, I was referred to Charles Rycroft, and I had an analysis with him.

After about a year, I plucked up the courage to ask him if he thought I would be able to do this work.

PLR: Had you seen someone in London before Rycroft?

PL: No, I was at that time in general practice. Rycroft gave the go-ahead, so I applied. I was interviewed by Winnicott, who was immensely charming. I was completely bowled over by him. At the end of the interview, as I went to leave, he said, "Do you know that you've got a hole in your pants?" There was something very spontaneous about it, really disarming. It was almost like a child saying, "Well, you've got a hole." I said, "Yes, I'm aware. I'm very hard up." [laughs] I was accepted, and I went through the analytic business. Again, I was lucky, I think, in my teachers, who included Melanie Klein, Winnicott himself, and Rycroft. Marion Milner supervised me; she rarely gave a lecture. Balint, Bowlby. They are the names that stand out.

PLR: Could you give me some feel of what it was like to be in analysis with Charles Rycroft?

PL: He was immensely capable and very rigorous as an analyst. He got an understanding of me. He was scrupulous and on the ball. He was, for that time, fairly free and flexible. The rule was five times a week; because I was hard up, he let me off with four times a week. [laughs]

PLR: Did the Training Committee know about that?

PL: Oh, no. [laughs] And he would talk about himself and what he thought about people in the Society in quite an open way.

PLR: Can you give me any examples of things he said that stay with you even now?

PL: Later on in the analysis, when he had become disillusioned with the Society, he referred to one leading Kleinian as having castrated more men in London than anyone else. He could be quite acid. When I wanted to go to Balint for supervision, he said, "He's a sadistic man, but brilliant."

PLR: Did that conform with your impression of Balint?

PL: It's a bit severe.

PLR: He was fierce, maybe.

PL: Yes. He was fierce. Sadistic is too strong. I'm saying all the good things I feel about Rycroft because there was a lot to be grateful for in the way he helped me to understand my childhood and put up with me. I must have been a diabolically difficult patient.

PLR: How so?

PL: I was very argumentative and would question what he did a lot. I was very slow to make progress. I can remember, after four years or so, with a sort of sigh, he said, "You know, there's one thing to be said for you"—as if there were nothing else [both laugh]—"you do seem to learn from your mistakes." Those little touches one remembers.

PLR: They kept you going.

PL: Kept me going. Yes, encouragements, or the odd compliments, which are not to do with interpretations, that I had from him—or from other people—I remember.

PLR: The human touch.

PL: They stick there. Because he was a very truthful man. But he was very arrogant. He felt he was intellectually superior not only to me but to nearly everyone. Although I was a difficult patient, I'm sure he provoked me into being competitive. He was rather a male chauvinist. He came from the minor aristocracy, and in spite of his flexibility compared with many therapists—he thought the Kleinians were very rigid—I found the whole business of analysis inhuman, in some ways, and impersonal. I could not for years get him to address me as Peter.

PLR: Even after the analysis?

PL: I think it was only after the analysis, when I kept up a relationship with him, that I could persuade him to call me "Peter." When I objected to being called Dr. Lomas, he started to call me Lomas, which was the manner of address in the public school.

PLR: So the class issue came into it?

PL: Yes, he did consider class. I think, in spite of his having had even Communist views in his early days, the class thing was strong in him. So the analysis was a mixed blessing. It helped me a lot. What I value most, in a way, was that he encouraged the rebel in me. He didn't discourage that because he himself has quite a rebellious streak. And he also left the Society.

PLR: Your careers contain some striking parallels.

PL: Yes.

PLR: Not only were you both trained as doctors before becoming analysts, but you both resigned from the British Society after taking an independent path. You've become prolific authors who have influenced culture outside of psychoanalysis.

PL: Yes. So there's a lot that was good and helpful which I've followed. But, on the other hand, he was very competitive and, although I don't think he would easily like to think of me as in his class . . .

PLR: As it were.

PL: [laughs] Not in any sense. I think he was probably competitive with me.

PLR: He recognized your gift, probably, and saw something of himself in you as well.

PL: It may be, but to say that I had a gift is not something that would come easily to him. So the very word sounds a bit strange. I'm leaving out my own psychopathology in this.

PLR: Would you be comfortable talking about that? I'm interested in how you feel psychoanalysis can bring about change in a person and its possible benefits.

PL: I think that simply understanding one's life is immensely helpful, although I now believe not nearly enough. Postmodernists talk about the story as if it were just made up. But I mean a story that one feels is true and believes is true and that I think has truth in it. In that sense, analysis changed the story of my life.

PLR: Can you say how it did that?

PL: It made me realize how much I had let myself be influenced by my mother, who was very possessive and who I think had separated me from my father. Analysis enabled me, as it were, to get back to my father and to value him in a way that I had not been able to. It brought me in touch with schizoid or obsessional defenses. I don't like jargon, but I find myself using it as shorthand.

PLR: This reminds me of Guntrip. Not only the background of clergy, but the schizoid defense.

PL: Yes. I feel that throughout my life I've probably become less schizoid. But an awful lot has happened to me since I stopped analysis. I have changed in ways I think are good. My wife tells me I'm easier to live with. That doesn't necessarily mean that I've improved. It might mean that I've become tame. But I think I'm less standoffish. What it has not done for me is to cure what I went for, God knows how many years ago. I went for anxiety. It has not cured my anxiety. I have to confess the anxiety is manifestly less, because it was very acute. I used to get anxiety attacks, sweat, and so on to such an extent that I thought the only thing to do was to go to a psychiatrist who would say, "Anyone in this state should be put away." I no longer have fears of that kind, but I've remained all my life an anxious person.

PLR: Would these attacks be triggered by certain situations, or was it a more general state?

PL: It's a general anxiety. I would like, as a result of therapy, to have felt a more secure person than I do now in many situations. In social situations I'm often ill at ease. The only specific one I can think of is that I'm particularly anxious in travel. But not cripplingly so. It's not stopped me from going anywhere, but I have an unpleasant degree of anxiety.

PLR: Concerning disaster that might occur?

PL: No, I think it's unfamiliarity.

PLR: Just being in a strange place?

PL: Yes, I'd rather be back in the womb.

PLR: Instead of out in the world?

PL: Nice and safe somewhere.

PLR: So it's an existential anxiety?

PL: Yes.

PLR: I imagine that your work as a therapist over the years has been a way of prolonging your experience of self-reflection. Have you learned even more from your work with patients than from your own analysis?

PL: I think so. I think the beauty of being pretty screwed up is that I don't have any problem of empathy with screwed-up patients. I sometimes feel, "Just you bring one that I haven't experienced, and that will be something." I can identify with most degrees of distress and confusion [laughs] and despair that people can bring. And they know that.

PLR: I'm thinking about Laing as another somewhat maverick figure in psychoanalysis who also brought this quality of contact with the psychotic side of life. I wonder how you feel about Laing.

PL: Well, if I have mixed feelings about Charles [Rycroft], I have more mixed feelings about Ronnie [Laing]. I knew Ronnie; he was analyzed by Charles. I had already given a paper to the Institute in which I talked about the work on some of these American schizophregenic families.

PLR: Bateson?

PL: Yes. I was reading Bateson probably at the same time as Ronnie was reading Bateson.[1] So I was very drawn when I read his book *The Divided Self* and immediately met him.[2] We worked together a bit on families. I admired Ronnie a lot for his ruthless determination to go to any lengths in any situation. He seemed to have immense courage as well as drive. But the ruthlessness had another side to it. I felt that he gradually became more caught up with his own narcissism and ambition. As I say, I admired him a lot. I had fun with him, too. But I wouldn't feel comfortable sending him a patient, except perhaps a very severely psychotic patient he might get to whereas another person wouldn't. I didn't feel he had the kind of ordinary, everyday compassion for people that I think therapy needs.

PLR: To whom would you have felt comfortable sending a patient?

PL: Winnicott, Marion Milner, Rycroft, of the names I've mentioned. Those are the three. And Enid Balint.

PLR: Let's talk more about Winnicott. I thought the anecdote about the hole in your trousers was quite amusing. [PL laughs] I guess you didn't make a point of dressing up for the interview. Or were those the only pair of pants you had?

PL: Well, I hadn't any better ones. They were my best. [laughs]

PLR: I think Winnicott might have appreciated that you weren't putting on a False Self.

PL: That's true. We got on well and always did get on well. Later on, he referred me patients. I think he took me under his wing a bit. I liked his fun. He used to invite people to his house to have talks and seminars, and he included me among them. When I went, there were about six of us; they're not famous names.

---

1. See Gregory Bateson (1956), "Toward a Theory of Schizophrenia." In *Steps to an Ecology of Mind.* New York: Ballantine Books, 1972, pp. 201–227.

2. R. D. Laing (1960), *The Divided Self: An Existential Study in Sanity and Madness.* London: Tavistock.

PLR: People from the Society?

PL: Yes. It might be a bit unkind to say that they were acolytes. They weren't figures of his standing. He would be the teacher. In a sense, one might say that it was generous of him to teach. He certainly was not afraid of confrontation with his equals, but I feel he was quite a vain man. But, then, aren't we all?

PLR: He was trying to build a following, perhaps.

PL: Yes. And he would get pretty cross if I didn't follow him.

PLR: Was there a time that that happened?

PL: Over a patient, on one occasion. He referred me a patient, and I didn't do with the patient what he wanted.

PLR: How so?

PL: Well, after a short while, I thought that the chief thing was for this young man to get separated from his family and their influence. And I encouraged him to do that. We also stopped the therapy, where Winnicott thought it should have gone on. I did not like him interfering. I was young then and very flattered when Winnicott referred me a patient. But I have a very independent streak in me. If someone comes into my room, I want to do what I want to do. I was once very annoyed with him because he again referred me a patient when I was quite young, and this was the daughter of a rather famous man, whom I won't name. Winnicott said, "It's very important that you do well with this girl, because this man could have an influence on psychoanalysis." I thought, "To hell! I'm only interested in this girl. Bugger the man and psychoanalysis!"

PLR: Well, Winnicott had his position as President of the Society. I suppose he was concerned about the institution of psychoanalysis, as well as the outcome of this particular treatment.

PL: I was very idealistic and impractical, probably. After he died, his wife, Clare, came to see me for therapy, which surprised me very much. I liked Clare. I had known her a little bit, from going to his house, and I saw her for a while. But I wouldn't want to talk about that.

PLR: That's private. But that shows quite a degree of trust on her part, and respect on Winnicott's side also. Let's talk now about the process by which you evolved out of psychoanalysis. You wrote to me that you don't consider yourself in the psychoanalytic camp any longer.

PL: No, I don't.

PLR: That must have been a gradual process. I wonder if you could talk about the reasons why you've resigned from the Society, since you were a practicing analyst.

PL: I felt that the Society was claustrophobic. There was too much adulation of Freud. It had too many elements of religion in it. It was a closed society; it was not open enough to all other intellectual goings-on. It was elitist. The psychoanalysts were the important people—they still feel like that—among therapists. Even now, when I use the word therapy, I think that to a psychoanalyst it means something watered down.

PLR: The alloy.

PL: The alloy. Not the gold. Whereas I don't feel that at all. I became more and more critical of the theory and the technique—in particular, the technique of noncommunication on the part of the analyst, not revealing himself or herself. I came to believe that the analytic relationship should be more ordinary, human, friendly, and everyday, with a greater sense of equality. That's what people needed. They needed to feel that the other person was human; they needed to feel that he cared; they needed to know if he *didn't* care! The good and the bad. Therapy became less of a power trip. It was in the pursuit of truth, and not just the truth inside the patient, but the truth of what was going on in the room—the reasons why the therapist was saying things that he should not hide. I didn't believe that he or she should hide behind any convention, technique, or theory. If the analyst was working according to that, he or she should say so. All these things made me increasingly feel that psychoanalysis was too narrow. The same things that go for healing in ordinary situations of life and help people are vitally important in therapy. And that's what my patients told me! I was also influenced by existentialism, which criticized certain aspects of Freudian thinking. Buber's I–thou, and so forth.

PLR: As opposed to *The Ego and the Id?*

PL: Yes. That's right.

PLR: Do you feel that the therapist's disclosure of who he or she is influences the unfolding of the transference in the relationship?

PL: It must have some influence. But I don't think that, by and large, unless it's done wildly, it's deleterious. The transference will still appear. If there were a donkey sitting in the chair—and I hope I'm not a donkey—there would still be a transference to the donkey. It's sometimes said that introducing things about oneself distorts the transference. But sitting there and saying nothing distorts the transference, if there is a pure transference to be distorted. I don't think one can get at the pure transference.

PLR: No. But it's a question of whether the possession of a good deal of realistic knowledge about the therapist might crowd out the patient's opportunity to create his or her own fantasy.

PL: That's a very legitimate concern. And it does modify the way I would disclose myself. For example, I might sometimes ask, "What are your fantasies?" before I would say, "In actual fact, those are your fantasies, but the real answer is so-and-so, as far as I'm concerned."

PLR: Could you elaborate on that?

PL: Well, suppose that the patient had a fantasy about me that I was ill that day. It just depends on the circumstances whether I would say, "No, I'm not ill," or whether I would say, "No, I'm not ill, but what made you think I might be?" Or I might say, "What makes you think I'm ill?" and we'd explore the patient's fantasies. Then I'd say, "If I am ill, I'm not aware of it. I'm feeling perfectly good, actually." [laughs]

PLR: That's the worst kind of illness. [PL laughs] So you allow your intuition to guide you in a given situation as to whether to answer the question directly?

PL: Yes.

PLR: I think I agree with you that the transference will continue to march on almost despite what the analyst does. Perhaps one can be too concerned about the dangers of self-revelation. But there is still the theoretical problem of infringing on the patient's fantasy. Do you continue to use the couch with some patients?

PL: I leave it to them, by and large. We talk about it. But nowadays more of my patients sit in the chair than lie on the couch. And some might vary, from one to the other. There are things to be said for both.

PLR: Of course, when the patient is on the couch, you're out of view.

PL: That's it. It's less like an ordinary experience. And I try to make therapy as near to an ordinary experience, like two friends meeting, as possible. I think there is a danger of therapy being used as a defense by supposing that it's not connected with ordinary life. People sometimes say to me, "Look, this isn't real," and I say, "Well, it's as real as anything else that's happened today in our lives."

PLR: I know you admire Ferenczi very much. Do you have any thoughts about the experiment of mutual analysis? Have you taken any steps in that direction?

PL: Not as far as he went. I greatly admire Ferenczi's openness, and I think he was tremendously courageous to do what he seems to have done, which was almost a formal mutual analysis. I don't do that. I might, with some people in some situations, disclose a problem to them. But it would be in a context. For example, somebody might say, "Well, I couldn't possibly do anything to help you." He is idealizing me and thinking that he is a poor, unworthy being. Everything in my life is absolutely sunny and perfect and composed. I've been analyzed. How could he do anything for me? Of course, I might fall off my seat laughing to think that he could think that. Or I might say, "Well, you're wrong. I could give you an example—a problem I have at the moment." Or someone might be making a particular point that she can't help me. I would say, "I don't know whether anyone can help me, but what do you think about this problem that I've got?" I don't often do that, but I have done it.

PLR: That's courageous in itself. I suppose that whether therapy should be like or unlike ordinary experience has to do with a frame that one might want to place around the analytic encounter, as indeed around the aesthetic experience. When we go to a play, we expect something profound to happen, but we know that the experience is in another realm, the realm of play and illusion. In a way, that is the source of its power.

PL: Yes.

PLR: So I'm again concerned that, in trying to link up with ordinary experience, something might be lost precisely because of the attenuation of the artificiality or the frame of the setting.

PL: I do understand that misgiving. There's no doubt that the therapeutic situation is a special one, which isn't exactly like what happens elsewhere. But, then, almost every situation in life is special in some way. So that doesn't make therapy especially special. But it does create expectations and hopes and enables people to have the possibility of behaving in ways that they couldn't have in any other setup. That I am not closely involved with them in ordinary life does ease the situation. But, even given that truth, I think it's wrong if therapy is made into a set of rules: Thou shalt not give thy patients cups of coffee. Thou shalt not go on walks with patients. Thou shalt not hug thy patients. Or swear at thy patients. Or whatever. I don't think there should be these kinds of rules.

PLR: Or commandments.

PL: Yes. Commandments. [laughs]

PLR: I know you're very concerned about the moral dimension of psychotherapy. I'd like to ask you now about the sense in which you feel that psychotherapy is a moral endeavor. What is the current direction in your thinking?

PL: I think that we try to make—*make* is too strong a word—we try to *help* people who come to see us to be better people. I suppose that, if someone is psychotic and his life is in ruins and he can't get up from the floor, then it seems quite suitable to talk about health and get him to walk. But most of the people who come to me are not of that kind. They can live. With them, what I'm trying to do is not covered adequately by the concept of health, but by a much older concept, which comes down from the Greeks, of a good life. We are trying to help people to live a better life, and that includes being better people. I would not be satisfied if someone came to me with anxiety; we had therapy; and at the end of it she didn't have anxiety but she was a rotten person whose behavior we didn't approve of because she went and ripped everybody off. I feel that, willy-nilly, what most therapists do, but don't openly acknowledge, is to try to enable their patients to be better people in the moral sense, and that they bring that into every aspect of their work. They bring it into their interpretations, which are usually thought of as neutral. Some may be neutral, but there's an ideology—a moral sense of the world—that comes into them. Men and women. How should men behave? And how should women behave? Almost everything has its implications.

PLR: Robert Coles recently suggested that Winnicott's idea of a good-enough mother has to be understood as a *good*-enough mother, that is, one who has a moral sense that she is able to communicate to her child.[3] And Winnicott said that, beyond the question of health, there is the question of what life itself is all about.[4] I think at the end of his life he too was moving in an existential direction in his work.

PL: Yes, Winnicott's work does have an existential ring to it. I'm not sure how far back one can go. I don't think we know very well what a baby's world is like, and it's hard to talk about it. But even going

---

3. Robert Coles (1997), *The Moral Intelligence of Children.* New York: Random House, pp. 90–97.

4. D. W. Winnicott (1971), "The Location of Cultural Experience." In *Playing and Reality.* London: Tavistock, pp. 99–100.

back to early childhood, I think that the mother is trying to bring up not just a healthy child, or a happy child, but a moral child. Even the mother who has gotten rid of puritanical and Victorian ideas of rigid right and wrong—"Spare the rod and spoil the child" and that kind of stuff—is concerned with this question of how should one live. How should I bring up my child to live? I want my child to be good—not goody-goody.

PLR: Certainly not perfect.

PL: And not perfect. But someone whom one would be proud of. And not simply because she is healthy or because she is successful, but because she is decent. "Decent" is a word I like. I've just been reading a very interesting book, *The Decent Society*.[5]

PLR: Someone who is intrinsically worth loving. That's what comes to my mind.

PL: That's right.

PLR: Or the Greek word *sophrosyne*.

PL: Yes, someone who has wisdom.

---

5. Avishai Margalit (1996), *The Decent Society*, trans. Naomi Goldblum. Cambridge, MA: Harvard University Press.

Charles Rycroft

A Science of the Mind

Peter L. Rudnytsky: Could you tell me how you came into psychoanalysis and what it's been like for you?

Charles Rycroft: I was accepted for training as an analyst in 1936, when I was 22, on condition I did medicine. I had the idea that psychoanalysis might be a science of the mind that would illuminate other things I was interested in. I also had the idea, when I read Freud's *Interpretation of Dreams*, that I would be quite competent at it. I thought it would suit me. I had quite a good academic record from Cambridge. Some people have told me that I was a catch. I had had no idea of this at the time, I may say.

PLR: What did you read at Cambridge?

CR: I did the Economics Tripos Part I, on which I got a bad First. A One/Two. Then I did the History Tripos Part II, on which I got a Second. During the time when I couldn't decide whether I could go through with medicine, I was a research student in modern history. So I did a fourth year at Cambridge. That got nowhere but was quite interesting. I didn't have enough foreign languages to go on.

PLR: Were you already interested in the scientific aspect of psychoanalysis?

CR: Yes. I had the idea that history and economics suffered from the fact that there wasn't any proper psychology. And I had the idea then—which I tend to question now—that psychoanalysis could and would provide this. I should explain that there was another factor in all this. When I was 18, I spent six months in Germany, which coincided with Hitler's coming to power.

PLR: In 1933?

CR: From January to August 1933. Hitler became Chancellor in the beginning of January. Something dreadful was going on, and that politically alerted me. I saw that there was something wrong with British society because it didn't seem to be taking what was going on in Germany seriously. That got me involved in critical theories of all kinds.

PLR: Did you encounter anything having to do with psychoanalysis while you were in Germany?

CR: No.

PLR: When did you read *The Interpretation of Dreams*?

CR: I suspect it was my second year at Cambridge. It might have been my first. Of the people I made friends with, a number had read Freud at school and thought I was terribly backward because I had never even heard of Freud until somebody lent me a copy of *The Interpretation of Dreams*. Around the same time, somebody lent me Jung's *Modern Man in Search of a Soul*.[1] Anyhow, I was eventually accepted on condition I did medicine, and I went on and did it. I had rather a checkered career. I had great difficulty at the beginning.

PLR: In medicine or in psychoanalysis?

CR: In medicine. Well, in psychoanalysis, in the sense that my first analyst was Ella Sharpe, and she and I didn't really hit it off. I spotted quite early on that I worried her. Indeed, there was one occasion when I made some mistake about times. I came down to the street from the flat I was in, and there she was, waiting for me. She obviously thought I was highly gifted. That was flattering and alarming. And she worried about me, which was equally alarming. It was the first time in my life that anybody had worried about me. [laughs]

PLR: What was she worried about?

CR: I think she thought I was a bit of a lost soul, which in some ways I probably was. As I look back on it, some of my problems were ones that psychoanalysis hadn't yet caught up on. My father died when I was a child, and that had all sorts of social consequences. During the

---

1.   C. G. Jung (1933), *Modern Man in Search of a Soul*, trans. W. S. Dell & Cary F. Baynes. New York: Harcourt, Brace & World.

time that I was in analysis with Sharpe, my sister's husband was killed in a car crash. There wasn't any competent male around other than me to deal with it. I had lots of problems about widowed women, and so on.

PLR: How old were you when your father died?

CR: Eleven.

PLR: And when your sister's husband was killed?

CR: I was 23. My sister was left a widow with two children at 22, which is something one doesn't wish on anybody. Sharpe must have recognized that I was stuck because I was sent off to see Edward Glover. He recommended that I go on with Ella Sharpe. Looking back on it, I think it was because of the dearth of suitable training analysts.

PLR: Were you studying medicine at that time?

CR: Yes. I was still taking my first exam for the M.D.

PLR: What years were you in analysis with Ella Sharpe?

CR: That would be 1937 to 1939. Then there was a war, and Ella Sharpe left London and my medical school left London. Temporarily, psychoanalytic training stopped for me. Eventually, I was back in London and started with Sylvia Payne. Sylvia Payne and I got on very well. It was quite satisfactory. She was a practical woman.

PLR: Did you have any military involvement during the war?

CR: No. I was in the Auxiliary Fire Service very briefly. When I got into clinical work, medical students were exempted, and I slept in hospital once a week for quite a long time.

PLR: I've heard that you had left-wing leanings in those days. Is that true?

CR: [laughs] Oh, yes. At Cambridge, I was very briefly a member of the Communist Party. There's an article by me, "Memoirs of an Old Bolshevik," in *Psychoanalysis and Beyond*.[2] It was written to amuse my daughters around the time they went to university.

PLR: Let's go back to Ella Sharpe for a moment. You seem to be saying that she understood something about you—that you were a lost soul—and that she was right to be concerned.

---

2. Charles Rycroft (1969), "Memoirs of an Old Bolshevik." In *Psychoanalysis and Beyond*, ed. Peter Fuller. London: Hogarth Press, 1991, pp. 207–213.

CR: Yes, I think she probably was. But whether she was right to let me know that she was concerned is another matter.

PLR: You started to describe an incident when there was a question about times. Was she worried that you had done something drastic?

CR: I suppose so.

PLR: Did you have suicidal feelings at that time?

CR: No, never.

PLR: But she was that worried about it?

CR: I gathered later on that she had had a number of suicides among her patients, and she was already ill herself. She had a bad heart. I think she fell down dead in Victoria Station one day when she was in her 50s.

PLR: But that must have been a decade later.

CR: Slightly less than a decade. 1946 or so.

PLR: It sounds as though you and she didn't really get along in the analytic relationship, and you wanted to change.

CR: I didn't know what to do. The whole thing was much less organized than it is nowadays. I wrote about this in a paper I gave as a lecture for Regent's College, "Reminiscences of a Survivor," in which I was asked to be indiscreet.[3] I never had a choice of analysts. I was just sent. I received a letter saying I had been accepted for training, and would I . . .

PLR: You would start with Miss Sharpe.

CR: [laughs] Yes, exactly. At some point, I must have received a letter saying I would start with Dr. Sylvia Payne, and I had never heard of her. That was all right. She understood my family background much better than Ella Sharpe did. I am from what used to be called the new poor in the 1930s. That is to say, people of aristocratic background who had had a lot of money, but whose money had somehow disappeared. Payne understood all that much better than Sharpe did—what sort of person my father was likely to have been, and things like that.

PLR: Whom were you supervised by?

---

3. Charles Rycroft (1995), "Psychoanalysis 1937–1993: Reminiscences of a Survivor." *British Journal of Psychotherapy*, 11:453–456.

CR: My two supervisors were Marion Milner, who was very helpful—quite an education—and a woman now quite forgotten called Helen Sheehan-Dare. Supervisions with Helen Sheehan-Dare were a total waste of time. I had already done some psychiatry, and I had a hopeless case. I was convinced that the patient was schizophrenic and quite inaccessible. Helen Sheehan-Dare wouldn't have any of this, and amazingly complicated obsessional material used to be exhaustively analyzed. A nice woman otherwise. Nonmedical.

PLR: I'm surprised that the Society directed you to seek medical qualification, since in principle there was no objection to lay analysts.

CR: I think there were two reasons. One is that the requirement made sure that I couldn't start practicing until I was at least 30. The other is that Jones suspected I was a dilettante, and it was a test of endurance or determination.

PLR: Was there still a preference for the leadership in the Society to be medically qualified?

CR: Yes, indeed. That's almost forgotten about now, but there was reputed to be some kind of a treaty between the British Psycho-Analytical Society and the British Medical Association by which the analysts would be given respectability and be the representatives of true analysis on condition that they remained a majority medical organization. I think the arrangement was that only 20% of the people should be lay. In my day, the idea that the President or any officer of the Society should be nonmedical just wasn't on.

PLR: Let's talk about what was going on in the Society. Melanie Klein, of course, had already arrived on the scene.

CR: You're going to be disappointed, but I didn't become aware of all these feuds and discussions until about 1946 or 1947. Payne never talked about them, though she was deeply involved. "Not in front of the children," was the habit in the analytical world. I must say it was quite a time, even after I started attending scientific meetings, before I realized how powerful all the disagreements were.

PLR: In what year did you qualify for membership?

CR: In 1947.

PLR: At that point, the Controversial Discussions had been concluded and the new training scheme was instituted.[4]

---

4. See *The Freud-Klein Controversies* (1991), ed. Pearl King & Riccardo Steiner. London: Tavistock. Analytic candidates could follow either Course

CR: That's right. The new training scheme came in, and I found that I had started as a final-year student. I attended lectures by Melanie Klein, Anna Freud, and Marjorie Brierley. I think she's one of the forgotten people who were terribly good.

PLR: What were your impressions of some of the people you've mentioned?

CR: [laughs] Ella Sharpe had a slightly portentous way of talking. In Margaret Little's book about her analysis with Winnicott, there's a brief account of her analysis with Ella Sharpe, which I found myself agreeing with.[5] She had an infuriating habit of taking a cigarette out and then waiting to light it because she didn't want to interrupt one. Very trying indeed. Payne did not give the impression of being formidable to meet. She was an extremely talkative woman, a fact I discovered after she had retired.

PLR: Even during analysis?

CR: No. In her professional life she was the model of discretion. Outside it, not. I had a patient years later who had been a great friend of Sylvia Payne, and this patient knew all about me. [laughs]

PLR: That seems to cross over between the professional and the personal.

CR: Yes, quite.

PLR: What sorts of areas were you able to explore with Sylvia Payne that you didn't get into with Ella Sharpe as much?

CR: [pause] The thing that comes to mind is this question of extricating oneself from the pressure of a depressed mother. My mother recovered from being depressed, but after the time we're talking about. She lived on until 99. I was helping to support her until I was 67.

PLR: That's even older than Freud's mother!

CR: [laughs] That's right, yes. There's a curious overlap. My social

---

A, the Kleinian track, or Course B, the track organized by Anna Freud; but the requirement that all candidates receive supervision from one non-Kleinian member of Course A eventually divided the British Psycho-Analytical Society into three groups for administrative as well as training purposes (pp. 906–907).

5. Margaret I. Little (1990), *Psychotic Anxieties and Containment: A Personal Record of an Analysis with Winnicott*. Northvale, NJ: Aronson.

background and Freud's are totally different, but we share this thing of growing up with elder half-brothers and nephews.

PLR: That's fascinating.

CR: I had one brother who was 27 years older than I, and another one who was 17 years older.

PLR: I think you said your father died when you were 11.

CR: Yes.

PLR: Freud's father, of course, lived on until Freud was 40, so that's a major difference, but Freud had fantasies that his half-brothers were the partners of his mother. Did anything like that occur for you?

CR: I don't think so. Well, actually, that's untrue. After my father died, the idea that my mother could have had an affair with my second brother did occur to me, but I think it was just a fantasy. Looking back on it, I think it was fortunate that my mother never saw a psychiatrist during my teens, because she would have had an ECT or something. She used to mutter things all the time about my half-brother Michael that I couldn't ever quite hear. It was very disturbing.

PLR: She would go on under her breath?

CR: That's right.

PLR: So your father had been previously married?

CR: Yes.

PLR: Had he divorced?

CR: No, he was a widower. The number of deaths around is really quite impressive, actually.

PLR: You said you wrote a paper called "Reminiscences of a Survivor."

CR: That's right. [laughs] Yes, quite.

PLR: One of the major themes in *The Interpretation of Dreams* is guilt of the survivor. Did you pick up on that when you read the book?

CR: No, I didn't. When I read *The Interpretation of Dreams* in preparation for my book *The Innocence of Dreams*,[6] I came to the conclusion that this man didn't understand his own dreams at all, which I gather is not an original opinion. I thought that Freud came out as

---

6. Charles Rycroft (1979), *The Innocence of Dreams*. London: Hogarth Press.

extremely snobbish, superior, aloof, and not quite straight sometimes. I don't think I could read it again.

PLR: Could you describe the difference between your approach to dreams and Freud's?

CR: I don't believe the hallucinatory wish-fulfillment theory of dreams. Guntrip says somewhere that dreams are a revelation of psychic structure. But there is still a wish, because all mental life has an element of wishing about it. One is kept going by desire of one kind or another, isn't one? One of the few original ideas I've had is that Freud's later theory of anxiety undermines his theory of dreams because he demonstrates that anxiety is not a specifically sexual manifestation. Therefore his insistence that anxiety shows sexual repression falls apart.

PLR: So there are dreams that are not merely wish-fulfillments?

CR: That's right. They are a process of working through and integrating.

PLR: I sometimes think of dreams as problem-solving activities.

CR: That's quite a good way of putting it. People do often have dreams in which they feel they've resolved a problem. I've always been a great fan of Karl Abraham. He had this idea, which amuses me, that when people recover from a depression, they have a dream in which they have an enormous defecation. They get the whole thing out of their system.

PLR: An enormous deification?

CR: Defecation.

PLR: Defecation. Oh, yes. [laughs]

CR: Not so very long ago, I had a patient who had had the most dreadful childhood. Both parents died when he was five. One day he had a dream in which the analytical session here, in this room, was also him sitting in the lavatory. In the dream, while talking about the satisfactory analysis he was having, he was also producing a stool. I said, "Surely this must mean it's the end of the analysis." [laughs] He laughed and said, "Well, in a way, that is quite true." The work had been finished, you see.

PLR: The working through. Was his analysis on the couch?

CR: Usually. He was one of those people who some days lie on the couch and some days don't.

PLR: I should think it would be more difficult to pass a stool if one were lying down on the couch. [laughs]

CR: Maybe he wasn't. Quite right.

PLR: We were talking about your experience as a survivor and linking it up with Freud and his half-brothers. You said your mother was depressed. Did you have any full brothers or sisters from your parents' marriage, or did you have only half-siblings?

CR: No, I had one full brother, Richard, who was older than I and went into the Navy. He is now dead. My half-brothers would be well into their hundreds if they were alive. And I've got two younger sisters, who are both alive.

PLR: Did your mother remarry after your father's death?

CR: No.

PLR: So you were the second son of that marriage?

CR: That's right.

PLR: Why did you have to look after the women in the family, if there was an older brother?

CR: He was useless. Richard was a bully. As he grew older, he grew nicer. But as a child, to my mind and my sisters' mind, he took advantage of my father's death to seize a degree of power that he didn't really have any right to. And, in any case, he was in the Navy and was usually stationed abroad.

PLR: Well, in the traditional scheme of primogeniture, that would have been the normal course of events. You would have had to go into the church!

CR: That at one time was under discussion.

PLR: Let's return to the experiences you had in the British Society. What can you tell me about Melanie Klein and Anna Freud?

CR: I didn't know them well. I went to some postgraduate seminars under Melanie Klein. They were quite impressive, but I came to disapprove of her very much. There was one case I presented to Melanie Klein, and she used to *tell* me what interpretations to make. Some of them I did. When this man's analysis came to an end, he thanked me for what I had done, but he said, "You know, those cuckoo interpretations you sometimes used to make . . . "

PLR: Who were the people you were most influenced by?

CR: I was tempted to say Winnicott, but I don't think I ever had a tremendous need to idealize anyone, which Payne didn't have either. She was always trying to reconcile, and I would have gone along with that. If one has to take sides, I'd be on Winnicott's side, as opposed to either Melanie Klein or Anna Freud.

PLR: Why don't we talk about your impressions of Winnicott?

CR: Brett Kahr interviewed me for his book on Winnicott, and he quotes me as having said that Winnicott was a prima donna.[7] Again, I find I'm not the only person to have thought this, though I've been a bit more outspoken about it than some. There was an enormous self-absorption. But he could be funny. [laughs] At Society meetings, which were always terribly crowded, I remember Winnicott coming up to me, shaking me vigorously by the hand, and saying, "Dr. Livingstone, I presume?" An anti-Semitic joke, I think.

PLR: Can you explain that?

CR: "Dr. Livingstone, I presume?" is what Stanley said when he met Livingstone in the middle of Africa. I think the implication was . . .

PLR: The only white person among all the blacks?

CR: That's right. [laughs] The Society after the war was predominantly Jewish. It wasn't exactly a problem not to be, but you had to be careful. I think that was what he meant. It was a relief to meet a blond Gentile in the woods. He was quite capable of making jokes, and some of them were arguably in slightly bad taste.

PLR: In the ideological alignments in the Society in the 1950s, were the Kleinians the dominant group?

CR: It was mainly Klein versus Winnicott and the Independents, with the Anna Freud group withdrawing a bit. Winnicott was already having heart attacks in the 1950s, so I was Acting Training Secretary for a while, which meant I did all the work. I can't remember Winnicott ever doing any work at all.

PLR: This involved the interviewing and selection of applicants?

CR: That's right. Part of the trouble was that the whole thing was very finely balanced, and one felt it could split up. I remember an incident that annoyed me very much, which must have taken place after I was Training Secretary. They then had a period in which there

---

7. Brett Kahr (1996), *D. W. Winnicott: A Biographical Portrait*. London: Karnac Books, p. 111.

were joint Training Secretaries, one of whom was an Anna Freudian and the other was a Kleinian. One of them, Mrs. Hedwig Hoffer, recommended a candidate to be analyzed by me on the grounds that I was Middle Group leaning toward B Group—B Group being the Anna Freud group, to which she belonged. Somebody else on the Committee found out that she had made the recommendation and compelled Mrs. Hoffer to write me a letter of apology for saying I was close to the B Group.

PLR: Was there some advantage in being seen as not leaning too far in either direction?

CR: If I had wanted to play politics, it would have been quite a good thing. I at some point realized that I might become more and more involved because I was in a politically acceptable position. It was very like what happened during the brief period when I was a member of the Communist Party. If they wanted to organize a meeting in Cambridge, I was sent along to arrange it because I looked so respectable. [laughs]

PLR: Was there any connection between your involvement with analysis and your disillusionment with the Communist Party?

CR: I don't think so. It was going to Russia that disillusioned me.

PLR: In the 1930s?

CR: In 1935. I had my 21st birthday on a Soviet ship in Hamburg harbor. I had gone to see *The Meistersingers of Nuremburg* at the opera house. At the end, the problem of returning to the boat arose, and some people in Nazi uniforms rowed us out. It has always struck me that one lives in a bit of a lunatic asylum. It's mad, isn't it?

PLR: Were you making this trip on your own?

CR: No. There was a organization called Society for Cultural Relations with the USSR, and with a friend of mine, John Madge, I was on the committee of the Cambridge branch. He had an elder brother, Charles Madge, who was one of the Auden circle and quite well known as a poet. The boat was intriguing. There were 25 people, some of whom became quite famous—or notorious. There were Anthony Blunt and Michael Straight. Straight was a Whitney by origin, and I have the idea that he edited *The New Republic* at one time. He once came up to me and said, "Do I look like a proletarian?" And I said, "No, you don't. You look like an American millionaire pretending to be a proletarian."

PLR: That's funny. Let's go back to the unfolding of events in the Society. You mentioned the anecdote about you and Winnicott as Gentiles. Was there also an issue of the dominance of women, especially on the Kleinian side?

CR: That was becoming so, but I can't remember its bothering me very much. A friend of mine, Armstrong Harris, now long dead, said, "The trouble with the Society is that it's full of soft men and hard women." There's quite a lot in that, actually.

PLR: Would you characterize Winnicott as a soft man?

CR: A very strange man. Ultimately, not, but he did give the impression of being soft, yielding, and maternal. But Aubrey Lewis, who was Professor of Psychiatry at the Maudsley in those days, used to say that Winnicott was the most aggressive man in London.

PLR: Did you find your understanding of psychoanalysis undergoing an evolution at that time?

CR: I think it always has. It still goes on.

PLR: Was that mainly in response to your own work with patients?

CR: I think so.

PLR: Could you talk about how your views have changed?

CR: For many years, I would have taken the view that there was a mainstream analysis and that Freud, Abraham, Ferenczi, Winnicott, Melanie Klein, and so on were all making contributions to its development. But, at some point in the 1960s, I started thinking that it wasn't so. There was too much divisiveness, and the groups were against one another. I became preoccupied with the idea that psychoanalysis is really about meaning and not about the causation of things. My withdrawal from the Society, which occurred many years before I actually resigned, stemmed from a meeting when I thought, these analysts really aren't any use, when it comes down to it. A man called James Home wrote a paper that developed the meaning theory of psychoanalysis,[8] and I agreed with an awful lot of it. But what struck me was not how wonderful the paper was, but how ghastly the discussion of it was. [laughs] Lots of people contributed to the discussion. All of them made very short declarations of faith in the natural scientific method and totally dismissed Home's paper. There

---

8. H. J. Home (1966), "The Concept of Mind." *International Journal of Psycho-Analysis*, 47:43–49.

were two exceptions to this. One was me, and the other was Peter Lomas. Peter Lomas got up and expressed wholehearted agreement with Home. I got up and said I thought that some aspects of analytic theory must be problems of meaning and some were problems of causality. That led me to resolve never to go to a meeting of the Society again. I never have either.

PLR: Was it that you simply didn't feel it was intellectually stimulating enough?

CR: No, I thought it was bigoted. And they were all hoping—this is my fantasy—that their loyalty to the scientific ideal of Freud would be recorded in the minutes. [laughs]

PLR: For posterity. Is there any sense in which you feel that psychoanalysis could be called a science?

CR: As I say in my *Critical Dictionary*, it's not a natural science.[9] It can't possibly be. There are all sorts of problems about people's awareness of futurity that don't fit in. But in that it's capable of organization, it is a science. It's a moral science, actually.

PLR: What about Bowlby's attempt to integrate the art of psychotherapy with natural science in the field of research? Do you think that has any validity?

CR: Yes, I do. I'm quite sympathetic toward Bowlby's attachment theory. I've written a piece about Bowlby in *Psychoanalysis and Beyond*.[10] It was on loss, mainly, which comes back to a theme raised quite early on in this discussion.

PLR: How do you feel about his work on loss?

CR: I think some of those statistics are a bit unsound. Bowlby is difficult. Although I absolutely agree with him about attachment, there's something seemingly unimaginative about Bowlby that puts one off. He came from a background rather similar to mine. His father was a baronet, as my father was. He was a second son, and his elder brother never had children. He is said to have hoped that he would get a knighthood before he inherited his brother's title. [laughs]

PLR: So it would be his own?

---

9.   Charles Rycroft (1995), *A Critical Dictionary of Psychoanalysis,* rev. London: Penguin, s.v. Science.

10.   Rycroft, "Bowlby: Attachment and Loss." In *Psychoanalysis and Beyond*, pp. 147–155.

CR: That's right. But in actual fact he was never knighted, and he died before his brother, so the whole thing came to naught.

PLR: I agree with you about the importance of meaning in psychoanalysis. But I would like to integrate the hermeneutic side of the work with something that we could still call a natural science, at least in the field of research. So I wouldn't like to discount the scientific element completely.

CR: Nor would I.

PLR: To come back to the paper by Home, was that the last time you attended a scientific meeting of the Society?

CR: I once gave a paper to the Independent group in an emergency. Walter Joffe, a former President of the Society, rang me up one day and said he had committed himself to giving a lecture but was too tired, and would I give it instead? I said I would, and he had a heart attack a few days later.

PLR: Did you have anything to do with the 1952 Club?

CR: I was one of the founders of the 1952 Club.

PLR: Even though you had qualified five years earlier?

CR: Yes. A group of us, which included Armstrong Harris, Masud Khad—who in those days was young and reasonably respectable—Barbara Woodhead, and Pearl King, had at first a dining club arrangement in which we would meet once a month or so and discuss cases. In 1952, it was decided to turn it into an organization with a bank account and programs. It was my idea to call it the 1952 Club. I insisted that we must have a name with no political significance. We weren't to style ourselves the Independents, or the Orthodox, or the Unorthodox.

PLR: Was Enid Balint one of the founders?

CR: No. She was eventually a member.

PLR: Can you tell me something about Masud Khan? You must have witnessed his career at close range.

CR: The high dramas of his career came after I had begun to withdraw from the Society. I think his whole history counts as sad, ultimately. He was the youngest son of a much older father, in his 70s, who lived into his 90s. He was adored by the father, according to him, at any rate. Masud was always so peculiar, but he comes under the category of younger sons of second marriages. [laughs] There's a life of him written by one of his patients, Judy Cooper.[11] When I first met him, he was very young indeed, in his early 20s. I must have been around qualifying. He was a very exotic character, with lots of money. Not altogether a truthful man, and some people say the story he gave of his origins and background is untrue. Masud was in analysis with Ella Sharpe, who died, with John Rickman, who died, and then with Winnicott. And then some people say he was in analysis with Anna Freud. I saw that in print recently, but I find myself querying that claim. I must have decided he was mad, at some point. He was a psychopath, a creative psychopath. He wrote a paper on collage, and, as I look back on it, that is what Masud himself was.[12] He was a picker-up of other people's ideas, which he didn't properly integrate. The whole of his mind was a kind of muddle of all sorts of people, including me, except that he hardly ever quoted me. Like many Moslems, he would get on to alcohol and start drinking too much. I knew both his wives. He married dancers. The second was Svetlana Beriozova, who was a prima donna of Russian origin. That was all a disaster. She's still alive, but if you want to write a paper on Masud and approach her, she does not help.

PLR: It makes me want to go see her!

CR: Yes, quite. Masud became an impossible person, eventually, and I gave up seeing him. Dropped him, as they say. It's an interesting question how much of Winnicott was written by Masud. I used to think it was quite a lot, but now I'm not sure.

PLR: Khan certainly went over a lot of Winnicott's papers, but I don't think we need to conclude that he wrote them.

CR: Indeed. I used to have the idea that I only had to say something about Winnicott's paper before it would be mentioned in the next paper by Winnicott.

PLR: I'm sure he paid attention to the discussions. It's well known that you were the analyst of R. D. Laing. Could you say something about your impressions of Laing and his career?

---

11.   Judy Cooper (1993), *Speak of Me as I Am: The Life and Work of Masud Khan*. London: Karnac Books. According to Cooper, Khan was actually the second child of his father's third marriage. His father was 76, with six children from his first marriage and none from his second, and his mother was 17, with a son born out of wedlock, at the time of their marriage.

12.   M. M. R. Khan (1979), "Role of the 'Collated Internal Object' in Perversion-Formations." In *Alienation in Perversions*. London: Hogarth Press, pp. 120–138.

CR: Laing was very bright. I've altered my views on him, since my views of analysis have changed so much. The practicalities of Laing's analysis with me were masterminded by J. D. Sutherland, who was head of the Tavistock Clinic and a Scotsman. Sutherland gave me a job at the Tavvy and gave Laing a job at the Tavvy, so that Laing's analysis would be paid for by the National Health Service. I don't think I would go for such a setup nowadays, and I now certainly would never take on a patient who, by the rules, had to come five times a week and lie on couches and whose treatment with me was conditioned by a third party. That gets absolutely hopeless.

PLR: You mean you wouldn't be comfortable seeing someone where the setting of the treatment was prescribed by the formalities of the training procedure?

CR: That's right. Looking back on it, I was already a bit disenchanted with the Analytical Society.

PLR: What years are we talking about?

CR: Late 1956 to early 1960. Of course, Laing's attitude to me changed. For a few years in the 1960s, he went around being very contemptuous of me. Then I started writing books. Laing, who was a snob in quite a conventional way, started saying nice things about me. One of the very last things he wrote was a review of *Psychoanalysis and Beyond*, which was most understanding.[13] I felt that this man really understood me terribly well. Since then, I've had dealings with his son, Adrian. His first wife is very devoted to me, as is clear on the rare occasions I see her. The second wife I've seen socially too. It's funny, somebody said that Laing was contemptuous of me because I had never read Kierkegaard. But I can remember reading Kierkegaard in the late 1930s. "The worst has already happened." I've heard somebody quote this as something that I've said; somebody else said it's Laing; but in fact, it's Kierkegaard.

PLR: Could you describe more precisely the interconnection between the changes in your theoretical understanding of psychoanalysis and your views of Laing as a person?

CR: I've become much more antiauthoritarian. I think classical analysis has an element of imposing conditions on the patient which the patient should really choose for himself, including frequency of attendance and length. A person having a training analysis in the British Society is committed to four years, and the analyst is committed to

13. R. D. Laing (1985), "Innocence of Vision." *The New Scientist*, November 28.

four years. It's very tempting for both the analyst and the patient to postpone mentioning difficult areas. I think that's a beautiful way of mucking the analysis up.

PLR: Do you think four years might be too long?

CR: Yes.

PLR: In some cases, I can see the value of it, but I'm not convinced that for a person who's relatively well-functioning, four years would be necessary. What can you talk about all that time?

CR: Yes, quite. [laughs] Years ago, I had transferred to me, by an analyst whom I knew to be a lesbian, a woman patient who had come to her to be treated for her lesbianism 10 years before, and they had got stuck. She had her first heterosexual affair a few weeks after starting with me, but then she was faced with whether, at 46, she was too old to have a child. That's the sort of thing long analyses get people into, isn't it? Life goes on.

PLR: Do you feel that homosexuality is something that should be treated?

CR: [pause] It's a bit like alcohol. No. It's up to the patient, isn't it? If a patient came to me to say that he was worried about his homosexuality, I would say perhaps we should investigate that, but I can't possibly say whether it needs curing or can be cured.

PLR: How do you see the analogy to alcohol?

CR: It tends to be very discouraging. The temptations to go back on it are too great. I've had some quite successful cases in my life, but not with alcoholics.

PLR: That would imply that alcoholism is a disease.

CR: Yes, I think one has to say it's a disease that's largely biological. It makes people ill and shortens their expectations of life. Homosexuality intrinsically doesn't, but there's something very mysterious about homosexuality. Biologically, it's dysfunctional. Sex must have something to do with reproducing children. One doesn't know at what point in human evolution the dissociation of sexuality from reproduction occurred. Until quite recently, most people swore that it never got separated in women, which is not true. Post-60s women do their best to dissociate their sex life from their reproductive life, and they often pay a price for doing so.

PLR: How so?

CR: The children they should have had, they haven't; and they start having children too old.

PLR: If you look at the scene today, particularly here in London, how do you see the future of psychoanalysis?

CR: I'm rather gloomy about it all. I'm not well enough informed about what goes on in the Society to speak with confidence. There's something terribly inbred about it. People tell me it's much better, but occasionally I hear reports that suggest it's just as impossible as it used to be. I met somebody four or five years ago who had organized a party at the British Psycho-Analytical Society. She said she had never met a more paranoid and evasive group of people in her life. She was absolutely furious, and, when she found she had a sympathetic audience in me, she presented me with a copy of the book that she had organized the party for. [laughs]

PLR: Do you consider yourself a psychoanalyst today?

CR: I sometimes write analyst, and sometimes write psychotherapist. When I'm asked in ordinary social situations, I usually say I'm a shrink.

PLR: Has your way of treating patients changed?

CR: The way I treat patients is partly an adaptation to age. All my patients know that I'm now quite elderly. Something that intrigues me very much is that the number of patients who say "thank you" to me at the end of a session has gone up enormously. Whether it's because of something I do, which I don't quite understand, that is of help to them, or whether they think it's nice for an old man to spend time bothering about them, I really don't know.

PLR: It sounds as though there's a greater degree of warmth in the room.

CR: I think so.

PLR: The human element in the psychoanalytic relationship is always with us.

CR: Yes, indeed. All the things that Daniel Stern and Colwyn Trevarthen are on to are enormously important in adult analyses.

PLR: That goes back to the scientific aspect of psychoanalysis.

CR: Yes.

PLR: But it has its impact on the way people treat each other in the consulting room.

CR: That's right.

Peter D. Kramer

The Communication of Perspectives

Peter L. Rudnytsky: I've read your work with great admiration and actually used *Listening to Prozac* in my course on literature and psychology. I can see that you've emerged out of a psychoanalytic tradition—or one that is very sympathetic to psychoanalysis—but you've gone in a somewhat different direction toward what you call the "psychopharmacological era."[1] I'd like to have a dialogue on the level of theory with you, but then I'm also interested in the personal dimension of people's work. You yourself have said that "psychotherapeutic theory is often veiled autobiography."[2] So I'd like to try to have a twofold conversation, if we could, about how the unfolding of your work has had this autobiographical element and to invite you to reflect on your theoretical stance toward psychoanalysis.

Peter D. Kramer: I think you've almost done it already.

PLR: Maybe we should stop then!

PDK: I do have a question. I have in mind a Freud project, which I don't think I will ever do. It's more like a thought experiment, which is to sort out what remains of Freud.[3]

PLR: I'm extremely interested in that myself.

1. Peter D. Kramer (1993), *Listening to Prozac*. New York: Penguin Books, 1994, p. 287.

2. Peter D. Kramer (1997), *Should You Leave?* New York: Scribner, p. 94.

3. See Peter D. Kramer (1998), "Freud: Current Projections." In *Freud: Conflict and Culture*, ed. Michael S. Roth. New York: Knopf, pp. 196–206.

PDK: I would love to have someone go through and say exactly what remains of Freud and then to say what the grounding is for what we do if that is what remains of Freud. We come into psychotherapy on a picaresque basis—there was this episode in history and therefore we use this technique. We go on with that technique and various things are accreted to it. And then, down the road, the scaffolding is removed. So why are we still doing the same thing? Why are people lying on the couch, and why are they free associating? It's almost as if the method is so powerful that it can exist floating in air with no theory—or constantly changing theory—to support it. There's always a different justification for doing the same thing. Isn't it a striking incongruity that we should always do the same thing even if the theory has changed?

PLR: But maybe we don't do the same thing.

PDK: Right. We don't do the same thing. Empathy is stressed over interpretation. But the method remains fairly fixed—the mechanics.

PLR: Your practice includes the use of medications, and that already introduces a difference into the relationship. The thought occurred to me just yesterday that, if we are to approach Freud as literature, which in some ways is what I'm afraid we're reduced to, that's much the same as approaching the Bible as literature. That is to say, the text no longer has a sacred status, but it continues to be extremely influential, and we still have to come to terms with it. I myself am seeking a synthesis between psychoanalytic theory of one form or another—which may not be Freudian theory—and what we can say on a scientific basis about human behavior.

PDK: I'm stuck on this project because I found psychoanalysis magical. That is, my own analysis included dramatic realizations that I was denying something that obviously was influencing me in a way that could almost be demonstrated to me. You've gotten yourself so far out on a limb that when the analyst finally says, "What about this?" you think, "Oh my God, that is the case," and that it relates to the Oedipus complex, and so on.

Let's say that we're doing some other kind of analysis that doesn't have much concern for the unconscious. It involves a great degree of empathy and support, attention to ego functions, and some real assessment of strengths and weaknesses. It talks about patterns in relationships that turn primarily on learning issues rather than on consciousness and unconsciousness. At that point, there's no magic. I think anybody in history would have been willing to say that people who are disturbed could make do with some support and a more realistic view of their patterns in life. That to me is very reasonable, but the whole magic of psychoanalysis is its implausibility. I was just reading something in Milan Kundera's *Slowness*, where he talks about love. He says, "If a woman tells me: I love you because you're intelligent, because you're decent . . . then I'm disappointed; such love seems a rather self-interested business. How much finer it is to hear: I'm crazy about you . . . even though you're a liar, an egotist, a bastard."[4] That's how I think about psychoanalysis. What's the point of it if it's so reasonable?

PLR: It's like what Walter Benjamin terms the loss of aura.[5] You're saying that the quality of magic or unreasonableness of psycho-analysis—the fact that it's not simply common sense—is part of what continues to exert a hold on us.

PDK: And it gives us a hope that we can be catapulted out of our neurosis rather than having some reasonable way to make incremental changes in it, which seems exhausting.

PLR: You write about your analysis in some detail in *Moments of Engagement* and use your confusion about the names of Penelope and Penthesilea as an example of the kind of thing you're talking about here.[6]

PDK: Yes, exactly.

PLR: I was wondering how long your analysis lasted.

PDK: That analysis lasted nearly two academic years. Those were the years I was in London. I started not long after I arrived. So that's my notion of analysis. Then I had an unfortunate episode where the doctor in England thought he had arranged for me to enter a training analysis in Boston when I began medical school. That turned out not to be true. Not only was it not true, but the interviewer at the Boston Psychoanalytic treated me as if I were mentally ill, as if this were some narcissistic fantasy on my part—that I, a medical

---

4. Milan Kundera (1996), *Slowness*, trans. Linda Asher. London: Faber & Faber, p. 43.

5. Walter Benjamin (1936), "The Work of Art in the Age of Mechanical Reproduction." In *Illuminations*, trans. Hannah Arendt, ed. Harry Zohn. New York: Schocken Books, 1968, pp. 217–251.

6. Peter D. Kramer (1989), "Myth." In *Moments of Engagement: Intimate Psychotherapy in a Technological Age*. New York: Penguin Books, 1994, pp. 7–15.

student, could enter a training analysis. It turned out that he was a protagonist or an antagonist in a struggle within the Boston Psychoanalytic, which was at that moment determining whether one could enter a training analysis in medical school or only upon completion. So it was quite disingenuous of him to treat this belief as a fantasy on my part. This was something that would very much have been on his mind and about which he knew a great deal.

I was instead offered to be a control analysis for a candidate at the Institute, which was all I could afford and, even at a low rate, rather stressful on my finances. I did that for a couple of years in medical school, and quite religiously. You had to show up four or five times a week, and it meant going at 6:00 in the morning or leaving surgery in the middle of an operation [PLR laughs]—raising your hand and saying, "By the way, I'm going to my analysis," which was outrageous. That analysis did not go well. It was interesting to me in that it showed me some of the shortcomings of psychoanalysis. I've written about that in an obscure piece I did.

PLR: Where did you write about it?

PDK: In *Psychiatric Times*.[7] It had a pentimento quality, which is to say that the analyst in training was being supervised by a training analyst, and I kept saying to this analyst that he seemed to me to be behaving as a woman would behave. He said, "This is your latent homosexuality." I'm not one who has been conscious of much latent homosexuality. I was aggressively heterosexual at the time—which may or may not be a sign of latent homosexuality—but it was a concept whose time had perhaps come and gone already. It turned out that his supervisor *was* a woman; and late in the therapy, when he himself had gotten very upset with psychoanalysis, he admitted that to me. He said that I had been right. He'd felt I was right, and he'd not been allowed to tell me that I was right. In a way, I thought it was wonderful that the analyst is so transparent to the patient; but in another sense, the bad faith in the encounter was curious.

That analysis stopped being an analysis at a certain point. He said, "Why don't you sit up, and we'll do conventional therapy?" I did a fair amount of medical school away from the home site, so that I was commuting and doing "analysis" maybe one day a week, when I'd come back to Boston to get some supervision. So that was not a very successful experience. But it did make me aware of a certain anger or resistance, and I always worry as I approach psychoanalysis whether I am the product of an incomplete analysis. I think that

---

7. Peter D. Kramer, "The Dyer's Hand." *Psychiatric Times*, May 1986, pp. 3ff.

is the proper attack on me from inside psychoanalysis as of 40 or 50 years ago—that there is some hostility or resentment there. I try to be aware of that, and at least on the surface my thoughts are rather sentimental and tender toward psychoanalysis. But I certainly take that accusation seriously. I did have another therapy very briefly when I was in residency.

PLR: You mention that in your writing. You said you needed a push of some kind.[8]

PDK: Yes. I went to this therapist who was known for being very tough and abrasive, and I said, "I want two things. I want to get married and I want to write a book." He said, "We don't always get to choose how we enter therapy. Sometimes therapies just seem the same every time, whatever you want. It may end up looking a lot like the past therapies you've had." But whether with that help or not, or simply with the help of case supervision, which I think has some of the qualities of psychotherapy, I did in fairly short order get married and write a book.

PLR: Was that also psychoanalytically oriented psychotherapy?

PDK: It was once a week or less and very confrontational, but if you had to say what theory was at the root of it, yes, it would be psychoanalysis. But more probably it was like John Rosen's wild analysis. He was a British analyst who would give you the interpretation right away and not let you wriggle out of it.[9]

PLR: Was the book *Moments of Engagement,* or was it your novel?

PDK: It was my novel that was never published.

PLR: So you didn't want to publish a book, you just wanted to write one?

PDK: It's actually sort of a stuttering entry. Which is to say that I was in residency and started collecting material for one of those acculteration-of-a-professional books. I was very lucky to get Peter Davison, the poet, as an editor. He said something gurulike to me one time when I handed him some work. He said, "This is fine, but I'm not sure this is what you want to write." This episode is in *Should You Leave?*[10]

---

8. Kramer, "Just Good Friends." In *Moments of Engagement,* p. 118.

9. See John N. Rosen (1953), *Direct Analysis: Selected Papers.* New York: Grune & Stratton.

10. Kramer, "Imperatives." In *Should You Leave?* p. 126.

PLR: Yes.

PDK: So I wrote this novel, and as a result of someone's reading it, I was invited to do reviewing. As a result of the reviewing, I started writing a column for *Psychiatric Times*. An editor at W. W. Norton who read the *Psychiatric Times* column then wrote me to ask if I wanted to write a book. In response to that, I wrote *Moments of Engagement*, which used some of the material that I had been working on for Peter Davison, though I hope in a more mature fashion. So that's the long story of my success.

PLR: You certainly found your métier as a writer.

PDK: That's what I would say—that I did start writing seriously on my own behalf things that were intended to be books not long after that therapy. I also left residency early to be with my girlfriend, whom I then married. So that therapy was very useful. It did exactly what it should have done, which was to help put into working form what had gone on in the two psychoanalyses. I don't think it was that therapy in a freestanding way. The therapist was good at pulling threads together and not asking me to regress.

PLR: Did you make a decision not to pursue psychoanalytic training after that second analysis where you were asked to be in analysis with a candidate?

PDK: I think there was some narcissistic injury there. But, in addition, what happened in the interim was that I went to Wisconsin and did an internship.

PLR: You had contact with Carl Whitaker there?

PDK: I had contact with Carl Whitaker, but in addition we had elective time, and I did my elective in psychiatry. I spent a couple of months at the Veterans' Hospital in Madison on the Psychiatry Service, which was headed by a monkey researcher, William T. McKinney, Jr.

PLR: Harry Harlow had been at Wisconsin.

PDK: Yes, that primate lab was associated with the person who was head of the V.A. The particular ward I was on gave residents a lot of autonomy but used medication quite intensively. In some ways, you were free to do what you wanted in psychotherapy because it wasn't clear that the psychotherapy was doing the work. There was a lot of interest in correct diagnosis and some quasi-medical things like hypnotic regression and amytol interviews. There was a medical-model aspect even to the psychotherapy. Carl Whitaker did come in and consult on a case with me, so I had a lot of exposure to different materials. Then when I entered residency at Yale, the first ward I was on was headed by a neuropsychiatrist. That's the episode I've written about in *Moments of Engagement*—the entry into that ward and the troubled or troubling resident.[11] So that by the time I got to think about psychoanalysis again, I had had a year and a half of exposure to family therapy, biological psychiatry, psychopharmacology, and so on. I think that between being reluctant to be infantilized and being intensely aware of different aspects of psychiatry—forgetting the narcissistic aspect—psychoanalysis then looked like a different undertaking.

PLR: It was no longer so crucial to you professionally.

PDK: Well, I just didn't have as much of a sense of whether I believed in it or understood the basis for it. I thought that to apprentice myself without being sure of my beliefs was a problem, although I did feel somewhat either inferior or dishonest for not doing it. That's something I was quite capable of feeling, so I don't want to put too much emphasis on that. And, of course, I did want to be a writer. The wonderful thing about Yale was that it gave you a sense of the variety of psychiatry. I had some interest in forensics that developed there; I did a lot of interviewing of patients in prisons. I was also interested in consultation-liaison medical-model psychiatry. I wrote an article about a patient I saw that also relates to a chapter in *Moments of Engagement*. She had collagen-wasting disease, which was treated with multimodal psychiatric intervention that involved my going to her home and taking an interest in the medication she was getting for blood pressure, and so on.[12] So by the time I tried to make decisions about psychoanalysis, I was very aware of the ferment in psychiatry. I had a very fine teacher for family therapy, Behnaz Jalali, whom I write about in *Moments of Engagement*. So it was just not clear where to invest one's extra time. But I did have a sense that the infantilizing aspects of the more rigid analytic institutes would not be congenial to me, and I didn't see the point either of going to an analytic institute that wasn't quite strict and rigid, because I thought the rest of it was more or less on a par with lots of other theories I could think of.

---

11. Kramer, "The Mind-Mind-Body-Problem Problem." In *Moments of Engagement*, pp. 43–65.

12. Kramer, "When It Works." In *Moments of Engagement*, pp. 155–184.

PLR: I hope that's not true. What you're describing is in some ways an indictment of psychoanalysis.

PDK: Well, it's an indictment of my induction into psychoanalysis as a student. I think there is a great deal to be said for self psychology, ego psychology, and object relations. But I think there was also a lot to be said at the time for family therapy.

PLR: Sure.

PDK: That's what I mean about there not being anything compelling about one course of study versus another. I guess I also thought, having been through two psychoanalyses and contemporaneously being in a third, that what I really needed to a large degree was to learn theory and read material, and that I could do without being in an institute, and maybe do it more freely. I had a sense that there was going to be some constraint if I entered into training.

PLR: Your sense of your second analyst as a woman having been borne out by the role of the supervisor in the case is similar to what you write about your experience with your first analyst Max's heart condition, where you had a perception of something that turned out to be true.[13]

PDK: Yes.

PLR: It also reminds me of a passage in *Playing and Reality*, where Winnicott says to one of his patients, "'I am listening to a girl. I know perfectly well that you are a man but I am listening to a girl, and I am talking to a girl.'"[14] He explains this in terms of the patient's mother having wanted a girl and always seen the patient as a girl. Through his countertransference he was picking up something about the internalized gender identification of the patient. So there's nothing I can see that immediately contradicts psychoanalytic theory in those experiences you describe, except to say that you were perceiving something that had some reality basis to it and wasn't simply projection or transference.

PDK: One of the valuable things I take from psychoanalysis is that we know a great deal about one another through subtle cues and that our integration of those cues is often extremely accurate. That theme plays right through *Should You Leave?* In a sense, our skill at find-

---

13. Kramer, "Myth." In *Moments of Engagement*, pp. 8, 14–15.

14. D. W. Winnicott (1971), "Creativity and Its Origins." In *Playing and Reality*. London: Tavistock, p. 73.

ing mates has to with that ability, which is something like transference or countertransference or intuition. I also take it very seriously when patients say things about me because, if they're careful and thoughtful, they likely will have put their finger on something. However neutral and invisible and abstemious we are, that may only make more important aspects of us emerge.

PLR: I'd like to ask you about your family of origin. Do you have any brothers or sisters?

PDK: I have a sister.

PLR: I don't think you mention her in any of your writing.

PDK: That's an interesting observation. Unfortunately, I feel as though I can't discuss that in print, except to say that she is implicitly very much in my writing. At a certain moment, I discovered that my fraternal concerns about her might be the subject of my writing in some way.

PLR: Could you elaborate on that?

PDK: I can't, except to say that some of the tender and caring and concerned aspects of being a therapist probably come from being an older brother. Occasionally, in the writing I might realize that there is a more exact correspondence to that brother–sister relationship. So I think implicitly she is very much present.

PLR: Does she have any major disabilities?

PDK: No, she's fine. She's as fine as the rest of us.

PLR: Good. Also, about your father. Apparently, he was seriously ill when you were five years old.

PDK: Yes. I always have trouble remembering the dates, but actually I was probably a bit younger than that. More like when I was three.

PLR: I believe you said that you feared he would die when you were three, but also that he became ill and was in a sanatorium—when you went to your grandmother's house—somewhat later than that.[15]

PDK: But I think it wasn't though. It was when I was three. He had tuberculosis twice.

---

15. See Kramer, "Myth." In *Moments of Engagement*, pp. 8, 10; and "When It Works." In *Moments of Engagement*, p. 162.

PLR: Did he recover?

PDK: Yes. He's alive as we speak.

PLR: That's wonderful. To change the subject, I was wondering what percentage of your patients are on medication of some kind.

PDK: It's hard to say, because I have two kinds of patients. I have patients whom I see mostly for 45-minute sessions, and then there are either patients of mine who have done with therapy and are now just on medicine or patients in therapy with someone else who are seeing me for medication. Those patients whom I see for half an hour or fifteen minutes every so often add up to a large number. But of the patients I see in psychotherapy, I'd say about half are on medication. I think fewer when I'm seeing more couples in therapy, and more when I'm seeing more individuals. So about half. If you looked at the charts in the drawer, probably the majority are on medication. I don't see anyone for 15 minutes for psychotherapy.

PLR: Those would be people whom you'd be monitoring.

PDK: Right. I might see them for a number of hours before we switched. That would be when things were going smoothly or they were already in psychotherapy with someone else.

PLR: Have you ever taken any psychopharmacological medication?

PDK: I took a sedative sleeping pill when I was in college once. It was a barbiturate, and I wrote down my reactions to it as I was going to sleep. I was rather fascinated and scared.

PLR: Was this something you were advised to take?

PDK: Yes. I was overwrought about exams or something. That's about it. I have occasionally taken melatonin to sleep. The answer is basically no, extremely no. The times in my life when I've had two drinks probably could be counted on the fingers of one hand.

PLR: I ask this because of the emphasis in your work on Prozac and other drugs, and one of the obvious differences between medication-based therapy and traditional psychotherapy is that . . .

PDK: There's no requirement to take the medicines.

PLR: Right. And so in some way the doctor is external to the patient's experience.

PDK: There are doctors like Donald Klein, who has probably taken anything he's ever prescribed. They really feel they need to know or like to know. I have a great respect for these medicines and don't want to give them to anyone who doesn't need them, including myself.

PLR: I'm not saying that you should take them. I'm just wondering about the phenomenology of the whole experience.

PDK: In the end, I think that *Listening to Prozac* is largely a book of social commentary. All my books ask what kind of a culture we are that requires or celebrates these treatments. What does it say that we tend to see the self in biological terms? But yes, it's a more external treatment. Medication, writing, and psychotherapy are closely allied in my way of seeing them. They all have to do with the communication of perspectives. When medicating goes well, I don't feel that something very alien is happening to my patients. Medications do seem a lot like cotherapists. I think the patients are having experiences, as they report them, that are familiar to me. And when they are ill, they are, to some extent, having experiences that are familiar to me in more minor form. Depression, especially, and anxiety— the mood states—don't seem to be very alien experiences. I don't suppose I've felt the panic of psychosis, but I think any human being has some sense of what anxiety and depression are.

PLR: Absolutely.

PDK: And one also has some sympathy with the more autistic states. At least I tell myself I have the flavor of most things in psychotherapy. I think the transformation via medication is to some extent like fluid changes in mood state that take place in people who are biologically more resilient. I think I know what it's like to be blue and then to be ebullient.

PLR: That's certainly understandable. Of course, you talk about how for many people these experiences on medication have the effect of bringing out their sense of themselves rather than causing them to lose touch with themselves.

PDK: I think that is the interesting report. People say this is the self, even though they've never been this self before.

PLR: They have a sense of their innate potential, which, once they discover it, they realize is what they were looking for.

PDK: Yes. And some sense of rightness of fit. That this seems like a stable spot.

PLR: Didn't you write that one of your reasons for going into this field was to alleviate the sense of depression?

PDK: No, though I do believe that I have a pronounced sympathy with depression.

PLR: You referred to having "a passion for protecting against insidious depression."[16]

PDK: But I meant in others. I thought you were saying in me. I was never aware of that.

PLR: Not necessarily depression in yourself, but having empathy with the experience of mood disorders or anxiety in other people.

PDK: There are lots of ways of becoming a psychiatrist, but one of them is that you are anyway the kind of person whom others approach. What's interesting is that to some extent I think of myself as quite cerebral, and I admire people who are more naturally empathic. But let's say that for a man—or for an intellectual man—I certainly was someone who, in college and afterward, was used as a resource by lots of people who, in retrospect, probably had minor mental illnesses. There was something that I had some natural sympathy for.

PLR: I think it's fairly common for people who become therapists to be children of depressed parents or to be trying to heal some kind of fragmentation in the family.

PDK: Right, and whatever quality that induces is obvious to others in the culture as well.

PLR: Another broad theme I wanted to raise with you is whether or not we can continue to adhere to the idea that everything we do is meaningful. In your words, "Psychoanalysis works best when every aspect of the patient's life can be deemed meaningful."[17]

PDK: Right.

PLR: On the other hand, you also say that "the fiction that all occurrences in life are meaningful has become difficult to maintain."[18]

PDK: Yes.

PLR: Many therapies today try to bring about major changes in peo-

---

16. Kramer, "Simple Gifts." In *Should You Leave?* p. 238.

17. Kramer, "The Mind-Mind-Body-Problem Problem." In *Moments of Engagement*, p. 62.

18. Kramer, "The Mind-Mind-Body-Problem Problem," p. 64.

ple without achieving insight. But do we need to abandon the idea that our experiences are intrinsically meaningful?

PDK: I think our experience of the world is that many things are meaningful. I'm a phenomenologist in that way. But when I was in therapy, if there was a strike on the underground and I showed up late, or if I lost an umbrella, it would still be interpreted to me. As I've gone through life, I realize that there's an inherent probability that one will lose umbrellas. Anything that happened was interpreted. I think that was very valuable. It kept my eye on the ball. Anything I said or did was taken to be a product of the unconscious. That was very useful, because it didn't allow me to say, "This aspect of my personality is protected in some way. Let's not examine it." I think that, once you don't allow the umbrella or the underground, you don't allow anything at all. It meant that there was a constant potential for the interpretation of personality that was not especially insulting because it was a part of the whole world. It led to a sort of regressed state in which one was aware of unconscious influence.

Once you say, as I think we must today, that large aspects of personality are based on either inborn temperament or the biological effects of experience—and even that the early environment has some genetic determinants—you can't in good faith maintain that everything in life is the result of unconscious forces. There are many intersecting vectors. The unconscious becomes a very complicated concept. And which unconscious are we talking about? Is it the Freudian unconscious or somebody else's view of what is unconscious? I think it becomes harder to do therapy. Any particular act or aspect of personality may have unconscious determinants; it may be that those unconscious determinants are very minor and account for a tiny degree of the variance. But once you start using that language—of the percentage of variance—it becomes very difficult to do psychoanalysis. It's not so much that there's no meaning; it's that it's hard to defend any particular account of where the meaning resides.

PLR: If you were late because of an underground strike, wouldn't it be up to you at a certain point to begin to consider whether there was any subjective motivation for that lateness? Or would the analyst pounce and challenge you? Doesn't interpretation become fruitful only once someone can begin to see something as an issue for himself?

PDK: Well, if you're late, the issue is always resistance. You could have read the papers; there was a strike pending. You could have gotten up early and listened to the radio. You could have gone on your bicycle, or whatever. In the end, the question is, "What were we talking about recently that was disturbing enough to you for you to want less time in the office?" As I say, in my case that premise turned out to be very useful. I'm probably a wriggly creature, or was at the time.

PLR: You were trying to get off the hook?

PDK: I had all kinds of reasons why something wasn't the case, and the point of analysis is that it is the case! I don't dare treat my patients that way.

PLR: Not even in your underlying assumptions when you interact with them?

PDK: Yes, that's true. I do hold in reserve the possibility that even quite plausible events are aspects of the resistance.

PLR: Or that there are many levels of meaning, and unconscious fantasy may be at work even in seemingly banal occurrences.

PDK: Yes. I do keep open that possibility.

PLR: If we accept that dreams are the result of the activation and synthesis of firing neurones, that doesn't necessarily prove that they are not meaningful subjectively to the person who has them.

PDK: That biological line of argument has never been convincing to me. Whatever we may say about dreams, patients' *accounts* of dreams in the consulting room are quite interesting. Of course, many of them don't require great detective work, such as Freud undertook in his Irma dream.[19] The dream speaks for itself. The patient will come in and laugh, saying, "A few sessions ago you said so-and-so. Then I had this dream," and it couldn't be more blatant.

PLR: In my view, we don't need to adhere to a wish-fulfillment theory to say that dreams are meaningful and engaged with psychic processes.

PDK: Yes. The dreams presented to me seem organically part of whatever material is there. I have no trouble in integrating them.

PLR: That to me exemplifies how we can accept a biological model of explanation without discounting a psychological interpretation of experience.

PDK: There has to be some encoding of dreams, and they must have

19. Sigmund Freud (1900), *The Interpretation of Dreams. Standard Edition*, 4:96–121. London: Hogarth Press, 1953.

some function. But I'm always at the "Anna Freud-stwabewwies" theory of dreams.[20] When my youngest child comes in and tells me his dreams, they seem to me very obviously to be about things that are on his mind or aspects of his personality that are troubling at the moment.

PLR: That would be no surprise to Freud.

PDK: That's true. You're right, it's not that they're necessarily wishes, but they have to do with anxiety and those sorts of issues.

PLR: One figure whom you don't mention in your work is Bowlby. Has he been at all important in your thinking?

PDK: I haven't read as much of Bowlby as I would like. I read some Bowlby in writing *Should You Leave?*, and I mention attachment theory there. I heard Bowlby speak a few times. It was a question of how much one could include. In *Should You Leave?*, I went back to theories that have been important to me over a number of years, starting in residency or before, and Bowlby just wasn't that sort of figure for me.

PLR: In talking about attachment and relational theory, you place a good deal of emphasis on Jean Baker Miller,[21] but I think that there is a tradition antecedent to hers.

PDK: I agree. I probably did not give enough credit to Bowlby, but I certainly thought of him in *Should You Leave?* when I was talking about alternative explanations of the unconscious.

PLR: It's merely a historical footnote.

PDK: But that transition—it's in Bowlby as well as in Kohut—which says that sexuality is not the only dynamic and a lot of what we're seeing is more readily explained by the vicissitudes of insecure attachment, is at once a modern truth and also one of the things that makes psychoanalysis less magical. To me, there's something sexier about sex than about attachment!

PLR: In that case, we shouldn't lose sight of Freud's emphasis on sexuality. But behind my question is the issue of whether or not we can establish psychoanalysis on a scientific footing, so as not to relegate it to being merely an antiquarian curiosity, and sort out which of its tenets still seem to have an empirical foundation.

---

20. See Freud's report of the undisguised wish-fulfillment dream of his 19-month-old daughter in *The Interpretation of Dreams*, p. 130.

21. See Kramer, "Only Connect." In *Should You Leave?* pp. 105–122.

PDK: There are some intellectual pursuits that are always on the horizon and never fulfilled. Linguistics has that quality in its promise to explain the human mind. I fear that is the case for the science of psychoanalysis. I'll say some things that are loosely associated with this train of thought. One is that I think Kohut was very bad at giving credit, and a lot of Kohut is Bowlby and a lot of Kohut is Carl Rogers.

PLR: And Winnicott.

PDK: Yes, the whole object relations school gets in in various ways. I wish there were a more honest account of the intellectual foundations of self psychology. But Kohut himself had a foot in both camps. He really was a Freudian, and he really had a belief in empathy. He tried to combine the two by saying that empathy is a form of awareness about the other, rather than saying that empathy is directly healing. Self psychology as it is practiced now is so decidedly empathic that a lot of the burden of healing is based on surrogate love. I think that we could have a science of that, but whether it would be a science of psychoanalysis is an interesting question. I've written an essay against the more extreme forms of self psychology, which you may not have in your bibliography.[22] It's a precursor for *Should You Leave?* in that it says that there are a lot of practical things we know about the other person. It's not as if everything about the other person can be discovered through empathy. Even choosing at what level to respond requires a very pragmatic view of the other on the part of the therapist.

My other fantasy project, like the Freud project, is a naturalistic study of psychotherapy. I'd look at what therapists—assuming they're pretty good—actually do in their offices. Then I'd look at outcomes and see who actually gets better. Then I'd go back and say what the theory must be that supports those things which work. Psychoanalysis is not especially open to that approach. To its credit, psychoanalysis likes very comprehensive—almost mathematically beautiful—theories that explain the whole of human behavior.

We're in an extremely eclectic era in which that type of comprehensiveness is not possible. Contemporary psychology needs to take into account genetics, early trauma, randomness in the system, the unconscious, what you ate yesterday. Psychoanalysis is a very diffi-

---

22. Peter D. Kramer (1993), "Empathic Immersion." In *Empathy in Medical Practice: Beyond Pills and Scalpel*, ed. Howard Spiro. New Haven, CT: Yale University Press, pp. 174–189. See also Peter D. Kramer (1993), "Amazing Grace," *Psychiatric Times*, March, pp. 3ff.

cult theory to think about. I think that scientific attempts like behavior therapy and doing PET scans on people are very primitive when it comes to psychotherapy. I like the work of Daniel Stern, which is certainly multifactorial, but how much of it is psychoanalysis and how much is accurate and comprehensive? The form of it at least has some relationship to contemporary science.

PLR: In my view, the problem with psychoanalysis is not that it attempts to be comprehensive, but that it rests on a rather shaky foundation. I would like to try to preserve or rescue the vision of psychoanalysis, but in a more contemporary context. You write about the possible integration of everything from cellular biology to animal ethology.[23]

PDK: I think that is Freud's posture. Whatever one may say that is negative about Freud, he did try to read widely and honestly, though "honestly" is always problematic. He stuck to the reality principle in creating his theories. There is no point in having a psychoanalysis that doesn't contain as much as possible of our beliefs about the world. Animal ethology, cellular biology, and so on—those are windows on the world. I don't think I'm smart enough to take all that into account.

PLR: I think you've come pretty close.

PDK: It's what I've tried to do on the level I'm able to do it.

PLR: That's how we all have to do it. You've written that there is currently "a new consensus about the human condition,"[24] which reminds me of E. O. Wilson's *Consilience*.[25] The Enlightenment idea of the possible congruence of knowledge across different fields of endeavor is not as fashionable in the humanities as it is in the sciences. My criticism of Freud would be that he imposed his own preconceptions on what he saw and wasn't really scientific in being able to revise his thinking in light of the evidence.

PDK: That's true, but his preconceptions were at least based on a wide range of reading. They took into account mythology, biology, physics—to the extent that he understood physics—and so on.

---

23. Kramer, *Listening to Prozac*, p. 282.

24. Kramer, *Listening to Prozac*, p. 18.

25. Edward O. Wilson (1998), *Consilience: The Unity of Knowledge*. New York: Knopf.

PLR: He had an encyclopedic erudition, and the strength I still see in Freud is his grounding in the humanities and his attempt to link that with a scientific perspective. Unfortunately, as Bowlby argued, he went astray in his choice of scientific models, such as Lamarckianism . . .

PDK: Yes, and his physics and everything else. He turned out to be wrong about everything, which is a problem. But he *is* my model in many ways. Like the "old Freud," I write in the morning and see patients in the afternoon. One way of seeing that second project—the naturalistic experiment—is that to some extent that is what takes place in my writing. I say to myself, "I'm doing something with my patients. What is it that I'm doing?" Using medicine as a cotherapist, making some assumptions about people's temperament when I treat them, and so on—these are ideas that come from my experience with patients. That is very much a Freudian posture—to take a small number of cases and think about them intensively.

PLR: That's admirable.

PDK: Well, it certainly is idiosyncratic nowadays.

PLR: I'd like to press you about two more things. One has to do with Max, your analyst, in *Moments of Engagement*, and the other is Lou Adler, the character in *Should You Leave?* To start with Lou Adler, you acknowledge that this is a fictional creation of yours, and yet in the references there is a book called *Pieces of Resistance* . . .[26]

PDK: Yes.

PLR: Which you say was published by Scribners in 1983. I don't believe there is any such book.

PDK: You're right, there isn't. And articles. Adler has a whole bibliography.

PLR: Did you feel that providing a fictional bibliography was necessary to the thick description of the character? Did you have any qualms about the possibility of misleading the reader?

PDK: I've certainly been accused of misleading the reader. But I think any careful reader would be worried about this "Lou." One thing that no reviewer picked up is that Lou has no gender. Lou is neither a man nor a woman. I mention Lou Andreas-Salomé. There are lots of cues that Lou might be a woman. I was to some extent playing off

---

26. Kramer, *Should You Leave?*, p. 299n62.

the great emphasis in the popular literature on the importance of whether one is a man or a woman by trying to take someone through the whole book without knowing the gender of this crucial character. It makes no difference to the advice being given whether the character is a man or a woman.

PLR: To be honest, the question of gender indeterminacy never crossed my mind. I perceived Lou as avuncular and definitely a male figure.

PDK: Lou is flirtatious; Lou is not the main breadwinner. If we are reading carefully, Lou is a modern man or a modern woman. I hope there was some useful gain that had to do with Lou's identity, and I didn't want to show my hand too soon. Plus I like the notion of fiction writing. A lot of *Should You Leave?* has to do with the craft of writing, and it is largely modeled on second-person fiction, which is quirky enough. But there is in addition a fiction of the following sort. The narrator responds to Lou's stories. Lou has written stories about Connie, and so on. Those stories exist only in the narrator's response to them. There is no story that precedes the story. It's a short story told in the form of a response to a short story, but that's the whole of the entity. There is an implicit comment on how we create the world, what our perspectives are on the world, the extent to which story telling is a way of mastering or interacting with the world. It is a deeply fictional book. If I can immodestly say this, it never got the intelligent review it deserved, except that I did get a nice review in an obscure journal called *Medical Encounter*, which begins with the reviwer saying to his wife, "I think what I'm reading is my favorite fictional book of 1997."[27] Later, in England and Scotland, it got reviews that mentioned John Updike, Philip Roth, and Iris Murdoch, by way of context.[28]

PLR: Those would constitute good reviews. I was simply wondering about the title of Lou's book in the footnotes, and I had to go to the Harvard library to track it down before I was absolutely sure it didn't exist.

PDK: I've often thought of writing a book myself called *Pieces of Resistance.*

---

27. Frederic W. Platt (1998), Review of *Should You Leave? Medical Encounter*, 14:18–19.

28. See the reviews of *Should You Leave?* by Julie Myerson (1998), "Night and Day" (UK) *Mail on Sunday*, September 20, p. 35; and Susie Maguire (1998), "Wise Counsel." *Scotland on Sunday*, September 9.

PLR: There is one by the literary critic Eugene Goodheart.[29]

PDK: I see.

PLR: But titles are not copyrighted.

PDK: No, they're not.

PLR: Maybe I could end by coming back to the figure of Max. You mention by name so many people whom you've been influenced by, yet you create a pseudonym for your analyst.

PDK: I didn't really create a pseudonym. Max happens to be his name. But it is a pseudonym in the sense that I don't give his last name. I suppose that was to give myself a degree of privacy, although Max did do some writing. At one point in England, I wanted to get access to his writing to see what I thought of it or put it together for publication. I didn't try very hard, but also was not allowed to do so. Max is not a pseudonym, but he is . . .

PLR: Fiction?

PDK: No, Max is not fiction. Max is pretty much as I experienced him. He is fictional to the extent that any attempt at writing or characterization is creative and only partly successful.

PLR: A kind of fictive attitude?

PDK: Yes.

---

29. Eugene Goodheart (1988), *Pieces of Resistance*. Cambridge: Cambridge University Press. See also Kramer, "Pièce de Résistance." In *Moments of Engagement*, pp. 67–79.

Stephen A. Mitchell

Between Philosophy and Politics

Peter L. Rudnytsky: You are at once a practicing analyst and a scholar of psychoanalysis who has looked at both the continuities and discontinuities between Freud and contemporary psychoanalysis. I hope we can talk about the issues raised in your work, but I'm also interested in the personal motivations that draw people to psychoanalysis. So, if I might, I'd like to begin by asking you what led you to become a psychoanalyst.

Stephen A. Mitchell: One could take it back to many different points, depending on how you wanted to enter into this. I grew up in suburban New Jersey, and for the last two years of high school I went to Horace Mann in New York. That was a difficult experience in various ways, but it opened the world up intellectually for me. I got very interested in literature, literary criticism, and Freud. So I was introduced to Freud.

PLR: Even in high school?

SAM: Yes. I was thinking about this for this interview, and it must have been after my junior year. I read the five-volume edition of Freud's *Collected Papers*.

PLR: The Riviere translation.

SAM: Right. I remember being very intrigued. So when I went to college, it was with the intention of being a psychology major and studying psychoanalysis.

PLR: Where did you go?

SAM: I went to Yale. The introductory psych course was terrific. It was taught by a guy who had Jungian predilections, and it was very exciting.

PLR: Who was the teacher?

SAM: Michael Kahn was his name. A Michael Kahn has written me some letters in response to my books over the last couple of years, and it suddenly dawned on me that this might be the same Michael Kahn who was my freshman teacher.

PLR: That's funny. Did he know that you were his student?

SAM: No. He wouldn't have known because it was a gigantic lecture course with 100 or 120 kids. So I wrote him a letter saying, "Could you possibly be the same Michael Kahn . . . ?" He said, "Yes, in fact I am. So glad to know because it makes me feel proud." It was nice.

PLR: That's the teacher's fantasy: "He was my student."

SAM: I did well by him. Anyhow, that was a great course. I became interested in Joseph Campbell. But then, in my sophomore year, I took six different semester courses in psychology to explore that as a major, and I hated it. It was very behaviorally oriented and quite antipsychoanalytic. So I ended up majoring in History, the Arts, and Letters, a very broad, cross-disciplinary major. That was absolutely wonderful. By my senior year, I had three interests. I was still very interested in psychoanalysis and psychology. I had become very interested in philosophy—Yale was very strong in philosophy—especially problems in 19th-century philosophy, which of course was the context in which Freud operated. And I was also very interested in politics. This was the mid-to-late 1960s. I got very caught up in the antiwar movement.

PLR: When did you graduate?

SAM: 1968. In that major, you spent the senior year writing a thesis, and my thesis was called, very grandiosely, *Man and the State.* I worked with a terrific professor of 19th-century philosophy.

PLR: Who was that?

SAM: Karsten Harries. He wrote a book on the philosophy of modern art as well. I audited lots of philosophy courses, and I had what amounted to a tutorial with Harries for my senior year. I loved him. When I graduated from Yale, I was unsure which way I wanted to go. In fact, I applied to Yale in philosophy.

PLR: To graduate school?

SAM: Yes. I was very interested in political goings-on. I had read Nietzsche. I was involved in the antiwar movement and talked to people about community organizing. The interests in philosophy and politics ended up collapsing back into psychoanalysis. One of Nietzsche's main concerns was demonstrating that the prior 2,000 years of Western philosophy had taken a wrong turn by thinking too much about what man *should* be instead of looking at what man was. The development of a perspective on what man should be involved a contempt for human nature and human experience. So philosophy began to dovetail back into psychology for me. And the more I learned about political action, the more I began to feel the same way about that. Sol Alinsky came to Yale and talked about what it was like to move into a community, help people organize themselves, leave, and then have it collapse again. Unless you could change people internally, there was no way you could involve yourself in effective political action. So politics too circled back into the study of man or human nature.

Intellectually, it was a hard choice, but I felt that the thing to do was to go to graduate school in clinical psychology at NYU, which was an extraordinary program in those days. It was run by a wonderful man named Bernie Kalinkowitz. This was the fall of 1968—after the spring of the Columbia revolution—a very exciting and wide-open time. Through supervision and tutorials, which were always the ways I learned most effectively, I obtained first-hand experience with clinical psychoanalysis. A lot of the people there had been trained at the White Institute. I began to feel more and more that there was something wonderfully satisfying about psychoanalysis. I was helping people with their difficulties in living, which seemed very important. But at the same time I got to think about all the most interesting philosophical questions in a way that was grounded in lived experience and not abstract. I felt that I was participating in a community and a process that I hoped would have social and political implications in the long run. So psychoanalysis was—and has remained for me—deeply satisfying on many different levels.

PLR: It has a philosophical dimension in its concern with issues of knowledge and being, and it's also tied in a concrete way to politics in improving the quality of people's lives for you even today.

SAM: Right.

PLR: So landing at NYU was decisive in introducing you to clinical psychoanalysis.

SAM: Right.

PLR: Who were your most influential teachers at NYU?

SAM: Bernie Kalinkowitz himself. One of my supervisors was a brilliant clinician named Avram Ben-Avi. He conveyed a feel for the complexities of people and the analytic process.

PLR: Was Robert Holt there at that time?

SAM: He was part of the group at the Research Center, and I wasn't directly involved with them. I minored in community mental health, which was a carryover from my political interests. Then I did my internship at the Columbia Psychiatric Institute, and I was on the community service for half of the year and analytic service for the other half. For a while I was thinking of getting more involved in the community mental health movement and going to medical school. If I were going to do that, I wanted to be in a position of influence administratively. That drew me in a different direction from the Research Center.

PLR: My thoughts are going in two directions. One is back to your familial motivations. The other is your experience of personal analysis, because obviously that is formative in one's choice of psychoanalysis as a profession. Maybe we could take the second part first. At what point did you begin analytic therapy?

SAM: It was the first year of graduate school. Bernie encouraged people to get into treatment. That seemed like a good idea to me. I also got married for the first time halfway through that first year. I had the usual complicated problems . . .

PLR: Associated with a first marriage?

SAM: Right. [PLR laughs] It was a good idea in many different respects. I got a lot out of it.

PLR: After you received your doctorate from NYU, did you go on to begin psychoanalytic training?

SAM: Yes, at the White Institute. My first analyst was a self-described Freudian. It was a more classical analysis. I was on the couch. When I went to the White, I had to enter treatment with one of their analysts, a man named Militiades Zaphiropoulos, who was one of the generation of people who had been in treatment with Clara Thompson. I don't know whether he knew Sullivan; he certainly knew Fromm and Frieda Fromm-Reichmann. I think of that as a classical interpersonal analysis—sitting up. I got a great deal out of both analyses. It was useful to have those two different analyses—different ideologies, different men.

PLR: Would you like to share the name of your first analyst?

SAM: Richard Mulliken.

PLR: I didn't know that the couch was not mandatory in training analyses at the White. Does that continue even today?

SAM: Yes.

PLR: Have you had further analysis since that time?

SAM: No.

PLR: So the second analysis continued while you were in training at the White.

SAM: Right. I was in training there for five years, and I was in analysis for four years.

PLR: Let's go back and pick up the familial aspects of the story. I'd be curious to know something about your background—what kind of work your parents did, brothers and sisters, and so on.

SAM: My father was—and still is, he's elderly now—a certified public accountant. He's a very smart man, mathematically oriented. If he had grown up in a different economic or social era, he might have gone into pure mathematics or physics. But for various family reasons and practicalities, he ended up in accounting, for which he was poorly suited in certain respects. He was never a businessman-type. My mother was a legal secretary when she was younger, and when she got married she stopped working and basically was a housewife. My father's father ran a hand laundry, which I worked at. It was my first job—folding towels and so forth. I loved him very much. He was a very important person in my life.

PLR: Your paternal grandfather?

SAM: Yes. I have one brother, five years younger. As we grew up, my mother worked a little in the office of my grandfather's laundry, but she didn't work in any significant way after she gave up the job as a legal secretary.

PLR: What does your brother do?

SAM: He's also an accountant. He's had a long and complicated job history, but he recently went back to business school and got an M.B.A. specializing in accounting. He's the comptroller for a growing national company that distributes pharmaceuticals.

PLR: Were your family long-time Americans, or did they immigrate?

SAM: My parents were both first-generation. Their parents were immigrants.

PLR: So your grandfather immigrated to this country?

SAM: From Russia.

PLR: What part of Russia?

SAM: The Russia-Poland area. Pinsk was the name of the town.

PLR: Not to be confused with Minsk. [laughs]

SAM: Right. [laughs]

PLR: And the religious background?

SAM: Jewish.

PLR: Do you think there was anything in the inner history of your family that led you to become a psychoanalyst?

SAM: Very much.

PLR: Is that something you could talk about?

SAM: One of the salient organizing facts of my family life when I was growing up was that my brother stuttered. This was a cause for great concern. My parents took my brother to various experts—child psychologists and that sort of thing. It's hard for me, looking back, to know whether this was just lousy treatment or whether he got ground up in my parents' dynamics or what happened exactly. But there was very much a sense that this was purely a psychological problem. Today thinking about stuttering has really changed. I don't know a lot about it, but I gather it's a much more complex phenomenon.

PLR: So the people who were brought in to treat your brother perceived this as a psychological problem, and your parents did also. Did they feel responsible in some way?

SAM: They felt responsible, but especially my father passed the responsibility around. So I got blamed. It cast a huge shadow on the impact we were having on each other. There were issues of competition and guilt and responsibility—all sorts of juicy dynamics. This left a central impact on me and was certainly part of what got me fascinated by how the mind works, how family dynamics work, and the relationship between the mind and the body.

PLR: That's quite an interesting story. Let me come back to the analyses you mentioned. I wonder if there's anything you could describe about either your first or your second analysis that captures something of what those experiences meant for you.

SAM: I could actually. Among the most impactful sessions in the first analysis were ones where I was completely silent. I don't know how long I was silent, but it felt like a long time. There was something very important about that for me—that that was okay, basically, with this analyst. My family—especially my father's family, but both sides of my family—are very production-oriented. You keep busy, you work hard, you do things . . .

PLR: You write books?

SAM: You write books. They're also very talk-oriented. My father and his father and his older brother were all very interested in politics. One was a communist, one was a socialist, my father was a liberal democrat. I was used to people yelling at each other.

PLR: Your father was one of how many brothers and sisters?

SAM: He had one brother and one sister. He was the youngest in his family. Everyone was very opinionated and impassioned in their beliefs. So there was all this talking and arguing and working hard and being useful. For me there was something really quite extraordinary about an extended stretch where it was okay for me just to come and lie on the couch, being with my own experience. I've thought about it subsequently in terms of Winnicott's great paper on the capacity to be alone in the presence of another.[1]

PLR: That's fascinating. How far into the analysis was it when that silent stretch occurred?

SAM: It was a long time ago. I think it was quite a ways into the analysis. I had—we had—to work to get to that point.

PLR: How did it feel? Was it comfortable or was there a sense of anxiety and tension?

SAM: The remarkable thing is that it felt comfortable, the way I remember it.

PLR: So your analyst simply permitted you to be silent. You described

---

1. D. W. Winnicott (1958), "The Capacity to Be Alone." In *The Maturational Processes and the Facilitating Environment.* New York: International Universities Press, 1965, pp. 29–36.

this earlier as a Freudian analysis, but that kind of acceptance of the need to regress or just to use the time in your own way is contemporary.

SAM: It's progressive Freudian, let's say.

PLR: I can't help but see a connection between the themes of talking and stuttering and silence—that not talking might be connected to the issues you've been alluding to.

SAM: Right. In terms of the significance of talking in the family?

PLR: And stuttering.

SAM: And stuttering. Right.

PLR: Was that explored?

SAM: I don't remember.

PLR: Okay. And was there something equally defining for you in the second analysis?

SAM: One of the things I got most out of the second analysis was that Zaphiropoulos is someone who has a tremendous verve. He really enjoys life. One of my [chuckles] most memorable experiences of the first year with him was when I went to the Institute Christmas party. There was a skit going on, and he was singing this song about psychoanalysis to the tune of "The Rain in Spain Falls Mainly on the Plain." I can't remember what the substitute lyrics were, but it was a riot. For me it took the air out of a lot of the pretentiousness that was certainly part of the White Institute and part of psychoanalysis.

PLR: It was the opposite of stuffy.

SAM: Exactly.

PLR: It's interesting that a moment outside the formal analysis was important in the experience of that relationship.

SAM: It dovetailed in many ways with my general sense of his take on things, which tended to be oriented toward the fact that life is short. I think of this as very much interpersonal and influenced by Fromm. You don't have a lot of time.

PLR: Play hard.

SAM: Exactly. [laughs] I remember one moment when we were talking about my longings in relation to my mother from when I was a little boy, and he said, "But what would you *do* with a mother now, at your age?" It was a very interesting question. It recontextualized things in terms of the discontinuity between old longings, which can be very powerful, and a new reality. Those moments caught for me the tenor of the work with him in general, which was an openness to explore experience but with a sense of what is to be done now.

PLR: A reframing.

SAM: Yes.

PLR: Just to bring the biographical side up to date, I gather that you're divorced from your first wife?

SAM: Yes.

PLR: And you're remarried?

SAM: Yes.

PLR: Any children?

SAM: Two.

PLR: From the first marriage?

SAM: From the second.

PLR: What does your wife do?

SAM: She's a psychoanalyst and the coauthor of *Freud and Beyond*.[2]

PLR: Of course, you've ended up at the White Institute.

SAM: Well, I don't know that I've ended up there. [laughs] I've stayed.

PLR: But that's your intellectual home in psychoanalysis?

SAM: I would say I have a split home between the White Institute and the NYU Postdoctoral Program. Both have been very important places.

PLR: One of the topics I wanted to raise with you is your perspective on the institution of psychoanalysis and the politics of the psychoanalytic movement. Are you a member of the International Psychoanalytic Association?

SAM: No.

PLR: Is that at all important to you?

---

2. Stephen A. Mitchell & Margaret J. Black (1995), *Freud and Beyond: A History of Modern Psychoanalytic Thought*. New York: Basic Books.

SAM: No.

PLR: In this country there are many avenues to psychoanalytic training, but in England, for example, there is only one institute, which is controlled by the IPA.

SAM: Right.

PLR: I think that the question of who can authorize someone to become a psychoanalyst is crucial. Have you had any dealings with members of either the American or the International Psychoanalytic Association where your affiliation with the White has been a factor?

SAM: Let me tell you about another experience that shapes my thinking about this. The book that I did with Jay Greenberg came out in 1983.[3] Around that time we were contacted by a fellow from Denver named Charles Spezzano. He and some colleagues were forming a psychoanalytic interest group with the idea of possibly starting training. They wanted to know whether someone would come out and teach for them, which I did. That whole experience had a huge impact on me. Denver was a city with lots of people very interested in psychoanalysis, but only one institute, which was the institute of the American and in quite a moribund state. The general feeling was that it had a stranglehold on psychoanalysis in that city. I taught at various times over the next several years. I'd go out and teach for 10 or 12 hours over two days. Then we did videotapes and phone hookups. It was some of the most exciting teaching I've ever done. I love teaching. This was before the lawsuit that opened the American to nonmedical applicants, so the institute had a waiver system. People would get into analysis with one of the senior analysts four times a week at the full fee and hope to be waivered in. Some of them had been waiting around for years and years and years. It was ridiculous. Charlie happened to be from New York, so he naturally had the impulse, "Well, we'll start our own institute!" I don't know what the count is now, but there used to something like 37 different institutes in Manhattan. No one in Denver had thought of that before probably because the presence of the American was so destructive and intimidating. Some of these people had had their interest in being trained outside the American interpreted as an acting out of oedipal dynamics.

PLR: The product of an incomplete analysis.

---

3. Jay R. Greenberg & Stephen A. Mitchell (1983), *Object Relations in Psychoanalytic Theory.* Cambridge, MA: Harvard University Press.

SAM: Right. [laughs] It seemed pernicious to me. I loved teaching these people. In terms of the sheer enthusiasm for the subject matter, you couldn't find a more exciting group.

PLR: It harks back to the early days of psychoanalysis, when people did it out of passion and not just as a career.

SAM: That's right.

PLR: Was this training sponsored by the White Institute, or was it completely freestanding?

SAM: It was completely freestanding.

PLR: So it was for people who already had clinical credentials in Colorado who were gaining analytic experence under your auspices?

SAM: That's right.

PLR: Did other people travel out from New York?

SAM: Yes.

PLR: Who else?

SAM: They were very interested in a comparative approach. Martin Bergmann went out there. Different people.

PLR: So for the money they were spending for their four-times-a-week analysis, they could fly you people out there and have a much better experience?

SAM: That's right. A number of years later, the lawsuit had its impact, so the Denver Institute opened up. There was a younger generation of graduates from the Denver who would have loved to have been involved with this new group, but they couldn't before the lawsuit because they were forbidden by the American to teach anyplace outside their institute. The mid-to-late 80s and the early 90s were a very heady time. What happened in Denver was like the spark that set off a whole movement. It was called the Local Chapters movement. It was connected with Division 39 of the American Psychological Association. There began to be programs in Boston, Chicago, Oklahoma City, San Francisco, Seattle. It was extraordinary. In my professional experience, it is one of the most exciting things to have taken place. As Charlie pointed out to me a while ago, it was very important symbolically to have two guys outside the American Psychoanalytic writing a book because this issue of authorization that you're talking about is so powerful.

PLR: People in the mainstream institutes had to take notice of it, but it also enabled people outside the American to validate their own sense of being analysts. Through Clara Thompson and Frieda Fromm-Reichmann, your lineage seems to me to go back to Ferenczi, who never became a "dissident" but who sponsored a view of psychoanalysis alternative to the classical Freudian one.

SAM: Right.

PLR: This leads us into the intellectual issues that I wanted to raise with you. What you've told me about your experiences in Denver reflects what I see as a tragic dimension in the history of psychoanalysis. The ideals of psychoanalysis come into conflict with the realities of partisanship, rivalries, excommunication, and so forth in a way not unlike what we find in church history.

SAM: Right.

PLR: In my own understanding, a lot of this dissension can be traced back to Freud. In what I've read of your work, you don't talk much about Freud's personality or the way his intellectual and analytic style might have had a negative or even tragic impact on the history of psychoanalysis. Invoking Hans Loewald, you speak of transforming Freud from "an improperly buried ghost who haunts us into a beloved and revered ancestor."[4] One question that I have is whether Freud should be regarded as a "beloved and revered ancestor" or whether he's not in some way . . .

SAM: The villain of the piece?

PLR: The Grillparzer play, *The Ancestress*, which Freud contrasted with *Oedipus the King*, is about a family curse.[5] I wonder whether Freud didn't bequeath a curse on the history of psychoanalysis that needs to be taken into account.

SAM: That seems too harsh to me for a couple of reasons. One is that Freud was such a towering genius. It's hard for me to be in the field and not to feel a debt of enormous gratitude forever in terms of the whole landscape that he opened up. The second reason is that I was

---

4. Stephen A. Mitchell (1993), *Hope and Dread in Psychoanalysis*. New York: Basic Books, p. 176. See Hans Loewald (1960), "On the Therapeutic Action of Psycho-Analysis." In *Papers on Psychoanalysis*. New Haven, CT: Yale University Press, 1980, pp. 248–249.

5. Sigmund Freud (1900), *The Interpretation of Dreams. Standard Edition*, 4:263. London: Hogarth Press, 1953.

reading Ferenczi's *Clinical Diary*,[6] which I find a very moving document, with some reading groups. I would ask them: "Here is Ferenczi caught in the grip of intense transference–countertransference struggles with different patients, some of which led to mutual analysis. Suppose that you're a supervisor and Ferenczi shows up in your office. What would you want to say to him?" It was an interesting exercise because there are a great many things that my colleagues today could say to Ferenczi that would have been enormously helpful and weren't part of his intellectual culture. He lacked the conceptual tools to deal with a lot of the things that we are now struggling with from a much more advantageous position.

I regard Ferenczi as a hero for getting involved in the work at the emotional depth that he did, with so little within his conceptual repertoire to help him understand what transference was and the way in which countertransference was going to pull you in and chew you up. He wrestled with boundaries and what it was okay not to do and not to provide, which is a common part of analytic supervision now. I have a feeling of great sympathy for Ferenczi's plight and what it's like to be a pioneer way out there ahead of the historical movement that you're opening up. I feel the same way about Freud. I think Freud was a very troubled man. A lot that has come out in recent years certainly suggests how manipulative he was politically. I'm horrified by some of the things he did clinically in the service of making money and encouraging donors.

PLR: The Frink episode?[7]

SAM: Yes. There's no question that he had enormous problems with father–son relationships. All of that is true. I have a lot of sympathy for the fact that Freud never had an analysis. The idea that he analyzed himself is preposterous within today's frame of reference. But what was he going to do? Where was he going to turn for an analytic

---

6. Judith Dupont, ed. (1985), *The Clinical Diary of Sándor Ferenczi*, trans. Michael Balint & Nicola Zarday Jackson. Cambridge, MA: Harvard University Press, 1988.

7. In the 1920s, Freud urged his patient Horace Frink, an American psychiatrist, to divorce his wife and marry one of his own patients, the bank heiress Anjelika Bijur, who was herself married. Freud was spurred by the hope that some of Bijur's money would trickle into psychoanalytic coffers. The imbroglio ended with the deaths of both abandoned spouses and Frink's decline into a major depression soon after the failure of his remarrige. See Lavinia Edmunds (1988), "His Master's Choice," *The Johns Hopkins Magazine*, 40(April):40–48.

experience? Again, he didn't have basic elements that are available to us now. It's hard for me to villainize Freud in that sense. I think you're right that some of his difficulties have been reverberating throughout the field since. But it's hard for me on balance to regard them as a curse. I feel that the blessings greatly outweigh the curse. Plus, most of the other disciplines that I know have the same rivalries and problems. I can't think of a discipline in which people don't savage each other through competitiveness and fratricidal struggles of some sort. I'm not sure it's particular to Freud's legacy.

PLR: I would agree with you that all fields of human endeavor exhibit some of the same conflicts and tensions that we find in psychoanalysis. But those tendencies are often exacerbated in psychoanalysis because people are reflecting theoretically on the very personal processes that they're engaged in. If that doesn't lead to better understanding, it can lead to a much louder explosion.

SAM: A holy war.

PLR: Yes. I would draw an analogy between Freud and the Denver Institute, on one hand, and Ferenczi and the Local Chapters movement, on the other. In addition to treating his patients, Ferenczi was engaged in a deep transference-countertransference relationship to Freud.

SAM: Absolutely.

PLR: In the *Clinical Diary*, Ferenczi has an entry called "Personal Causes for the Erroneous Development of Psychoanalysis."[8] I think that Ferenczi was moving toward the idea that a successful analysis occurs when a dialectic of forgiveness can be introduced into the analytic relationship. Freud was never able to experience contrition for the way he treated people and turned intellectual disagreements into personal antagonisms.

SAM: Disloyalties.

PLR: He didn't allow other people to pursue their own paths of development while remaining within his sphere of influence. He posed a choice between loyalty and rebellion, and that to me is tragic.

SAM: Have you known people in powerful positions who have been able to be more magnanimous toward the younger generation?

---

8. Dupont, ed. *The Clinical Diary of Sándor Ferenczi*, pp. 184–187.

PLR: Let me give an example, which raises the broader question of psychoanalysis and science that I want to explore with you. Darwin was extremely generous toward Alfred Russel Wallace, who sent him a paper on the theory of evolution before Darwin had published *The Origin of Species*. Darwin shared the credit with Wallace, and Wallace was equally magnamimous in ackowledging Darwin's genius.[9]

SAM: Right.

PLR: So here we have a great figure who did not seem to find it necessary to turn scientific explorations into a personal rivalry. That leads me to wonder whether Freud's personality didn't lead psychoanalysis in an unfortunate direction by abandoning a scientific ethos by which people revise their hypotheses if they find that they are contradicted by evidence. Freud was very much committed to things that he believed were true and often imposed his preconceptions on the data. He was unwilling to change his mind even when there was good reason for him to do so.

SAM: I think you're right about Darwin. But most of the powerful people I've run into in the world are more like Freud than like Darwin. Freud certainly had a streak of heroic megalomania that allowed him to imagine he had explained everything.

PLR: But don't both the triumph and the tragedy of psychoanalysis stem from that Messianic quality of Freud's character?

SAM: I don't know. Since I was trained at an institute that was not Freudian at all, you might think the White Institute or NYU Postdoctoral Program would be free of that legacy and that curse. Ironically, the internal politics and the generational battles I saw in those places were just as pernicious and crushing as they were anywhere else. Often, underneath an ideology of openness, there was an enormous concern with political correctness and control. That's part of what makes me feel the issues are more universal than personal to Freud. I don't find the argument about science persuasive. If you make a basic contrast between science and hermeneutics, I'm more inclined to see the epistemology of psychoanalysis as hermeneutic and constructivist. It's true that a lot of the passion has to do with the close proximity of theory to personal lives, but I don't know that the way around that is to appeal to scientific evidence.

PLR: But are the kinds of conflicts you describe within the White

---

9. See Frank J. Sulloway (1996), *Born to Rebel: Birth Order, Family Dynamics, and Creative Lives*. New York: Vintage Books, 1997, pp. 103–104.

Institute inevitable in any human endeavor? Do we simply have to accept them and analyze them and live with them, or can people in psychoanalysis and other fields learn, as it were, to get along?

SAM: [laughs] I'm disinclined to universalize anything. So I don't see them as inevitable. The book that Greenberg and I did, my interest in comparative psychoanalysis, and my founding editorship of *Psychoanalytic Dialogues* have all been aimed at developing a level of discourse among people who look at psychoanalysis from differing points of view that is constructive rather than destructive.

PLR: I support that completely, of course. But it causes me to repose the question of whether Freud's intellectual style and its subsequent reverberations in the history of psychoanalysis aren't things that we need to regard critically. I don't want to posit an inherent conflict between the scientific and the hermeneutic.

SAM: I agree. It's more complex than that.

PLR: By extension, if Darwin's personal style was allied to a willingness to revise his thinking in light of the evidence, didn't Freud paradoxically steer psychoanalysis in a direction that was antiscientific despite his desire to ground psychoanalysis in natural science?

SAM: I think there's no question that it was antiscientific in that ultimately his authority was law. Again, my involvement with the journal has sought to encourage reasoned arguments and the sharing of clinical experience as forms of persuasion.

PLR: If that's the case, it's hard for me to rest content with the description of Freud as "beloved and revered," because part of what we need to do is take him to task.

SAM: I wouldn't want to have him as just beloved and revered.

PLR: That is important. To go back to something a while ago, I thought you were going to say that, thanks to your training at the NYU Postdoctoral Program and the White Institute, you were able to have a freer relationship to Freud because you weren't caught up so directly in the shadow of authority that hung over the more orthodox institutes of the American.

SAM: Yes, that's one of the implications of what I was saying.

PLR: In addition to your point that some of the same problems were recreated in the world of interpersonal psychoanalysis?

SAM: To me those go together. Seeing them recreated outside the

American also frees me to see Freud in terms of his advantages and disadvantages. It also frees me from seeing him as the villain of the piece. The American produces people who become very devoted but also people who have suffered greatly from many of the policies that have been handed down from Freud.

PLR: How have they suffered?

SAM: That organization is totally oriented toward authority, with all the qualification rituals and so forth.

PLR: A stultification has set in so that a lot of the people who have been trained in that world want to escape from it themselves?

SAM: Yes.

PLR: Let's explore the scientific issues in more depth. In both *Object Relations in Psychoanalytic Theory* and *Relational Concepts in Psychoanalysis*, you resist a simple choice between the drive model and the relational model. You argue that it's impossible to adjudicate between their respective claims. For example, you say, "It is neither useful nor appropriate to question whether either psychoanalytic model is 'right' or `wrong.' . . . [T]hese premises are not subject to empirical verification."[10] And in *Relational Concepts*, you say that each of the models "has interpretive power and breadth, but arranges the same data differently."[11] You add that it's "misleading and simplistic" to regard the contemporary shift in understanding babies as a "scientific advance."[12] It seems to me that the thrust of your work is that these are alternative visions of reality that are powerful and valid on their own terms, and there's no external frame of reference to which we can appeal to try to choose between one or the other. Is that what you think?

SAM: Yes, although that puts it more starkly than I would want to. People choose between the models based on many different things, including scientific methodology. If you're excited about infant research, that's going to make the relational model much more compelling. I'm not a hermeneutics person to the extent of saying "forget science." But a scientific methodology gives you additional data

---

10. Greenberg & Mitchell, *Object Relations in Psychoanalytic Theory*, pp. 404, 406.

11. Stephen A. Mitchell (1988), *Relational Concepts in Psychanalysis: An Integration*. Cambridge, MA: Harvard University Press, p. 59.

12. Mitchell, *Relational Concepts in Psychoanalysis*, p. 131.

rather than conclusive proof. Each of us organizes many different influences, including what's been generated by science, to make a choice between these two models. So I think it's relevant, but not the definitive platform on which the models are adjudicated.

PLR: Can they be adjudicated?

SAM: No, I don't think they can in any absolute sort of way. The models are not falsifiable.

PLR: If I were to offer a tendentious analogy to creationism and the theory of evolution and say that "both models have interpretive power and breadth, but arrange the same data differently," would you still maintain that it's "neither useful nor appropriate" to decide whether one is right or wrong?

SAM: I don't know that you could disprove creationism. How could you disprove creationism?

PLR: I'm asking you. [SAM laughs] Are you willing to say that it's a toss-up?

SAM: No. But I'm also not saying that it's a toss-up between the drive and the relational models. I think the relational model is better; I don't think it's "right." The way that I think about this is influenced by Richard Rorty. To ask whether a theory or a concept is right or wrong is not useful. It can't be proved in an ultimate way. The more useful question is, what reasons do we have to believe this as opposed to that? I think there are lots of very good reasons to believe the theory of evolution; I don't think there are many good reasons to believe creationism, which to me is preposterous.

The same is true of the relational theory compared with the drive theory. I think the drive theory is anachronistic; I don't think it's Wrong, with a capital "W." It was a great explanatory framework at a particular point in intellectual and clinical history. Now it doesn't work very well. The success of the relational turn in psychoanalysis is mostly due to the fact that it's more useful. It explains people—clinicians as well as patients—to themselves much better. It's also more consistent with a whole range of movements in other intellectual disciplines. So I'm happy to say that I think it's a much better theory. It's a more useful theory. Is it "right" as opposed to "wrong"? I don't think you can say, because I don't know how it could be decided.

PLR: Do you accept the analogy between relational theory and Darwinian evolution versus the drive theory and creationism?

SAM: Yes.

PLR: But you wouldn't want to say that one is right and one is wrong because they're both simply constructions of reality and, invoking Rorty, there's no external empirical or scientific court of authority to which we can appeal to settle the disputes between them?

SAM: Right.

PLR: So science has no independent standing for you as a way of resolving these questions?

SAM: No, not completely. I think science bears on the question of the persuasiveness of psychoanalytic concepts and issues. There's a chapter in my new book about this.[13] If the things that I believed began to run counter to a current of scientific research, it would cause me to rethink what I believed.

PLR: So scientific research has a contribution to make?

SAM: Yes, it has a bearing.

PLR: But that implies that there is a type of work that we could call scientific as opposed to what is not scientific.

SAM: Sure. An empirical methodology.

PLR: But ultimately that is just one more construction of reality for you?

SAM: No, that makes it all too level.

PLR: That's the point. I would argue that we need a scientific methodology in order to distinguish what has become anachronistic from what continues to be vital in psychoanalysis. In conjunction with being skilled readers and listeners and interpreters, which requires being open to the evidence, we need the scientific model as an underpinning. That's what permits us to sort things out in the way that I think you want to do. Fundamentally, I don't agree with Rorty. In one passage, you say that the closed-energy and tension-reduction models have been "superseded" by the current understanding of babies.[14] That implies that we've rejected them on the basis of research. Or, citing Joseph Lichtenberg, you refer to the "disconfirmation of the motivational principle of tension-reduction in experimental research

---

13. Stephen A. Mitchell (1997), *Influence and Autonomy in Psychoanalysis.* Hillsdale, NJ: The Analytic Press, pp. 203–230.

14. Mitchell, *Relational Concepts in Psychoanalysis*, p. 135.

on animals and infants."[15] Again, you're invoking scientific research that is falsifiable to sort out these conflicting models. So it seems to me that even though, on a theoretical level, you don't want to appeal to something external to the explanatory system, in practice you're doing that. Why not just say so?

SAM: Because I don't agree with you.

PLR: Isn't that being scientific?

SAM: No, I don't think it is. Any theorist worth his salt who believes in any of the major psychoanalytic schools can explain any piece of scientific data.

PLR: So a Freudian and a Jungian, for example, could each explain everything in the framework of his theory?

SAM: Right.

PLR: Is there a way to sort out whether one is right and one is wrong?

SAM: No. Each individual can sort out what's useful and for what purposes. Then, if you look at the court of history, you can say that this particular approach has been generative of interesting ideas, including some that explored certain aspects in terms of scientific methodology and found confirmation. If you put that all together, that to me is the way people choose among theories.

PLR: So it becomes a pragmatic decision. One possible response to that would be that, in many quarters, the verdict of history on psychoanalysis has been negative. Although I've shared some of the excitement of people who work clinically, I've also been affected by the numerous critiques of psychoanalysis by people who would say that because psychoanalysis has abandoned the claim to be scientific—or because Freud's efforts to prove that it was scientific have not been borne out—it doesn't work. There may not be any reason to think that psychoanalysis is more efficacious than other modes of therapy or has anything more than a placebo effect. From the standpoint of scientific psychology, one is in danger of saying that psychoanalysis itself has become anachronistic. I think that psychoanalysis needs to meet those arguments on their own terms. Psychoanalysis is not anachronistic only because much of it can be supported by good empirical research, even though that may not be the final justification for how we work clinically.

---

15. Mitchell, *Hope and Dread in Psychoanalysis*, p. 50.

SAM: Well, it depends on what you're calling psychoanalysis. Many of the current therapies are spinoffs of psychoanalysis. That is a verdict from the court of history. I like the kind of work generated by such people as Robert Wallerstein, who are trying to evaluate psychoanalysis.[16] I think that efforts to look at the long-term impact on people's lives, particularly if you include physical health, on a cost-efficiency basis are very useful. But I've never seen any that found ways to measure the analytic process that resonates with my own sense of the experience.

PLR: A lot of it may have to do with what we consider to be the purpose of a psychoanalysis. Freud started out by thinking he was curing symptoms, but psychoanalysis turned out not to be very good at that. In consequence, it became something that derived its ultimate justification from allowing people to find meaning in their own lives. This may have an indirect benefit on particular symptoms or problems.

SAM: It takes it out of the medical model. How do you evaluate the kind of meaning or the extent to which people find meaning in their own lives? How you measure that empirically is enormously complicated. I'm speaking as someone who spent several years doing a doctoral dissertation.

PLR: On what?

SAM: This was in the community mental health days. I studied the fit between the individual and the environment in hospitals. I explored the idea that adult patients might return to hospitals not because of physical disease processes but because their emotional needs were being met there better than in the other environments in which they lived. It followed the line of research at that time, and I've known many other people who've spent time doing this sort of project. It's very hard to study the really important problems—like the meaning of people's lives—in a way that's also tight methodologically.

PLR: I agree that insofar as we're dealing with existential issues and psychoanalysis is a discipline of interpretation, we are in the realm of the hermeneutic. But good clinical practice rests on a sound scientific foundation. What I regard as Freud's great errors as a clinician, which include imposing his fixed ideas on his patients, are

---

16. Robert Wallerstein (1986), *42 Lives in Treatment*. New York: Guilford Press.

linked to his lack of a genuinely scientific understanding of how infants, for example, experience the world. I think there is an underlying current in your work that is somewhat negative toward empiricism.

SAM: Yes.

PLR: You speak of people "clutching tightly" Daniel Stern's *The Interpersonal World of the Infant*.[17] To my mind, that attitude cuts out a very important argument in favor of psychoanalysis and perhaps the only way we have of sorting out what continues to be vital and valid from what we need to leave behind.

SAM: I strongly disagree. If you read Daniel Stern closely, he says, "I'm making a lot of this stuff up. I'm taking empirical studies of babies' perceptual and cognitive capacities, and I'm making up a story about what their subjective experience is like." Stern is actually quite careful about that.

PLR: We're going to have a productive disagreement on this. Is the only difference between better and worse stories, or can we say that certain things have been disproved and superseded on the basis of empirical research? The drive theory is contradicted by everything we know from Bowlby's findings on attachment, for example.

SAM: Right.

PLR: So we can no longer accept a closed-system model of tension reduction. In the same way, the arguments for creation theory have been disproved. It's not simply that we have two narratives here between which we're free to choose. I'm not willing to say that it's just a pragmatic argument. There's a scientific foundation that underlies the difference between the two narratives.

SAM: I think that part of the problem with this conversation is that you're setting up the dichotomy too starkly. It's as if there's something that you're calling scientific, and then there are just stories that are all equivalent. I'm not arguing in favor of stories that are all equivalent. But I also don't believe that there's something called "science" that's in the ultimate position of sorting out what's right and what's wrong.

PLR: These issues are linked to how we understand reconstructions in analysis and whether the choice between various interpretations is determined strictly by the fit in the here-and-now. Donald Spence, of course, asserts that the truth of interpretations in psychoanalysis

---

17. Mitchell, *Hope and Dread in Psychoanalysis*, p. 68.

depends on their "rhetorical appeal" rather than "evidentiary value."[18] To me, that goes down a very unprofitable road.

SAM: I wouldn't agree with Spence. I think there's a third possibility that entails a flexible correspondence between the experiences of one's life and the narrative that the interpretation offers. It can open up new possibilities without claiming to be a final account.

PLR: So there is "evidentiary value" of a sort?

SAM: The discipline to which I find it most useful to compare psychoanalysis is history. History isn't just a bunch of stories or a question of "rhetorical appeal." There are many competing theories based on very different presuppositions about how the world works. If you take a clever proponent of a particular approach, such as Marxism, it's going to be very difficult to disprove.

PLR: Even if we accept that history involves stories concerning the past, that doesn't mean that every story is true. Take the example of the denial of the Holocaust.

SAM: Some stories are much more persuasive than others, and part of what makes a story persuasive is that it arranges evidence in a compelling way. I think the same is true of psychoanalysis. Let's go back to creationism. If I look out my window at the lightning and try to imagine what it was like to be living 2,000 years ago, creationism is a great theory. What else are you going to believe?

PLR: You could believe in Zeus.

SAM: Exactly. [laughs] I don't understand a lot of the theory about electricity, but you can't believe in Zeus any more. But it was a great theory a couple of millennia ago. It worked. I feel that drive theory doesn't work. Part of the reason it doesn't work is the kinds of evidence we've been talking about.

PLR: But once you're willing to say there's such a thing as scientific evidence at all, you've acknowledged that there's a court of appeal outside the stories. In *Born to Rebel*, Frank Sulloway says that "science is not a subject, but a *method*."[19] He uses statistics to test competing hypotheses about revolutionary scientific and political movements. He makes a very strong case against the Marxist theory

---

18. Donald Spence (1982), *Narrative Truth and Historical Truth: Meaning and Interpretation in Psychoanalysis*. New York: Norton, p. 32.

19. Sulloway, *Born to Rebel*, p. xvii.

that social class is a determining factor in whether people—often from the same family—align themselves for or against revolutionary changes. He shows that birth order is much more important.

SAM: Right. I'm familiar with the book.

PLR: His project suggests how there may be a way of framing the conversation in terms of scientific criteria, and not just better or worse stories. In *Hope and Dread*, you argue that "our era is postscientistic," and "human knowledge is no longer regarded as an incremental march toward a singular, complete understanding."[20] But in his recent book *Consilience*, E. O. Wilson takes issue with Rorty and the constructivist view.[21] There is a countervailing current of people mainly in the scientific community who still believe in a freestanding reality and a unified vision of truth. That may mean that our era is not postscientistic.

SAM: That's equivalent to saying it's not true that evolutionary theory has become the dominant ideology because there are still those who believe in creationism. Again, this is in chapter 7 of my book.[22] There I draw a contrast between science and scient*ism*. I think that science is important, but scientism was a deep faith at the time of Freud that science was somehow going to provide us with the answers to life. Generally speaking, that's not a persuasive view for many people at this point. It may still be for scientists, but that's like asking creationists if they're persuaded by the theory of evolution. To ask Wilson if he's convinced that science is no longer going to solve all the problems of life is like asking the fundamentalists whether it's true that creationism isn't going to solve the problems of life and give the ultimate answers. You're asking the wrong guys; you're asking the true believers.

PLR: So you're equating Wilson with the creationists?

SAM: The analogy we were working with is the movement from one ideology to another ideology—creationism to evolution theory; science to postscience, let's say.

PLR: I don't accept the idea of postscience.

SAM: We live in a postscientistic era.

---

20. Mitchell, *Hope and Dread in Psychoanalysis*, pp. 18, 20.

21. Edward O. Wilson (1998), *Consilience: The Unity of Knowledge*. New York: Knopf, p. 190.

22. Mitchell, *Influence and Autonomy in Psychoanalysis*, pp. 203–230.

PLR: Do we live in a postscientific era?

SAM: No.

PLR: What is the difference? Do we live in a scientific era?

SAM: Well, we live in an era in which science is useful for lots of different things. It has an enormous place in society. But I think it's an era in which many, many people—if not most people—feel that science doesn't provide them with a framework of meaning in the way that it did 20, 30, or 40 years ago. Before science there was religion.

PLR: I think it's unfair to say that science is a religion for Wilson. It's the opposite. Science involves the ability to change one's mind on the basis of new evidence rather than maintaining the same beliefs regardless of what we learn.

SAM: But Wilson has a set of beliefs in the methodology of science.

PLR: That is true.

SAM: Are those beliefs in the methodology of science as ultimately providing the answers to things ever going to be changed?

PLR: I think there are good reasons to hold those beliefs.

SAM: But that gets back to Rorty's categories.

PLR: I can see why you would say that. But, in my way of looking at it, Wilson is a scientist for the same reason that creationism is not a credible belief. To say that the choice between competing world-views is simply a matter of alternative constructions, which can be adjudicated on the grounds of whether they tell compelling stories . . .

SAM: You keep reducing my point of view to something trivial.

PLR: I don't mean to do that, of course.

SAM: You make it seem as though we're just talking about narrative forms that are decided in relation to "rhetorical appeal," to take that phrase from Spence. That's not what I believe. I don't think the choice is between your view of science and competing narrative constructions.

PLR: So you want to allow for an empirical court of appeal?

SAM: I don't think it's a court of appeals. The empirical is a part of the universe that we live in. It's useful information. "Court of appeal" puts it outside on a platform that I don't think it belongs on.

PLR: We've probably kicked this around long enough. Let me come back to the way you cast Freud. At one point, you say that Freud believed in a "singular Truth" and thought that the psychoanalytic method "would gain access to undisputable and clear phenomena."[23] That implies he had an unproblematic view we have somehow advanced beyond. It seems to me that he is self-contradictory throughout, not just in chapter 3 of *The Ego and the Id*, about which you write: "Unlike the vast majority of Freud's writings, this chapter seems conceptually flawed, torn by internal tensions."[24] To me, internal tensions are everywhere in Freud, including the tension between a scientific or classical and a postmodern or hermeneutic view of the world. Do you really think that Freud believed in a "singular Truth"?

SAM: What I was talking about was the idea that, if you took a piece of clinical material, Freud believed that there was a true, singular understanding of its significance.

PLR: Is that how you read "Constructions in Analysis"?

SAM: Yes, definitely.

PLR: So the reconstruction that the analyst offers . . .

SAM: Is either true or not.

PLR: But isn't there a sense in which it's a jointly constructed fiction that may or may not correspond to a memory in the patient's past?

SAM: That's not the way I remember that paper.

PLR: Or the Wolf Man case?

SAM: I would have said Freud thought these things happened.

PLR: I think that the whole concept of primal scenes turns on an indeterminacy as to whether we regard them as fantasies or actual occurrences.

SAM: But that's a different question. When Freud made an interpretation about the meaning of something in the present in relation to a childhood experience, it might have been a real event or it might have been a fantasy. But Freud felt it was a definite childhood experience; it was that child's psychic reality. There's a correct way to interpret the meaning of current situations with respect to a singular piece of childhood reality. It's a complex theory; it's based on mul-

---

23. Mitchell, *Hope and Dread in Psychoanalysis*, pp. 51, 49.

24. Mitchell, *Relational Concepts in Psychoanalysis*, p. 48.

tidetermination, so you've got different things feeding in. And it's based on what Waelder called multiple function.[25] Let's take some clinical material. Do you want to think of this clinical material as more like a jigsaw puzzle or more like a Rorschach card? I think Freud thought of it as a jigsaw puzzle. There's one correct way to assemble the pieces.

PLR: The archeological metaphor?

SAM: Yes. Or shards, let's say, of a pot. Here are the pieces. There is one correct way to put them together. If someone else came along and said, "No, let's rearrange them this way," one of them is right and one of them is wrong. That's what I meant by "singular." A contemporary constructivist would be more likely to say that a piece of clinical material resembles a Rorschach card. This gets back to the question of whether something is right or wrong. With a Rorschach card, there's no one response that's right. But there's a phenomenon called form level. It's not at all just competing constructions of reality. You have to have good form level. It has to be persuasive. You have to get the tester to be able to see what it is that you're talking about, but it's not a question of "Card 3, what is that?"

PLR: I think many people reading Freud in the humanities would tend to see him as more complex than the jigsaw-puzzle model. In "Constructions in Analysis," and indeed throughout his work, there is also the Rorschach model. He starts out with an archeological confidence that his constructions are reconstructions, but he ends up by saying that his constructions may be no more than delusions like those of his patients.[26]

SAM: It's true that some readers have said I'm unfair to Freud and present him in a unidimensional way. There are lots of ways to read Freud, I'm sure, and I don't read German. I'm interested in the critique of people like Bettelheim and Loewald, who said that Freud was butchered by Strachey. So the Freud that I'm talking about is the Freud of the Strachey translation as interpreted within American clinical psychoanalysis. To me there's no question that, as applied to the clinical situation, Freud was understood to be saying that interpretations are either right or wrong. The constructions either capture something of the psychic reality of that person as a child (in

---

25. Robert Waelder (1936), "The Principle of Multiple Function." *Psychoanalytic Quarterly*, 35:45–62.

26. See Lis Moller (1991), *The Freudian Reading: Analytical and Fictional Constructions*. Philadelphia: University of Pennsylvania Press, pp. 19, 25.

which case, the material opens up and the associations flow) or they don't (in which case the material falls flat). Freud definitely believed in a correlation criterion. If you read his work in the original German or apply it to literature, maybe it's different.

PLR: The issues of translation are important, but I don't think that they're crucial in this connection. I simply wanted to propose that the way Freud comes through in some of your writing has the effect of creating a distance between us and him, where he had a belief in "undisputable and clear phenomena," whereas today we are more aware of the complexity of narratives or constructions. I think many people in the humanities would contend that Freud is contemporary in that respect. I've criticized Freud for imposing his preconceptions on his patients' material, but it's to his credit that he was aware at times of the tentativeness of the interplay between his reconstructions and what "really happened."

SAM: One way of thinking about Freud that I find useful is Habermas's notion of him as on a dividing line between two worlds.

PLR: That's what I was alluding to earlier. Therefore I don't think it's quite fair to say that Freud believed in a "singular Truth," because his practice shows how equally postmodern he was. In the last sentence of *Totem and Taboo*, he says of the killing of the primal father, "In the beginning was the deed,"[27] but that's a quotation from Goethe, which alludes to the Gospel of John, "In the beginning was the word." So the assertion that something really happened is itself a rhetorical gesture that reinscribes it as fictional.

SAM: I find that interesting, but I'm not sure I buy it. Also the quotations you're taking out of my work are in particular contexts. Comparative psychoanalysis is a treacherous business. There's nothing I've ever written about which the people who are deeply into any of the positions don't feel that I'm being wildly reductive.

PLR: I'm simply calling attention to my own responses to what I've read, not so much trying to advocate any one position. But let me briefly mention Winnicott, who is someone I've been much influenced by. I think you're a little unfair to Winnicott, in a way analogous to your treatment of Freud. You say at one point that he had "total confidence" in the "universal validity" of his theories as an "unerring guide."[28] I find Winnicott

---

27. Sigmund Freud (1913), *Totem and Taboo. Standard Edition*, 13:161. London: Hogarth Press, 1955.

28. Mitchell, *Hope and Dread in Psychoanalysis*, p. 72.

in his best work to be highly provisional and subjective. To me he embodies an alternative to Freud precisely because of his lack of "total confidence." I can see why you would say that he believed strongly in his models, but I think he offers a dialectical view of the analytic encounter in which the analyst doesn't have all the answers.

SAM: To their credit, I think all these people were constructively inconsistent. That description of Winnicott certainly sounds like an overstatement, if that's what I said. But there are two issues with Winnicott that are difficult not to collapse together, but extremely important to keep separate. One is Winnicott's manner of being in the clinical situation. I agree with you about his manner of being. I think his demeanor was very different from that of Freud and the way classical analysis was practiced. But that is separate from Winnicott's understanding of development. One of the principal features of his understanding of development is that the self is generated in a particular medium. It has to be a medium in which the other adapts itself to the spontaneous gestures of the self in question. He was a wonderful medium to encourage development of the self in question. Margaret Little described him as "yeasty."[29] He was good at enouraging growth and that sort of thing.

PLR: Fermentation.

SAM: Yes. But he did that because he felt certain that there was a developmental need that required a particular kind of parental interaction. So, on a theoretical level, he was totally convinced of the correctness of his views, and that's a different issue from his clinical manner of being.

PLR: That's fair. In my view, Winnicott was right, so I am probably totally convinced of the correctness of his views.

SAM: [laughs] That's good.

PLR: To say that any living organism cannot exist without a facilitating environment—Balint uses the metaphor of oxygen—is to my mind irrefutable. It's empirically true. Therefore, if we allow Winnicott the latitude to talk about this metaphorically in terms of the primary caretaker, his understanding of what goes on in psychoanalytic therapy is well founded.

SAM: But you share with Winnicott a belief in science!

---

29. Margaret Little (1985), "Winnicott Working in Areas Where Psychotic Anxieties Predominate: A Personal Record." *Free Associations*, 3:9–41.

PLR: I do, but you've acknowledged that in his clinical practice he wasn't dogmatic, and to me that is very important. I agree with Winnicott theoretically, but he introduced a major break from Freud by rejecting the model of the authoritarian analyst who thinks that the business of the analyst is to tell the patient the truth about the patient rather than letting the patient find it out for him- or herself.

SAM: Where I have problems with this view is that there's ultimately a condescending dimension to it. The passage from *Holding and Interpretation* that I discuss in *Hope and Dread* describes a powerful example of a man whom Winnicott was driving crazy.[30] This guy was trying to engage Winnicott, to get him to stand in one place and say what he thought. Winnicott was convinced, because of his scientific theory of development, that what this man needed was for him to adapt himself to the patient, and that's a problem.

PLR: I suppose that no analyst is right for every patient. But I would still contrast Winnicott, and the Independent tradition generally, with both Freud and Klein in upholding the fundamental belief that the analyst is someone who is there for the patient to use as the patient wishes rather than someone who knows better than the patient.

SAM: Absolutely. I think Winnicott has had more influence than anyone since Freud on how American clinicians understand the analytic situation, and in a very beneficial way.

PLR: And on you personally?

SAM: He's been a big influence, but I don't know that he's the greatest.

PLR: Who would you say?

SAM: Fairbairn.

PLR: I share your admiration for Fairbairn. What I'm noticing in this conversation is that I'm pressing you to choose between things. What you're often doing, it seems to me, is trying to have it both ways and say there isn't a necessary contradiction between alternative views. Maybe I'm splitting and you're integrating.

SAM: That's kind of ironic because Arnold Richards, in his long review of *Relational Concepts*, accused me of being a dichotomizer.[31] So I'm glad to hear that I'm a synthesizer.

---

30. Mitchell, *Hope and Dread in Psychoanalysis*, pp. 69–72.

31. See the review essay by Janet L. Bachant & Arnold D. Richards (1993),

PLR: I want to say that certain things are right and certain things are wrong, even though I'd like to maintain an attitude of tentativeness and humility in the search for knowledge and my dealings with people. But for me there is a reality out there, at least in principle.

SAM: I believe in a reality out there also.

PLR: But not a truth?

SAM: Not a truth. Thomas Nagel calls it "perspectival realism."[32] The distinction is important. Some of the time when you think I'm trying to have it both ways, I'm actually trying to open up a third possibility. That happened in our conversation earlier, where if it's not science, then it's just stories no one can choose among.

PLR: You want to inhabit potential space?

SAM: That's right.

PLR: I do too. But for me, if there's reality, then there's truth. We're not simply constructing.

SAM: But if there's a reality, then there are perspectives on that reality. How can you get to that reality except through a perspective? There's no "view from nowhere," to use Nagel's phrase.

PLR: It's always possible to find people who will assert things that no one can convince them are untrue. That's perhaps an insurmountable problem. The example of creationism is a case in point. But the fact that certain people refuse to accept scientific evidence does not to me lead to the conclusion that we cannot decide whether the biblical version of creation is literally true or not. I agree with you that on some level all we have is intersubjectivity, but if there is a reality out there, which is not simply contructed . . .

SAM: The reality is not simply constructed. Our *takes* on it are constructed.

PLR: I agree. But being scientific for me entails being willing to revise our perspectives on reality in light of experience, which falsifies our way of thinking because it comes from outside our framework.

SAM: [laughs] You're not going to convince me of that.

Psychoanalytic Dialogues, 3:431–460; and Stephen Mitchell's reply, pp. 461–480.

32. Thomas Nagel (1986), *The View From Nowhere*. New York: Oxford University Press.

PLR: That's fine. But let me throw a couple of juxtaposed passages at you. They touch on different topics, although the underlying theme is the one that we've been exploring: whether we can synthesize or must choose between alternatives. On one hand, you say, concerning Freud, "Certainly, it is essential that psychoanalysts never discard Freud's thought"; however, you say one page later, "Sometimes it is better to start with a fresh canvas."[33] To me, those are contradictory aspirations. If it's better to start with a fresh canvas, that must mean discarding Freud's thought, at least in some respects.

SAM: Of course. I didn't mean the totality of Freud's thought or what Freud said about everything.

PLR: But when you say, "It is essential that psychoanalysts never discard Freud's thought," it sounds as though we can never start afresh because we're always writing on Freud's palimpsest. There's no tabula rasa because Freud's thought is always there and should always be there.

SAM: If you pull out a sentence here and a sentence there, you can make them contradictory. I can't imagine teaching psychoanalysis without beginning with Freud. The aspect of Freud that I would never want to discard is the problems that he was struggling with. What I'd like to discard are a lot of the answers.

PLR: So Freud is an indispensable point of reference, but we must discard Freud's thought at least insofar as some of his conclusions are concerned.

SAM: Absolutely.

PLR: Then we agree. That leads to a related topic, which is the tension between evolutionary and revolutionary perspectives on the history of psychoanalysis. As with the drive/structure example, I see you saying that both are true and we need not choose between them, while in practice you come down on one side. You write: "Calling these changes revolutionary emphasizes the differences; calling these changes evolutionary emphasizes the continuities. Neither view is more correct. It is a question of emphasis."[34] That contradicts what I take to be the thrust of your work, which is that there has been a radical change in contemporary psychoanalysis—a revolution in theory and a revolution in metatheory.

---

33. Mitchell, *Hope and Dread in Psychoanalysis*, pp. 90, 91.

34. Mitchell, *Hope and Dread in Psychoanalysis*, p. 84.

SAM: This goes back to the question of what we mean by true.

PLR: Or correct. You say, "Neither view is more correct."

SAM: Right. I don't think it's Correct, with a capital "C."

PLR: What about with a small "c"?

SAM: [laughs] I think the revolutionary perspective is a much more useful way to think about contemporary psychoanalysis. It accounts for more things that I find interesting. But talk to Arnold Richards. He'll tell you, "No, no, no, it's evolutionary. It was all in Freud."

PLR: But from your point of view, isn't one model more correct than the other?

SAM: It depends on what we mean by "correct."

PLR: You say it's a "question of emphasis." The inference I draw from that is that an equally plausible case could be made for the evolutionary perspective.

SAM: No, I think the revolutionary is more plausible.

PLR: But not more correct?

SAM: You can make the words mean what you want. To me, "correct" implies the correlation theory of truth. Here's the way to look at something, and it matches the way it really is. But I don't think there's any way to get at the way it really is so as to figure out which one matches better. I like the revolutionary model because it encompasses more of the things that seem important to me.

PLR: So your assertion that "neither view is more correct" rests on a philosophical premise that we finally cannot in any absolute sense choose between competing narratives. But in practice, or pragmatically, you are willing to speak of a revolutionary change.

SAM: Yes, and I've taken a lot of heat for it. The way that many of these positions get defined becomes polarized. I find a lot of hermeneutics and constructivist theory too antiscience and too antiempirical, in a way that seems silly to me. It rejects areas of experience that ought to be taken into account. I would say that mine is a middle view. I'm not willing, as you are, to say that we're going to take those empirical data and make them the ultimate court of appeal. So I'm not in the science camp. I'm not going to give them that power, because I don't think they stand outside competing frames of reference. But I'm not a hermeneutics guy who says, "I don't want to read or hear about any of that stuff because it's all a question of what we make up anyhow." I'd like to read your interview with Mary Ainsworth, because I met Bowlby in the early 1980s and found what he did very interesting. But I then lost track of the attachment research. I picked it up again when I was invited to give the Bowlby Memorial Lecture last year at the Bowlby Institute in London.

PLR: Is there such a thing?

SAM: It's called the Institute for Attachment-Based Psychoanalytic Psychotherapy.

PLR: Who runs it?

SAM: His son, Richard Bowlby, is important there. So is John Southgate, and Suzy Ohrbach is connected with it. I was invited to speak there because they see very strong connections between what they're doing and what we're doing. I spent some time getting into the attachment research literature. That's one area of empirical research I find dazzling. It's able to get at meaningful things in a methodologically consistent way. But much of the research that I've come across doesn't interest me at all.

PLR: I think that pragmatically we agree almost 100%.

SAM: Right.

PLR: I wanted to ask you about Bowlby, whom we mentioned in passing, because to me he is extremely important. I think he would have agreed with me about science and the need to reject the drive model because it can't be supported empirically.

SAM: Right.

PLR: He was largely criticized and ignored within psychoanalysis because of his attempts to establish his understanding of human development on an empirical foundation. But, for the same reason, his work has been influential not only within psychoanalysis but also within the broader field of scientific psychology.

SAM: When he spoke at the White Institute, I was the discussant. The paper that I presented in London dealt with the relation between attachment theory and psychoanalysis. I think he was rejected for a lot of bad—political—reasons, but also for some good reasons, in the sense that the scientific-behavioral way he was getting at attachment is not very helpful clinically. That's why I've always preferred Fairbairn, from graduate school on. I thought Bowlby was *right*, but I thought that Fairbairn was much more useful.

PLR: I don't see a contradiction between Fairbairn and Bowlby.

SAM: I don't either. I think it's really interesting to look at them together.

PLR: But you think that there are some good reasons why the psychoanalytic people turned away from Bowlby?

SAM: Not that they turned away. But part of the problem with Bowlby's concepts was that they were too simplistic to be used clinically.

PLR: Can you give me an example?

SAM: I think that his writing about attachment didn't get enough at the texture of internal experience. Fairbairn's notion of internalized bad objects and the relationships between the libidinal ego and antilibidinal ego has a texture to it, and you can take a case and use that to develop a picture of the inner world.

PLR: Whereas Bowlby's concepts of ambivalent attachment or anxious attachment don't have the same purchase?

SAM: They don't. I've read a lot of bad papers applying attachment theory to clinical cases. It's like sliding stuff into categories. People say, "Here's an example of ambivalent attachment." I find Mary Main's work very interesting, but that gets into much more complex material.

PLR: I think we agree about the value of the entire tradition that comes out of object relations and attachment theory. I see them as very compatible.

SAM: Yes.

PLR: I would only want to invoke Bowlby, as someone whose last work was a biography of Darwin and who has been hailed by Frank Sulloway, among others, as scientific, whereas Freud is faulted by the antipsychoanalytic camp for being unscientific.[35] I don't think all the recent critiques of Freud can be ascribed to defensiveness. At least some of them are fairminded but simply take issue with Freud in various respects.

SAM: I don't think Sulloway is fairminded. Sulloway has a very antagonistic attitude toward psychoanalysis.

---

35. See Frank J. Sulloway (1991), "Darwinian Psychobiography." *New York Review of Books*, 10 October, pp. 29–31.

PLR: What do you think is the cause of that?

SAM: I have no idea. But he disparages psychoanalysis, as does Stephen Jay Gould.

PLR: It may be because they don't think it's scientific.

SAM: But that's a lousy reason. To say, "It's not scientific, so I'm going to disparage it," is silly. It's shutting yourself off from a whole domain of knowledge that, as far as I'm concerned, is very valuable.

Frank J. Sulloway

On Darwin and Freud

Peter L. Rudnytsky: My project involves interviewing people who have worked in the field of psychoanalysis, whether as analysts or scholars, and when Phyllis Grosskurth suggested that I contact you it seemed like a great idea. What I think you can bring to bear in a very valuable way is a perspective from outside the discipline, which people in psychoanalysis need to take into account more than they do. I expect you and I will find that we agree about many things, but probably there will be times in our conversation when I show greater sympathy with psychoanalysis than you do. Your two books—the Freud book of 1979[1] and now *Born to Rebel*[2]—take Freud and Darwin as central figures, and one thing that I want to explore with you is the role of Freud and Darwin in your thinking and how your assessment especially of Freud has changed. Your admiration for Darwin seems to have been consistent, but clearly there has been an evolution in your thinking about Freud in the two decades since you published *Freud, Biologist of the Mind*. I'd also like to hear about how you got interested in Freud and Darwin and how you see your theoretical work connected to your own life experience. So maybe we could start with something autobiographical and then move on to issues of theory and substance.

---

1. Frank J. Sulloway (1979), *Freud, Biologist of the Mind: Beyond the Psychoanalytic Legend*. New York: Basic Books.

2. Frank J. Sulloway (1996), *Born to Rebel: Birth Order, Family Dynamics and Creative Lives*. New York: Vintage Books.

Frank J. Sulloway: My first academic interest was in Darwin and stemmed from a project that retraced his five-year *Beagle* voyage (1831–1836). At this time I was a junior at Harvard College. I raised about $30,000 and put together an eight-person film crew that went around South America during the summer of 1968 and made a series of films. Our script was constructed entirely in Darwin's own words. We took his letters, diary, and various published versions of his account of the *Beagle* voyage and strung all these materials together into a self-narrated documentary.

When I came back from this four-month trip, I decided to write my undergraduate thesis on Darwin and the *Beagle* voyage. I was very interested in trying to understand how he had become an evolutionist. After I had completed my undergraduate thesis, I was awarded a traveling fellowship for the following year, and in the course of this fellowship year I did a lot of reading in the field of psychology, and particularly on the subject of creativity. One of the authors I decided to read was Freud. I hadn't previously read any of Freud's works, at least any that I remember. I felt that, if one was to understand how the mind works, Freud was a reasonably good place to start. The first work about Freud that I read was Ernest Jones's biography of him.[3] Many ideas that Jones took for granted, such as that there are oral and anal stages to childhood sexuality, struck me as puzzles. As a true believer, Jones would simply say something like, "Then Freud discovered the polymorphously perverse nature of childhood sexuality." The biography didn't go always into the rationale behind the theories.

Having had some training in the history of science, which was the field in which I was about to begin my graduate studies, I was naturally curious about the origins and historical context of Freud's ideas. So I decided to read Freud's correspondence with Wilhelm Fliess. I was immediately struck by the fact that Freud was discussing infantile sexuality in these letters at a time when he was not yet supposed to know about this idea. Well before the self-analysis, there's a letter of December 6, 1896, in which he asserts that the child must be sexual.[4] A few weeks later Freud connects the child's polymorphous perversity to sexuality in animals, including the sense

---

3. Ernest Jones (1953, 1955, 1957), *The Life and Work of Sigmund Freud*, Vols. I–III. New York: Basic Books.

4. Jeffrey M. Masson, ed. & trans. (1985), *The Complete Letters of Sigmund Freud to Wilhelm Fliess, 1887–1904*. Cambridge, MA: Harvard University Press, p. 212.

of smell.[5] He also refers to Albert Moll's similar ideas on this subject.[6] Freud is talking, of course, about the notion of "abandoned erotogenic zones." I knew from my background in the history of biology that behind this general discussion was a well-known biological assumption, namely, Ernst Haeckel's biogenetic law.[7] Without having to spell it out to Fliess—who, like Freud, had a strong background in biology—Freud was saying that a child *has* to be sexual because the child recapitulates the sexual history of our ancestors.

According to the biogenetic law, the child recapitulates, during the early stages of individual development, the *mature* stages of our ancestors. From our present-day perspective, these mature stages of sexuality can be viewed as "polymorphously perverse"—representing the kinds of erotic interests that dogs have, for example, in feces—erotic interests that are typical of animals generally. The child's form of sexuality is, as Freud put it, a form of "zoophilia."[8] When I first read these discussions in Freud's letters to Fliess, I thought, "Gee, that's an interesting historical point. Freud appears to have had his first insight into one of his two most celebrated discoveries from the general perspective of late 19th-century evolutionary thought."

PLR: The other discovery being about dreams.

FJS: Yes, the other being his insight into what he believed to be the hidden meaning of dreams. So Freud, at least in his thinking about human development, clearly was borrowing from this great intellectual tradition—namely, 19th-century evolutionary thinking in its special Haeckelian version—and I'd never seen a reference to this influence. I certainly didn't see it in Jones's biography. And since this important insight occurs many months before Freud is supposed to have discovered infantile sexuality through his self-analysis, it didn't appear to me as though he had really discovered infantile sexuality via that route. Or, if he did, he discovered something other than the basic concept.

In any event, none of this evidence linking Freud's thinking about

---

5. Letter of January 11, 1897. In Masson, ed. *Freud–Fliess Letters*, p. 223.

6. Letter of November 14, 1897. In Masson, ed. *Freud–Fliess Letters*, p. 279.

7. Ernst Haeckel (1866), *Generelle Morphologie der Organismen: Allgemeine Grundzüge der organischen Formen-Wissenschaft, mechanisch begründet durch die von Charles Darwin reformierte Descendeztheorie*, 2 vols. Berlin: Georg Reimer. See Sulloway, *Freud, Biologist of the Mind*, p. 199.

8. Letter of January 11, 1897. In Masson, ed. *Freud–Fliess Letters*, p. 223.

psychosexual development to evolutionary biology had been discussed by any of Freud's biographers or by other historians of psychoanalysis. I'm sure they had read this section of the correspondence with Fliess, but it apparently meant nothing to them. It meant a lot to me, though, and it clearly meant a lot to Freud, who appealed to similar notions throughout his career and who possessed, of course, a strong background in evolutionary biology. So this particular observation about Freud's intellectual development sucked me in. I thought to myself, "I'll write a paper on this topic." This was in 1972.

At this same time I was taking a graduate seminar at Harvard University with Jerome Kagan, a developmental psychologist of considerable note, and I started a paper on Freud's intellectual development for Kagan's seminar. The more I burrowed into Freud's collected works and correspondence, the more references I kept finding to the idea that ontogeny recapitulates phylogeny. So I started following up these references back to the books Freud was reading and citing in this general context. I consulted Albert Moll[9] and Richard von Krafft-Ebing,[10] for example, and found that the same kind of evolutionary logic was present in their writings about sexuality. Krafft-Ebing believed that sexual perversions were throwbacks to the forms of sexuality present in our ancestors; so sadism, for example, was believed to a reflection of the aggression males once used when procuring a mate.[11] Krafft-Ebing and others thought that, in humans, these kinds of "atavisms" emerge in pathological cases. This, of course is the same basic logic to which Freud had appealed during his own radical change of thinking in 1896 and 1897, when he went from believing that children are asexual (and hence will be traumatized by premature sexual experiences) to accepting that sexuality in childhood—albeit "polymorphously perverse"—is normal. In other words, Freud had begun to think that childhood sexuality possesses an energy of its own (libido) and that this energy doesn't need to be awakened by stimulation from the outside world. This more dynamic conception of childhood sexuality replaced the theory that Freud soon abandoned when his seduction theory of neurosis finally collapsed in the fall of 1897.

---

9. Albert Moll (1897), *Untersuchungen über die Libido Sexualis.* Berlin: Fischer's Medizinische Buchhandlung.

10. Richard von Krafft-Ebing (1886), *Psychopathia Sexualis, with Especial Reference to Antipathic Sexual Instinct: A Medico-Forensic Study*, trans. from 10th (1898) German edition by R. J. Rebman. London: Rebman, 1899.

11. Krafft-Ebing, *Psychopathia Sexualis*, pp. 199–200. See Sulloway, *Freud, Biologist of the Mind*, p. 295.

My research project on this aspect of Freud's intellectual development just grew and grew and grew. I took an incomplete in Kagan's course to pursue this historical reconstruction of Freud's ideas. [PLR laughs] My study became a long paper, and then it became a short book. Finally, I decided to do my doctoral dissertation on this topic, and it went on to become a rather long dissertation—eventually over 1,000 typewritten pages. About four years later, when I was finishing this dissertation, I said to Kagan during one of our regular meetings, "You know, I still have an incomplete in your seminar course." Kagan, who had followed all of my developing ideas on this subject, said to me, "I guess you've done enough work now. I'll give you an A." [both laugh]

PLR: You almost had the fate of evolutionary theorist William Hamilton and didn't receive a degree for your work![12]

FJS: Actually, I was a Harvard Junior Fellow at that time, and during the old days Junior Fellows didn't take degrees. They were evidently considered above that. By the mid-1970s, however, it had become customary for Junior Fellows to take a degree. Anyway, what started as an innocent little paper eventually became my first book. This was an interesting process of intellectual discovery because it lured me in, deeper and deeper. I had no intention of writing a long work on Freud, but I stumbled into a hornet's nest of historical and scientific problems as I tried to make sense out of Freud's intellectual development and his scientific heritage. Because the more traditional analysts who had engaged in Freud scholarship up to that point, including very capable people such as Ernest Jones and Kurt Eissler, did not have a background in either intellectual history or the history of science, they appeared to have missed a lot. This was not generally true of Henri Ellenberger, who missed practically nothing, but Ellenberger's scope in his *Discovery of the Unconscious* was so broad that he wasn't really focused on Freud as a developing individual but rather on Freud's broader place in the history of psychiatry.[13] So there really was a niche open there.

---

12. See Sulloway, *Born to Rebel*, pp. 57–59. While a graduate student at the University of London in 1963, William Hamilton proposed a theory of genetically encoded "kin selection" (along with a related notion of "inclusive fitness") as a solution to the longstanding conundrum of why, according to the laws of natural selection, inherently selfish organisms should engage in cooperative behavior. Although it has since proven extremely influential, Hamilton's work was initially deemed insufficient to be awarded the doctoral degree.

13. Henri F. Ellenberger (1970), *The Discovery of the Unconscious: The History and Evolution of Dynamic Psychiatry*. New York: Basic Books.

PLR: You followed a niche-picking strategy.[14]

FJS: Mine was definitely a niche-picking strategy. So that's how I got interested in Freud. I must say, having spent seven years on that project, that the more I looked into Freud's ideas, the more disillusioned I became with psychoanalytic theory. Not, however, with Freud as a historical figure. Back then I still thought that psychoanalysis was a terribly interesting theory, even if it was deeply flawed. And I had a lot of admiration for Freud, although it was certainly mixed with criticisms as well. Trained as a historian, I tended to view Freud, including the substantial errors that he appeared to have made, as one might view Aristotle.[15] There's practically nothing in Aristotle's scientific works—in his theoretical biology or his physics—that's valid today, although the observational aspects of his biology have fared better than his cosmology. But a historian writing about Aristotle with the distinct advantage of having a knowledge of 20th-century science wouldn't ridicule him for his stupidity. So I felt that my job was to study the origin of Freud's ideas and not to denigrate Freud for being so stupid as to accept a principle such as the biogenetic law, which is now known to be totally wrong and that was, even during Freud's lifetime, also known to be wrong. This simply wasn't the spirit in which I wrote my book.

When I finally finished the book I did feel, however, that I had invested a great deal of time in understanding the development of a theory that was not particularly useful for solving the problems that had gotten me interested in Freud in the first place. These problems involved scientific creativity and human development more broadly. The more exposure I acquired to academic psychology, the more I realized that almost none of these people were wasting their time with Freud. All I had succeeded in doing in the course of my researches was to show, through historical analysis, why serious behavioral scientists ought no longer to be interested in Freud. So after finishing my book on Freud, I went back to Darwin.

PLR: What was it exactly that you become disillusioned with in the course of writing your book?

FJS: It wasn't so much the methodology as the theories. I subsequently became much more critical of Freud as a hypothesis-tester

---

14. Sulloway has developed the notion of niche picking as a sibling strategy. See *Born to Rebel*, pp. 95–96.

15. See Sulloway, *Freud, Biologist of the Mind*, p. 500.

and methodologist. But that wasn't the source of my disillusionment in the late 1970s.

PLR: Is this disillusionment reflected in the book?

FJS: Yes, there's a certain ambivalence purposely reflected in the book. I was trying to be balanced. I didn't want to pull a Jeffrey Masson, who became disillusioned with Freud's theories and then concocted a strange historical scenario in which Freud goes astray through intellectual cowardice (a preposterous thesis if there ever was one).

PLR: You were before Masson though. [laughs] *The Assault on Truth* was not published until 1984.[16]

FJS: Well, yes, but I had met Masson and knew something of his opinions about Freud, and I did not want to pull a Jeffrey Masson-like intellectual stunt. In other words, I didn't want to be a sensationalist, especially at the expense of historical balance. I was trying to give Freud his due and at same time to make the argument that almost every major assumption in the psychosexual theory of development that underlies the rest of his psychoanalytic theorizing—in the interpretation of dreams and so on—is based on outmoded 19th-century assumptions that are now known to be dead as a doornail.

PLR: The sense that Freud's thinking is based on outmoded concepts doesn't come through to me in *Freud, Biologist of the Mind*. The death instinct is described as logically coherent and justified rather than being attacked in your book.[17]

FJS: The book takes for granted—perhaps too much so in some places—that the educated reader is aware that such notions as the inheritance of acquired characteristics (which is a necessary prerequisite for the biogenetic law), and the biogenetic law itself, are now known to be totally wrong ideas. Actually, in several places I am quite explicit on this important point.[18] On this subject one doesn't have to beat a dead horse, or at least that was what I thought at the time. Once I had shown, for example, that the death instinct possesses a peculiar biogenetic logic, which has to do with regression to past life forms and so on, I had really made my point. Such a theory, no matter how conceptually elegant, couldn't possibly be true.

---

16. Jeffrey Moussaieff Masson (1984), *The Assault on Truth: Freud's Suppression of the Seduction Theory.* New York: Farrar, Strauss & Giroux.

17. Sulloway, *Freud, Biologist of the Mind*, pp. 395, 409.

18. Sulloway, *Freud, Biologist of the Mind*, pp. 439–442, 497–498.

PLR: I agree with you completely about the untenability of Freud's Lamarckianism. But it seems to me that the discussion in your book sometimes conflated Darwinian and Lamarckian theories of evolution. You showed Freud's participation in a scientific tradition, but you didn't make a concerted effort to differentiate between the parts of his thought (if any) that might be considered Darwinian—and therefore soundly based—from those based on untenable concepts. You were concerned with Freud as a "biologist of the mind" in a broad sense. You used the relationship to Fliess to demonstrate that Freud was influenced by a set of contemporary assumptions that explained his thinking in another way but didn't necessarily undercut it.

FJS: The critique of Freud is definitely there in the book. It's perhaps not as developed as I would make it if I were rewriting the book now. In the last chapter, I'm quite clear about the fact that there are fundamental defects in the whole theory of psychosexual development and in the hydraulic theory, which are explained by Freud's unfortunate reliance on outmoded assumptions drawn from 19th-century biology. I go on to ask: What, then, can we give Freud credit for? I gave him credit for tackling the most interesting psychobiological topics of the day and for identifying them as fruitful, but not for solving them. I made my allusion to Aristotle and other great thinkers in this connection. Most of these philosophers and scientists, working within the conceptual limitations of their day, were wrong on a lot of issues, but we still give them their due as great thinkers.

Back in the late 1970s I tended to think of Freud as someone who deserved credit for having a brilliant mind and an ability, given the assumptions of the day, to spell out exactly where these assumptions would lead a logical thinker, even though it turns out that most of these assumptions were wrong and led Freud in the wrong direction. There are always a lot of people around in any given historical period who don't ever grasp the big picture. They don't know how to draw all the available information together. Then someone comes along, like Freud, who reads voraciously and synthesizes all the existing literature. Suddenly this one person has a very sharp picture and creates a coherent theory, which now becomes a target for potential refutations. Then this new theory is either confirmed or not. That's the stage at which I left Freud in my book.

The great tragedy of psychoanalysis is that, having staked out fertile territory and having proposed, through Freud's own concepts, an extraordinary theory that united it all, its practitioners then failed to do what is normal and indeed essential in science. The second step of science after one has developed a hypothesis is to test that hypothesis. Freud and his followers generally failed to take that second step, and this failure proved fatal to the whole enterprise.

PLR: I'm prepared to agree with you about a lot of this. Perhaps the project needs not to be abandoned but to be grounded more securely through the type of testing you're talking about.

FJS: That's an interesting issue. Almost no one, in my opinion, is effectively doing that, mainly because the discipline does not train its practitioners to do formal research, and the people in medicine who have been adequately trained in scientific methodology are too busy doing their own research to do what psychoanalysts should be doing for themselves.

PLR: Psychoanalytic theory isn't monolithic. It may be necessary to discard many components in order to reground it. To anticipate something we might talk about later: Bowlby is someone I know you admire greatly and whom I also admire very much. In my view, he came as close as anyone to laying a foundation for contemporary psychoanalysis.

FJS: There are two crucial issues relevant to the intellectual fate of psychoanalysis—both past and present. One is the nature of the theory, which was badly flawed from the start. The other is the nature of the personnel who are attracted to the discipline and who then, through the form of education that it offers, fail to learn the basic methods of science. Even the most faulty of theories eventually is corrected or discarded as long as a discipline's practitioners engage in hypothesis testing. Psychoanalysis did not do this, and, as a result, the field has become mostly a dead end for research. Bowlby was an exception, not because he stayed in psychoanalysis but because he effectively left psychoanalysis. He clawed his way to the real world of modern science, which is an extraordinary thing for someone to have done given where Bowlby started out. I once asked him how he did it, and he told me that he owed a great debt in this connection to his Cambridge University education in natural science.

PLR: I don't think it's fair to say that he left psychoanalysis.

FJS: For all practical purposes he was ostracized from the psychoanalytic movement in England. His psychoanalytic colleagues had almost zero interest in his work, and his closest colleagues, such as Mary Ainsworth, eventually became academic psychologists.

PLR: I've interviewed Mary Ainsworth for this book.

FJS: I'd like to read that interview. I'm not saying, by the way, that

Bowlby didn't still feel some intellectual continuity between what he was doing later in his life and the field where he started out.

PLR: He never renounced his identity as a psychoanalyst.

FJS: True enough, but we must keep in mind that there are two key factors that drive any theory forward. One is the theory proper and the other is the methodology—the testing. At the level of methodology, Bowlby effectively moved into the world of science.

PLR: But he retained close ties with John Sutherland and others in the object relations tradition of psychoanalysis. When you refer to Bowlby, you invariably call him a psychiatrist or a psychologist, never a psychoanalyst. I agree that the cold shoulder given Bowlby was extremely unfortunate. I would simply say that, insofar as the project of grounding psychoanalysis in something compatible with a scientific perspective is tenable, which I hope it is, Bowlby is a crucial figure in pointing the way to that.

FJS: Well, I heartily agree. But it's also fair to say that the people who are the heirs to this tradition—the psychologists who work on attachment behavior—have mostly done their research through academic channels.

PLR: I think there's been a healthy cross-fertilization.

FJS: The main problem, as I have said before, is that psychoanalysts don't get any real training in science. So they don't know how to do hypothesis testing, experiments, or epidemiological studies. They know how to read a book and how to pick up on an interesting theory or idea and either be convinced or not be convinced of it. But the cutting edge of research in behavioral science areas like those in which Bowlby was interested is now found in work done by academic psychologists, not psychoanalysts. These academic psychologists are not interested in rescuing psychoanalysis because, in general, they don't think there's anything worth rescuing.

PLR: I can say that Mary Ainsworth has a different perspective on psychoanalysis. She is quite well disposed toward it.

FJS: What about Mary Main? She's a mainstream academic.

PLR: Stephen Mitchell cited her work very favorably in talking to me, but I don't know what she would say about psychoanalysis. It would be interesting to find out.[19]

---

19. Mary Main's views on psychoanalysis are contained in "Discourse, Prediction, and Recent Studies in Attachment: Implications for Psychoanalysis."

FJS: Yes.

PLR: In a passage from *Freud, Biologist of the Mind*, you say that "Freud established perhaps the most comprehensive evolutionary explanation of the origins of human behavior that has yet been formulated in science."[20] That's high praise indeed. I know that it reflects a certain stage in your thinking, but I picked it out to suggest that the critique of the Lamarckian and Haeckelian dimensions of Freud's biology wasn't something that you pressed in that book.

FJS: Well, it depends on which parts of the book one reads. Moreover, the sentence you have quoted is not inconsistent with my conclusion that this grand evolutionary vision was basically flawed in fundamental ways. It's also true, however, that my main intent in the book was not to conclude whether Freud was right or wrong but rather to illuminate his intellectual development. Probably the main reason I didn't emphasize the issue of validity more is that my training was as an intellectual historian, and one of the most basic principles that gets drummed into students in this field is "Don't commit the fallacy of Whiggish history." Whiggish history is the end result of seeing events and ideas as leading up to the present, which is considered "correct." Everything that isn't on this path to truth, virtue, and justice is considered wrong.

In Theodore Shapiro & Robert N. Emde, eds. (1995), *Research in Psychoanalysis: Process, Development, Outcome*. Madison, CT: International Universities Press, pp. 209–244. Main's chapter, which traces the progression from Bowlby's ethological-evolutionary theory of attachment, to Ainsworth's Strange Situation procedure, to Main's own Adult Attachment Interview, shows Main to be fundamentally sympathetic to psychoanalysis. Main notes that "we have the capacity for attending to, processing, and drawing inferences from input that does not reach the usual levels of awareness," and this "has implications for the development of defensive processes and is in keeping with analytic theory" (p. 214). She cites empirical evidence that a given parent's response to the Adult Attachment Interview—responses classified by experimenters as secure, dismissing, preoccupied, or disorganized—"strongly resembles the infant's response to the [same] parent in the Strange Situation" (p. 225)—responses that are classified independently as secure, avoidant, ambivalent/resistant, or disorganized. Main compares an insecure parent's behavior toward his or her infant to that of a patient who, according to Freud, "does not *remember* anything of what he has forgotten or repressed, but *acts* it out" (p. 255); and she argues that these "dyadic adjustments begin in the earliest weeks of infant life" (p. 236). I am grateful to Frank Sulloway for the reference to Mary Main's paper.

20. Sulloway, *Freud, Biologist of the Mind*, p. 367.

PLR: But if you're a historian of science, isn't such a perspective to some extent unavoidable?

FJS: Of course, which is why I tried to make my views crystal clear in several key places. For example, I stated that "various unconfirmed aspects of Freud's theories may be correlated almost point by point with his erroneous premises" and that "acceptance of Freud's historical debt to biology requires a rather uncongenial conclusion for most psychoanalytic practitioners, namely, that Freud's theories reflect the faulty logic of outmoded 19th-century biological assumptions."[21] In the last half century, however, the history of science was influenced greatly by an attempt to get away from this Whiggish view and instead to consider erroneous beliefs as being just as worthy of study, understanding, and even empathy as those beliefs that have triumphed over them. This is the kind of relativistic perspective that has been in the ascendancy, culminating in the view among some historians of science that erroneous theories must be judged exactly the same way as theories that have withstood the test of time.

PLR: But you don't buy that, do you?

FJS: Oh no, I don't. But I *was* influenced enough by the general principle of "Don't commit the Whiggish fallacy" that I bent over backwards not to pounce on every mistake Freud made and then turn around and declare the guy was clearly an idiot. I was trying to reconstruct the intellectual context that made Freud's ideas seem plausible or reasonable to him and his contemporaries, even if those ideas are now known to be incorrect. If such ideas were reasonable at the time, then it was legitimate for Freud to propose and develop them. Now, there comes a point at which every true scientist, after proposing new hypotheses, has a responsibility to take the next step in science. This is something that Patricia Kitcher has written about in a very interesting book.[22] The gist of her argument is that Freud drew in very eclectic ways from a variety of disciplines, but that, as these disciplines revised their understanding of the mind via hypothesis testing, Freud refused to change his own. That, in a nutshell, was the fundamental flaw of psychoanalysis.

PLR: I would agree with a lot of that. Did it make any difference for your work that the Fliess letters were published only in abridged form at the time you were writing your book?

---

21. Sulloway, *Freud, Biologist of the Mind*, pp. 497, 499.

22. Patricia Kitcher (1992), *Freud's Dream: A Complete Interdisciplinary Science of Mind*. Cambridge, MA: MIT Press.

FJS: Most of the really nifty stuff in the Fliess letters that wasn't published in 1950, in the original expurgated edition, was alluded to either by Max Schur[23] or by Ernest Jones[24] in their biographies of Freud. When the unexpurgated edition came out, I was actually surprised how much of the excised material I had known about either by reading Schur or Jones or by reading Fliess himself, and seeing what the logic of Freud's thinking was, as well as the empirical support that he eagerly provided for this logic.

PLR: Certainly the Emma Eckstein episode was known through Schur's work.[25]

FJS: There were also many allusions in Jones and Schur to Freud's efforts to develop a theory of psychosexual stages in terms of Fliess's two biological periodicities (23 and 28 days) and to use the temporal crisscrosses between these two cycles as a mechanism for determining when a repression or a fixation would be most likely to occur. What's important about the intellectual collaboration between Freud and Fliess is not the specifics of the theories that Freud was playing around with, which can be viewed, superficially, as ridiculously silly and wrong at one level—and so have been generally dismissed by historians of psychoanalysis—but rather the broader set of underlying biological assumptions that goes with these theories. The most important of these assumptions, or, more precisely, the most important *consequence* of these assumptions, is the idea that children are spontaneously sexual because their development is guided by a sexual biology that drives conception, gestation, growth, and even death. If that were true, then a proper understanding of human sexual development required a biological paradigm to go with it. From their perspective, the details of what Freud and Fliess were jointly working on might have been wrong, but the gist of the paradigm underlying those details had to be right. This intellectual collaboration was taking place at a time when Freud's thinking was moving from an almost complete reliance on the environment (trauma) as a cause of

23. Max Schur (1972), *Freud: Living and Dying*. New York: International Universities Press.

24. Jones, *The Life and Work of Sigmund Freud*.

25. Max Schur (1966), "Some Additional 'Day Residues' of 'The Specimen Dream of Psychoanalysis.'" In *Psychoanalysis: A General Psychology: Essays in Honor of Heinz Hartmann*, ed. Rudolph M. Loewenstein, Lottie M. Newman, Max Schur & Albert J. Solnit. New York: International Universities Press, pp. 45–85. See also Schur, *Freud: Living and Dying*.

neuroses to a theory of the child's being a sexually active source of its own neurosis. This same basic concept was at the heart of Fliess's own theory of human development, because he believed that the periodic ebb and flow of sexual chemistry causes the organism to develop the way that it does. The best evidence for this theory, according to Fliess, was that spurts in growth occur at even multiples of 23 and 28 days and are accompanied by manifestations of the sexual chemistry that propels them.

PLR: You saw a lot of Freud in Fliess.

FJS: They saw a lot of themselves in each other. All I did was to show that this was the case in spite of the repeated denials of analysts-turned-historians who were saying that Fliess was only a sounding board for Freud and nothing more. It was certainly ironic and an eye-opener to go back to Fliess's published works and find discussions of infantile sexuality in a book that came out almost a year before Freud's self-analysis.

PLR: Wasn't Fliess's book on the nose published in 1897?[26]

FJS: Freud read it in manuscript even before, in 1896. The book discusses thumb-sucking as a form of sexual pleasure that intensifies on days when biorhythms reach their peaks. Various aspects of bowel movements were also sexual, according to Fliess. That set of Fliessian ideas is basically the starting point for Freud's later theory of psychosexual stages. These discussions seem a bit strange unless one understands them in terms of the biogenetic law. This was the basic theory of sexual evolution held by many biologists and some psychiatrists at this time. Sexual evolution, according to Darwin's German proselytizer Ernst Haeckel, developed from a single-celled organism that invaginated to form a mouth—the oral stage of sexuality. After the evolution of a gastrointestinal tract, more sophisticated genitalia emerged, which were associated with the anal region. Eventually there evolved a phallic stage. That's the general theory that Freud and Fliess were playing around with, and that's why they both attached sexual significance to the mouth, the alimentary canal, the anus, and so forth. Unless one understands this important historical point, one cannot understand either their 17-year scientific relationship or the development of Freud's own ideas.

---

26. Wilhelm Fliess (1897), *Die Beziehung zwischen Nase und weiblichen Geschlechtsorganen: In ihrer biologischen Bedeutung dargestellt.* Leipzig: Franz Deuticke.

PLR: When you became interested in Freud, was there any sense that you were trying to understand things about yourself? Did you use the study of psychoanalysis in a way that could be called self-analytic?

FJS: I was not motivated to study Freud for that reason. When I read *The Interpretation of Dreams* I initially played around with self-analysis, as any reader would, and I analyzed some of my own dreams. It was fun to do. But this wasn't a primary motive for my study of Freud's ideas. I certainly didn't turn to Freud because I felt, "Gee, I really want to come to grips with my own life." Still, one couldn't read Freud and not try him on, so to speak, just to see how the theory worked.

PLR: Did you find any connections between yourself and what you read in Freud? Were there certain moments when you felt that what you saw in his work was true for you?

FJS: Basically, no. I'm sure there were some insights that I had about myself that I probably got by reading Freud. But they weren't unique to my having read Freud. They were probably general insights that I might well have had if I had been doing a lot of in-depth reading in developmental psychology. I didn't say to myself, "Oh, my God, I've repressed the memory of blah-dee-blah. No wonder I've had this paralyzed arm all my life, and now it's gone away." [laughs] There wasn't anything like that.

PLR: It never really connected with you in a personal way.

FJS: After the initial period of experimentation, during which I did make some connections, I don't really think so. At a more general level, however, I thought the theory in all its complexities was fascinating. I sometimes used to think, "If Lamarckian inheritance and the biogenetic law had been true, this theory might very well have been predominantly true." It has a logical beauty and coherence to it, as long as those biological principles are allowed to operate and one can appeal to inherited memories. The theory offers, in a more psychologically palatable form, the kind of biologizing of the human organism that evolutionary psychology and behavioral genetics have offered since the 1970s and 1980s. But that's a much more complicated set of theories to get into. Freud did it all at a much simpler level. Essentially, the phylogenetic past became life writ large today. As Freud once commented about the biogenetic inevitability entailed in his theory of psychosexual stages: "In all this the phylogenetic foundation has so much the upper hand over personal accidental experience that it makes no difference whether a child has ever really sucked at the breast or has been brought up on the bottle and never enjoyed the tenderness of a mother's care. In both cases the child's development takes the same path."[27]

PLR: I don't think that many people who become excited on reading *The Interpretation of Dreams* are relying on the biogenetic law as an intermediate link between what they see in Freud and what they find in themselves.

FJS: No, one certainly doesn't have to. But, as Freud well knew, there comes a point when every orthodox Freudian interpretation is subsumed by his theory of psychosexual development, and at *that* key point the ultimate meaning of a dream, slip of the pen, or neurotic symptom is largely dictated, or at least significantly constrained, by these biogenetic assumptions. People who read Freud's works, including *The Interpretation of Dreams*, and who do not understand these underlying biological assumptions really do not understand Freud's theories as he intended them to be understood. These readers are mistaking a "pure psychology," as Jones and others (including Freud himself) have sometimes tried to characterize psychoanalysis, for a distinctly psychobiological set of theories.

PLR: In my own thinking about Freud, the libido theory is not so crucial. There are other dimensions that are more productive and fruitful. You credit Freud with being able "to recognize the truly dynamic and infantile source of man's unconscious."[28] That doesn't necessarily involve sexuality, but it does assume the lifelong influence of early experience. You refer elsewhere to Darwin's having said that the first three years of life are the most important, and you link that claim to Freud's belief in the "pertinacity of early impressions."[29] I think one can put aside the debate about what is sexual and ask simply whether the role of early childhood experience is crucial and occurs below the level of consciousness, as Freud thought—and as Darwin seems to have thought as well. Does that seem plausible to you?

---

27. Sigmund Freud (1940), *An Outline of Psycho-Analysis. Standard Edition*, 23:188–189. London: Hogarth Press, 1964.

28. Sulloway, *Freud, Biologist of the Mind*, p. 128.

29. Frank J. Sulloway (1991), "Darwinian Psychobiography." Review of *Charles Darwin: A New Life* by John Bowlby. *New York Review of Books*, October 10, p. 29.

FJS: Let's make it absolutely clear that if people reject Freud's sexual theory, they are not Freudians. Freud himself made this clear in his disputes with followers who broke away from him after 1908 or so. To Freud, psychoanalysis was not just a belief in the unconscious and the power of early experiences. These were ideas that many of his contemporaries also endorsed. There are some comments in my book, such as the one you just read about the dynamic unconscious, where I was writing, as a historian, of Freud's own thinking about what he was doing. I was not necessarily endorsing something that I consider a valid Freudian discovery. For example, I might say something like, "Freud had an insight into the polymorphously perverse nature of infantile sexuality." This doesn't necessarily mean that *I* believe what Freud believed. I'm simply saying that Freud in his own mind had an "insight."

I didn't realize until after I had published my book on Freud that a reader might infer from such passages that I was endorsing Freud. It was only when Fred Crews wrote his article "Beyond Sulloway's *Freud*" and picked up on almost every one of those phrases that I finally became aware of it.[30] When I might be writing, for example, about Freud's remarks in a letter saying "Here I discovered the meaning of dreams," I took it for granted that this is what *Freud* thought he had discovered, not necessarily some fundamental truth that I was also endorsing. There are some forms of language in my book that Crews took to mean that I bought hook, line, and sinker that Freud had really discovered a bunch of things that were real. But I generally meant these statements to be understood in a more metaphorical way, without necessarily implying that I was passing scientific judgment on Freud's ideas. With hindsight, I think that some of this phraseology was simply careless, and I now wish that I had been clearer on this issue.

PLR: I think it's admirable that you are able to look back at something that was, after all, published 20 years ago and see Freud differently from the way you did then. It wouldn't be healthy if you wanted to affirm every word. For my own part, I think it's important to distinguish between being a Freudian—which I'm not—and adherence to a psychoanalytic mode of thinking that I believe to be intellectually sound. I'm simply trying to clarify what you were saying then and how you see things now.

---

30. Frederick Crews (1986), "Beyond Sulloway's *Freud*: Psychoanalysis Minus the Myth of the Hero." In *Skeptical Engagements*. New York: Oxford University Press, pp. 88–111.

FJS: If I were to revise this book, there are places where I would definitely want to modify my language to clarify that I am not necessarily endorsing the validity of psychoanalysis. In most instances, I was simply trying to recreate how Freud felt about what he was doing.

PLR: Certainly, when you use the word "recognize" you imply that he was discovering something that was really there. And you do say that he recognized "the *truly* dynamic and infantile source of man's unconscious." In conjunction with the encomiastic statement I cited earlier about Freud's having established "the most comprehensive evolutionary explanation of the origins of human behavior" or your quotation from Philip Rieff that Freud produced "the most important body of thought committed to paper in the 20th century,"[31] I think all that conveys strongly that you agreed with much of what Freud had said and were trying to show its logical coherence.

FJS: There's no question that I had an enormous admiration for Freud as a grand theoretical synthesizer, as generally conveyed in the comments you are referring to. I wouldn't change in a major way my views on that subject. But I would, if I were revising my book, alter some of those discussions that appear to be endorsing the specifics of the theory. What I did endorse, as I stated explicitly in the final chapter of my book, was that Freud awakened interest in many important areas of research, including infancy, childhood, irrational behavior, and so forth. I did not give him high marks, however, for his particular theories on these subjects. Again, if I were revising my book today, I would try to make a sharper distinction between Freud the theorist, seen in the context of his times, and the theories themselves.

PLR: I was struck by Darwin's seeming to agree with Freud about the importance of the first three years of life. So if we're going to reject Freud on this, we're also going to have to reject Darwin.

FJS: That's easy. Darwin wasn't an expert on this topic. [laughs]

PLR: Maybe both of them were wrong. It seems there are three major components of Freud's assertion. One is that there is such a thing as the unconscious part of our minds. Second, that the unconscious has its roots in infantile experience. The last is that the unconscious is dynamic. If we take those three claims separately, I wonder whether in your current thinking as a historian of science, as a social scientist more generally, or simply as a human being, you would agree with any or all of them.

---

31. Sulloway, *Freud, Biologist of the Mind*, p. 358.

FJS: I certainly believe that there are unconscious aspects to thought, but I do not believe in Freud's dynamic unconscious as a kind of sealed-off area of the mind in which a whole other psychic life, dating mostly from early childhood, is imprisoned by the powers of repression. That theory, and the psychobiological mechanisms that Freud used to justify it, are deeply flawed by the outmoded biology that went with them. I don't see any way to rescue Freud's theory of the unconscious.

PLR: But you accept the existence of unconscious phenomena?

FJS: There probably isn't a living psychologist worth his grit who doesn't accept that there are "unconscious" mental phenomena.

PLR: So that much is agreed. Are we talking about something that is not voluntarily accessible to consciousness?

FJS: Not exactly. I'm thinking more of the subtle things one encounters, for example, in tachistoscopic experiments which show clearly that the mind can perceive something communicated as a subliminal message flashed quickly across the retina but that it doesn't recognize consciously. This is not the same thing as there being an unconscious (repressed) idea to which the mind has no direct access. It's just that there are threshold effects in the perception of information within the brain. Information is processed at some levels that are inaccessible to consciousness and at other levels that *are* accessible. But none of this bears on Freud's much more controversial claim that the unconscious is formed by pathological repression. The closest I would come to agreeing with Freud's concept of pathological repression has to do with people whose minds exhibit "dissociation" of a pathological sort. I am not a psychiatrist, however, and I do not really know how to integrate that kind of medical evidence with Freud's far more grandiose claims about repression sealing off a portion of the unconscious mind in normal individuals. In general, I think Freud's argument that the bulk of the interpretable meaning of adult behavior is closely linked with this sealed-off world of the dynamic unconscious is untenable.

PLR: I'm not sure that we need to say "sealed-off world of the dynamic unconscious."

FJS: I'm just repeating *Freud's* own way of talking about it—the theory as he understood it after 1900 or so. Maybe a psychoanalyst today would express this idea differently, but then this person would not be endorsing Freud's own model of the mind or his related theory of why the mind develops neurotic symptoms. In any event, I don't think there's anything going on in the mind like Freud's own notion of the dynamic unconscious. Moreover, I certainly don't think such a hypothetical mechanism is the key to understanding dreams, slips of the pen, and so forth, although some slips of the pen do appear to involve the more innocent and lackluster form of "unconscious" thinking that is widely accepted in psychology. So there's a whole range of levels at which one can talk about unconscious phenomena, some of which are compatible with current psychology and some of which are not. Unfortunately for Freud, the ones that really count in his theory of psychopathology, as well as in his theory of human development, are the ones that are incompatible with the modern scientific understanding of the brain.

PLR: I suppose the fundamental question for me is whether there is some part of our minds that remains forever mysterious to ourselves. As Jonathan Lear has argued, "There is something which would count as a global refutation of psychoanalysis: if people always and everywhere acted in rational and transparently explicable ways."[32] I'm thinking in this connection of your excellent piece in the *New York Review of Books* about Bowlby's biography of Darwin, the gist of which you incorporated into *Born to Rebel.*[33] Again, I'm trying to use Bowlby as a way of rescuing or preserving what I think is valuable in psychoanalysis. I want to see whether we don't share more common ground than one might imagine at first glance.

FJS: Let me just say something at the outset about Bowlby's treatment of Darwin and my own endorsement of it. Much of what works in that treatment of Darwin's life has nothing to do with the first three years of life or with the Freudian unconscious. It has to do with the entire pattern of Darwin's childhood relationships with his sisters, and his father, and the mother whom he lost when he was eight. That's what makes Bowlby's psychological explanation far more plausible than Freud's various attempts at psychobiography. Bowlby was trying to get away from the notion that everything of psychological importance takes place during the first three years of life and through the operation of repression in whatever form—primary (organic) or secondary (psychological). His explanation of Darwin's illness as a form of panic anxiety does not require him to

---

32. Jonathan Lear (1998), "On Killing Freud (Again)." In *Open Minded: Working Out the Logic of the Soul.* Cambridge, MA: Harvard University Press, p. 25.

33. Sulloway, "Darwinian Psychobiography," pp. 28–32; and *Born to Rebel,* pp. 140–145.

endorse the notion that there is a whole sealed-up portion of the psyche that motivated Darwin to think and act without even being aware of the reasons why.

PLR: The question of the importance of the first three years is different from the question of repression.

FJS: Well, they're two issues that, in Freud's mind at least, went together. The close linkage of these two ideas was demanded, by the way, by Freud's biogenetic conception of human psychosexual development, which led him to claim that all secondary (and psychological) repressions are preceded by primary and organic (or biological) repressions occurring during the first three years of life. In any event, these two ideas are largely irrelevant in Bowlby's own approach to Darwin, which entails looking at the entire period of Darwin's youth and at his family to see the characteristic ways in which he related to his parents and siblings and asking whether these family relationships had a lasting influence on his character and later on his science.

And the answer to these questions appears to be manifestly yes. This conclusion isn't so much psychoanalysis as it is simply good, sensitive psychobiography in which Bowlby considered the entire panoply of childhood experiences as a continuous and collective source of developmental trends. So, in Bowlby's theoretical account, Darwin could have experienced the life that he did in his own family up to the age of three and then been adopted by another family. In that case he would probably have turned out to be a rather different person, though not dramatically different, because we know from behavioral genetics that about 40% of the variance in personality is heritable. But many of Darwin's characteristic peculiarities—such as his extraordinary deference to his sisters and his feeling that he was in constant need of tutoring by them—were behavioral patterns that he seems to have developed to a significant degree through interaction with his sisters.

PLR: Again, I don't think there's a great difference between our views here. I'm asking with genuine curiosity, how important are the early years? I'm taking off from your statement that Freud recognized the "dynamic and infantile sources of the unconscious."

FJS: I certainly wouldn't make that statement today, except on Freud's behalf to summarize the gist of his theory, which was how I meant it to be taken.

PLR: Let's consider the question of repression. In the Bowlby review, you connect Darwin's statement about his sister, "'But what will she blame me for now?' I made myself *dogged* so as not to make myself care what she might say," with his beloved phrase to describe genius, "It's *dogged* as does it"; and you go on to suggest that "from Bowlby's perspective these valuable qualities of Darwin as a scientist can be seen as part of his response to his intimidating father and overzealous older sisters."[34] It seems to me that the surfacing of the word dogged in two different contexts is something that a psychoanalyst would say confirmed his sense of how life works. A pattern of childhood experience—even if it was set at the age of eight rather than the age of three—shaped Darwin's character in a way that had a lifelong effect. The word then can be called a signifier or symptom that came to his mind for reasons that are determined unconsciously in a truly revealing way.

FJS: I'm not sure I agree with your comment about this particular thought process being determined unconsciously. More important, I don't view the material you've quoted from my Bowlby review as being particularly psychoanalytic or even "unconscious." That's just good biography. It involves tracing characteristic patterns of behaving within the family and seeing whether they have a broader manifestation in someone's adult life. In my review, I added pertinent examples that Bowlby hadn't actually used, such as the phrase "it's dogged as does it" as Darwin's definition of genius. In the second half of the review I made a concerted attempt to show that Bowlby didn't know as much about Darwin's life as he perhaps would have liked, and one can actually make a stronger case for his psychobiographical argument than he himself was able to do. My review was therefore a critique of Bowlby's biography in the most complimentary sense. In so doing, I threw in some additional biographical evidence, and I thought his arguments and my own were all pretty commonsensical. This additional evidence drew on Bowlby's ideas about the importance of attachment relationships, but there was nothing deeply "repressed" or "unconscious" about the psychological mechanisms posited by this argument. This kind of argumentation goes on throughout most of Bowlby's biography and in my own analysis at a level that Darwin himself would have appreciated and understood, had we probed him on it. Now, there *are* a few interesting "psychoanalytic" issues such as the wonderful story about Darwin's playing a word game very much like Scrabble where somebody added the letter "m" in front of the word "other" to form the word "mother."

---

34. Sulloway, "Darwinian Psychobiography," p. 31.

PLR: Exactly.

FJS: And Darwin, the story goes, stared at the word and repeatedly said: "MOE-THER; MOE-THER; there's no word 'MOE-THER.'"[35] Unfortunately for psychoanalysis, that's not necessarily evidence of the operation of Freud's dynamic unconscious.

PLR: Why not?

FJS: Because people don't have easy access to Freud's dynamic unconscious, and we all have little mental blocks here and there that have nothing to do with pathological "repression." If someone can point out the connection between a mental lapse and an "unconscious" idea to the person who exhibits the lapse and this person instantly, as in Darwin's case, recognizes the connection, the motive for this lapse is not repressed in the Freudian sense.

PLR: The point is not whether Darwin was able to recognize the lapse when it was brought to his attention, but that he committed it in the first place. When someone told Darwin, "But that's *mother*," he must have said, "Oh my goodness, now I see that it's the word."

FJS: But there's nothing repressed about that realization.

PLR: Surely his inability to recognize the word in the first place is evidence of repression.

FJS: Not necessarily. Just to be very clear, my point is that Darwin's lapse is not necessarily "repression" in the sense that Freud would have understood it. It's clearly evidence of a mental block or a dissociation, and we can use some word like repression to describe it, but the lapse has nothing in common with the kind of organic pathological repression associated with everything present in Freud's dynamic unconscious. With the *dynamic* unconscious that lies at the heart of Freud's theory of the neuroses and his theory of psychosex-

---

35. Gwen Raverat (1952). *Period Piece*. New York: Norton, 1953, p. 245. Raverat, Darwin's granddaughter, facetiously comments: "I feel that the Psychologists might get a great deal of fun out of this anecdote—I beg their pardons, I don't mean fun, but Important Information; clues to the conception of the *Origin of Species*, on the one hand, or to his ill health on the other; both of which developments could doubtless be proved by this story to be the direct consequences of the early death of his own MOETHER." Raverat does not expressly state that "mother" was formed by adding "m" to "other," but this seems the most likely explanation. Her spelling of "MOE-THER" presumably reflects Darwin's own misprision that caused him to stumble over the word. I am grateful to Frank Sulloway for this reference.

ual development, a person almost never attains direct awareness of the motive lying behind a mental lapse or slip. All that a person can be consciously aware of are the indirect repercussions of such a repression, through dreams, symptoms, "resistance," and so on. Therapists almost never encounter an instance where they say directly to a patient, "Actually, because *this* happened when you were a year and a half, you're a repressed homosexual." And the patient responds, "Right on. Now I see the light." That simply doesn't happen with Freud's dynamic unconscious.

PLR: But that is a caricature. There are plenty of examples in *The Psychopathology of Everyday Life* where the meaning of a slip becomes clear to the subject as soon as it is pointed out, but the motive is still held by Freud to be a repressed sexual or aggressive wish. Your supposition about what doesn't happen in therapy may divert our focus from what was happening in Darwin. Darwin's "mental block," as you call it, that prevented him from recognizing the word mother is precisely a symptom that provides indirect evidence for the workings of repression.

FJS: Darwin didn't require years of psychotherapy to appreciate that he had a mental block concerning the memory of his mother. He discussed this point in his *Autobiography* and gave a plausible explanation for his block, namely, the refusal of his sisters, out of grief, to mention his mother's name after she had died.[36]

PLR: The fact that there was a conspiracy of silence within the family concerning this traumatic event helps to explain why it should have precipitated a repression. That's perfectly consistent with a psychoanalytic view. The death of his mother was obviously emotionally charged and the subject of intense conflicts, both in the family and in Darwin's own mind.

FJS: I'm simply trying to say that Bowlby's account is not a Freudian account.

PLR: Can we call it a psychoanalytic account?

FJS: I don't even think it's particularly psychoanalytic. Let's consider the work of somebody like Mary Main, who is a second-generation attachment theorist with no training in psychoanalysis that I know of. She might easily have read a Darwin biography and written an

---

36. Charles Darwin (1876), *The Autobiography of Charles Darwin, 1809–1882. With the Original Omissions Restored*, ed. Nora Barlow. London: Collins, 1958, p. 22.

article giving the same general account of Darwin's intellectual and emotional development as Bowlby provided and that has no formal relationship to psychoanalysis other than having borrowed and further developed the concept of attachment through Bowlby. This kind of explanation is not psychoanalytic; rather, it's psychobiographical. That's the common ground between the two approaches. In any event, psychoanalysts almost universally rejected Bowlby's ideas about attachment, in the 1950s and 1960s, as being antipsychoanalytic and anti-Freudian.

PLR: There's no doubt that Bowlby's ideas initially aroused a lot of opposition among his colleagues. After all, he challenged both the one-sided emphasis on fantasy of Melanie Klein and the libido theory of Freud. But that doesn't make him antipsychoanalytic. In particular, he retained close intellectual and personal ties with the Independent tradition of psychoanalysis, whose best-known representatives include Winnicott and Michael Balint. As Bowlby himself wrote, "Historically attachment theory was developed as a variant of object-relations theory."[37] I don't want to engage in speculation about what Mary Main might or might not have done.

FJS: Fair enough, but I'm just using that hypothetical example to illustrate my general point.

PLR: To me the concept of the dynamic unconscious has a lot of validity to it. Even though I'm prepared to cast aside the libido theory and even to be skeptical about the role of the very earliest years of experience in shaping how our minds work, this example of Darwin's not recognizing the word mother is important to me in showing that the dynamic unconscious plays a part in human life. I don't understand why you feel the need to insist that it's not the Freudian unconscious. You also quote from Bowlby a letter of condolence that Darwin wrote to somebody about the death of his wife where he says, "I truly sympathize with you, though never in my life having lost one near relation I dare say I cannot imagine how severe grief such as yours must be."[38] You yourself connect this bizarre statement to the facts that Darwin's mother died when he was eight and that her death was not discussed in the family. At two crucial moments Darwin revealed a block about something of great emotional importance in his experience.

---

37. John Bowlby (1982), "The Origins of Attachment Theory." In *A Secure Base: Clinical Applications of Attachment Theory*. London: Routledge, 1988, p. 29.

38. Sulloway, "Darwinian Psychobiography," p. 30.

FJS: Yes.

PLR: In a footnote to *Born to Rebel*, you say, "I use the term 'repressed' advisedly and in a different manner from the the traditional psychoanalytic usage. Bowlby has reformulated the concept of repression as 'selective exclusion.'"[39] I don't mind using the term selective exclusion if that's what you want to call it, but it seems to me that these two examples furnish strong evidence for the existence of a dynamic and repressed unconscious. As Bowlby himself acknowledged, his concept of "defensive exclusion" is "no more than repression under another name."[40] In Darwin's blindness during the word game, there's a process of repression and interpretation going on, from which one can infer the workings of the dynamic unconscious within the self. To me that's very powerful. Of course, it's anecdotal evidence, but it provides strong support for a cornerstone of psychoanalysis.

FJS: Clearly, you have much more of a fervor about all this than I do. It sounds like you're trying to find a way to say, "Well, gee, some of this is still salvageable."

PLR: Absolutely.

FJS: I don't feel that need one iota. I do think, however, that there is *some* common ground with psychoanalytic theory in phenomena involving what Bowlby would call selective exclusion. I simply don't think this kind of evidence proves a dynamic unconscious à la Freud at all, and this is a very important distinction for the viability of the theory as a whole.

PLR: I'm afraid we may be going around in circles. But let's take one more crack at it. You've agreed that Darwin experienced a "mental block" on at least two occasions and that these "blocks" were connected to the death of his mother when he was eight years old. Yet you insist that these examples do not provide evidence for a dynamic unconscious. It's interesting, by the way, that Bowlby referred not merely to "selective exclusion" but to "*defensive* exclusion" and equated the latter term with repression. Bowlby's approach is grounded in information-processing theory, but it's also (as I've said) entirely consistent with psychoanalysis. In the essay "The Origins of Attachment Theory" from which I quoted earlier, he wrote, "[T]his

---

39. Sulloway, *Born to Rebel*, p. 491*n*62.

40. Bowlby (1981), "Psychoanalysis as a Natural Science." In *A Secure Base*, p. 71.

revolution in cognitive theory not only gives unconscious mental processes the central place in mental life that analysts have always claimed for them, but presents a picture of the mental apparatus as being well able to shut off information of certain specified types and of doing so selectively without the person being aware of what is happening."[41]

Bowlby then went on to point out that the information warded off by emotionally disturbed or detached individuals is

> of a very special type. So far from its being the routine exclusion of irrelevant and potentially distracting information that we engage in all the time and that is readily reversible, what are being excluded are the signals, arising from both inside and outside the person, that would activate their attachment behaviour and that would enable them both to love and to experience being loved. In other words, the mental structures responsible for routine selective exclusion are being employed—one might say exploited—for a special and potentially pathological purpose.[42]

Thus, in a case such as Darwin's, which turns on the family's inability to mourn the death of his mother, we are dealing with a manifestation of "pathological" exclusion, and this is fundamentally different from the subliminal phenomena involved in the tachistoscopic experiments you referred to earlier. In this connection, Bowlby reiterated that "just as Freud regarded repression as the key process in every form of defence, so I see the role of defensive exclusion."[43] Despite the difference in terminology, Bowlby clearly comes down on Freud's side in the debate over repression. So let me ask you again: Doesn't Darwin's failure to recognize the word *mother* in the word game, as well as his declaration that he never "lost one near relation," tend to prove the existence of a dynamic unconscious?

FJS: I don't think it proves a dynamic unconscious in the way that most psychoanalysts construe that concept, and without that version of the concept, psychoanalytic theory doesn't really work.

PLR: Again, why doesn't it prove a dynamic unconscious?

FJS: Because I think that people who endorse a *dynamic* unconscious, as opposed to unconscious mental processes more generally, are

---

41. Bowlby, "The Origins of Attachment Theory." In *A Secure Base*, p. 34.

42. Bowlby, "The Origins of Attachment Theory." In *A Secure Base*, pp. 34–35.

43. Bowlby, "The Origins of Attachment Theory." In *A Secure Base*, p. 35.

positing something that is significantly sealed off by repression from the awareness of the individual—something that causes, as a consequence of this repression, major forms of neurotic illness.

PLR: When Darwin didn't see the word mother, wasn't that sealed off from his awareness at that time?

FJS: Yes, for a few seconds. But the moment someone said to him, as must surely have happened, "Look, Charles, that spells 'mother' and you had a mother, didn't you?" he would have repsonded [snaps his fingers], "Absolutely." There's not much more you need in order to understand that story, except to say that Darwin appears to have had a mild tendency to dissociate topics about his mother from his most conscious level of thought. Darwin didn't need to undergo five years of psychoanalysis to reach some other deeply hidden level of thought that might finally have freed him from that particular hang-up. Additionally, there is no plausible evidence at all that this dissociation on Darwin's part caused him to have any pathological symptoms. Rather, his mental block and his neurotic symptoms (excessive anxiety) appear to have a common basis in patterns of family dynamics of which he was consciously and fully aware whenever he was reminded of them.

PLR: I think that when someone showed Darwin that the word spelled mother, and he realized with bewilderment that his blindness had somehow to be connected with the death of his mother, he might well have decided—had he lived in the 20th century instead of the 19th—that he needed psychoanalysis. The emotional effect of this early loss and the conspiracy of silence in the family could not possibly have been alleviated by pointing out one manifestation of its consequences.

FJS: True, but none of Darwin's symptoms need be viewed as the outcome of repression in *Freud's* sense of the term or, indeed, in any sense of the term.

PLR: The repression is exhibited by Darwin's failure to see the word when it's staring him in the face.

FJS: I don't like calling it a repression in that sense. You can have a block about something without its being repressed in a pathological manner. For example, Darwin's "repression" can be regarded primarily as a symptom of his disrupted attachment to his mother rather than as a cause of any neurotic problems. That is, the repression itself may not be pathological. And if the repression isn't pathological, then it is not really a demonstration of the validity of Freud's ideas or of any neo-Freudian ideas that impute a pathological outcome to such mental processees.

PLR: As I've said, I'm not too particular about the term we use. Even if we attribute Darwin's blindness to "disrupted attachment," it's still a function of his "neurotic problems." The actual repression is only a symptom; its underlying cause is the family's inability to acknowledge or mourn the death of his mother. You can see why I think this example is powerful.

FJS: Well, for some events in life and their psychological interpretation there are indeed some ideas that might be called "psychoanalytic" that are perhaps useful. But I don't think they're nearly as powerful a tool in understanding the life course, and the sources of psychopathology, as most psychoanalysts believe. More important, it is imperative to distinguish such ideas as primary and secondary repression from one another and from their supposed consequences in symptom formation, dreams, and memory lapses. In Freud's theories, these ideas were all intimately linked together in an explicitly causal model. In modern psychology, they are not necessarily linked in the same manner. So one can believe in "secondary repressions," which Darwin may have experienced, and not believe that anything like a Freudian account is useful in understanding Darwin's life.

PLR: I'm perfectly willing to settle for "secondary repressions," if that's what you want to call them, since I have no investment in defending Freud's outmoded biology. It's precisely because Bowlby helps us to sort out what continues to be valid in Freud's thought from what has not stood the test of time that I find his work to be so valuable. In your book on birth order you yourself show how the microenvironment of family dynamics shapes a person's outlook for the rest of his or her life. It's a wonderful and thoroughly original argument.

FJS: This argument, of course, wasn't in any way psychoanalytic.

PLR: I know, but it's compatible with psychoanalysis.

FJS: It's about life experience, which may or may not fit with a psychoanalytic account. I tend to think it doesn't, although it certainly accords with a psychoanalytic approach in many important ways.

PLR: Your book brings something to the forefront of consideration that had previously been neglected. It's a great work, and I'm pleased to hear you say we share at least some common ground.

FJS: To the extent that psychoanalysts are interested in human development there are lots of common areas to discuss about dynamic (that is, conflict-laden) influences in the family. But there is a hard core of old Freudian notions that most analysts still employ that I don't use in explaining how birth order shapes personality. These older psychoanalytic notions are linked strongly to the theory of a dynamic unconscious; whereas when I write about the influence of birth order or parent–offspring conflict on personality development, I am discussing everyday interactions that, over time, become differences in personality. There is no need, in this kind of account, to believe that anything about personality development involves unconscious mental processes that have been repressed.

In my account of birth order and family dynamics I begin with Darwinian organisms that are wired to learn strategies. If a boy grows up with a sister, he tends to experience fewer physically aggressive interchanges with that sibling, and perhaps more affection in the relationship as well, because that's an emotion that is generally more appropriate for brothers and sisters to express toward one another. These kinds of differential experiences, depending on variations in family composition, appear to rub off on personality. A younger brother of an older brother, for example, is more likely than the older brother to be tender minded, fun loving, and unconventional. These kinds of differences arise as a result of differences in sibling strategies, as offspring attempt to adapt themselves to the family milieu. These kinds of nonpsychoanalytic explanations help to elucidate some of the environmental components of human development. Of course, we must also recognize that a substantial portion of the variance in human personality is due to the genetic roll of the dice that primes the pump, so to speak, and accounts for about 40% of this variance.

PLR: You are referring to temperament.

FJS: Yes, I am thinking of the kind of work Jerome Kagan has done on shyness, for example.[44] Of course, to provide a full explanation one must also factor in all the within-family variance that can be explained by family dynamics, and the various interactions between genetics and environment, and then one must consider influences from outside the family—mentors, good school experiences, and so

---

44. Jerome Kagan & J. Stephen Reznick (1986), "Shyness and Temperament." In *Shyness: Perspectives on Research and Treatment*, ed. Warren H. Jones, Jonathan M. Cheek & Stephen R. Briggs. New York: Plenum, pp. 81–90; Jerome Kagan, J. Stephen Reznick & Nancy Snidman (1988), "Biological Bases of Childhood Shyness," *Science*, 240:167–171.

on. Then one can, in theory, hope to explain the bulk of the observable variations in personality. From a scientific standpoint, what else does one need? We've done most of the job of providing an explanation without having to appeal to tortured interpretations of dreams in order to discover some set of walled-off repressions from the first three years of life that are driving all subsequent stages of development in ways that are supposedly a mystery to anyone who has not spent years in psychoanalytic therapy. We just don't need this kind of psychoanalytic explanation!

PLR: I agree with so much of what you've contributed that it would be churlish of me to argue with you. [FJS laughs] What I'm trying to do is to get you to agree with some of what I want to say, just as I can agree with what you say.

FJS: I'm a younger sibling, so I don't have a great need to agree. [laughs]

PLR: On the other hand, it might also be a problem if you insisted on being perverse just for the sake of stubbornness. [FJS laughs] You should be open to evidence and willing to agree if there's good reason to do so.

FJS: True, but it's not as if I haven't considered these issues.

PLR: Of course not. But when you speak of "tortured" dream interpretations, does that mean that all dream interpretations are useless? Your description implies that any use of it is an abuse. In *Freud, Biologist of the Mind*, you don't give any attention to the death of Freud's father. You mention it only once in passing in the context of Joseph Campbell's hero myth.[45] The fact that Freud's father died in October of 1896 as all the other things were going on in Freud's life isn't something to which you attach any explanatory weight. Nor that he lost an infant brother when he was less than two years of age. You don't examine any of Freud's dreams for the light that they might shed on his inner life. Your contribution is to put Freud in the context of the biological thinking of his time. That involves approaching the history of psychoanalysis with the tools and methodology of the history of science. I don't have a quarrel with that. But it leaves out of account those perspectives—whether they be Freudian, contemporary psychoanalytic, or even simply psychobiographical—that try to get at the inner experience of the person.

---

45. Sulloway, *Freud, Biologist of the Mind*, p. 447.

FJS: I wasn't writing a personal biography of Freud. I was writing an intellectual biography.

PLR: But the personal motivations and the scientific theories are intertwined.

FJS: That's true of Bowlby's biography of Darwin. When you're writing that kind of a biography, you go back and forth between the emotional life and the intellectual life as much as is necessary to tie the two stories together. Bowlby treated more of the emotional life of Darwin than I did of Freud. But I *did* consider aspects of Freud's personality and emotional life whenever I thought they were especially relevant to his development as a psychoanalytic theorist.

PLR: Your presentation of the relationship to Fliess focused on the intellectual content of Fliess's ideas and how they influenced Freud. You argue that it's the "forgotten context" of Fliess's ideas, and "not Freud's intellectual and emotional 'bondage,'" that explains his acceptance of Fliess's scientific work.[46] In other words, you take issue with the psychoanalytic model of looking at the Freud–Fliess relationship as a transference relationship.

FJS: Yes, I certainly do.

PLR: That would involve setting it in the context of a lifelong emotional pattern, at least on Freud's side. Let's say we were to take Charcot, Breuer, Adler, Jung, and the other major male figures in his life and trace his reactions to them. I think doing that would have the effect of highlighting the irrational elements in his thinking and the less attractive features of his personality. Your presentation of the Freud–Fliess relationship focuses so much on the intellectual plane that it leaves out the emotional dynamic, whether we want to call it transference or something else. The death of Freud's father isn't factored at all into what's going on in his relationship with Fliess. Just as your interest in Freud wasn't connected to anything in your own life—you didn't come to psychoanalysis in any kind of introspective mode, but saw it simply as a problem in intellectual history—so your treatment of Freud leaves out the subjective or phenomenological sense of his inner experience.

Richard Webster's book, which forms the successor to yours as a major critique of Freud, highlights Freud's compulsive need for fame and the Messianic quality to his thinking.[47] Freud's megalomania

---

46. Sulloway, *Freud, Biologist of the Mind*, p. 147.

47. Richard Webster (1995), *Why Freud Was Wrong: Sin, Science, and Psychoanalysis*. New York: Basic Books.

caused him to disregard evidence, not to engage in peer review, to be contemptuous of those who dared to disagree with him, and so forth. All that is very deplorable in Freud, but these failings can perhaps be attributed to Freud's insecure relationships to his parents. At least we can see that the formation of his theory is connected to his personal psychic needs. Webster's argument could therefore paradoxically be said to vindicate the essential tenets of psychoanalysis, even though he's pointing out Freud's flaws as a human being.

FJS: Just to reiterate, *Freud, Biologist of the Mind* was an intellectual biography, and I used and appealed to the psychology of Freud's own life whenever I thought it was relevant to the broader story of understanding how this particular man developed this particular set of theories at this particular time. Like Webster, I placed enormous weight on the psychological theme of Freud's grandiosity and need for fame. I built the third part of my book, which deals with the myth of the hero, around this whole topic. I felt that the various character traits in Freud that were responsible for his Messianic sense of ambition and his intolerance of criticism had exerted a major influence on the content and style of his science and on the nature and style of his friendships.

PLR: So we agree. Then why not say that Freud's relationship to Fliess is to a great extent transferential?

FJS: I didn't think that was necessary or useful to be said.

PLR: But you took issue with that interpretation.

FJS: I took issue with the attempt by psychoanalysts-turned-historians to sweep Fliess completely under the carpet as an embarrassment to the story of the hero by using the notion of transference.

PLR: But it doesn't have to be an either/or, does it?

FJS: No, but I should make it clear that I do not believe that the notion of "transference" adds anything to what is already obvious about Freud's relationship with Fliess. Theirs was a very strong friendship and scientific collaboration long before Freud's father died. One simply doesn't need to appeal to the death of Freud's father to understand why that friendship was steaming along and why the two were so busy exchanging scientific ideas. Besides the obvious fact that the two men liked each other enormously and had corresponded for nearly a decade before Freud's father died in 1896, there was also a shared world view and a shared scientific logic to their friendship. It is also true that a big part of that friendship rested on an emotional component, as does any long-term relationship. There they are, two grandiose guys who are feeding each other's ego. [PLR laughs] Equally or perhaps even more important, however, is that their friendship and collaboration nurtured an exciting way of thinking that involved Darwin's legacy to the 19th century—a legacy that both of them understood, but that Kurt Eissler, Max Schur, and Ernest Jones didn't. It was this Darwinian and biogenetic logic that made Freud think that Fliess wasn't a crackpot—that he was in fact a genius—and it's also the same logic that made many of Fliess's contempories agree that he might well be a genius. Many other contemporaries did consider Fliess to be a crackpot, but Freud wasn't in this other group. It is important to keep in mind the big picture in assessing this friendship. Fliess was an ear, nose, and throat specialist with a passionate interest in biology, and Freud was himself an accomplished biologist. So the two of them could bounce biological and other scientific ideas off one another. They had a deep and shared interest in various books on late 19th-century biology and medicine that are rarely mentioned in Freud biographies but that lined Freud's own bookshelves and that he read, annotated, and cited. This was the common intellectual bond that underlay their friendship.

Then this shared scientific outlook began to focus more and more on Freud's own work. Freud and Fliess began to collaborate. As long as one can tell the full story about this intellectual resonance in their friendship, one doesn't need to say much more about it to understand the birth of psychoanalysis and to trace key aspects of this new system of ideas back to Fliess's own theories and publications.

Believe me, if I had thought I could get useful mileage out of some dream Freud experienced, or a specific interpretation that he reached about one of his dreams, or the fact that his father died in 1896, I would have made the most of such information, as I occasionally did for other apsects of Freud's life and as I have sometimes done in my work on Darwin's life and ideas. But I didn't see a way to engage in such discussion without degenerating into the kind of convenient speculation, so common in psychoanalytic biography, where commentators weave a tale that says whatever they want it to say, using endless "reconstructions" of biographical evidence. Peter Swales has occasionally played this game in some of his articles, building on material offered by Freud himself (as in the *"aliquis"* episode that Freud reports in *The Psychopathology of Everyday Life*).[48] I don't

---

48. Peter J. Swales (1982), "Freud, Minna Bernays, and the Conquest of Rome: New Light on the Origins of Psychoanalysis." *New American Review*, 1(2/3):1–23.

think one really needs or benefits from this kind of quasipsychoanalytic speculation. It could be right. It could also be totally wrong. Who knows? I believe that these kinds of arguments are just taking up space on paper without really getting us anywhere.

The real issue, then, is, to what extent should one appeal to psychobiography in doing biography? Forget about whether it's psychoanalytic or not. To what extent do biographers need to appeal to complicated explanations about the interior life of their subjects? One has to consider this issue on a case-by-case basis. I don't ever rule it out, but I tend to draw on it very selectively. For me, psychobiographical claims have to seem reasonable and eminently plausible. They also ought to be testable—if not for the individual case being considered, at least for other cases more generally.

PLR: I'm all in favor of hypothesis testing in science, but, when it comes to offering an interpretation in therapy or of a work of art, I don't think one can resolve questions of meaning in the same way that one might be able to test a hypothesis about the relative influence of social class and birth order on orientations toward an intellectual revolution. As Bowlby argued, psychoanalysis is both a natural and a historical science. This distinction originated with Wilhelm Dilthey and is fundamental to hermeneutic theory. Psychoanalysis is a natural science in its attempt to formulate general principles of personality development and psychopathology, but it is a historical science in its attempt to understand and treat the problems of specific individuals. And, as Bowlby has written, whereas in the natural sciences "we are dealing with statistical probabilities," when it comes to history or literature "the individual example is the very essence of the case."[49] I thus don't see an incompatibility between the type of hypothesis testing that you advocate and exemplify in researching certain types of problems and the necessarily more subjective types of interpretation that also need to be undertaken with attention to evidence, tact, and an appeal to something shared in the public arena.

My concern is that in your espousal of a natural-science model, with its reliance on statistical methods, you may be losing sight of the equally important perspective brought to bear by the humanities. The writing of history or literary criticism, for example, isn't simply free association when it is done well. In fairness to Peter Swales, moreover, I would point out that his interpretation of the

---

49. Bowlby, "Psychoanalysis as a Natural Science." In *A Secure Base*, pp. 75–76.

"*aliquis*" parapraxis as a piece of disguised autobiography, indicating that Freud may have had an affair with his sister-in-law, Minna Bernays, is supported by copious archival research and external evidence. I think we can fault the excesses of psychobiography—whether psychoanalytic or otherwise—without concluding that the idea of trying to explain the interplay between intellectual development and the inner life is futile. I hope we are agreed on this. But in addition to the intellectual bond between Freud and Fliess, to which you rightly draw attention, there was undoubtedly a strong emotional component. According to Webster, the theory of hysteria is completely unsound, and, if we look back to Freud's adoration of Charcot, we can see that he brought to the relationship with Fliess a predisposition to validate his own sense of Messianic identity by projecting it onto someone else. I think there is a lot of good evidence for that.

FJS: I think there's just as much evidence to say that they had simply a strong friendship—nothing more, nothing less. I don't see Freud as projecting anything onto Fliess. By all accounts, Fliess was a fascinating person. For this reason, Freud didn't need to project anything onto him. He would need to project onto Fliess only if Fliess were an idiot, because then Freud's biographers would have to explain why this brilliant man, Freud, was associated with someone who had all these embarrassingly wrong ideas.

PLR: From my point of view, transferences play a part in all close relationships, in which an irrational component is inevitably present. That Fliess was intrinsically fascinating doesn't preclude the possibility that Freud projected his own fantasies onto him. The same could be said of Charcot or Jung. Both were distinguished men, but that alone doesn't explain why Freud should have responded to them as intensely—and, indeed, irrationally—as he did. And what about the Eckstein episode, in which Fliess failed to remove a meter-long piece of gauze from his patient's nasal cavity after an operation? Surely that didn't cast Fliess in a very good light. Didn't Freud need to do some pretty serious rescuing of his idealization of Fliess in the aftermath of that?

FJS: Well, in what way? Yes, it was an embarrassing episode and Freud certainly made apologies for Fliess. Almost anybody would do that for a good friend.

PLR: Or one might begin to think, "This guy wasn't all that I cracked him up to be. I need to be more critical."

FJS: One does well to keep in mind that Freud himself made mistakes in medical practice that were just as bad as Fliess's. Freud, for example, admitted to one mistake in medical judgment that actually killed one of his patients.[50] In any event, the friendship went on for a considerable time after this episode. One really ought to try to separate the fact that, as a physician, Fliess slipped up from the fact that, as an intellectual, he had ideas that were very interesting and compelling to Freud and many others. For these and other reasons, I don't see the Emma Eckstein episode as being all that important to their relationship. True, Fliess made a major mistake in leaving a big wad of gauze inside his patient's nose. That was clearly a sign of some incompetence. Still, because we don't know that much about Fliess's medical career, we also don't know if this was an isolated episode. I think Freud probably treated it as though it was a one-time, rather embarrassing mistake. Indeed, Freud blamed the patient's hemorrhage after the gauze was removed on her pathological need for sympathy, or some such thing. Now, other commentators can choose to make Fliess's blunder into a big deal, and virtually every psychoanalyst who writes on Freud has done so. But the same people have been so busy trying to denigrate Fliess in the service of his "transference" role in Freud's life that they have completely missed, in my opinion, the forest for the trees. The forest involves their scientific collaboration.

PLR: A lot of people who are critical of Freud also make a big deal of the Emma Eckstein episode. So it cuts both ways. The fact that Freud blamed Emma for causing her own hemorrhage, instead of holding Fliess accountable for his blunder, is precisely my point. And if Freud's defense of Fliess was motivated to some degree by guilt over his own medical blunders, that supports a transference interpretation. As Max Schur long ago argued about Freud's dream of Irma's injection, which he saw as connected to the Eckstein episode, "the main wish behind Freud's Irma dream was not to exculpate *himself* but Fliess. It was a wish not to jeopardize his positive relationship with Fliess."[51] Freud's identification with Fliess gets to the emotional or irrational components of their relationship.

FJS: What's irrational about it?

PLR: That Freud was unable to see how far-fetched Fliess's ideas were about the connection between the nose and the female sexual

---

50. See Freud (1900), *The Interpretation of Dreams. Standard Edition*, 4:111–112. London: Hogarth Press, 1953. As Peter Swales points out in this volume, the name of the patient in question was Mathilde Schleicher.

51. Schur, *Freud: Living and Dying*, p. 12.

organs. And that he blamed Emma for her postoperative bleeding.

FJS: You sound like Kurt Eissler! We can also express this question in a very different manner. Why did Fliess hang around with somebody whose ideas were often as far-fetched and wrong-headed as Freud's were? Does the answer to this question require that we assume that Fliess's father had recently died and that he was undergoing some sort of transference during his efforts to come to terms with his father's death, which then prompted him to project his greatness onto Freud? Of course not.

PLR: As a matter of fact, Fliess's father died in 1878, when Fliess was nearly 20. We don't know what kinds of psychological effects this loss may have had. But it would certainly be plausible to think that Fliess had a lot of emotional needs invested in Freud too. We're looking at it from Freud's point of view. The dynamics of transference don't come into play only after the death of Freud's father. They can be seen as early as Freud's first letter to Fliess, dated November 24, 1887, when he wrote in the opening paragraph that "you have left a deep impression on me which could easily lead me to tell you outright in what category of men I place you."[52] Even when he barely knew him, Freud cast Fliess as a hero, the same "category" in which he aspired to place himself. This is transference. Were we to try to tell Fliess's side of the story, we would, of course, have to learn a great deal more about his life. But just because the circumstances are different, that doesn't make him immune from transference.

FJS: My whole point is this: Fliess's ideas seem far-fetched today, but I don't view them as far-fetched in their historical and biogenetic context. These seemingly wacky ideas were no more far-fetched than Freud's ideas were, and some people actually thought that they were far more plausible than Freud's theories. Freud eventually became more famous, but that doesn't necessarily make him more right. The notion that a 28-day period is fundamental to human physiology has lots of support from the obvious evidence of the menstrual cycle in humans to Darwin's arguments that the gestation stages for animals tend to be in multiples of a week. The place that Fliess went badly astray was in his conviction that he was objectively documenting these periodic phenomena in clinical and other life-course data, but this conviction is no more weird or irrational than the extremes to which Freud sometimes went to interpret his patients' symptoms and dreams. We have all read patients' accounts of the dogged way

---

52. In Masson, ed., *Freud–Fliess Letters*, p. 15.

that Freud would wait for one little clue and then say, as he did to Clarence Oberndorf, "Well, your dream about going in a carriage with a white and black horse means you want to marry a black woman."[53] That's just gratuitous and even a bit arrogant. That style, however, is no different from Fliess's style. Freud was a conquistador, but so was Fliess. Some scientists display this grandiose style; others don't. Moreover, there are times when scientists who manifest this style come up with brilliant ideas that are actually true.

In 1896 or 1897, neither Freud nor Fliess could know whether the other was right or wrong because neither was using rigorous methods of hypothesis testing. There was no adequate check on their ideas. One doesn't need to go into the question of whether a transference was going on. Theirs was simply a friendship between two people who were both very smart and very ambitious, who shared this "conquistador" style, and who could not find too many other people to listen to their far-reaching ideas. By bonding together, they were able to further each other's career by a constant cross-fertilization of ideas. In addition, although neither of them was terribly critical of his *own* ideas, they tended to help each other in important ways by providing a critical sounding-board for the other's speculations. This, in any event, is the gist of the collaborative relationship that I portrayed in my book. Unfortunately, almost every attempt to "do the transference thing" in Freud biography is motivated by the same faulty logic you have expressed: Why did Freud, a brilliant man, spend so much time with this idiot named Fliess?

PLR: I don't think I said that exactly.

FJS: You referred to the "irrational components" of their relationship. It's on the tape! And then you said that "Freud was unable to see how far-fetched Fliess's ideas were." Some psychoanalysts have even called Fliess "paranoid" on account of his "pathological" theories.[54] That's the wrong way to think about their relationship.

PLR: But I have stressed that these "irrational components" were involved on both sides. As far as I'm concerned, whatever may be said

---

53. See Abram Kardiner (1977), *My Analysis with Freud: Reminiscences*. New York: Norton, p. 76. The dream was presented to Freud during the first analytic hour by Oberndorf, a Southerner raised by a black nanny. Oberndorf refused to accept Freud's interpretation that his reluctance to marry stemmed from an uncertainty whether to choose a white or a black woman. The analysis foundered, and Freud came to view Oberndorf with disdain.

54. Sulloway, *Freud, Biologist of the Mind*, p. 141.

of Fliess, Freud certainly had a paranoid streak. After all, the relationship came to an end over Freud's accusation, in his letter to Fliess of August 7, 1901, that "you take sides against me and tell me that 'the reader of thoughts merely reads his thoughts into other people,' which renders all my efforts valueless."[55] A decade later, the Schreber case,[56] where Freud attempted to explain paranoia as a result of repressed homosexual impulses, is still haunted by the shadow of Fliess. But in your account, it's as though Freud and Fliess had a purely scientific collaboration in which there was no irrational element. And though I'm quite willing to agree with you that not all Fliess's ideas were ludicrous, while some of Freud's were indeed outlandish, it remains true that Fliess is a nearly forgotten figure today whereas Freud was arguably the most influential thinker of the 20th century. Thus, I think that the question of why Freud valued Fliess so highly continues to be worth asking. For me there's no inherent conflict between an intellectual friendship and emotional needs.

FJS: But that's a completely different issue from needing a "transference" to explain the irrational element in their friendship. This concept assumes that there was something irrational about that friendship and collaboration. Yes, there was something emotional about it, but that truth is unfortunately seized on by analysts to take another unwarranted step, namely, to say that the friendship was irrational; and this fundamentally unjustified next step is then used in an an effort to sweep Fliess under the carpet.

PLR: Where I would come out is not to sweep Fliess under the carpet, but to point to a lifelong pattern in Freud's intellectual style that in many ways reflects poorly on Freud. The relationship to Fliess was one of the most important in Freud's life, but the way that he behaved toward Fliess is consistent with what we know about his behavior toward many other males in his life.

FJS: What part of the relationship reflects poorly on Freud?

PLR: If we take the relationship to Jung as a comparison, Jung was clearly a person of immense gifts.

FJS: I don't really agree. I am reminded of the old adage that "Jung makes Freud look scientific." In any event, let's go back to Fliess. What in *that* relationship reflects badly on Freud?

---

55. In Masson, ed., *Freud–Fliess Letters*, p. 447.

56. Sigmund Freud (1911), *Psycho-Analytical Notes on an Autobiographical Account of a Case of Paranoia (Dementia Paranoides).* In *Standard Edition*, 12:9–82. London: Hogarth Press, 1958.

PLR: I agree with you about Jung, but scientific rigor is not the sole criterion for greatness. As far as Freud and Fliess are concerned, I suppose that what casts Freud in the most negative light, besides the Emma Eckstein business, is the controversy over plagiarism that erupted in the aftermath of the relationship. As even Ernest Jones conceded, Freud was dishonest in not admitting to Fliess that he had divulged his ideas about bisexuality to Swoboda, who then passed them on to Weininger.[57]

FJS: I'm not sure myself that this particular episode reflects terribly badly on Freud. Moreover, by that time (1902–1904), the relationship was already estranged. Hence this episode does not shed much light on the earlier period, when their collaboration was so remarkably intense. Also, there are some other interesting historical aspects to the issue of bisexuality that makes this episode, in which Freud supposedly facilitated the plagiarism, appear to be blown out of proportion. First of all, the idea was not unique to Fliess, though he certainly liked to think it was. The notion of bisexuality had been written about by lots of people before him. Fliess didn't discover this idea; he didn't own it. Freud was therefore free to talk to anybody about it. There's nothing unusual about his communicating these ideas to a patient.

What is unusual is that, when Fliess wrote to Freud to try to find out how Weininger had learned about bisexuality, Freud did not immediately admit to Fliess that he had been the conduit for this information. But I can well imagine that, in such a situation in which people have become estranged and one (Fliess) suspects the other (Freud) of doing something improper, Freud's first inclination was to try to smooth over the situation by making light of it and by avoiding all the embarrassing details. And I think that is just what happened. Freud wrote his letter to this effect, and then he received another letter from Fliess that called his bluff.

Freud's disingenuousness was not exactly in the category of a white lie—it's more serious than that. But it wasn't a felony either. All in all, I don't see Freud's momentary duplicity as reflecting particularly badly on him. Normally, when one hears a statement like "the Fliess relationship reflects badly on Freud," this judgment is being applied to the earlier period, where psychoanalysts have long felt the need to explain why Freud tolerated this guy. Naturally, for psychoanalysts, the answer has got to be "the transference" and Freud's father's death, and then we are back into the standard psychoanalytic whitewashing technique.

---

57. Jones, *Life and Work of Freud*, 1:315.

PLR: I think one could explore these issues without whitewashing Fliess or anyone else. I mentioned Jung. We know that one of Freud's fainting spells occurred in the Park Hotel in Munich—a city he associated with Fliess, and possibly in the same hotel room where they had their final quarrel. It had to do with Freud's claim that Jung had not cited his work. Freud told Jones that there was "a piece of unruly homosexual feeling at the root of the matter."[58] As far as Adler and Stekel are concerned, he wrote to Ferenczi, "Adler is a little Fliess *redivivus*, just as paranoid. Stekel, his appendage, is at least called Wilhelm."[59] These examples suggest that Freud had a compulsive tendency to cast his relationships in repetitive patterns.

FJS: This is an interesting issue. Freud was obsessive about priority, as are most original people. Fliess was that way too. So we have two highly ambitious personalities duking it out for scientific priority as highly territorial and self-confident people typically do. It is not surprising that, when the relationship finally foundered, it did so over the issue of scientific priority. Freud had begun using some of Fliess's ideas, especially in his thinking about psychosexual development and repression, and he had a substantial lapse in 1898 when he failed to recall that Fliess had told him about one particularly important idea on the subject.

PLR: It had to do with bisexuality.[60]

FJS: Again, this particular idea—at least in its most basic form—wasn't unique to Fliess, but Fliess was the vector by which Freud first became exposed to it. Normally, in a scientific collaboration one would cite the other person if that other person had supplied some particularly important point of information that would otherwise have remained unknown to the first person. It would be like my saying, "I thank my friend Stephen Jay Gould for enlightening me on the issue of rapid evolutionary change," when I might have gone to several other people and gotten much the same information. But if Steve Gould had first told me about this important point I would probably have felt obligated to cite him, especially if he, like Fliess,

---

58. Jones, *Life and Work of Freud*, 1:317.

59. Letter of December 16, 1910. In Eva Brabant, Ernst Falzeder & Patrizia Giampieri-Deutsch, eds. (1993), *The Correspondence of Sigmund Freud and Sándor Ferenczi, Volume 1, 1908–1914*, trans. Peter T. Hoffer. Cambridge, MA: Harvard University Press, p. 243.

60. Freud (1901), *The Psychopathology of Everyday Life. Standard Edition*, 6:143–144. London: Hogarth Press, 1960.

had put some original twist on it. Freud didn't do that. Clearly, he was ambivalent about the fact that in their joint scientific thinking they were collaborating more and more. As I expressed this issue in *Freud, Biologist of the Mind*, there came a point where the question began to be: Whose theories explained whose? The two men's ideas had become so intertwined. For example, Freud's whole theory of psychosexual development was initially inspired and informed by Fliess's notion of periodic sexual thrusts. Infantile sexuality was very much a Fliessian construct. They began having conversations in which Fliess would say, "Maybe it isn't your interpretations that are responsible for the patient's recovery. Maybe it was because you conducted your analysis on a periodic day." The two psychosexual theories were competing to explain much of the same information about pathological fixation points, the onset of repression, the specific manifestations of neurotic symptoms, and the reasons for recovery and relapse. All the key disputes in that relationship, and the eventual estrangement, were really about priority, and territorial boundaries generally. So it's not surprising that many of Freud's subsequent disputes with colleagues involved the same basic issues. The bugaboo in Freud's character and failed friendships was not really Fliess. It was Freud's intense need for originality.

PLR: Quite right. But the relationship with Fliess is caught up in that dynamic of Freud's. One can see it in the "*non vixit*" dream, where Freud dreams of outliving Fliess and he recalls a childhood fight with his nephew John in which both boys claimed to "have got there before the other."[61] This is not to minimize either Fliess's intellectual contribution or the importance of that relationship to Freud on its own terms, but it does suggest that it fits into a broader pattern in Freud's life.

FJS: In that event, it's not that Fliess reflects "badly" on Freud, but instead that, in engaging in a relationship with Fliess, Freud sometimes exhibited behaviors that reflected badly on himself.

PLR: Exactly. That's what I'm trying to say. But if there's any silver lining to this cloud, it's how those of Freud's actions which reflect badly on him can be explained in terms of psychoanalytic theory. We can see that his conflicts over priority go back to his childhood.

FJS: Well, we can "see" that only because Freud, who held a theory to this effect, gave us the selective biographical information that confirmed his theory. Moreover, almost any theory of human development

---

61. Freud, *The Interpretation of Dreams. Standard Edition*, 5:483–484.

can explain the same general thesis. We don't need Freudian theory to understand that Freud's desire to be first, and to be intellectually dominant, must have had *something* to do with his early life. We could go over to Harvard University, call the entire Department of Psychology together, supply them with these same biographical facts and ask, "Can you account for the behavioral continuity in this pattern?" They're virtually all going to say "yes," and, to my knowledge, none of them except Philip Holzman has ever been psychoanalyzed. So you're going to be outvoted 30 to 1 on the question of whether psychoanalytic theory—either orthodox or revisionist—is in any way required to explain this aspect of Freud's adult behavior! The real question is, can psychoanalytic theory make a point that all those smart Harvard professors cannot make about the same biographical evidence? Show me that the theory can, and I'll perk up with considerable interest.

PLR: I guess I'd like to talk to Philip Holzman. [laughs] But this meeting of the Harvard Psychology Department falls into the category of hypothetical examples. The notion that Freud deliberately filtered the evidence about his life in order to lend credence to his theories seems far-fetched to me. After all, Freud tried to persuade Marie Bonaparte to *destroy* the Fliess correspondence, which provides the record of his self-analysis.[62] You seem to be of two minds about whether Freud's struggles for priority went back to his childhood. On one hand, you criticize the psychoanalytic approach as incapable of explaining anything; but, on the other, you say that its genetic model is a commonplace shared by other psychological theories. I would say that psychoanalysis is participating in a common discourse, and, if what can be argued from a psychoanalytic point of view overlaps with what people might argue from somewhat different explanatory frameworks, so much the better. But just as Darwin's symptoms of repression in adulthood are tied to the death of his mother, it's important to me to maintain that the patterns in Freud's life can be traced back to his early experiences and unconscious conflicts. The "guilt of the survivor" motif is one that he himself linked to childhood experience. A plausible case can be made that what was driving Freud's behavior was rooted not simply in his character but also in his early experience. Although on one level he was able to articulate this awareness consciously, the behavior that he exhibited repeated the pattern despite his intellectual insights. He told Fliess that he rejoiced in the "*non vixit*" dream at having outlived him and about his need to find the loved friend and hated enemy in the same person.

---

62. Masson, Introduction to *Freud–Fliess Letters*, pp. 4–11.

I'm not saying that psychoanalysis is the only vocabulary available to talk about these things, but it seems to me to be an illuminating way of framing the data.

FJS: It doesn't do much for me. I've read so many of these tortured interpretations and reinterpretations of Freud's dreams that it all seems a bit like bad food warmed over too many times. I don't know of a reliable way to evaluate the truth of such claims. Maybe there's some genius out there who can do this sort of psychospeculation delicately and with a reliable flair for getting at the truth, but most people who do it simply end up with stories that so blatantly confirm psychoanalytic theory that it's almost sickening. Of course, there's a ready audience for those stories among the true believers, but this circumstance is neither here nor there.

PLR: As I've said, I want to be rigorously critical about psychoanalysis. But the criteria for evaluating truth claims in humanistic fields such as history and literary criticism, to which psychoanalysis as an interpretative discipline is closely allied, cannot be the same as in the natural sciences. To be sure, much of what Freud maintained is no longer credible and has to be tossed into the dustbin of history. So for me it becomes imperative to try to sort out what has withstood the test of time from what hasn't. In your essay "Reassessing Freud's Case Histories," you say: "Psychoanalytic theory is perhaps unique in the history of science in that it contains within itself an elaborate historical account of its own intellectual origins. Freud has become his own most famous 'case history.'"[63] I agree with that. Of course, it's impossible to test the interpretation of a dream as though it were a scientific hypothesis.

FJS: One cannot test *any* of these hypotheses when doing biography. One can't even test these hypotheses in the clinical setting, as Adolf Grünbaum and others have persuasively argued.[64] That's why the most important methodological step in psychobiography is to draw from those healthy domains of science which study human development. If we were to survey academics and ask them what we need to know, almost none of them would tell us that it is psychoanalysis.

---

63. Frank J. Sulloway (1992), "Reassessing Freud's Case Histories: The Social Construction of Psychoanalysis." In *Freud and the History of Psychoanalysis*, ed. Toby Gelfand & John Kerr. Hillsdale, NJ: The Analytic Press, p. 159.

64. Adolf Grünbaum (1984), *The Foundations of Psychoanalysis: A Philosophical Critique*. Berkeley: University of California Press.

PLR: I think it depends on the discipline. I would agree that any psychoanalytic proposition that has been scientifically refuted is not likely to be useful in writing psychobiography or anything else. Too many people in the humanities go on using such concepts as the death instinct, primary narcissism, the pleasure principle, and so forth, which in my view are clearly outmoded. But once we have laid a firm scientific foundation, there are still questions of meaning that science alone cannot answer. This is where the humanities come in. The problem with Grünbaum is that he thinks everything can be reduced to a natural-science model. For him, there is no difference between the "history" of a particle in physics and the history of a human being. Many people writing biography today still find psychoanalysis has a contribution to make.

FJS: Yes, and humanists more generally are indeed drawn to it. But, pardon me, what the hell do they know? They're not scientists. They're not in a position to test and validate such theories. That's why the last refuge of psychoanalysis is in the humanities, where its practitioners are less equipped to tell the difference between a valid and an invalid scientific theory. If we are ultimately going to do biography right, we need a reliable theory of human development. The specialists who work on this enormously complex problem are developmental psychologists, behavioral geneticists, and the like. None of these people use psychoanalytic theory in any formal sense. They may occasionally fall back on notions that would also be employed by psychoanalysts. That doesn't necessarily make these psychologists' accounts psychoanalytic, but it does mean that there's occasionally a common ground—one that lies mostly in common sense.

PLR: Exactly. And that's something. I can't say I share your attitude toward the humanities. But I'm all in favor of learning from developmental psychology and other branches of sciences. Indeed, Daniel Stern, a psychoanalyst renowned for his work in developmental psychology, explicitly states that when these two perspectives come into conflict, "it is psychoanalysis that will have to give way."[65] And there's no doubt that some of Freud's interpretations are tortured. It seems to me that when he interpreted the dreams of others, he was often high-handed and imposed his preconceptions on what he heard. As Richard Webster points out, he conjectured that the dream of one of his female patients about a butcher could be explained by his own

---

65. Daniel N. Stern (1985), *The Interpersonal World of the Infant: A View from Psychoanalysis and Developmental Psychology*. New York: Basic Books, p. 17.

associations to the phrase "Your meat-shop is open," referring to a man's trouser-fly, and asserted that an unnamed vegetable must be asparagus, with its phallic connotations.[66]

FJS: The same objection is true of Freud's interpretations of his own dreams.

PLR: There I disagree. Earlier I used the example of the *"non vixit"* dream, where Freud traced his relationship to Fliess back to his early childhood, in which there was a literal competition over priority with his nephew John, toward whom he felt an ambivalent mixture of love and hate. This interpretation of his relationship to Fliess and his survivor guilt makes much more sense to me than does his interpretation of his patient's dream. Freud's explanations are generally far more compelling when they arise out of his own experience than when he's talking about somebody else.

FJS: I would agree, but this still doesn't mean that any of the interpretations that he offers are correct. They are simply less blatantly arbitrary.

PLR: But how can we determine that?

FJS: We can't—that's the whole point. All Freud's free associations to his dreams were influenced by his theories. Moreover, we know only about those free associations he chose to tell us about. As a result, we cannot make a determination about the validity of Freud's theories through any of the anecdotal evidence that is available about Freud's life or, for that matter, about anybody else's life. We must do scientific research to get a handle on these kinds of questions, which include memory confabulation, correlations in behavior over time that are not strictly "causal," and various other enigmas of human development. Unfortunately, we will find almost none of this research being conducted by psychoanalysts, so they're not going to help us where it really matters.

PLR: I admire your commitment to the scientific method. But I think it would be a delusion to suppose that controversies over the interpretation of historical events can ever be settled empirically. The same goes for psychoanalysis. To take a concrete instance, how are we going to prove that there was something significant in Darwin's failure to recognize that when you put "m" before "other" you get the word "mother"? Or when he said he had never experienced the loss of a near relation? The facts of what happened to Darwin are not in

---

66. Webster, *Why Freud Was Wrong*, pp. 267–269.

dispute, but the meaning is up for grabs. Surely we have to rely on our judgment here.

FJS: Right, but there's no amount of theory now known in psychology—and there will probably never be such theory in the future—that will allow us to take a biographical example such as these two and say that we've proven anything. They are purely anecdotal examples, and science doesn't prove anything by means of anecdotes. So all we can really say is that an anecdote is consistent with some other body of research where we *are* able to prove things. In psychology, almost all these kinds of proofs are conducted at the population level rather than the level of the individual. For this reason, the proofs are generally statistical. This is what Bowlby did when he argued that individuals who lose a parent at a certain age tend to develop a cluster of problems, including being more prone to anxiety and panic attacks.[67] The proof of the pudding in such hypotheses now lies in large epidemiological studies with adequate controls. From these kinds of controlled studies, scientists can say statistically that some of those hypotheses are valid and some of these hypotheses are invalid. But one can still never prove that such hypotheses are true in any individual case, no matter how intuitively plausible the evidence may seem.

PLR: We don't disagree about that. Where we seem to differ is in your confidence that questions of value and meaning can be settled with statistics. As you've just said, statistical studies are done at the population level. But in the human sciences, as Bowlby pointed out in a passage I quoted earlier, "the individual example is the very essence of the case." What is more, Bowlby went on to state that history, "whether it deals with societies or persons or ideas, is always concerned with appallingly complex sequences of highly specific interacting events which no amount of science can enable us to explain adequately, let alone predict."[68] Thus, Bowlby by no means relied exclusively on quantitative methods. From my point of view, the problem with your approach is not that it's scientific—I'm all in favor of science—but that you want science to answer questions about individual cases that call out instead for hermeneutics.

FJS: I have a discussion of this methodological issue in *Born to Rebel.* Anecdotes, as I stress, don't prove anything, though one may usefully employ them to illustrate points that one has already proven

---

67. John Bowlby (1980), *Loss: Sadness and Depression*. London: Hogarth Press.

68. Bowlby, "Psychoanalysis as a Natural Science." In *A Secure Base*, p. 75.

by other means. Anecdotes, moreover, can be an important source of hypotheses. I am far from wishing to reduce human behavior to statistics, nor did I mean to imply that Bowlby went that route either.

PLR: Fine. So there is a congruence between what we can glean from the human and the natural sciences. You asked me earlier what humanists know . . .

FJS: I meant "knowing" about the intricacies of human development, as understood by science. Humanists know lots of things, and they often have remarkable sensitivity and perception on certain topics. But I was commenting about knowledge in science, not about "knowing" in general, which often involves forms of knowledge that are untestable and hence unscientific, or at best prescientific.

PLR: Surely there's also something to be learned about psychology from literature. Let's say we're confronted with a Shakespeare play and are trying to determine what a passage means. Or what the play as a whole might mean. These are issues of interpretation, and I don't see how questions of meaning can ever be sorted out using the model of hypothesis testing.

FJS: No, they can't. And as far as I know, nobody ever said that they could be.

PLR: But it still seems to me that the endeavor to understand and interpret works of literature is a valuable enterprise. Trained people can judge whether it is done more or less successfully, even though they might not agree about a given interpretation. It's like being a juror in a court case—or even assessing the outcome of a statistical study—where one tries to weigh all the available evidence and to come to a conclusion, but one can never exclude the possibility of being in error in any given instance. The techniques of interpretation in the humanities, without being incompatible with the sciences, have a contribution to make in the effort to understand the meaning of experience in literature and perhaps even in life.

FJS: The similarity between the fields, as I see it, is as follows. Both science and nonscience have to start somewhere, and the first step is to try to reach a reasonable hypothesis about the subject of study. So, if one is interpreting Shakespeare, one studies his plays in great detail. Then one tries to put everything together and come up with an interpretation, and that's fine as far as it goes. The problem is that, in the humanities, one normally cannot test the validity of such hypothetical interpretations, whereas in science the ball game has only just begun when one has finally reached a plausible interpretation. It's at this crucial point that scientists engage in a second step of research, namely, hypothesis testing. This formal step is missing from most humanistic research because there is no way to carry it out using humanistic or hermeneutic methods. It is this second step that allows us to determine whether a plausible (or implausible) "interpretation" of the data has any validity. Humanistic claims are therefore scientific claims without the science to back them up. Such claims are conjectures, nothing more. Humanists often think they are testing their ideas, but such informal methods are almost always exercises in "confirmatory" hypothesis testing—that is, looking for supporting evidence.

PLR: I don't think that claims in the humanities can be equated with scientific claims. They may rest on a scientific foundation and should not be contradicted by any known evidence, but they're of a fundamentally different order. And a good reader, like a good researcher in any field, is open to evidence that disconfirms his or her initial expectations. In my view, psychoanalysis is a hybrid discipline. In its ideal form, if there be such a thing, it has to be accountable to the criteria of science . . .

FJS: Quite right. But it unfortunately isn't.

PLR: Well, but it could be.

FJS: In theory, yes; but given the personnel who work in this intellectual domain, the prospects are dim. The problem lies with the training. One can't become a psychoanalyst without partaking of the institutional mechanisms the discipline has established, and that, to put it bluntly, is usually the end of someone's career as a scientist.

PLR: Well, it could be detrimental, but I'd like to think it need not be fatal. [laughs] Let me quote you something from Edward O. Wilson.

FJS: He's a kind man, so perhaps he can help you.

PLR: That's a virtue. [FJS laughs] He says: "Psychoanalytic theory appears to be exceptionally compatible with sociobiological theory. . . . If the essence of the Freudian revolution was that it gave structure to the unconscious, the logical role of sociobiology is to reconstruct the evolutionary history of that structure. When Freud speculated in *Totem and Taboo* on the primal father, primal horde, and the origins of the incest taboo, he created a sociobiological hypothesis, but a poor one."[69] I'd agree with that.

---

69. Edward O. Wilson (1977), "Biology and the Social Sciences." *Daedelus,* 106:135–136.

FJS: So would I, as I explicitly argued in *Freud, Biologist of the Mind.*[70]

PLR: In principle, then, psychoanalysis is compatible with science. Maybe you've decided that psychoanalysis is not productive or interesting for you, but to me it's critical to ask what still holds up.

FJS: What precisely is there that still holds up? I'd love to know.

PLR: I'm arguing that the idea of a dynamic unconscious still seems to be valuable.

FJS: I'll mostly reject that claim for the various reasons I have given. What's the next one on your list?

PLR: I tried to defend that idea by pointing to the sequence of incidents from Darwin's life brought forward by Bowlby.

FJS: I don't view those incidents as evidence for the dynamic unconscious, at least in the theoretically and medically strong form that Freud espoused and that was central and necessary for his whole theory of psychosexual development and psychopathology. These kinds of biographical stories are far more plausibly seen as evidence for a far milder version of the unconscious, one that Freud would not himself have considered "psychoanalytic."

PLR: We may not agree about the terminology, but in some form it surely exhibits repression.

FJS: Once again, I don't like the word, just as Bowlby didn't like it either, because it implies certain aspects of Freud's theoretical system that have not stood the tests of subsequent scientific inquiry. In any event, we are certainly not dealing here with repression as part of the dynamic unconscious, as Freud himself understood it. It's such a watered-down version of the original idea. Freud would be outraged.

PLR: I don't think so. And as I've tried to demonstrate, I think you're wrong in claiming that Bowlby rejected the notion of repression— though he preferred to call it "defensive exclusion"—just as he clearly agreed with Freud about the dynamic unconscious. Unfortunately, we can't resuscitate either of them to ascertain whose interpretation of their respective positions is closer to the mark. And I'm still interested in considering the role of early experience. I think Freud himself is a good example of the utility of genetic explanation, since we know so much about his life and his early childhood—sibling loss . . .

---

70. Sulloway, *Freud, Biologist of the Mind*, pp. 5, 367, 500.

FJS: Right there you are committing a gigantic methodological error. You have a pet idea, and then you go to one life—Freud's—to confirm it, just as Freud himself did.

PLR: I'm testing a hypothesis. And you yourself just said that "biographical stories" were "evidence" of *something*, even if we disagreed about exactly what that was.

FJS: No, you can't test a hypothesis with evidence drawn from the life of a single person.

PLR: We could falsify it, I suppose.

FJS: No, you can't even falsify it. Although you may be able to find a case that doesn't fit your hypothesis, that doesn't disprove your hypothesis. You can't do anything scientific with a single life. Even evidence from multiple biographies does not, per se, provide a *scientific* perspective on such claims. One needs to perform statistical tests on such evidence, using large samples carefully controlled for the kinds of covariates (and alternative hypotheses) that are relevant to the claim under consideration. Let me provide a concrete example. Let us suppose that the early death of a sibling, as in Freud's case, is thought to lead to "survivor guilt," which, in turn, is thought to cause ambivalence in adult relationships, which, in turn, is thought to nurture an excessive credulity toward wacky ideas, as well as a desire to steal those ideas. We could test this idea by examining a large population of subjects according to their beliefs in a variety of pseudoscientific ideas and popular superstitions. We might then look for a significant correlation between such beliefs and the early death of a sibling, as well as a significant correlation between both of these variables and an objective measure of ambivalence in adult relationships, perhaps by using an instrument drawn from the research on attachment theory. Finally we might try to replicate and extend these results (assuming they turned out to be favorable to our initial hypothesis) by studying priority disputes in science. There we would expect people who lost siblings in childhood to be overrepresented. In addition, we would expect the same people to exhibit a lack of critical thinking when faced with new and highly speculative ideas (such as Fliess's theories) that have subsequently turned out to be incorrect.

Because behavior is "overdetermined," as Freud liked to point out, none of these relationships, if they exist at all, will be perfect. Indeed, we know empirically that such relationships, even when valid, tend to explain only a modest percentage of the evidence, which is why we need to employ large samples and formal statistical tests in our empirical analyses. Finding a case in which little ambivalence existed in adult relationships, and in which desire for priority did not go hand-in-hand with uncritical thinking about a friend's ideas, is no more a disproof of the theory than confirming evidence is a proof of these same claims. Such anecdotal evidence cannot decide the validity of our theory, and a hundred anecdotes are no more useful than is one in this regard. All that such anecdotes can do is to suggest plausible hypotheses, some of which may be testable (and thereby become amenable to scientific analysis) and some of which may not be.

The problem with the general anecdotal approach that you are advocating and trying to employ yourself is that, with scores of relevant examples, one invariably ends up overweighting "confirmations" and underweighting "inconsistent evidence" concerning the hypothesis that originally motivated the research. Many experimental studies have shown this to be the case, and the remarkable progress of modern science, since scientific methods were introduced into research in the 17th century, dramatically demonstrates the superiority of formal methods of testing over those generally employed in the humanities. Humanists may be content to engage in suggestive "interpretations" in their own academic research, but when they fall desperately ill it is modern medicine, not 16th-century medical hermeneutics, that saves their lives.

Not only do psychoanalysts and people within the humanities more generally not understand that anecdotes are not the basis of science (or truth), but they often have an additional incorrect belief that people can conduct formal testing within the psychoanalytic situation. This is an issue that Grünbaum has written about very effectively.[71]

PLR: What you've described sounds to me less like a scientific hypothesis than a polemical narrative. I agree that science is progressive in a way that art is not, but that doesn't mean we can dispense with everything that isn't science. I'm open to weighing the evidence critically.

FJS: The scientific method is hardly a "polemical narrative." Rather it is a set of formal procedures for *minimizing* polemics by allowing them to be resolved as efficiently and rapidly as possible. In your own humanistic researches, I am sure that you are open to weighing evidence in a critical manner, but weighing the evidence when the *N* equals 1 doesn't count for much in science. You're not doing science, even if you *are* engaged in reasonably rational thinking.

---

71. Grünbaum, *The Foundations of Psychoanalysis*.

PLR: Which is not necessarily incompatible with science. If you can't perform a scientific experiment when $N = 1$, the corollary is that quantitative methods can't possibly tell us how to interpret any individual case, which is the most important thing in history or any of the other *human* sciences. This goes back to what I was saying before about psychoanalysis as a hybrid discipline.

FJS: But what ends up happening with this kind of one-step protoscience is nicely exemplified by the many attempts written by true believers to salvage psychoanalysis. Christopher Badcock in England, for instance, has tried to show in this general manner that psychoanalysis is compatible, after all, with current Darwinian biology.[72] What we often get from such attempts, however, is merely a translation of current ideas about evolution back into standard psychoanalytic terms, which is little more than an attempt to save the phenomena, so to speak. That's what happens when people think they are doing hypothesis testing and allying themselves solidly with modern science, but are not really doing science at all. Under these circumstances, people just rationalize the evidence in ways that suit their fancy, and the only really relevant evidence to them is *confirming* evidence.

PLR: I don't know Badcock's book, but his project sounds very worthwhile to me. It's not a matter of "saving the phenomena" or translating everything back into "standard psychoanalytic terms," but of seeing what in psychoanalysis can be integrated with modern science. You seem to imagine that your own thinking is unclouded by subjectivity, while proponents of psychoanalysis are incapable of evaluating a hypothesis in the light of the evidence. But though this may have been true of Freud, who embraced science in theory while often betraying it in practice, I've agreed that much of what he said needs to be rejected.

FJS: That's not going to help you much, however. The problem is that, since you are not doing science yourself, you're at the whim of whatever the last decade or two of psychoanalytic "research" has said on the subject. Unfortunately, in psychoanalysis people go from one fad to another. Morris Eagle and David Wolitzky have written a very good and relevant paper about theory change in psychoanalysis.[73]

---

72. Christopher Badcock (1994), *PsychoDarwinism: The New Synthesis of Darwin and Freud*. London: HarperCollins.

73. Morris Eagle & David Wolitzky (1989), "The Idea of Progress in Psychoanalysis." *Psychoanalysis and Contemporary Thought*, 12:27–72.

Yes, the theories do change over time, but almost never for the reasons that cause theories to change in the hard sciences.

PLR: But, as I've been arguing all along, psychoanalysis is not entirely a hard science. It is equally grounded in hermeneutics. If we're seeking to understand an individual case, scientific methods alone are insufficient.

FJS: Psychoanalysis is not a hard science at all. It's not! It's not even a soft science!

PLR: Insofar as Bowlby's work reflects a tradition that grows out of psychoanalysis, I see it as compatible with science.

FJS: Yes, there are topics that some psychoanalysts work on that scientists also work on. But the fact that the problem areas overlap doesn't make psychoanalysis a science or its practitioners scientific.

PLR: If something can be refuted by scientific investigation, I do not want to continue to employ its ideas or premises.

FJS: I'm sure that's true. But the problem you and other humanists face is that, if you're not an active participant in science, you must passively sit and wait for the real scientists to come up with their results.

PLR: Well, we're all indebted to the work of others. We're all experts only in limited areas. When we consider what we think we know, we can't help relying on authorities to a great extent. If I am persuaded by your work on birth order, for example, it's not because I have done all the computations and statistical analyses myself. But I have read your work and I am convinced that the evidence you offer is good evidence and that it's been presented in a logical and a valid way. Surely that's acceptable to you, isn't it?

FJS: Yes, at one level. I appreciate the fact that you respect my work on this subject and have, to a considerable extent, been convinced by it. But the fate of my ideas on the subject of birth order and family dynamics will ultimately be decided by the scientific community. If this community goes against me, the support of nonscientists such as you won't help me one bit.

PLR: I would say that the fate of your ideas, like that of Freud's or anyone else's, will be determined by their reception by the culture as a whole, a process in which scientists are important, but by no means the only, arbiters. Admittedly, I'm not doing either the clinical or the experimental work on the epistemology of psychoanalysis myself, but I am trying to be conversant with it. I feel justified in concluding that certain things can be dismissed because they've been refuted, and certain other things seem to hold up pretty well.

FJS: I made these comments about the nature of science only because you indicated that you believed you could do some kind of testing in an *informal* way. For the reasons I have given, I don't believe this is possible. In addition, I don't believe that the feedback you may get from psychoanalysts is worth much, because it is inherently unscientific. Unfortunately, most scientists are working on other problems, so you won't get much feedback from them either.

PLR: I'm interested in feedback not only from psychoanalysts but also from people who question psychoanalytic assumptions. That's why I'm talking to you. I was asking whether we might be able to use Freud's life as evidence for psychoanalytic theory.

FJS: I think this effort, however fascinating, is just *doomed* to failure, because the evidence, being anecdotal, can only suggest hypotheses, not confirm or disconfirm them.

PLR: I respect the scientific model of hypothesis testing for which you are arguing, but there are questions of value and meaning that science alone can't answer. As I've already stipulated, any proposition that can be refuted by scientific investigation must be rejected.

FJS: Well, building theories based on single biographies has got to be number one on the list of things to reject. It's just a bad strategy—inherently unscientific. You can go about constructing a biography out of anecdotes, but this procedure will never in any really effective way change your psychoanalytic thinking. You're more likely to confirm your thinking than to refute it.

PLR: How might we set up an experiment to examine whether or not the experiences of the first three years of a person's life have an influence on his or her subsequent development? It's hard for me to imagine how that could be tested. Wouldn't we have to rely on natural experiments?

FJS: The natural experiments one must use have to be epidemiological studies. This kind of research involves studying large numbers of individuals who have gone down different developmental pathways. Such research requires the simultaneous control of all relevant covariates. Then one asks, is there continuity in behavior as measured during the first three years of life and then when measured later on? It's difficult to do these kinds of studies because one must take into account genetic inputs and other factors. Probably the most rigorous way to tackle this question is through a behavioral genetics design in which developmental psychologists measure and study behavior longitudinally. Such studies have already been done. As a result of such research, the evidence is already available, and it strongly indicates that the first three years of life do not have the kind of predominant influence on behavior that Freud himself believed.

PLR: And Darwin.

FJS: Darwin's comment on this whole subject was a little more open ended. For him, the influence of the first three years was not as great as Freud believed. And one should bear in mind that this comment was something he only said once. How exactly did Darwin put it?

PLR: I have the passage here. He said: "It is a virgin brain adapted to receive impressions, and although unable to formulate or memorize these, they nonetheless remain and can affect the whole future of the child recipient."[74]

FJS: That claim is not terribly far reaching. He was just saying that the brain absorbs a lot of information and experience in the first three years. He was not saying that the first three years are the absolute key to life as an adult. Freudian theory makes a much stronger statement on this subject.

PLR: Well, Darwin did say that these experiences, even though they may be below the level of consciousness, "can affect the whole future of the child recipient." That sounds pretty Freudian to me. But I'm simply asking, what can we learn from the study of Freud's life? We know so much about it.

FJS: Once again, I think that's really the wrong place to start if you want to understand human development more generally. Individual lives can suggest interesting hypotheses, and such lives can illustrate theories of human development that have been validated by other means; but individual lives cannot be employed to test hypotheses, such as Freud's claims about the importance of the first three years of life.

PLR: We may have here a difference in our disciplinary training. Again, you seem to be saying that the only function of history or literature is to illustrate truths already established in the sciences, but

---

74. Quoted in Sulloway, "Darwinian Psychobiography," p. 29.

they are not sources of knowledge in their own right. I'm interested in working in a way that exhibits consilience and a convergence of knowledge, but the humanities have a distinctive contribution to make. And the humanities work—as therapy does—with individual cases. We need good scientific theories to bring to bear on our work with each unique case. But, when we try to interpret a dream or the experience of a relationship, it's very hard to reduce that to something statistically demonstrable. We're dealing with something inherently elusive and subjective. Perhaps I could use this as a transition to ask you a question about Paul Robinson's chapter on your work.

FJS: I haven't actually read it, although I know it's largely negative. [laughs]

PLR: Robinson says, "According to Sulloway, Freud will be great if he can be made to resemble Darwin. It will not do to suggest that his achievement was more like that of Augustine or Rousseau."[75]

FJS: I think that's silly.

PLR: Could you explain why? I think Robinson raises an important issue. In highlighting Freud as a cryptobiologist, you situate his work in relation to one important domain of cultural discourse, but you don't look at Freud in relation to a tradition of introspection or consider his literary and philosophical background.

FJS: That's true, but your quotation from Robinson implies that I think Freud has to be salvaged by allying him with Darwin. That wasn't the goal of my book. In many ways, I saw Freud and psychoanalysis as beyond the point of being salvageable. In any event, the book's goal was simply to understand Freud, not to make him somehow more palatable by making him into a Darwinian (which he was not).

PLR: There's nothing in Robinson to suggest that it's a matter of trying to "salvage" Freud. His point is that what you value in Freud is his biological thinking and his participation in the Darwinian tradition, and nothing else.

FJS: I think that's a somewhat misleading reading of my book. My goal was not at all to make Freud great by making him look like Darwin or by highlighting his debt to biology. My goal was to understand why Freud developed his various ideas, and how the most

---

75. Paul Robinson (1993), *Freud and His Critics*. Berkeley: University of California Press, p. 67.

important of these ideas grew out of a 19th-century evolutionary tradition. The net result of this analysis was to highlight the problematic character of Freud's theories, not to make Freud "great." Robinson has missed the whole point.

PLR: I think Robinson was responding to those passages, which we've already discussed, where you say that Freud offered "the most comprehensive evolutionary explanation of the origins of human behavior" or your quotation from Philip Rieff that he produced "the most important body of thought committed to paper in the twentieth century."[76] Surely your understanding of Freud, which included paying tribute to his greatness where you felt it was appropriate, led you to connect him above all to Darwin.

FJS: Let me try to clarify this point, because it is an important one. There's no question that I valued those aspects of Freud's thinking that were rooted in natural science much more than I did those which were rooted—to take the extreme opposite—in wild speculation and mysticism. There is, as you know, that side to Freud. There is also a side to Freud that is nonscientific in a more virtuous sense, and that is his vast knowledge of literature, archeology, and the humanities more generally. I didn't write a lot about the contributions of literature, linguistics, philosophy, and so on to psychoanalytic theory because I have a particular viewpoint on this whole subject, one that I believe is both useful and defensible. The core of Freud's psychoanalytic theories—the key postulates that really make them work at a causal, natural-science level—is drawn largely from the medical biology and psychiatry of his day. These key postulates involve such notions as fixation, regression, "organic repression," ontogenetic developmental processes recapitulating phylogenetic developmental processes, and, finally, hydraulic forces that move dynamically within the nervous system. This core set of "metapsychological" ideas is very consistent, well articulated, and well thought out. In addition, these key ideas are linked to certain underlying assumptions of his day that Freud and others considered quite plausible. For example, given the enormous influence that Helmholtz's theory about the conservation of energy exerted in Freud's day, Freud's model of the nervous system made this particular idea central to all of his psychoanalytic theorizing.

Now, laid over this core paradigm in the corpus of the *Standard Edition* of Freud there is a widespread appeal to literary illustrations and allusions and other examples of high culture. The question

---

76. Sulloway, *Freud, Biologist of the Mind*, pp. 367, 358.

is, did Freud's extensive knowledge of literature, philosophy, and the culture of the day filter back into the core of his psychosexual theory and influence it in a fundamental way?

PLR: That's an excellent question. How would you answer it?

FJS: In *Freud, Biologist of the Mind,* I deliberately and specifically identified all the things that I thought illuminated and explicated the core of the theory. Given the enormity of this task, I did not spend much time discussing aspects of Freud's intellectual style that he used only to illustrate the theory or to embellish it in a culturally erudite fashion. In answer to your question, I was never able to find evidence that Freud's knowledge of linguistics, for example, exerted a fundamental influence on some of the deep assumptions of his theories the way that John Forrester, among others, has argued.[77] I don't find Forrester's account very plausible. It ignores a fundamental fact about Freud's career, namely, that he spent the first half of it as a neurobiologist and neuroanatomist, not as a psychoanalyst and certainly not as a linguist.

For me, the bottom line about Freud's intellectual development is that he trained from the age of about 18 through his mid-40s in neurobiology and to some extent evolutionary biology. Those were the fields in which he intended to make his career, with all the natural scientific values and identifications that went with these fields of study. Freud read a vast amount in these disciplines, and it was out of these biological and medical fields that he knew he would have to draw all the basic assumptions and working principles for a theory of human development that was really adequate to the task. In other words, Freud firmly believed that the theory of human development had to be a *scientific* theory and, for this reason, it had to draw its deepest roots from psychobiology and medicine. So he fashioned his key assumptions out of those biomedical domains, and *that's* the story I tried to chronicle.

By contrast, Freud did not go the route of thinking to himself, "Well, I'll contemplate Goethe's writings for a few days and draw some fundamental assumptions about human nature and human mental functioning from them," because he knew that one couldn't formulate a scientific paradigm out of Goethe's ideas. He could and did use Goethe, who was one of his favorite authors, to his advantage in other ways, just as he used other German writers for the same

---

77. John Forrester (1980), *Language and the Origins of Psychoanalysis.* New York: Columbia University Press.

literary purposes, but none of these authors became crucial sources of the key assumptions and principles of psychoanalytic theory.

PLR: Goethe, of course, like Leonardo, was a scientist as well as a humanist and served Freud as a model in this respect. And let's not forget that Freud wrote *On Aphasia*[78] and used linguistic as well as biological models throughout his career. You don't have to be a Lacanian to know that psychoanalysis is called the *talking* cure! Because you see everything through the lens of Freud's desire to construct a scientific theory grounded in biology, you don't present his self-analysis as a psychological process of self-discovery in its own right. For you, literature serves merely to illustrate or embellish an already established scientific truth. But don't the literary and philosophical dimensions of psychoanalysis have to be considered along with Freud's scientific ambitions? When Freud wrote to Fliess on October 15, 1897 that "a single idea of general value" had occurred to him, he immediately cited Sophocles' *Oedipus* and Shakespeare's *Hamlet*, and he invoked these two works again in *The Interpretation of Dreams*.[79]

FJS: Those are literary examples, and damn good ones, which Freud used to illustrate an insight that he had derived by thinking about (a) the things his patients were telling him and (b) the theory of psychosexual development.

PLR: And also what he was finding in his own self-analysis.

FJS: Yes, although I think a lot of that personal exercise consisted of reading into his own life experiences an organizing and explanatory structure that he was then in the course of deriving from other sources.

PLR: But there's a process of investigation occurring on several tracks—his clinical work, his reading, and his analysis of his own dreams and early life history. I think it's significant that, when he pulled this all together, he did so by mentioning Oedipus.

FJS: How could any educated person, once he had finally reached that particular insight, not mention Oedipus? I don't view a knowledge of Sophocles' *Oedipus Rex*, which Freud had read as a gymnasium student, as in any way *causing* the development of

---

78. Sigmund Freud (1891), *On Aphasia: A Critical Study*, trans. E. Stengel. Madison, CT: International Universities Press, 1953.

79. Masson, ed., *Freud–Fliess Letters*, p. 272; and see Freud, The *Interpretation of Dreams. Standard Edition*, 4:262.

psychoanalytic theory. The relationship with Fliess and the associated collaborative insights into a dynamic and biogenetic conception of psychosexual development—these are primary causal determinants of Freud's thinking. In particular, his familiarity with Haeckel's biogenetic law caused Freud to develop a sweeping paradigm about human psychosexual development—to recognize, for example, that the child will be "polymorphously perverse." Freud could have read a million novels and Greek tragedies and never reached that crucial conclusion about childhood sexuality. But such ideas arose almost inevitably from a familiarity with 19th-century medical science, particularly sexology, where they were already being discussed by such people as Albert Moll and Wilhelm Fliess.

PLR: The kind of discussion we are having here exemplifies why I think that quantitative methods are insufficient in historical research. We have to use our judgment in weighing various possible influences on Freud's thought. Because you are steeped in the history of science rather than in literature, you believe that Albert Moll was more important to Freud than Sophocles, Shakespeare, or Goethe. Didn't Freud's reading of *Hamlet* and *Oedipus* cause him to think along certain lines?

FJS: Please don't misunderstand me. I have not said, nor do I believe, that quantitative methods are sufficient for understanding history. What I have said is that anecdotal evidence—the main thrust of historical argumentation—is insufficient when it comes to formal hypothesis testing, which is the main thrust of scientific argumentation. After a careful study of Freud's readings in the emerging discipline of sexology, as it was then being developed by such figures as Albert Moll and Richard von Krafft-Ebing, I reached my conclusion that Moll's work was more influential on Freud's ideas about psychosexual development than was the work of Shakespeare or Goethe. Freud needed the general ideas in this emerging field to make theoretical sense out of otherwise puzzling or unconnected empirical findings, including those garnered from his study of literature. Without this theoretical perspective, together with the medical evidence supporting it, Freud's reading of *Hamlet* is exceedingly unlikely to have caused him to formulate a theory that the whole of human development, and its various psychopathological glitches, is *Hamlet* writ large.

PLR: Or that incest is a fundamental component of human desire?

FJS: No, I don't believe that kind of causal imputation about *Hamlet* is the correct historical scenario. If it were, and if, on average, one psychiatrist in a thousand was likely to think about psychopathology in similar terms, Freud's own ideas would have been anticipated by tens of thousands of medical practitioners during the three centuries that preceded his own development of these ideas. *Hamlet* and *Oedipus Rex* are simply not enough. But having grown up in the context of the late-19th-century Darwinian viewpoint on human development, someone like Freud could say [snaps his fingers] that this kind of perspective supplies one with a scientific theory about human development. *Then* the examples from literature take on a new and very different meaning. The fundamental causal chain proceeds, then, from biology and medicine to clinical psychology (including Freud's self-analysis) and then to the relevance of admittedly powerful literary illustrations.

I think this whole question of cause and effect in Freud's thinking comes down to the following difference in opinion between us. People such as I, who have a natural sciences background, would like to ground their story of Freud's intellectual development in the natural sciences. People who are trained in the humanities naturally want the humanities to play a more central role in the story. Now, as I'm sure you will agree, it doesn't matter what any of us may want; all that matters is what actually happened. And Freud himself was solidly grounded in, more than anything else, the natural sciences, the domain of knowledge that gave his theories, as he once commented, their "indispensable organic foundation without which a medical man can only feel ill at ease in the life of the psyche."[80] That was Freud's core identity. He was trying to develop what he personally considered to be a natural science. He was extremely concerned that his theory be a reductionist scientific theory. He would have hated the notion that psychoanalysis is a fundamentally hermeneutic discipline, although hermeneutics played an important role in his thinking and methods.

PLR: You've warned against the danger of giving too much weight to confirmatory evidence. Yet you don't seem to realize that there is anything problematic in equating your version of the story of Freud's intellectual development with the truth. "What actually happened" to Freud, to use your words, as in history generally, is by no means transparent but is inevitably subject to interpretation. In addition to the passage you quoted, Freud also wrote in the 1935 Postscript

---

80. Letter of April 19, 1908. In *The Freud / Jung Letters: The Correspondence between Sigmund Freud and C. G. Jung* (1974), ed. William McGuire, trans. Ralph Manheim & R. F. C. Hull. Princeton, NJ: Princeton University Press, pp. 140–141.

to *An Autobiograpical Study* that, "after a lifelong *détour* through the natural sciences," his interests had "returned to the cultural problems which had fascinated me long before, when I was a youth."[81] So I think your conception of Freud's "core identity" as simply that of a natural scientist is too narrow, though this was of course one component of his extraordinarily complex make-up. As early as *Studies on Hysteria*, Freud said that it struck him as strange that his case histories "should read like short stories and . . . lack the serious stamp of science."[82] Hence, not only was Freud more than a natural scientist, but his texts have to be understood with the tools of literary criticism.

FJS: That particular remark in *Studies on Hysteria* is neither here nor there. Such a statement is equivalent to Freud's saying that anecdotal evidence, in and of itself, isn't science even though it's often great literary material that helps to illustrate the general truths of science. He felt that what he was doing was strange precisely because he was trained in natural science and strongly identified with this training.

PLR: That's true, but he was employing a discourse that came out of literature.

FJS: Not exactly. Like any clinician, Freud found it necessary to illustrate general medical principles by using stories, and that was a far cry from having been trained to explore the neuroanatomy of *Petromyzon*. But arriving at the kind of certainty of scientific knowledge exemplified by the neuroanatomy of *Petromyzon* is really the level at which he ultimately wanted to do science, even if he had to reach that level of theoretical certainty by illustrating his theories with case histories that seem like episodes from a novel.

PLR: Again, you're reducing literature to the status of a decorative illustration rather than treating it as a source of knowledge in its own right. Freud was a *writer* as well as a scientist, and he often found himself taking the side of the poets against the scientific wisdom of his day.

FJS: But that's not causal. Rather, it's largely *tactical*, in my view, at least. With any behavioral theory one can think of, there has almost

---

81. Sigmund Freud (1925), *An Autobiographical Study. Standard Edition*, 20:72. London: Hogarth Press, 1959.

82. Josef Breuer & Sigmund Freud (1895), *Studies on Hysteria. Standard Edition*, 2:160. London: Hogarth Press, 1955.

always been some poet or other who's said much the same thing. So if one happens to be in the scientific minority by having advocated a set of unpopular theoretical viewpoints, one can usefully cite a famous poet who said much the same thing and then say, "Well, you see that everything I have found was said before me by great poets." That sort of effective tactic is neither here nor there when it comes to the origin of Freud's biomedical theories.

The fact is that Freud, as I have said before, was trying to base his theories solidly in natural science. At the same time, he was also a smart, highly literate fellow who naturally did his best to dress up his theories by illustrating them with as many literary embellishments as he could. If one is attempting to write an intellectual biography of Freud, one needs to go beyond Freud's literary allusions to account for the fundamental axioms that empower his theory of psychosocial development. These fundamental ideas include his theories about fixation, repression, regression, psychosexual stages, the whole of the libido theory, and so on. In addition to all this, one needs to account for the origins of those closely related ideas that make up Freud's theory of dreaming, where one encounters his appeal to mental hydraulics, dynamic mechanisms such as condensation and displacement, and similar concepts that Freud borrowed mostly from contemporary neurphysiology. These ways of thinking are closely allied to Freud's *Project for a Scientific Psychology*.[83]

How this complicated theoretical system of interlocking ideas works to explain the neuroses—*this* is the very core of psychoanalytic theory. This set of biomedical ideas is also the heart of what, as a biographer, one needs to account for. What I tried to do in my book was to focus directly on this conceptual core and pay careful attention to the influences that allowed this intellectual core to emerge. There is no way that this conceptual core to Freud's psychoanalytic theorizing can be explained by his readings of poets, playwrights, novelists, or philosophers. The key ideas at this core came from 19th-century medical biology. Believe me, if I had found some Greek tragedy that Freud had read and that I felt had exerted a fundamental, causal influence on his development of his theory, I would have said so.

PLR: How about *Oedipus Rex*?

---

83. Sigmund Freud (1895), *Project for a Scientific Psychology*. In Marie Bonaparte, Anna Freud & Ernst Kris, eds. (1950), *The Origins of Psychoanalysis: Letters to Wilhelm Fliess, Drafts and Notes: 1887–1902*, trans. Eric Mosbacher & James Strachey. New York: Basic Books, 1971, pp. 355–445.

FJS: [pause] I think that, if Sophocles had never lived, Freud would still have developed the Oedipus complex as a theoretical notion. Now, what he would have called this complex is another matter entirely. Obviously, he would not have been able to avail himeself of Sophocles' name for the mythical Theban king. But Freud would surely have found another name for this concept.

PLR: I doubt that the Oedipus complex by any other name would have smelled as sweet. [laughs]

FJS: Still, Freud did not need Sophocles to come up with the basic concept. Other people in Freud's day had discussed this whole issue, including Westermarck, who dealt with the question of incest avoidance from an anthropological perspective.[84] Freud could have read all about this general topic without ever having had any knowledge of that wonderful Greek tragedy by Sophocles. So I don't view Freud's knowledge of this play as being at all central to his most fundamental psychoanalytic claims. Of course, the fact that the play is so well known and provided a universal illustration of the concept is clearly important at another level, but it does not appear to have caused Freud to have hit on the idea in the first place. It certainly did, however, allow him to communicate this idea in a particularly effective manner. At least that's my view on this matter.

PLR: But Westermarck's theory that the incest taboo stems from an innate aversion among people reared together is the opposite of Freud's, for whom it is a prohibition on unconscious desire. And when Freud wanted to assert the universality of his vision of early childhood experience, the Oedipus myth as presented by Sophocles was indispensable to him.

FJS: I agree, although I would say that the Oedipus myth was "particularly useful" to Freud rather than being "indispensable."

PLR: Still, the Oedipus complex exemplifies Freud's fusion of scientific and literary cultures. This fusion becomes part of psychoanalysis.

FJS: Again, I agree, as long as we are clear that this fusion occurred largely at the level of *communicating* the theory rather than causing the theory to arise in the first place.

PLR: Freud's style of drawing universal generalizations on the basis

---

84. Edward A. Westermarck (1891), *The History of Human Marriage*. 3 vols. London: Macmillan, 1921.

of particular cases is itself indebted to a strategy that we could call philosophical or literary. He finds something to be true of himself, he finds it in a patient, and he sees it to be enacted in a literary work, and therefore he can say that it is the fate of all of us to have this desire.

FJS: I don't know if I really buy that interpretation. First of all, a style of reasoning that generalizes from a single case is also generally called bad science. Freud had his considerable shortcomings as a scientist. These shortcomings included drawing generalizations consistent with a preconceived theory, which he then failed to test adequately, rather than simply generalizing from too few observations. It was the preconceived theories that tended to make single observations so powerful in Freud's mind. The Oedipus complex is a case in point. To conceive the idea of the Oedipus complex one doesn't need much more than to think that the child is sexual but must repress most of that premature sexuality. As Freud first conceived of them, the child's forms of sexuality are perverse and in conflict with civilization. This, incidentally, was one of Fliess's bioenergetic and biogenetic theories, as Freud himself acknowledged in print.[85] The energy for higher social and mental functions comes from the repression of sex during childhood, which repression, in turn, produces "sublimation" of this sexual energy. Therefore, if the child is truly sexual, the child will inevitably have sexual feelings toward the opposite-sex parent, and this kind of sexual attraction clearly has to be repressed. Well, now you're talking about the Oedipus complex.

PLR: Does the biogenetic law explicitly involve incest?

FJS: No, not directly. Freud was the one person who came to the conclusion that one could merge the two concepts together and end up with the basic logic of *Totem and Taboo*.[86]

PLR: The two concepts being?

FJS: The first one is that ontogeny recapitulates phylogeny—not just *any* phylogeny, but the sexual phylogeny of our species. This means that the child is destined to pass through adult sexual stages of all our ancestors.

PLR: And the second concept?

FJS: Then Freud needed the notion of the repression of incestuous

---

85. Sulloway, *Freud, Biologist of the Mind*, pp. 175–179.

86. Sigmund Freud (1913), *Totem and Taboo. Standard Edition*, 13:1–161. London: Hogarth Press, 1955.

feelings. Of course, Freud reached that particular idea in part through his clinical work, although his preconceived theories also played a role in the kind of clinical "evidence" he encountered. He became convinced that repression is a source of all neuroses. Then he became convinced that the only targets of repression are sexual feelings. This meant that the only true cause of neuroses in Freudian theory had to be the repression of sexual feelings or experiences. Now enter the biogenetic law. Given this evolutionary principle, what becomes repressed is inevitably the "polymorphously perverse" nature of sexuality in childhood. What, then, are some of the specific forms that this perversity takes? Oral, anal, and also incestual. Finally, oedipal conflict could be related directly back to Darwin's ideas, in *The Descent of Man*, about mankind's original living conditions in a "primal horde" ruled by a single dominant male.[87]

PLR: And so the emphasis on incest—right or wrong—is Freud's contribution?

FJS: Yes, to a certain extent, although, like so many of Freud's ideas, this one has its precursors (in the work of Westermarck, for example). For Freud, the importance of incestuous impulses arose almost the moment he abandoned the seduction theory and accepted Fliess's alternative viewpoint, namely, that the infant possesses its own internal, periodic sexual chemistry. Sooner or later, Freud was bound to realize that one of the great potential conflicts inherent in such a self-generating kind of infantile sexuality was that sexual impulses may be expressed toward a parent. According to Freud, these sorts of inappropriate sexual impulses were going to have to be repressed, and that, of course, is the essence of the Oedipus complex. In short, as soon as Freud started down that biogenetic route, this particular aspect of his theories was in the cards.

PLR: If it was all so inevitable, one might wonder why no one else had arrived at this synthesis already. Did Fliess talk much about fantasy? He certainly had the concept of infantile sexuality, but I wonder whether Freud's emphasis on fantasy isn't distinctive.

FJS: I don't think there's any evidence from Fliess's writings, one way or the other, about what he thought on the subject. I guess he would have tended to be less interested than Freud in fantasy and to have interpreted sexual fantasies as the sublimated derivatives of the biorhythmic processes that he believed to be driving the developmental system.

---

87. Sulloway, *Freud, Biologist of the Mind*, p. 372.

PLR: So Freud's idea that "there are no indications of reality in the unconscious"[88] is again something that, right or wrong, would have been distinctively his?

FJS: Yes, there's no evidence that Fliess had any thoughts on that particular subject. Still, Fliess's general theory of human development strongly implied that psychic reality (fantasies) could be just as clinically relevant to psychopathology as life experiences. As soon as Freud began to elaborate a psychosexual theory of development that included an active Fliessian core to it and is "recapitulatory" in the Haeckelian sense . . .

PLR: Not the Hegelian sense? [laughs]

FJS: No, Haeckelian.

PLR: I know.

FJS: Well, I am glad we don't have to haggle over Hegel. [laughs] Within this biogenetic perspective, the issue of the extent to which a child's sexual experiences are largely psychological rather than just physical was inevitably going to arise. It's really not much of a conceptual leap. The crucial step for Freud was when he decided that fantasy could sometimes have an importance even greater than reality. Why did he take that step? I think he did so for a very simple reason: there weren't enough cases of childhood sexual abuse or "seduction," as he often termed those experiences, to create the number of "neurotics" found in society because (a) seduction couldn't be *that* widespread and, more important, (b) many people who were known to have had sexual experiences as children did not become ill as adults. Those two conclusions, which Freud spelled out in his September 21, 1897 letter to Fliess, killed the seduction theory deader than a doornail.[89]

There were a couple of different sources of evidence that caused Freud to change his mind on the issue of whether or not sexual experiences in childhood inevitably led to neurosis. Freud later credited Havelock Ellis in this regard. Freud claimed that it was his reading of accounts of childhood sexual activity like those described by Ellis in 1903 that finally made him realize that the seduction theory was wrong.[90] But it clearly wasn't Ellis who was the original source of

88. Letter of September 21, 1897. In Masson, ed., *Freud–Fliess Letters*, p. 264.

89. Masson, ed., *Freud–Fliess Letters*, pp. 264–266.

90. Sigmund Freud (1905), *Three Essays on the Theory of Sexuality, Standard*

those accounts. It was somebody that Freud apparently did not want to mention. I am convinced that Freud had in mind Albert Moll's book *Untersuchungen über die Libido Sexualis*.[91]

PLR: Of 1897?

FJS: Yes. In that book, which Freud read in two unbound parts in the spring and fall of 1897, Moll stated very clearly that, of the numerous kids in German boarding schools who had childhood sexual experiences—Moll had personally conducted a systematic study on this subject—very few later developed perversions or other problems. In Freud's theory, a neurosis is a "repressed perversion," so the same conclusion applies to neuroses. If, for example, one encounters a large sample of people who engaged in homosexual experiences as children, almost none of whom developed perversions or other problems as adults, even fewer of them ought to have developed neuroses, because the number of people who would have subjected these experiences to pathological repression is smaller than the total number. So, on the basis of this new evidence, Freud's seduction theory was suddenly in big trouble.

Felix Gattel, Freud's erstwhile friend and collaborator, was doing some of the same kind of research that Albert Moll was conducting in his systematic interviews with normal individuals. Gattel's research involved conducting clinical interviews in Krafft-Ebing's clinic. Krafft-Ebing was a world-famous psychiatrist who specialized in the problems of sexual perversions. The same difficulty cropped up in the research that Gattel conducted at Krafft-Ebing's clinic: people who weren't hysterics or other kinds of neurotics commonly reported sexual experiences in childhood. It's obvious why Freud later didn't want to credit Albert Moll, by the way. The two were rivals, and Moll later attacked psychoanalysis, so that seaied his fate in the psychoanalytically oriented history books. But I think it was primarily Moll's book, reinforced by Gattel's similar findings, that triggered Freud's final abandonment of the seduction theory. As for Gattel, he and Freud later had a falling out over guess what—the issue of scientific priority. For that reason, Freud was hardly inclined to credit Gattel for having helped to torpedo the seduction theory.

PLR: In a footnote to *Freud, Biologist of the Mind*, you refer to Freud as a birth order "hybrid," whereas in *Born to Rebel* you treat him as

---

Edition, 7:190–191n. London: Hogarth Press, 1953. See Sulloway, *Freud, Biologist of the Mind*, pp. 312–313.

91. See Footnote 9.

a classic firstborn.[92] Did your thinking about Freud's birth-order dynamics change?

FJS: Yes.

PLR: Could you explain why? He had two half-brothers and a nephew who were older, though he was the eldest child of his own parents' marriage.

FJS: When I wrote my book on Freud, I was thinking much more along the lines of Freud's own emphasis on the pertinacity of early impressions than I later concluded was justified. It's pretty clear from statistical evidence involving people whose birth-order status changed in the course of their lives that what I call the influence of "functional" birth order is continuous and relatively evenly proportioned throughout childhood. If one goes through half of childhood as a functional firstborn and then becomes a functional laterborn, about half of that portion of one's personality that is shaped by birth order will have been molded by each of the two family niches occupied during childhood.

PLR: How could someone become a functional laterborn?

FJS: It could happen via some disruption of the original family system, which would then make a biological firstborn into a younger sibling, if one's parents remarry and one acquires stepsiblings, for example. The important point is that there's no magic first three years that account for, say, 80% of the variance in personality, with the remaining years of childhood not really mattering all that much. Incidentally, it is because Freud believed in the role of early experience that he emphasized his rivalrous relationship with his nephew John, which lasted until Freud was three years old, when John's family moved to England. When I was first thinking about the possible importance of birth order, I viewed Freud's life more the way he did, in which case the first few years are presumed to count a lot. But in my later research I obtained abundant empirical evidence from people whose functional birth orders changed owing to a disruption to the original family system. This kind of biographical information showed that the first three years didn't count as much as Freud (or I) had thought.

PLR: So if someone becomes a functional firstborn because of sibling loss, that wouldn't be terribly significant? How does your approach weigh the impact of such a potentially traumatic event?

92. Sulloway, *Freud, Biologist of the Mind*, p. 363n2; and *Born to Rebel*, p. 56.

FJS: The crucial issue is, at what age does a person's family niche change? Because the influence of family niches is a continuous developmental process in which each year of childhood counts almost as much as every other year, what one really wants to know is how much of childhood, proportionally, did a given person spend in any given family niche. Freud put a great deal of emphasis on the first three years, so he tended to view himself as a birth-order hybrid. On the basis of my theoretical presuppositions, by the way, I would love to have been able to claim Freud as a psychological laterborn, but he really wasn't.

PLR: And the half-brothers from his father's first marriage?

FJS: The problem with counting them as Freud's elder siblings from a *functional* birth-order perspective is that they were 21 and 23 years older.

PLR: So, in effect, they weren't siblings?

FJS: Right. Freud was functionally a firstborn relative to his own younger siblings. As for Freud's nephew John, there's no evidence that the two of them lived together in the same house. They merely played together on occasion. So Freud appears to have been reading far more into that relationship than was really there. In my computerized data base of the historical evidence used in *Born to Rebel*, which includes more than 6,000 people, I list Freud as the first of six children. In this connection, I followed a formal rule in *Born to Rebel* by which people were coded according to their functional birth order. I was later criticized by one reviewer for not coding everybody according to biological birth order, but that's absurd. In any event, because most people's biological and functional birth orders are the same, that distinction affected such a small percentage of my sample that it made absolutely no difference for the overall results. This distinction affects about 3% or 4% of the sample. Alan Woolf made a big deal about this issue in his review of my book in *The New Republic*.[93] He was all worked up about the fact that I was studying not literally *birth* order but, rather, sibling-rearing order. This is the kind of nit-picking sophistry that one sees in a reviewer who wants to be critical about a book but who doesn't really have anything intelligent to say on the subject and so grasps at straws. Had Woolf read the foot-

---

93. Alan Woolf (1996), "Up from Scientism: What Birth Order and Darwinism Can't Explain." Review of *Born to Rebel* by Frank J. Sulloway, *The New Republic*, December 23, pp. 29–35. See also Frank Sulloway's letter to the editor and Woolf's reply, *The New Republic*, February 3, 1997, pp. 4–5, 48.

notes and appendix to my book, he would have seen the full evidence substantiating the importance of functional birth order and the sometimes misleading value of biological birth order.

By the way, the formal classification rule I followed was that a person had to establish a functional birth order during the first six years of life and had to remain in that functional birth order past the age of 16. If, for example, one grew up as a functional firstborn for the first three years and then became a functional laterborn for the rest of one's childhood, I counted this person as a functional laterborn. But if a person passed his or her seventh birthday and this person's birth order changed, I excluded the person from the sample. I also conducted a separate statistical analysis of such cases in which functional birth order changed and found that my classification rule accorded well with the evidence regarding attitudes in adulthood toward radical changes. In particular, firstborns who were raised as functional laterborns were significantly more likely than other firstborns to support radical social and scientific revolutions.[94]

PLR: So you abandoned the hybrid category?

FJS: Well, I didn't quite abandon it. Instead I refined it through empirical testing. By means of such tests, I was able to show that sibling strategies (for which birth order is merely a proxy) exert a continuous, steady, and cumulative impact on personality throughout the course of early life. This result, by the way, is an effective test of the importance of the first three years of life on personality development. For this and other reasons (for example, the evidence from behavioral genetic studies), I no longer believe in the fundamental importance of the first three years of life the way I once did. Sometimes such seemingly plausible ideas just don't turn out to be true. That's what science is all about.

PLR: Maybe we should let that be the last word. Thanks.

---

94. Sulloway, *Born to Rebel*, pp. 47, 465–81.

Roy Schafer

This Is My Calling

Peter L. Rudnytsky: In reading your work, I noticed that you said your "passionate and faithful adherence" to psychoanalysis began in your sophomore year of college.[1] Could you tell me how that came about?

Roy Schafer: Yes. I took a Psych 1 course at City College in New York City. It was a filler in my schedule. I was planning to be a physics major, with no particular enthusiasm, only because I had gotten good marks in high school. That was during the Depression. I considered it a high ideal to be able to become a high school teacher with a steady income because poverty was the first consideration. But the relatively new faculty at City College, assembled by Gardner Murphy, were young, bright, progressive psychologists. We were assigned, in addition to all the standard works, Freud's *General Introduction to Psychoanalysis*. And that was it for me. I had the experience that "this is my calling, and I have to find some way to be in psychology." I wasn't specifically thinking of becoming an analyst, because once I started taking psych courses I was taking social psychology, physiological psychology, and so forth from enormously bright, cutting-edge sorts of guys. The whole field fascinated me, except animal psychology, which I didn't much care for—and I still don't. But before long I felt that I wanted to become an analyst. Through Murphy, who knew a number of analysts, I had a chance to talk to one or two, who discouraged me, because I was not planning to go to medical school. At that time, it was a real barrier.

---

1. Roy Schafer (1974), "The Evolution of My Views on Nonnormative Sexual Practices." In *Tradition and Change in Psychoanalysis*. Madison, CT: International Universities Press, 1997, p. 249.

PLR: Of course.

RS: So I thought, "Well, I hate the idea of going to medical school, and I'll do something in psychology." Clinical psychology was not yet a field, but there were a few people working in child guidance clinics or state hospitals doing testing. And that was already interesting enough. So I said, "I'm going to go ahead and do it anyway." This was against family opposition because they found out that it was not a field. There were virtually no jobs. It was a ridiculous way to "throw myself away." I was an A student, and it was a "waste" of myself.

PLR: Did their attitude apply to psychology generally or to psychoanalysis in particular?

RS: It applied to psychology generally, but my specific interest at that point was in becoming an analyst. It seemed hopeless. The war was on then. It was in the early 40s; I hadn't been drafted yet. And, before I graduated, along came David Rapaport from the Menninger Clinic. He needed a research assistant in his work on testing. He had a grant, and he had a sponsorship that would enable him to get me a draft deferment until the project was finished. Which they did. I went to Menningers'—again against family opposition—and I worked with Rapaport for a little over two years. We finished the research, and I was drafted shortly before V.E. Day. I was still going through various forms of basic training when V.J. Day came, so I never served in combat.

Then the Menningers started a massive program of training psychiatrists that by now had caught on in a way that it never had before. There was a form of discharge from the Army for agricultural workers and others called "for the convenience of the government." So I was discharged in a year. I came back to the Menninger Clinic with only a bachelor's degree, and I was teaching not only psychiatrists but psychologists, who were getting paid five times as much as I was, how to do testing in this progressive way. We were then the cutting edge. Nobody else was doing what we were doing. And I was proficient at it. Then I hoped at least to get analyzed. It didn't work out at the Menninger Clinic because there was all the competition from the new psychiatrists. I tried to go to graduate school in psychology at Berkeley, because that was the hot place, and get analyzed by Erik Erikson, who had lectured at the Menninger Clinic. That didn't work out because his time was filled. Then the Director of Psychotherapy at Menningers' moved to the Austen Riggs Center as Director and asked me to come as his psychologist. He offered me analysis as an inducement. He was idealized by everyone. So I went.

PLR: Was that Robert Knight?

RS: Yes.

PLR: When did you go to Austen Riggs?

RS: In 1947.

PLR: And when did Erikson move to Riggs?

RS: Erikson moved in 1950, after the huge Loyalty Oath fight. The only two people I know of who stuck it out were two psychoanalysts, Nevitt Sanford, who stayed in California, and Erikson, who lost his job at the University of California and came to Riggs. So that was it. I was getting training in psychotherapy from a psychoanalytic point of view. Working with Rapaport, I had learned the new ego-psychological theories inside out because he was using them on the tests. Then the staff at Riggs and a few Menninger analysts who moved to New Haven decided to start an analytic institute.

PLR: The Western New England?

RS: The Western New England. It took a while, but in 1954 they began classes. They started me in classes, though there was as yet no provision for my getting clinical training. A couple of years later, the American Psychoanalytic Association, at their initiative and with the support of some influential people, set up a program called Research Candidate Waivers. Under this program, applicants would be accepted who had already demonstrated they had a contribution to make in psychology or other fields; they would bring psychoanalysis to those fields and not become practitioners. I had already not only been listed as collaborator on two basic books on testing[2] but had also written a sequel of my own.[3] So I had something to show for it. I was very young at the time. I went to Menninger when I was 20. I wrote my book when I was about 24.

PLR: How old were you when you graduated from City College?

RS: Twenty. In fact, I was lacking one course, but I took a substitute course with permission in Kansas, and I graduated.

PLR: Wasn't Rapaport also a psychologist, rather than an M.D.?

---

2. David Rapaport & Roy Schafer (1945–1946), *Diagnostic Psychological Testing*, Vol. I & II. Chicago: Yearbook Publishers.

3. Roy Schafer (1948), *The Clinical Application of Psychological Tests*. New York: International Universities Press.

RS: He was a psychologist, an immigrant from Hungary.

PLR: Did he practice as an analyst?

RS: He was never qualified as an analyst or as a member of the American Psychoanalytic Association. He knew as much about psychoanalytic theory as anybody around, but that's all he was interested in. His main writings, after he wrote on testing, were on theory. Then he moved to Riggs, and he taught theory in the Institute. I was in his classes, and I was very advanced. Just about the time I was ready to graduate, about five years later, he wanted to give up his introductory theory courses, and they turned them over to me. So I started teaching shortly before I was qualified.

PLR: Was this already in New Haven?

RS: Yes. I moved to Yale in 1953, and the Institute started in 1954. I taught the courses Rapaport had set up for quite a number of years before I was able to get out of them and teach some other courses.

PLR: Did you enter graduate school at some point for the Ph.D.?

RS: While I was at Riggs, I enrolled at Clark University because I could take courses once a week there in a condensed way. I got my Ph.D. in two years, in 1950. That was long before I applied to the American Psychoanalytic.

PLR: Did you first encounter Robert Knight in Topeka?

RS: Yes.

PLR: When he offered you analysis, was that with himself?

RS: Yes.

PLR: Could we backtrack a little and talk about your family? You said they were hesitant about your career choice.

RS: Yes.

PLR: Do you have brothers and sisters?

RS: I have an older brother, and two younger sisters who are identical twins. He's two years older, and they're two years younger.

PLR: What sort of work do they do?

RS: My brother is a retired music professor. He studied to be a concert pianist. Then he had a career for a number of years in musical comedy, working as an assistant. He even had a number of musical comedies of his own produced, but they were not hits. Then he went back to classical music, and he ended up teaching in the City University system until his retirement some years ago. One of my sisters got a Ph.D. in clinical psychology at the University of Chicago. They both worked initially as secretaries. The other one remained a secretary, got married, and stayed home with the kids. After her husband died, she went to work. She became a university assistant administrator, first at Adelphi, then at NYU. She has remarried and now lives with her husband in Atlanta; they're both retired.

PLR: Could you tell me a little bit about your parents?

RS: My parents were essentially uneducated Jewish immigrants from eastern Europe—Lithuania in my mother's case, and between Russia and Romania in my father's. They both had miserable childhoods. My father was a hardworking semicapitalist. He was one of five partners in a laundry business that never flourished.

PLR: This was in the Bronx?

RS: Yes. During the Depression it flourished even less, because they took in a lot of unemployed family members. So the payroll stayed very small. But we *lived.* We didn't starve. We had a working-class income. My father was also a truck driver for his laundry plant. My mother stayed home until my sisters were in school. Then she went back to work as a dressmaker. She was an expert dressmaker in a union shop in the garment district. They were very full of aspirations for the children, especially for the boys. For the girls, the traditional ideal was to get married and have a family. So my mother, who was the dominant force in this, discouraged them from getting higher education. They took the commercial course and worked as secretaries. My parents liked families to stay together. They liked achievement. Achievement was on their mind. They never got educated and never really knew what I was doing. But they were proud to have my books on the front hall table where people would see them. And they played up my brother's musical accomplishments.

PLR: I wonder what accounts for your discovering Freud in the way that you did and finding psychoanalysis to be your calling.

RS: It's hard to spell that out. What I can say is that my major and prolonged experience in childhood and adolescence was unhappy. A lot of low mood. I was always an achiever in school. I didn't have to be a hard worker because I wasn't in demanding schools, but I was very conscientious. It was part of my character to be the good son because my brother, who was first-born, was the more spoiled one, in conventional terms.

PLR: You mean he was the favorite in some way?

RS: He was my mother's favorite. He thought I was her favorite, because she held me up as an example to him. If I can take time to tell a funny story, we discovered this in our 50s. My mother was then widowed, and we were traveling together to visit her. I casually remarked in the course of conversation, "You were always her favorite." He said, "*I* was her favorite? No, *you* were her favorite."

PLR: It sounds like the Smothers Brothers!

RS: [laughs] So we discovered, after 40 or 50 years of going through this, that we had opposite conceptions of her. But by conventional standards he was the spoiled one. My mother always favored him. She herself had amateur show-business aspirations. She liked to sing at meetings of Jewish women, family parties, and stuff like that. So she lived through his musicality. That made it difficult for me. On the other hand, she cultivated him, so it was a circular process.

PLR: So you became, so to say, the good son.

RS: That was my niche. It fits in with inborn temperamental factors. He was a very fussy baby from birth; I was a very docile baby from birth. That kind of thing.

PLR: Did you then have a certain kind of closeness with your father that your brother didn't have?

RS: No. My father was a pretty shut-in man. His own childhood had been pretty bad. He was hardworking and devoted, but uncommunicative. His idea of play, insofar as we played at all, once we were old enough to be in school, was to be intellectually competitive. He would throw out multiplication problems at the dinner table to see who could do the mental arithmetic. [both laugh] It wasn't long before I was better than he was. [laughs] And that caused some awkward moments.

PLR: So your discovery of Freud provided a way of looking at the world that rang true.

RS: Yes, and of understanding myself and other people. And, when I took these other psych courses, a way of understanding the social world and the physiological world. It really opened up a vibrant life to me, which I felt I hadn't had previously.

PLR: I think that anyone who becomes a psychoanalyst or dedicates himself to the field in some way is doing it in order to engage in self-exploration.

RS: Yes, although, when you analyze yourself or other people, there's also a reparative urge to cure your parents, particularly your mother. It's very common.

PLR: I think the depressed mother is common.

RS: Yes, but it can also be to understand the narcissistic mother.

PLR: If we move back to your experience in analysis with Robert Knight, could you give me some sense of what that was like?

RS: It was a very bad analysis because it was within a small staff in a small town. Stockbridge is now much more cosmopolitan, but at its heart it's still a narrow, provincial town. There were no Jews living in town. There was one Jewish tailor. There were no Jews in the country club. In other words, there resulted a very in-grown, incestuous kind of atmosphere among the staff, most of whom were outsiders. And to be in analysis with your boss, whom you saw at staff conferences, at social functions, and heard people talking about—it's the wrong way to be in analysis. He also let me end it early, really for no good reason at all, I think, except maybe he was finding it burdensome too. As an analyst, I know how much he must have felt constantly scrutinized. Anyway, I had to go into analysis later in New Haven. I had a better analysis.

PLR: How long did the first analysis last?

RS: Two years. It was too short. Although he was a brilliant clinician by everybody's standards, I think he was a pretty uninspired analyst. Analysis is not doing ordinary psychotherapy. It's a very different kind of thing. My second analyst was a real analyst. Robert Knight was a good psychoanalytic psychiatrist. But not many people agree with my view of him. He was extremely idealized. Tall, silver-haired, fair, judicious, good-looking. He had all the attributes.

PLR: Was he a WASP?

RS: Oh, yes. A midwestern WASP. Golfer, athlete.

PLR: So there was the non-Jewish factor. A country-club type.

RS: Yes.

PLR: Was he idealized by his analysands, or just by people on his staff?

RS: By some of his analysands whom I've talked to.

PLR: I noted a passage where you wrote about your first analysis in which you said that you hated your analyst.

RS: I never said that. Hated him personally? No. Like any analysand, I must have in part unconsciously hated him.

PLR: This is from *The Analytic Attitude* [reads]: "I had to a significant extent continued to hate my analyst for having been, as I experienced it, remote and ungiving; that aspect of my negative transference had simply not been dealt with adequately in that analysis."[4]

RS: I'm not referring there to an ego-syntonic emotion. When the analysis ended, I was trying to idealize it. I was still under the aura.

PLR: So, at the time, you felt it was actually a good experience for you?

RS: I tried to think so, but within a couple of years I knew that it was not. And so it was in retrospect that I realized that. It's different from coming out of analysis knowing that you hate your analyst.

PLR: Isn't it more disturbing to come out of it thinking that one has had a good experience—as you say, trying to idealize it—and not even recognizing that there were areas of dissatisfaction?

RS: It's not rare. [laughs] Not rare in the field. One of the hard things that a conscientious analyst has to do is to keep bringing out the negative feelings. A lot of patients, especially at the end—when they want to justify their analytic experience or to quiet their insecurity about the future—will want to leave on a good, unambivalent note. So you have to be vigilant up to the *last second*!

PLR: Doesn't it seem unanalytic to want to be unambivalent?

RS: Well, in terms of what's going on unconsciously the patient is ambivalent throughout analysis. Initially, the ambivalence can often be used to hide the good feelings because of defensiveness, but later on the emphasis can shift very much. You hear resentments, bitching, that kind of stuff. But to find really deep transference hatred you have to look very hard. I sometimes joke, "We're in a crazy profession. We work our asses off to get our patients to hate us!" [PLR laughs] But it takes a lot of skill, tact, careful timing, and a long perspective. You have to analyze your own countertransference because it's nice to work in a cozy atmosphere. So you have to fight yourself as well as the patient.

PLR: It's easy to think the positive transference is what makes the analysis go forward and not to see it as a defensive coping mechanism.

4. Roy Schafer (1979), "On Becoming a Psychoanalyst of One Persuasion or Another." In *The Analytic Attitude*. New York: Basic Books, 1983, p. 285.

RS: Oh, yes. Often it seems to make the analysis go forward.

PLR: Didn't Freud try to present it that way in the concept of the therapeutic alliance?

RS: He did in terms of getting the analysis started, but after that he thought the basic transference took over so that the patient was locked in with you for all kinds of reasons. And then he knew there was a lot of hatred and a lot of guilt.

PLR: Is all emotion that arises in the analysis a transference experience? This would imply something that is not reality based since it has its source in the past of a person's life and is not justified in terms of the present context.

RS: In my current orientation to clinical work, which is very much along the lines of the contemporary Kleinians of London, I take the following position. There certainly can be realistic things to have feelings about. They don't deny it, and I don't deny it. Nobody would deny that. But it is not likely that anything significant, however justified, does not at the same time have connections to all kinds of infantile sources. So that when we look at anything that comes up from the standpoint of transference, we're not saying that it's nothing but transference. What we're saying is, "For analytic purposes, what is the transference in this reaction?" Suppose I forget to tell a patient I'm taking a long weekend. I tell him at the last minute, and he's offended. Now, that's a sign of countertransference, probably. I usually give advance warning. There could be all kinds of reasons why he could be annoyed by that. He could have made plans, and now it's too late. So he'll get irritated. But there's a lot to analyze—potentially. You may not be able to. First of all, he's likely to be conflicted about being irritated. So there's a defensive response to work out. Then it's likely to get tied in with how he's been overlooked, neglected, undervalued, felt that his parents wished to get rid of him, or whatever the transference might be. That's going to enter into it. It may not be worth pursuing in a particular case. But it's a question in your mind: "What is the transference?" So that's the position I would take.

PLR: You seem to have had a change of heart about the Kleinians. In *A New Language for Psychoanalysis*, you said that "the Kleinians have carried the reification of metapsychology to a grotesque extreme."[5]

---

5. Roy Schafer (1976), *A New Language for Psychoanalysis*. New Haven, CT: Yale University Press, p. 3.

RS: Yes.

PLR: That was back in 1976. But now you've edited a book on the Kleinians and spoken in positively glowing terms about Betty Joseph and Hanna Segal.[6] What accounts for this change in your views of the Kleinian contribution?

RS: There are a number of things. I still maintain what I said about the basic Kleinian metapsychology as it existed then. A lot of it still exists, and I don't think it's good theory. But the modern British Kleinians have developed a technique that has a lot in common with the best of modern ego psychology, although it's conceived in different terms and is executed differently. But it's not strange, which is why in England the Freudians are no longer so antagonistic to the Kleinians. And that's why people in this country—in San Francisco, Cleveland, some parts of New York, and other places—are getting more and more interested. They're importing British Kleinians to lecture, to give honorific talks, and so on. The Kleinians have changed their emphasis almost exclusively to technique. And technically they have changed. Whereas in Melanie Klein's heyday the emphasis was on making quick and lengthy interpretations back to infantile experience, they don't do that now. They're hardly interested in the past or reconstruction, except in a general sense that what they interpret now must have its origins. Patients are always talking about their past.

So in my own analytic work, as in theirs, a lot of the dialogue pertains to the past, but the emphasis is on what is happening now. How can we understand it? Not how can we understand its origins, but how can we understand its present fabric? From that, certain general things about the past can be assumed. Memories are not trusted, because it's known that memories change during analysis and personal history is untrustworthy anyway. So they hear them and take them into account, but they don't base too much on memory in and of itself. Whereas formerly they extrapolated back into the past freely, they don't do that now. So I feel at home with that.

The last factor I would mention is that my own work on action language, the analytic attitude, and narration had already led me to develop my own technical way of working, a way that was not vastly

---

6. See Roy Schafer, ed. (1997), *The Contemporary Kleinians of London*. Madison, CT: International Universities Press; and Schafer (1995), "Blocked Introjection/Blocked Incorporation." In *Tradition and Change*, pp. 111–120; and Schafer (1992), "Betty Joseph Live." In *Tradition and Change*, pp. 157–160.

different from what they were doing. I was working more and more with the transference, with the here-and-now situation, and not being as intellectualistic as I had been about explaining things in terms of the past. So having discovered the turn they had taken since the late 1970s, I believe I have learned an enormous amount from them in honing my skills further. I didn't feel the shift so much as a personal revolution. The bigger revolution was to begin to use their language in talking about clinical practice. But I don't think they have a good theory.

PLR: What about non-Kleinian object relations theory? You don't write as much about Balint, Fairbairn, or even Winnicott, whom you do, of course, cite occasionally. It seems as though the Kleinians have had a greater impact on your thinking than has the Independent tradition of object relations theory. Is there some reason for that?

RS: Well, there have been interesting pieces by those people, and I've read some, including Fairbairn's *Psychoanalytic Studies of the Personality.*[7] I also for a while was very impressed by Charles Rycroft when he was in his heyday, writing theoretical papers. He was the first person I looked up when I went to England in 1975 on the Freud Professorship at University College, London. He was gracious enough to take me to his club for a chat. But I always felt that the others were spinoffs from Melanie Klein. Winnicott and Fairbairn were basically Kleinian in orientation. Winnicott's first collection of papers, *Through Paediatrics to Psycho-Analysis,*[8] was clearly Kleinian. And then he gradually developed what I call his own poetic form of psychoanalysis.

PLR: I think that Winnicott was greatly influenced by his relationship with Melanie Klein, and his second analyst was Joan Riviere; but there is a difference, in my view, between the Kleinian tradition and the Independent tradition that has to do with the role of the environment. In my way of understanding it, which is perhaps not as sympathetic to the Kleinian tradition as yours, the Kleinian conception of infancy—and by extension of the analytic relationship—concentrates so exclusively on the role of fantasy that it doesn't give enough attention to the way the inner world is formed out of a field that includes the primary caretaker. In the example that you gave

---

7. W. R. D. Fairbairn (1952), *Psychoanalytic Studies of the Personality*. London: Routledge & Kegan Paul.

8. D. W. Winnicott (1958), *Through Paediatrics to Psycho-Analysis*. New York: Basic Books.

of your hypothetical patient whom you failed to notify of the cancellation until the last minute, which had a possible countertransferential motive on your part, the patient would presumably be justified in some kind of inference to that effect. So one possible technical way of handling that would be to say, "I'm sorry that I failed to notify you until the last minute." Some analysts would even consider the possibility of acknowledging the interference of a countertransferential dynamic there.

RS: Mm, hmm.

PLR: One might wonder whether, if the analyst masks that and only analyzes the inner world of the patient's transferential response, that could have a traumatizing effect. People need validation that their perceptions have a certain basis in reality. If that wasn't granted in childhood and it again isn't granted in the analytic encounter, I would be concerned about a possible negative consequence. Of course, one wants to analyze the transference, but isn't there also a need for the analyst to give credit, as it were, where it's due or to acknowledge making a mistake?

RS: Well, I do do that, but I do it selectively, depending on the patient, especially because if you do it quickly you may lose some good analytic material.

PLR: That's interesting.

RS: But we've come to a point here where I would like to go into another aspect of my thinking.

PLR: Sure.

RS: There is an important distinction in this regard between a theory of technique and a theory of personality development and psychopathology. A general theory of personality development and psychopathology has been the ambition of everybody—ego psychologists, Melanie Klein, Winnicott. It doesn't dictate the specifics of technique. So, although the Kleinians are free to acknowledge that especially early childhood events, but also later events, affect a person, their interest is in what unconscious fantasies are stimulated by or play an influential role in shaping the experience of reality. Because they assume—as I assume, and I think the ego psychologists do too—that nothing significant in the so-called real world is experienced without being influenced to some extent by the shaping role of unconscious fantasies.

PLR: I think that's indisputable from a psychoanalytic point of view.

RS: Now, Heinz Hartmann tried to develop a theory that would give recognition to the fact that not everything impinges directly on the unconscious. We develop what he called relatively conflict-free, or autonomous, ego functions.[9] So you can think objectively about situations even when they are personally disturbing to you. And sometimes that's what analysts do. So this was an attempt to recognize theoretically—at least in terms of degree—that not everything has equal access to unconscious influence. I think Hartmann's was a worthy attempt. Hartmann was brilliant and a major figure in that regard. But there are problems with that theory too. What you describe, though, is not a real issue for me. I don't disagree with you. I think that a true-blue Kleinian of today would say to you in response, "Well, yes, but you can't say what that real experience is for any particular individual without knowing how his unconscious fantasies played a role in processing it." So if you said, "Well, certainly a trauma is going to have a big influence," the Kleinian would say, "Sure, but what influence? It could be very different from what you expect." Ego psychologists say the same thing. Anna Freud said the same thing.

PLR: There may be a convergence of perspectives and, as it were, a greater search for common ground in contemporary psychoanalysis. But my concern is that at times the Kleinian position seems to be that fantasy is autonomous, while the role of experience is negligible. Let me read you a passage from Klein's "The Importance of Symbol Formation in the Development of the Ego": "Sadistic phantasies directed against the inside of the mother's body constitute the first and basic relation to the outside world and to reality. The child's earliest reality is wholly phantastic."[10] What do you think about those assertions?

RS: I think Klein had no basis for saying that.

PLR: Right. And what about her belief in the death instinct? In her view, the fundamental relationship of the infant to the primary caretaker is one of hostility, and anything good comes only from the external world if one is lucky.

---

9. Heinz Hartmann (1939), *Ego Psychology and the Problem of Adaptation*, trans. David Rapaport. New York: International Universities Press.

10. Melanie Klein (1930), "The Importance of Symbol Formation in the Development of the Ego." In *The Writings of Melanie Klein*, Vol. 1, ed. R. Money-Kyrle. New York: Free Press, 1984, p. 221.

RS: That's a postulate, as far as I'm concerned, that she used to help her understand other things. The position that would be taken now—and I think there's authority for this in Klein too, because she wrote a lot and, as in Freud, you find different things in different places—is that there are dual instincts, as Freud said, but that at the beginning the strength of aggression relative to libido is predominant. It keeps a lot of the libido functioning in a subordinate position. But then, with any kind of nonpathogenic experience, the aggression can be progressively modulated and the libido is not overwhelmed as much; so that in the depressive position, which regularly (except in extreme situations) succeeds the first position, the emphasis is much more on libido. It's on loss, reparation, concern, and so on. But the aggression is still always active. If you follow Freud and a good many Freudians, they would say the same thing. Now I don't hold with instinct theory, but I think that there is always in everyone's unconscious functioning a good deal of aggression—and aggression-related phenomena like guilt—as well as libido. To understand things, you have to keep track of the manifestations of both.

PLR: But if you don't accept Freud's instinct theory, on what basis do you explain libidinal and aggressive phenomena? If one could show that an infant from the earliest moments of life is engaged in cognitive activity, wouldn't that be sufficient to disprove Klein's contention that "the child's earliest reality is wholly phantastic"?

RS: Well, nobody has access to the infant's mind. Infants do show, according to modern developmental research, including that of Daniel Stern, amazingly early learning of some sort.[11] But the psychic content of that learning is a matter of postulation.

PLR: That's true.

RS: That goes to your more general question. I don't think it's something to be decided by evidence. I said to you what I believe. You always have to look for aggression and libido in some form, not necessarily primitive. But they're probably operating. You don't even have to assume they're equal all the time. But how did they get there? I'm not even sure that's a valid question. If somebody wants to make a theory about how they got there, he sets up certain axioms. Aggression is reactive to frustration. Or aggression is reactive to pain. Or it's there from the beginning but it takes certain experiences to be activated. Whatever. You make up the basic story. It's a matter

---

11. Daniel N. Stern (1985), *The Interpersonal World of the Infant: A View from Psychoanalysis and Developmental Psychology*. New York: Basic Books.

of narration. It's not an evidential thing. From then on you look at phenomena in those terms. But the only evidential aspect that's involved is that by any conventional standard—and here you fall back on convention—you always find in people aggression and libido. Love or sex and self-destruction or destruction. If you look back—and you know this from literature—you can't find a civilization that does not refer to these things. So we know there's something there, and from then on it's a question of what axioms you set up. I don't look for evidence in that area.

PLR: I want to give a greater role than you do to extraclinical research. I agree that we can't know in a direct way what's going on in the mind of an infant. But I think one can demonstrate that an infant exhibits recognition and other signs of learning based on experience from very early on. If you want to use Hartmann's terms, a conflict-free ego sphere is being formed.

RS: No, conflict-free is an assumption. You don't know.

PLR: No, we don't. But there is certainly evidence, it seems to me, that the infant is learning from reality-based perceptions.

RS: Yes, all the studies of attachment show that.[12]

PLR: Exactly.

RS: But that attachment is unambivalent is another matter.

PLR: I'm not saying that.

RS: But that's where assumptions come in.

PLR: We probably have a divergence of emphasis here. I am much closer to Stern's position that the "observed infant" and the "clinical infant" have a lot to say to one another.[13] Klein's statement seems to me to be wholly speculative and, in fact, to be subject to refutation if we can show that the child is learning from day one. If the child's relation to reality is not entirely based on fantasy, that has crucial implications in understanding the importance of the environment in early development and then in any subsequent relationship, including that of analysis. It's an example of how a theoretical position can

---

12. See Joseph D. Lichtenberg (1983), *Psychoanalysis and Infant Research.* Hillsdale, NJ: The Analytic Press; and Susan Goldberg, Roy Muir, & John Kerr, eds. (1995), *Attachment Theory: Social, Developmental, and Clinical Perspectives.* Hillsdale, NJ: The Analytic Press.

13. Stern, *The Interpersonal World of the Infant,* p. 14.

be refuted on the basis of evidence. Why do we no longer accept the drive theory if not because there's no evidence that the mechanism of energy-reduction that Freud postulated actually exists? Empirical studies seem to me to play an indispensable role in sifting out which theories in psychoanalysis continue to be vital and which theories are outmoded. Does that seem true to you?

RS: No, because I think you overestimate the empirical basis of Daniel Stern's work. Stern is reading theory into the infant, in my opinion. You may not think so. He knows that there is some form of contact or communication that goes on because the child is responsive to what's in the mother. If you go back to Melanie Klein's statement, she says that the infant's *experience* of the mother's body is wholly fantastic. There is a mother's body recognized to be in the infant's experience. But what Klein is postulating is that there are already fantasies about that body. Now, she also postulates inborn fantasies, so that's where it becomes more and more "fantastic," if I can use the word here. That's where I think Melanie Klein's theoretical ambitions were not in good hands. She was a very astute clinician. She developed an enormous amount of insight into children and adults. People are still learning from her work, but they're distilling it all the time. And they're not emphasizing these early reconstructions.

PLR: Perhaps the core issue for me is whether psychoanalytic theory, either of a particular school or considered as a totality, is something that can be assessed within any framework outside that of psychoanalysis itself, or can it find its validation only from within its own way of thinking?

RS: That's what I believe.

PLR: I expect you would agree that the implication of the latter view is that psychoanalysis is not scientific in any respect.

RS: Yes, I object to its being called a science.

PLR: In fact, you say that "psychoanalysis is an interpretive discipline, not a natural science."[14]

RS: Yes.

PLR: I agree that psychoanalysis in its clinical practice is an interpretive discipline. But I think that it can be consistent with natural science. As a theory of development, psychoanalysis has to take sci-

---

14. Schafer (1980), "Action and Narration in Psychoanalysis." In *The Analytic Attitude*, p. 255.

entific research into account. The choice, to my mind, is not between science and no science, but between good science and bad science. Freud, in particular, had a great deal invested in certain versions of natural science—Lamarck's theory of the inheritance of acquired characteristics or Haeckel's so-called biogenetic law that ontogeny recapitulates phylogeny—that have since been discredited. But that doesn't mean that sound science doesn't have a lot to contribute to psychoanalysis, as attachment theory does. A good theory has practical benefits and thus can aid rather than contradict the hermeneutic dimension of psychoanalysis.

RS: If you put it that generally, I would agree, but I would say that it's true of every area of human inquiry. I think that the study of history, languages, literature, philosophy, anthropology—anything that brings other points of view with the evidence that is gathered according to those points of view—is a potential source of stimulation. Ernst Kris, who was one of the great theoreticians of ego psychology, said about child developmental studies that they are a good source of hypotheses for psychoanalysis, but not a good source of evidence.[15] And that's how I look at it. All these fields raise questions. Nobody can encompass all learning, but the more educated an analyst is—and Freud tried to be such a person—the greater range of interpretive possibilities he or she can encompass and bring to bear.

So I think that the empirical studies of attachment behavior raise certain questions, and insofar as people have been using another kind of theory of infantile development, they are now—the ego psychologists under Anna Freud's thumb wouldn't even hear of attachment theory—beginning to take it very seriously. But I'm questioning that whole spate of theories, and I don't know yet what would be an adequate solution to the problems. There are ideas that have been useful in doing analysis, and experience is shaped partly by those ideas. They provide a body of assumptions and procedures and inferences and rules of interpretation that allow you to do an analysis. That's as far as I'm willing to go.

PLR: You referred to Kris, but you cite another incident involving Kris when he would go to his wife between sessions and exclaim, "It's true, it's all true!" You juxtapose this with Betty Joseph's statement that "the analyst must always 'rediscover' with each analysand the

---

15. Ernst Kris (1950), "Notes on the Development and on Some Current Problems of Psychoanalytic Child Psychology." In *Selected Papers*. New Haven, CT: Yale University Press, 1975, pp. 54–88.

soundness of the principles guiding the treatment."[16] But if every-thing is true—if we're only rediscovering things we already believe—aren't we in danger of turning psychoanalysis into a religion? If there's no possibility of testing from outside the framework within which one is working, isn't one simply guided by a faith in which each person's set of beliefs is finally as good as anyone else's?

RS: Speaking from within my point of view, I don't think the demand that there be an openness to some kind of scientific testing is made of any other interpretive discipline. The demand is not made of literature, philosophy, history, or anthropology. There are systems of beliefs that are competitive, both within the system and between systems; and by discussion, by challenge, and by reflection people have refined their ideas of psychoanalysis since 1905. I consider that to be development. Whether psychoanalysis is truer now than it was then, in the sense of being a natural or physicalistic science, I don't think is a relevant question. I know that most people feel that somehow psychoanalysis ought to be a science, but I don't see any foundation for that.

PLR: I tend to agree with Bowlby's position that the practice of therapy or analysis is an art, but the theory of psychoanalysis can be consistent with natural science.[17] One risks basing an entire system on a set of assumptions that don't hold up, for instance, Freud's Lamarckianism. No serious scientist today would lend credence to that view. That view then led Freud, like Klein, to talk about phylogenetic memory traces. Therefore he could say that, if something didn't happen in reality, then it must have happened in fantasy, because we inherited that fantasy. You risk piling up one dubious assumption on top of another, which can be avoided by placing one's theory on a solid foundation.

RS: Okay, but then what I think you're talking about is a general theory of personality development and psychopathology. There are all kinds of claims made, many of which can be tested only by some kind of empirical scientific method, like child development studies in psychology.

PLR: That's what I think too.

---

16. Schafer (1996), "Authority, Evidence, and Knowledge in the Psychoanalytic Relationship." In *Tradition and Change*, p. 188.

17. John Bowlby (1978), "Psychoanalysis as Art and Science." In *A Secure Base: Clinical Applications of Attachment Theory*. London: Routledge, 1988, pp. 39–57.

RS: I agree with that. But I don't think that, when an individual comes to you, you can automatically apply any of that to that person's case.

PLR: Not automatically.

RS: It's something you would keep in mind. You would listen. Even when some of those generalizations from scientific studies seem to be consistent with the patient's material, you still want to know what his experience of it is. And especially what the unconscious experience is, which is more primitive.

PLR: I'm not challenging the centrality of unconscious experience in the process, but there seems to be a difference in our metatheoretical frameworks. For example, you say at one point: "In our discipline . . . each well-developed school is sufficiently self-enclosed and self-validating to fend off criticisms to its own satisfaction. It is only within its borders that it allows assessments of validity."[18] That to me is antiscientific, because as Frank Sulloway would say—he is no friend of psychoanalysis, of course, but I think his position is still worth considering—"the essence of science does not lie merely in replicating one's theory and praxis. Rather, it lies in replicating them *outside of one's immediate social group*."[19] If one finds validation only from within psychoanalysis, then there is a danger that everything will become self-enclosed.

RS: Okay.

PLR: That's okay with you?

RS: Yes, but what typically happens is that the people doing these studies then try to extrapolate directly into psychoanalysis as though they're testing ideas that they used in clinical analysis, and I think that's incautious of them. Daniel Stern does that.

PLR: He extrapolates incautiously from observational studies into the clinical setting?

RS: Yes, and I think that what, in fact, he's doing is importing his

---

18. Schafer (1994), "The Practice of Revisiting Classics: An Essay on Heinz Hartmann's *Psychoanalysis and Moral Values.*" In *Tradition and Change*, p. 201.

19. Frank J. Sulloway (1992), "Reassessing Freud's Case Histories." In *Freud and the History of Psychoanalysis*, ed. Toby Gelfand & John Kerr. Hillsdale, NJ: The Analytic Press, p. 185.

psychoanalytic preconceptions into the infant's mind, because he can't know what's there.

PLR: But if we can demonstrate that the infant is learning from experience from the very beginning of life, then its relation to the external world is not entirely based on fantasy, and that's a useful starting point.

RS: I don't think anybody has ever said that.

PLR: Well, Klein said it.

RS: Not with that meaning. It depends on how you read it. We get into a theory of reading here, which I know you're very familiar with.

PLR: All right. I don't know whether we need to belabor that issue. Before we finish, I'd like to ask you about your second analysis. I wonder if you would talk about that briefly and say how it was a different experience from the first one.

RS: Well, I had an analysis with a man in New Haven named William Pious, who was very wise and a popular teacher in the institute. I had a much deeper emotional experience than I did in my first analysis, and it had a much more transformative effect on me. Not just at the time, but over the subsequent years. Apart from my having known him a little from Menningers' and New Haven, he was not part of my personal or working life. That made it possible for me to have a much more profound transference experience of the interpretations. So the analysis meant a great deal to me.

PLR: At one point you quote Rilke, who spoke of "the emptying out of love in anonymous work."[20] That seems to me to capture something of what you've tried to do in your own analytic career.

RS: I think so. I mention Loewald's similar writings.[21] I make a point of anonymity because there are those now, especially in the object relations school in New York, who feel that a much greater openness on the part of the analyst can facilitate analysis. I think the transformative effect has to be in the interpretations and not in the social relationship. But that's a different idea of what analysis is and what you do.

---

20. Roy Schafer (1991), "Analytic Love." In *Retelling a Life: Narration and Dialogue in Psychoanalysis.* New York: Basic Books, 1992, p. 308.

21. See Hans W. Loewald (1970), "Psychoanalytic Theory and Psychoanalytic Process." In *Papers on Psychoanalysis.* New Haven, CT: Yale University Press, 1980, pp. 297–298.

PLR: That's classical.

RS: I'm much more classical.

PLR: Thank you. I think we've had a wonderful conversation, and I appreciate your time.

Jessica Benjamin

Reparative Projects

Peter L. Rudnytsky: I think it's fair to say that, despite having written two subsequent books, you're known above all as the author of *The Bonds of Love*.[1] So perhaps we could structure our conversation by talking about how you came to write *The Bonds of Love*, assuming that the main ideas are somewhat familiar to our readers, and then by talking about the evolution in your thinking in the dozen or so years since that time.

Jessica Benjamin: I started thinking about the issues that are in *The Bonds of Love* in the fall of 1966 after I had spent the summer finding out about the Frankfurt School and reading such books as Marcuse's *Eros and Civilization*[2] and Norman O. Brown's *Life Against Death*.[3] I probably also read Freud's *Totem and Taboo*[4] and *Civilization and Its Discontents*,[5] and I was very excited about psychoanalysis.

1. Jessica Benjamin (1988), *The Bonds of Love: Psychoanalysis, Feminism, and the Problem of Domination*. New York: Pantheon; (1995), *Like Subjects, Love Objects: Essays on Recognition and Sexual Difference*. New Haven, CT: Yale University Press; and (1998), *Shadow of the Other: Intersubjectivity and Gender in Psychoanalysis*. New York: Routledge.

2. Herbert Marcuse (1955), *Eros and Civilization*. Boston: Beacon Press.

3. Norman O. Brown (1959), *Life Against Death: The Psychoanalytical Meaning of History*. Middletown, CT: Wesleyan University Press.

4. Sigmund Freud (1913), *Totem and Taboo. Standard Edition,* 13:1–161. London: Hogarth Press, 1955.

5. Freud (1930), *Civilization and Its Discontents. Standard Edition*, 21:64–145. London: Hogarth Press, 1961.

PLR: Where were you at the time?

JB: I was at the University of Wisconsin in Madison. There was a group of people interested in the Frankfurt School who were part of the left-wing antiwar scene, which was quite heavily Marxist. It was very theoretical compared with the rest of the American left.

PLR: So you went to the University of Wisconsin?

JB: Yes. I had spent two years at Bard College, where the key influence on me was Hannah Arendt's husband, Heinrich Blücher, who had organized a Jaspers-oriented "Common Course." So Bard was more of a great ideas place. Madison was a left-wing hotbed of European and American Marxism. I was always very Euro-oriented and studied with George Mosse a bit. My senior year I did mainly independent study and reading in intellectual history. I wrote a paper at that time on the idea of play in Nietzsche and Schiller. I came across it many years later and found it so incomprehensibly dense [laughs], so much in the footsteps of the Frankfurt School, that I could barely stand to read it. I felt great sympathy for Professor Mosse, who had had to put up with reading it. [laughs] At the same time, the antiwar movement was going on, and we had our first feminist group, which quickly fell apart because many women couldn't befriend themselves with the idea that we might have issues of our own that were independent of the war. A few of us ended up reading *The Second Sex*.[6] That was a big, eye-opening moment.

PLR: The feminist group fell apart or the antiwar group fell apart?

JB: The feminist group fell apart, because most of the women felt that we were just an auxiliary, help-the-boys movement, while a few of us were already seeing down the road to where feminism was going. We wanted to go in that direction, to find some other sense of ourselves. There was a huge argument, and everybody who felt there wasn't any independent purpose for a women's group left; only about three of us stayed.

PLR: So it wasn't a feminist group until that happened?

JB: That's right. Historically speaking, it's much more accurate to

---

6. Simone de Beauvoir (1949), *The Second Sex*, trans. & ed. H. M. Parshley. New York: Knopf, 1952.

say that it was a women's group that fell apart and became a small feminist group. As I said, we ended up reading Simone de Beauvoir. From that time, the problem of the other's consciousness has always remained with me.[7] But I recall having had, at the time, the insight, which I was just able to formulate because of reading de Beauvoir, that all the binary opposites that were present in Western thought were indeed hooked up to gender. I remember thinking to myself, in that wild and wooly way of an undergraduate when you have no anchor for your thoughts and you don't know whether they're important or not or anybody else has ever thought them, "Wow, this must go all the way back through the history of Western philosophy and reason! There's some kind of secret relation here. What is it about masculinity and femininity?" I remember having this inchoate but important experience and knowing that I didn't yet have any of the tissue needed to support that flimsy bone structure. It percolated in the back of my mind for the next 20 years.

PLR: Let's pause for a moment and backtrack even further. You went to Bard before you went to Wisconsin. Where did you grow up?

JB: I grew up in Washington, DC. I was the younger child in a family where my father had been an extremely active Communist. My mother had also been a Communist but supported the family while my father was a full-time Communist until I was born, at which time he left the party. That was really the framing and shaping experience in my family life. Another important influence was that my brother had studied political philosophy; he went to the University of Chicago as a graduate student to study with Leo Strauss. He was the person who told me, when I was picking a second language, not to bother with Spanish but that I should learn German because it would come in handy when I wanted to read philosophy later.

PLR: How much older is your brother?

JB: Almost nine years. So my family was very political and discursively active and, of course, *meschugge* like everybody else around, maybe even more so. I think the main thing that I experienced growing up was that we were at odds with the rest of the social world around us. There was no question of my being in any kind of comfortable relation to that social world, especially once we moved to the suburbs when I was 11. Before that we lived in an apartment project that was a hotbed of Communists who all settled there after

---

7. Benjamin, *Shadow of the Other*, p. xi.

World War II. My mother managed it and gave apartments to all these young families with children who couldn't get apartments anywhere. Any time some fellow travelers or C.P.-types came along, they could count on getting an apartment there. So for a time when I was young, it was actually a very cohesive community. But once that dissolved, I had an extremely uncomfortable relation to my suburban peers in the 1950s and 60s. It was pretty intolerable. Although I rebelled against my family, I had an outsider position, and I always had a sense that I was not going to conform to the gender rules. Not that anyone in my family expected me to because, after all, my mother supported the family, which wasn't that unusual for Communists. Communist families were not feminist families, but they had very strong women who didn't comply with gender arrangements. My father began to earn money only much later.

PLR: What did your mother do?

JB: Well, she managed this apartment project. But she did a lot of things. She worked for the government before she got thrown out—left, rather, before there was going to be any problem. Many of our friends were thrown out of the government at that time. If you look at Carl Bernstein's memoirs, you get a fairly good picture of the community I grew up in, except that his parents and many other people's left the Party later.[8] The fact that my father was more critical of the Party probably also had a huge influence on me.

PLR: So he had left by the time you were born?

JB: Yes, or pretty close to it, in 1946. To be around people who were so political had a huge influence on my growing up, but at the same time I felt that they were emotionally not in tune with whatever was going on at any given moment. My path of rebellion was going to be through psychoanalysis and then through feminism because those were ways of reinstating the value of the individual person. So when I discovered psychoanalysis, and discovered it in a version where I could hook it up to things that I continued to believe politically, I was completely overjoyed.

PLR: This happened while you were still in college?

JB: Yes. It was the perfect solution to this mammoth problem I had. And then I went to Frankfurt in 1967, thinking I was just going to visit. I was supposed to study intellectual history out at Berkeley,

---

8. Carl Bernstein (1989), *Loyalties: A Son's Memoir*. New York: Simon and Schuster.

but I realized that I couldn't be cooped up in graduate school and have to sit in the library 40 hours a week and write research papers. That was too personally repressive for me. Also, I knew that, as a single woman, it would be difficult because I had already seen what it was like among the graduate students in Wisconsin. Joan Scott was the only woman in our circles who was a successful graduate student. Everyone else was a wife of a graduate student, and I was worried about being the only woman who was independent and ambitious. These were prefeminist times, and the women were either putting their husbands through graduate school or at most getting teaching degrees. It was a very uncomfortable situation compared with that in Germany at the time. Although many of the women in Germany later fell by the wayside, as students they were treated in a way that felt to me quite different from the American reality.

PLR: So you had been accepted at Berkeley but decided to go to Frankfurt for a year?

JB: I was in Frankfurt visiting with friends and I thought, "This is great! I can stay here and study and I won't have to do anything I don't want to do." Because you could sign up for all the seminars, and you didn't have to write papers. You read two pages of Hegel a week, so you weren't overwhelmed with busywork the way you are in the American educational system. You did something intensively and in depth, and the rest of the time everybody sat around and argued politics, drank beer, and made the revolution. [laughs]

PLR: Did you speak German at the time?

JB: No, I didn't speak it quite yet. I knew that the great thing was that I would learn German. That was how I sold it to Berkeley—and to my parents and everybody else. They saved my fellowship for two years, at which point I understood that I really didn't want to do that any more.

PLR: How did you support yourself in Frankfurt?

JB: My parents helped me out, and I tutored English. Then I got involved in the children's pedagogy movement that was very psychoanalytically inspired. At that time in Germany, there were no nursery and few kindergarten programs. Kids had no day care. The entire educational system in Germany was very authoritarian until it was transformed by the student movement. Everyone was reading these little pirated editions of experimental psychoanalytic writings from the 1920s and 1930s that we typed and mimeographed ourselves until we got copiers.

PLR: Was Aichhorn's work influential?

JB: Yes, but not for me. I read Vera Schmidt, and Anna Freud's report on children from Theresienstadt.[9] The psychoanalytic world in Germany was eventually going to be transformed by this ferment, but nobody knew it yet. At the time, it was just a student movement with antiauthoritarian children's centers. So that's what I became involved with, and it brought together all the different issues in my life—the value I placed on the individual in any project of social transformation, which hadn't been emphasized in my own home. So this was a very reparative experience for me. Simply taking care of children was very reparative for me because the idea that children were important and you should spend your time with them instead of on the revolution was not a big one in my nuclear family or my extended family history.

PLR: Did you feel that enough time hadn't been spent on you as a child?

JB: No, certainly not enough time had been spent on me as a child. [laughs] That's a gross understatement. So I felt that this was a great way to be reparative, to stay within the political milieu that I still believed in, and to learn more about psychoanalysis. Originally, I thought I might even stay in Frankfurt. You could get a degree in social pedagogy, which was very psychoanalytically oriented, and then become a child analyst; that was what I thought I was going to do.

PLR: So you were in a degree program?

JB: Yes. I had switched out of sociology and philosophy by that time and into pedagogy. I did my *Vordiplom*, which is a kind of pre-Master's degree.

PLR: Did you meet your husband there?[10]

---

9. Vera Schmidt, a Russian analyst, founded a children's home in Moscow in 1921. Her work is discussed by Anna Freud (1930), *Introduction to Psycho-Analysis for Teachers: Four Lectures*, trans. Barbara Low. London: George Allen & Unwin, 1931, pp. 77–78. On Theresienstadt, see Anna Freud & Sophie Dann (1951), "An Experiment in Group Upbringing." *The Psychoanalytic Study of the Child*, 6:127–168. New York: International Universities Press.

10. Anson Rabinbach, Professor of History at Princeton University, is the author of *The Crisis of Austrian Socialism: From Red Vienna to Civil War* (1983). Chicago: University of Chicago Press; *The Human Motor: Engines, Fatigue, and the Origins of Modernity* (1990). New York: Basic Books; and

JB: No, I met Andy later. He had studied as a graduate student in Wisconsin with Mosse, but he arrived there the summer I left. Then he went to Vienna to do his research. We had exactly the same backgrounds and interests, but our paths didn't cross until we finally met at Hampshire in 1976, when I came to teach courses on the Frankfurt School so he could go on leave. So we did ultimately meet through our German connection, but later. The thing about Frankfurt was that once again there was a problem because everybody was into Marxism and nobody was into feminism. I was part of the very early women's movement there, which was a very difficult and conflicted experience because again the women felt that anything that they might do for themselves wouldn't really be political. I had one extremely good friend who lived with me in this little commune, and we were constantly arguing in favor of feminism with a group of 40 to 50 women who were all violently opposed. The startling thing was that when I left in December of 1971 and they had their first meeting again in January of 1972, they all came out as feminists, especially the lesbians who had been in the closet. It was as though I had to get out of the way because they could not face me and say that for months now they'd been thinking I was right. [laughs] I happened to be in Frankfurt a few years ago for a woman's 50th birthday party, and she came up to me and said, "I have always felt so guilty about this." [laughs]

PLR: You sowed the seeds of feminist consciousness.

JB: I brought all the literature over from the United States and got it distributed. But I missed out on a lot of good stuff here. On the other hand, I don't regret having been part of the German student movement. It was an unbelievably exciting experience.

PLR: And you didn't know about Anna O. at that time?

JB: No, the great thing was finding out later that Anna O. had lived literally around the corner from me and only four or five blocks from the *Kinderladen*—the antiauthoritarian children's center.[11]

PLR: Did you have any psychoanalysis in Frankfurt?

JB: Yes, I did. Actually, it was a very bad psychoanalysis with an analyst who suffered from the difficulty of obtaining training in post-Nazi Germany. He was also terribly alarmed by my feminism and

---

In the Shadow of Catastrophe: German Intellectuals between Apocalypse and Enlightenment (1997). Berkeley: University of California Press.

11. Benjamin, *Shadow of the Other*, p. 1.

became more and more defensive. I no doubt gave him a hard time, but he really had no clue about how to handle feminism and was terrified by it.

PLR: Was it conducted in English?

JB: Yes. He had been an antifascist and had good political credentials. But he had been trained by Alexander Mitscherlich, and Mitscherlich wasn't trained by anybody, as is well known. My analyst fell out with him and was not part of the institute in Frankfurt. Institute analysts had a two-year waiting list, but he had time.

PLR: Were you thinking of yourself as a future analyst at that time?

JB: I was, but when things finished so badly I became discouraged and came back to the United States.

PLR: Why did you leave Frankfurt?

JB: I left Frankfurt because I couldn't stand being away from the United States any more. I think it was an important act of separation and rebellion from my family to go over there in the first place, but at the same time I felt too cut off from any secure base. The whole student movement was terrifyingly cut off from the older generation. There was hardly anyone who had a connection to his or her parents. My boyfriend actually had a pretty good relationship with his mother, who was an apolitical, working-class woman. But most of the people I was surrounded by had frozen their connection to the older generation in a very frightening dissociative process. The amount of aggression being unleashed in the movement was frightening to me. There was a move toward authoritarian, Communist politics that was also very frightening. So the whole atmosphere changed. I tried very hard to create a feminist cohort that I could feel comfortable with, but I couldn't. At the antiauthoritarian children's center, the parents became more and more convinced that they should study Marx and forget about child-rearing, which was exactly what I was there to prevent! So I was very disillusioned.

PLR: It sounds as though you had an experience in that setting that was similar to your childhood experience in that there was a radical political ideology and a neglect of the needs of children.

JB: Well, these people were not neglectful. A lot of them were quite wonderful as parents. But they were young and they were very taken up with the idea that there was something important that they ought to do, and I felt it as a threat to our other project. Like anybody in our generation, they were already much more attuned to making a different kind of world for their children. Of course, there are always a few people who neglect their children, but by and large what I felt wasn't that but a lack of support from them for my personal reparative project. It wasn't theirs, because they didn't come from political families. They were trying to make up for something else—Nazism. Our reparative projects didn't mesh.

At the same time, the dissociative process by which the Germans separated from their parents was frightening to me. The people I had known in the United States had a level of connection to whomever they were rebelling against and to one another that was substantially different. The Germans were emotionally crippled. They have since worked this through in amazing ways. Much to my surprise, some of the craziest people politically changed their whole understanding of what they were about in a very deep way by going into analysis during the late 1970s and 1980s, when things fell apart there, but without losing their political involvement. So I'm appreciative of what they've done. On the other hand, they were coming from such an authoritarian family structure and were so frightened of any kind of personal communication that they were infinitely less open and less warm than Americans. I still feel close to many people there and to what they've accomplished. Psychoanalysis still has a serious place there in a culture that preserves some remnants of what the 1960s created much more than ours does. So it's a different world in Germany, and I'm glad I had a chance to be part of it; but I also couldn't bear it at a certain point, and I had to get back here and feel I was with my people.

The interesting thing was that it was only after I returned and there was a lot of water under the dam that I realized the degree to which I couldn't be in a place that had no Jews. It wasn't that the people I was with were anti-Semitic. If anything, they were philo-Semitic. I recall that I went back to visit friends in June of 1982, when the invasion of Lebanon was going on. There were these horrible posters all over the university comparing Begin to Hitler. It was a Saturday, and I saw some people sitting around in blue jeans looking as though they were still from the 1960s. I thought, "Oh, those are the people who are putting up those posters." When I got closer, I realized they were parents from my children's center. I was so happy to see them, and they had been going around tearing down the posters. [laughs] So I never had to lose faith in the people I was close to. But there wasn't a Jewish presence in the culture, and it was very strange.

PLR: Where did you go when you returned to the States?

JB: I went to New Haven for about a year and a half and did a bunch of different things there. I worked at the mental health center doing a scrub job, I taught sociology of women at Southern Connecticut State College, and I applied to graduate school.

PLR: Why did you go to New Haven?

JB: I had some friends there from Madison, and I thought the women's movement in New Haven would be a good place to settle into easily, as opposed to New York, which I knew would be difficult.

PLR: That was in 1971?

JB: Yes.

PLR: Did your analysis end abruptly?

JB: My analyst went off to take a professorship in Würzburg.

PLR: So you didn't give him two weeks' notice and break it off?

JB: No, *he* left *me*. I would have worked it out with him if I could have. But what happened was very devastating, so I knew that I needed to do analysis again. He had a very traditional notion of penis envy. He thought I was trying to steal his penis. I did go to see somebody else for a consultation, a young guy who lived way out of town. I told him the story, and he said, "It's fine with me if you have the penis. You speak English much better than I do, so you'll have it for a while." But he was moving to Switzerland, and I was really devastated that he wasn't available.

PLR: What was the name of your first analyst?

JB: Dieter Wyss. He wrote a couple of books, including a history of therapy that was translated into English.

PLR: Was there any specific incident in the analysis that crystalized the difficulties you were having?

JB: I guess I could typify it by saying that, when I came to see him for my last session and I was very upset about his leaving, he sat up abruptly at a certain point and said, "We have to end now. I have to go eat my dinner. This is what always happens between us." The implication was something like, "You're always wanting something more from me, and that's our conflict, but I have to go take care of myself now. You're just draining me too much."

PLR: That could be interpreted on a level of dependency needs rather than phallic conflicts.

JB: The whole thing was about dependency needs, but he chose not to address those.

PLR: He had a phallic monist perspective.[12]

JB: Yes. His interpretation that my dissatisfaction had to do with penis envy and wanting to steal his penis was getting the wrong organ. [laughs]

PLR: It seems that, at that point, you were dissatisfied with the analysis but didn't have a theoretical vocabulary to articulate the difficulties you were having.

JB: That's right. My analyst wasn't addressing the transference at the level it needed to be addressed, but I was nowhere close to where I was later. I had no theoretical understanding. Even the things that I read didn't give me any clue.

PLR: So even though you were an advanced feminist thinker for that time by comparison with the group of women you were associated with both in Madison and in Frankfurt, in the context of analysis you didn't have an alternative framework available to understand that your analyst's vocabulary of penis envy might not be adequate.

JB: I knew that penis envy was a really bad idea from a feminist viewpoint, but I didn't have a psychoanalytic understanding that would have allowed me to see that it might function as a metaphor for something else. I could say that it was wrong, but I couldn't analyze it and see what deeper level of need might be underlying it.

PLR: Let me ask you a theoretical question, and then we can pick up the biographical thread. You've said that "perhaps the starkest denial by psychoanalysis of the mother's subjectivity is Freud's insistence that children do not know about the existence of the female sexual organs."[13] Do you think that young girls—or young boys, for that matter—have an innate awareness of the vagina?

JB: I think it's absolutely proven that young girls do.

PLR: I've heard anecdotal reports that a number of grown women do not recall having been aware of their vaginas as children.

JB: There's been lots of discussion about this, but what people say is that first of all you're very aware you have a vulva and, second, you're

---

12. Benjamin, *The Bonds of Love*, pp. 166–167.

13. Benjamin, *The Bonds of Love*, p. 166.

very aware you have an opening of some kind. The idea that this opening goes all the way back and what it actually does can be very obscure.

PLR: Is it distinct from the urethral opening?

JB: I think that it may not be understood to be distinct, but why does it need to be, since, after all, girls don't really know how the urethra works? It's much the same with the boy, who doesn't have to understand the distinction between urine and semen. The point is whether there's a sensation, and a lot of people say that girls do experience sensation. What's striking is that once their vulvas and their vaginas are labeled, they know exactly what's going on. It's not just about whether or not girls have sensation; it's about the silencing effect of their not only being denied a language but being signaled that this must not be spoken.

PLR: Would you say that boys have a similar awareness of the anatomy of girls?

JB: I think it has to do with whether or not you talk to them. My two boys were extremely annoyed to hear that there was something they didn't have. Their first reaction at the age of 24 months or so was exactly the way I described it in "Sameness and Difference."[14] Boys' first reaction is the same as girls': "There can't be something I don't have. I have everything." So then they try to figure out what part of their body could correspond to the anatomy of the other sex. What Irene Fast says is that most likely they're going to make an analogy between the vagina and the anus.[15] So then they're going to assume that that's what little girls have, and that is a problem. In order for boys to assimilate everything that girls have, they frequently have to use a language that has a much more pejorative meaning.

PLR: So your view is that children of both sexes start out thinking that they have everything?

JB: It's not so much that they know innately they have everything. On the contrary, there are different levels. It's plausible to me that at some deep, unconscious level everybody knows everything, as Chasseguet-Smirgel argues.[16] Then it seems to me that there's also

14. Benjamin, *Like Subjects, Love Objects*, pp. 63–65.

15. Irene Fast (1984), *Gender Identity: A Differentiation Model*. Hillsdale, NJ: The Analytic Press, pp. 67–69.

16. Janine Chasseguet-Smirgel (1976), "Freud and Female Sexuality." *International Journal of Psycho-Analysis,* 57:275–286.

a later level of genital representation in which, as Little Hans shows, boys have this inchoate, unthought known that there is something that corresponds to the something that they have and that is where they want to put it.[17]

PLR: That would be a Horneyan view.

JB: Yes, but it's specifically something that Chasseguet-Smirgel says in relation to Little Hans. She points out the contradiction in Freud's denial of the vagina because Hans is looking for something to penetrate. So that's one level of experience. Then there's the level of experience where somebody actually tells the boy, "Girls can have babies, and you can't." Their first reaction to that, as Little Hans says, is, "No, that's not true. I can too." And then later: "Well, I know I can't, but I still think I can." At a certain point, for instance, girls say, "I have a penis, but it's inside." That's a very interesting statement because part of what it says is, "I have it in my mind." But they don't say, "I have it in my mind"; they say, "Where is it? It's somewhere in my tummy." A patient told me her daughter thought the penis was inside-out inside her, so that it really was the exact complementary organ to the penis, only involuted.

PLR: That's the standard view of Renaissance anatomy.[18]

JB: And that's what they try to do in transsexual operations. I think that those mental representations are tremendously important because they're the basis on which we have empathy for the other. You have to have some approximation in your mind of what the other person might be feeling or what he or she might be like in order to have attunement. It just doesn't work otherwise.

PLR: I agree completely.

JB: The whole basis of sexual attunement is those identifications. The irony is that, whereas most Americans think that if these opposite-sex identifications are radically severed or scotomized, that creates heterosexuality, in actuality that's what undoes heterosexuality.

PLR: It creates a hommo-sexuality, in Irigaray's sense.[19]

---

17. Sigmund Freud (1909), *Analysis of a Phobia in a Five-Year-Old Boy. Standard Edition*, 10:40–41. London: Hogarth Press, 1955.

18. Thomas Laqueur (1990), *Making Sex: Body and Gender from the Greeks to Freud*. Cambridge, MA: Harvard University Press, pp. 63–113.

19. Luce Irigaray (1974), *Speculum of the Other Woman*, trans. Gillian C. Gill. Ithaca, NY: Cornell University Press, 1985, p. 98.

JB: Exactly. Daphne De Marneffe did some fascinating experiments with young children and anatomically correct dolls.[20] The children are able to say whether they themselves are boys or girls, but at the age of two they're not able to point out the dolls correctly. They don't get the significance of genitalia until later.

PLR: What about hair and other markers?

JB: That's what they use, of course. According to Coates, in her comments on De Marneffe, the one-and-a-half or two-year-old child's experience goes something like this: "Why are you showing me a naked doll? Show me a doll with clothes and hair, and we'll have something to talk about."[21] [laughs] Freud's whole idea that categories of maleness and femaleness are based on genitalia is ludicrous because the constancy of the identification based on genitalia comes much later. This delay also opens up the space for fluidity. Since children don't know exactly what boys and girls have or what makes them different, they can handle all sorts of surprising things. My younger son was in nursery school from age two to three, and a year or so later we were talking about the teacher that he'd had, and he referred to this teacher as "he." I realized, "How wonderful! All year he thought he was being taken care of by a man. How good for his identifications!" Why did he think this? Just because this teacher had short hair. He didn't know that the name Maureen was for a "she." [laughs] Why would a two-year-old know that Maureen is a female name?

PLR: No inherent reason. We have to unlearn a lot to think the way children do.

JB: I think the wonderful thing about so much of the empirical research people have done lately is that it shows how differently kids perceive the world from adults. Little Hans reveals in every possible way that he envies what women have and identifies with his mother, and Freud misses that. He can focus only on the idea that girls want to be like men. This has been pointed out 100 times, but it's still astonishing each time you look at it.

PLR: It's very important. That was a detour into theory. So you landed in New Haven and stayed there about a year and a half.

---

20. Daphne De Marneffe (1997), "Bodies and Words: A Study of Young Children's Genital and Gender Knowledge." *Gender and Psychoanalysis*, 2:3–34.

21. Susan R. Coates (1997), "Is It Time to Jettison the Concept of Developmental Lines?" *Gender and Psychoanalysis*, 2:35–54.

JB: I applied to graduate school and got into NYU. I decided not to apply in clinical psychology because my Frankfurt experience had made me so antiempiricist. I didn't see how I could get through a program like that, and enrolling in the Ph.D. program in sociology gave me the maximum number of transfer credits. I didn't understand how difficult it would be to get clinical training without the Ph.D. in psychology. More deeply, I wasn't sure I wanted it because I had had such a negative experience in analysis. That was the underlying issue for me—could I repair that experience?

PLR: You entered the NYU program in sociology in 1973?

JB: Yes, and I started my analysis with Emmanuel Ghent at the end of 1974.

PLR: Were you thinking of an academic career at that stage?

JB: I was, but in the back of my mind I always had the idea that maybe I could still become an analyst. I started to write my dissertation in 1975–1976. It was called *Internalization and Psychoanalysis*, and it was a critique of the Frankfurt school idea that internalization is the basis on which one develops the autonomous ego. So it was a critique of the idea of autonomy as well as of internalization, and that was where I first adumbrated the theme of recognition. Some of the key ideas found their way into an essay I published in *Telos* in 1977.[22] While I was writing the dissertation, I got the job at Hampshire for a year and was commuting up to Massachusetts in the middle of each week. I got involved with Andy at the end of 1976, and he encouraged me to think more about what I really what I wanted to do. I'd been teaching for a year, and I felt that, if I was going to have all these unhappy undergraduates coming to talk to me, I wanted to talk to them about their real problems and not whether they should write about Lukács or not.

PLR: What year did you finish your degree?

JB: I finished the dissertation in November of 1977 and got my degree in 1978.

PLR: How did you end up seeing Emmanuel Ghent for analysis?

JB: That's a complicated story, but somebody I knew knew him, and so I went to see him. I didn't know what I was lucking into in terms

---

22. Jessica Benjamin (1977), "The End of Internalization: Adorno's Social Psychology." *Telos*, 32:42–64.

of his orientation and what he represented. I recall that I saw several people at the time, and he was the most analytic.

PLR: Had he published anything at that time?

JB: No. In fact, he was mainly still composing. He was always out at Bell Labs at night. He was one of the first people to use the computer for music composition. I liked that.

PLR: He was at the NYU postdoctoral program?

JB: Yes. That's what I meant when I said I didn't realize what I was lucking into. I was getting connected to that whole possible world.

PLR: And that was a truly reparative experience?

JB: Yes, it was. Despite all the things I've said about Wyss, I also had some very good experiences with him in the early part of my analysis. It is very striking how different I felt that kind of analysis was. It was a classical id-analysis. What I discovered that interested me the most is that that type of approach allows for what might be called a dissociation in the service of analysis. Through the process of free association, you can go places that you wouldn't go if you were emotionally connected, and you discover things that would otherwise hit too much resistance. It's like a trance state or a drug state, I suppose. Certain connections are made, but in a symbolic way rather than a truly felt way. That symbolic level can be dissociated from your emotional life. The same is true of dreams. You can have dreams where you don't feel anything but then are horrified when you wake up. This analytic technique has certain drawbacks, but it also has certain advantages in getting to material that is otherwise unavailable.

PLR: And that happened in the first analysis?

JB: Yes. My second analysis, on the other hand, was emotionally connected. I didn't go places that I wasn't emotionally connected to, and I sometimes had a hard time going to the places that were painful. That allowed for a greater reality because I was no longer engaging in a dissociative process. But I was also aware that there were parts of myself that I knew about because of my prior analysis that I could then make use of once I had this much deeper sense of emotional connection and being attached to the analyst in a safe way.

PLR: Did the connections you made in a hypothetical way in the first analysis gain an emotional grounding the second time around?

JB: Some of them did. And some of them had an emotional grounding at the time.

PLR: Can you give an example?

JB: What I would say is that the container for an emotional content wasn't created in the first analysis, so things emerged about my very early childhood that were very important to me, but they lacked a certain framing.

PLR: Can you say what they were?

JB: For instance, I became aware of some experiences that I had of early abandonment. But I didn't become aware of them in a way that I could use. That has to do with the fact that they weren't anchored in a secure transference. It's like having particles floating around that aren't attached to other molecules, but you're aware of them. So I became very aware of certain experiences and I truly understood how they were affecting me at one level, but at another level I couldn't fully make use of what I had discovered because of the transference situation. My sense is that there are aspects of sexuality and aggression that appear partly as breakdown formations. It's very difficult to say whether they would appear in the same way if you were in a more cohesive relationship. But through the freedom and lack of moral judgment that you can attain only by negating attachment, you can sometimes become aware of the potential for certain ideation that you just wouldn't reach in any other way.

PLR: You're talking about your first analysis?

JB: Yes. What I'm saying is that the detachment also creates a lack of censorship, including a release from superego inhibitions that can get in the way, precisely because it doesn't have to be reparative and you are not relating to your analyst as another subject. The relationship remains grounded in fantasy, and you never know who or what the analyst is in a certain way.

PLR: It's more of a classical analysis.

JB: Yes. It's not that you don't have perceptions of the analyst, but you're not able to implicate them in the relationship; so on some level the relationship remains fantastic, and that allows more dissociated voices to emerge. Obviously, the opposite is also true—that only through safety and a lack of dissociation other voices can emerge. I'm very struck by that difference.

PLR: Can one have a secure attachment to a classical analyst?

JB: Well, I think that people have had and do have them because there's such a range of how people behave within what's called classical analysis. There were always people who made those attachments possible while theoretically toeing the line, and there were always people who didn't. The way I see it, some people were impersonating analysts, and some people were being analysts. As Winnicott said, some people have these interminable analyses where they're not being grabbed.[23] The real part of them isn't there. I think that that was true for a lot of analysts too. The ones who weren't impersonating allowed those attachments to be formed. But for some patients, that's not enough. Nowadays in the United States, there are very few people for whom that will work. It's too far from how we are.

PLR: Presumably, these dissociated fragments of experience or voices have emotions underlying them on some level. So if you have a dream where you don't feel an emotion at the time, it may simply not have been able to emerge in connection with the ideation. One would like to imagine an analyst who could allow the freedom for these provisional trains of thought to emerge while also offering an emotional connection in which they could be experienced in the transference.

JB: This happens in any good analysis. A person will tell you she's just had some thought flash across her mind that seems unrelated, and that's how the process works.

PLR: Precisely. So how did you launch into analytic training?

JB: I went to a place in Brooklyn called the New Hope Guild, which was willing to train people who didn't have prior mental health degrees. They had a small externship program in which I took some classes and saw patients one day a week with supervision. So I jumped in and saw patients starting in 1978.

PLR: How did your analytic career unfold after the New Hope Guild?

JB: Then I was admitted into the New York University Postdoctoral Program in Psychotherapy and Psychoanalysis. I went there between 1980 and 1986. I was extremely fortunate in my peer group. You wouldn't believe the number of really interesting and terrific people who were in my entering class, which included Lewis Aron, Adrienne Harris, Beatrice Beebe, Neil Altman, and Marcia Levy-Warren. These are all people you can see on the Division 39 program now. It was a hot, exciting class. But, at that time, Postdoc was made up of Freudians and interpersonalists who were in a terrible war with each other. A friend of mine put this once very beautifully. The interper-

---

23. D. W. Winnicott (1969), "The Use of an Object and Relating Through Identifications." In *Playing and Reality*. London: Tavistock, 1971, p. 87.

sonalists represented ignorance masquerading as liberalism, while the Freudians represented knowledge contaminated by authoritarianism. It was a polarized situation. Most of us feel that we didn't get the education we would have liked, and we wish we could be students there now in the relational track.

PLR: When was that founded?

JB: In 1988. Two years after I graduated.

PLR: So your analysis with Emmanuel Ghent continued and became your training analysis?

JB: Yes. A great many of us who organized the relational track were students or analysands of his, and he really was the prime moving force in that.

PLR: What about Stephen Mitchell?

JB: He brought Steve Mitchell in. Somehow Steve Mitchell had been allowed into the interpersonal track a few years before that, and so Emmanuel Ghent, Stephen Mitchell, James Fosshage, and Philip Bromberg, all of whom had been hired by that time, were able, with the help of the graduates, to form this new relational orientation. We brought in all kinds of new people. Many of us became faculty fairly soon.

PLR: So then your clinical practice became the focus of your work?

JB: After I made the decision not to teach, I had to find a means of support. I tried to get a postdoc so I could retrain. I found out that I could only get an NIMH postdoc on an individual basis. I couldn't get into the training programs. So I applied through a very arduous procedure and made up my own research project on mothers and infants. With some help from Beatrice Beebe and a few other people, I did get this grant and went to Albert Einstein College of Medicine.

PLR: How many years was it?

JB: It was a three-year grant. So for three years I was at Einstein learning about infancy and doing my own research project.

PLR: What years were these?

JB: From 1979 to 1982. During that time, I was starting to build up my private practice a bit, but I was also being supported in a minimal way through this postdoc. I ended up hooking up with Beatrice Beebe and working on her research project because there was nothing else I could do at Einstein. She was at Yeshiva at that time.

Einstein was a very disappointing experience for me. I didn't know how to get into the clinical part of what was going on there. Nobody wanted to give me a supervisory hour because I wasn't a psychology intern. And the psychologists at Yeshiva didn't want me to take their Rorschach course because they were afraid I would try to get licensed and there wouldn't be enough patients in New York to go around!

PLR: Hadn't you already started the NYU program?

JB: Yes, but I would have been happy to have more training in a hospital setting. So eventually I stopped hanging out at Einstein and just did some work on Beatrice Beebe's project. During that time I had my first child; I was doing my analytic training and seeing a few patients; and that was enough. Then, in 1982, I agreed to give a talk at the Postdoc on a panel on women's issues in psychoanalysis. I started writing the paper that became the chapter called "Woman's Desire" in *The Bonds of Love*. That was where I worked out the theory of rapprochement and the father. As I think about it, my kid was still only nine months old. By the following year, when he actually hit that phase, I could see that everything I had postulated was true, which was rather odd.

To backtrack, and this is very important, in 1978 I came up with the idea that we should do a conference on *"The Second Sex*: Thirty Years Later." I did that through the New York Institute for the Humanities, which also gave me a small fellowship for a year. The conference was a traumatic experience for me because that was when identity politics was unleashed. Our purpose was to bring together the various elements of the women's movement—the more theoretical and the practical, the gay and the straight—to see if we could resolve some of the conflicts. On the contrary, identity politics came to the fore in a way that we didn't understand because it was unprecedented.

The most dramatic part of the experience was that, while some of the most important and well-known feminists of that time were on the podium, Audre Lorde excoriated everyone in the white women's movement and said that all during the 1960s we were having women of color clean our houses and take care of our children so that we could go out and be feminists. This was actually incorrect from my point of view. Because we were younger, we had been in the civil rights movement and the antiwar movement while Audrey Lorde was raising her children and having a private life. She also presented the radical separatist idea that you could not dismantle the master's house with the master's tools. This was again the anti-intellectualism that I was so familiar with in American life and feminism. It was tied up with identity politics and represented everything I had been spending my life arguing against. The vituperativeness of this talk terrified everyone. Monique Wittig was at the foot of the stage begging Audrey to stop. There were open microphones with 50 people standing in front of them who all wanted to get on the bandwagon and say how their identity had been left out of this conference and therefore they had been silenced. There was little one could do at that point to include a more diverse group of women. Afterward that changed, and many people who had declined our invitation or whom we hadn't thought of inviting because they hadn't shown the slightest interest in feminism then became involved with women's studies. Women's studies was only just getting off the ground in a major way, and there was still a difference between being devoted to this area of study and those women who were later going to seize on its popularity.

This conference in 1979 was a key moment for me because as a result I felt even more profoundly identified with psychoanalysis. What I wrote in *The Bonds of Love* analyzes the kind of identity politics that emerged in the early 1980s. It describes the stratagems that people use to get themselves into a position of power through their victim status. This was not a wholly new thing. It had gone on covertly for a long time, but it erupted overtly in stunning fashion at the conference. That's the hidden political subtext of *The Bonds of Love*—to address that phenomenon.

PLR: It seems to me that you have a very interesting double vision—on one hand, you're writing as a feminist and critiquing the dominant ideology while, on the other, you also have an unusually keen awareness of the way that the excluded position can itself be hardened into militancy.

JB: From a Kleinian perspective this is very easy to understand. The excluded group can easily fall into a retaliatory reversal, which leaves them stuck in the paranoid-schizoid position. What I wanted to do was to analyze the whole process of reversal. I had begun by writing about sadomasochism. This was part of my work in 1979 on de Beauvoir. It all coalesced for me—the synthesis of Winnicott and Hegel and my preoccupation with recognition—around my analysis of *The Story of O*. It allowed me to understand how these reversals work through a process of what I've later come to call split complementarity. This refers to the way a system is maintained by each partner's taking one half of the relation. That was crucial to my analysis of domination. I understood that domination involved an alienation of recognition, but it was the further insight into splitting and the formation of split complementarity that allowed me to grasp the dynamics of the process. And I had been writing about these ideas in the year preceding. I see nothing more destructive for any liberatory movement, especially feminism, than to fall into a complementarity embracing the victim position in a dynamic of doer and done to.

PLR: This is fascinating, but one might say that the evolution of your position lends credence to the critique of psychoanalysis as an antipolitics. That is at least a possible reading of Freud—that he turns from the political to the psychological, while then using the psychological to explain the political.[24] Is that an accurate account of your position?

JB: No, because my position was much more that if there was going to be any hope for politics we had to become aware of this dynamic, which is central to any liberatory tendency. It's true that I personally felt I couldn't cope with it any more, so in that sense you could say I was turning away from politics. I couldn't cope with what the feminist movement became in the 1980s. As I've said, this whole flag-waving, "I'm this identity" was an anathema to me. I found it equally unacceptable around Judaism, the idea of a chosen people entitled to forget the rights of others. I'm a born-and-bred universalist, and I can't bear these forms of particularism that are based on the victim position.

PLR: A card-carrying position, you might say.

JB: Yes. On the other side, that doesn't mean that I want to suppress particularity. During the 80s I was very obsessed with the issue of the universal versus the particular. Obviously, the position from which I began involved a critique of universalism, even though I didn't know that category. I should backtrack and say that one of the important influences on me was that when I met Andy in the 1970s he was already very deeply into Foucault and had worked out a Nietzschean critique of the ideology of goodness. It included a critique of the universality of the proletariat and of Lukács's collapse of the particular into the universal where one class is socially determined to be the liberatory class. All this was very helpful to me because, as soon as you look at feminism and apply the same principles, you can see the same problem of raising the particular to the universal. While everyone was claiming to save the particular, in fact what they wanted was simply to reverse the terms and make their particular the linchpin of some universal position. They then denied

24. William J. McGrath (1986), *Freud's Discovery of Psychoanalysis: The Politics of Hysteria*. Ithaca, NY: Cornell University Press, pp. 230–275.

its universality, but it clearly had the same absolutist characteristics. You then were stuck back in Hegel's struggle to the death for recognition of my particularity against your particularity. [PLR laughs]

The only issue ever—whether you're in psychoanalysis or out in the world—is, how are you going to get out of that power struggle of my ego against your ego, of my particularity against yours? Only by recognizing the commonality of our egos. After I had painstakingly worked this all out psychoanalytically, I discovered that Derrida had done it with a flick of the wrist in his paper on "Violence and Metaphysics."[25] I was coming from a very different position, namely, the concept of recognition. Derrida does it through a critique of Levinas, who insists on the absolute, irreducible quality of the other.

PLR: But don't you agree with Levinas?

JB: No, I don't, though I'm not all that familiar with his writings. But as I understand it, the issue is: If the other is absolutely other, how could you recognize him or her? It's only on the basis of some commonality that you can bridge difference.

PLR: Does that lead you to a position that could be called essentialist?

JB: No, or no more than anyone else. Essentialism is not escapable except by avoiding any declarative utterances.

PLR: Essentialism refers to a belief in a common human nature.

JB: All right. I believe in a common human nature insofar as I believe that the difficulty of recognizing the other is a common human problem.

PLR: And the possibility of overcoming it depends on attunement or the capacity to see a part of one's own experience in someone else's experience.

JB: I see where you're going. In that sense, it does lead me to an essentialist position. But I don't believe that there's an *essential* quality of otherness. That reification seems to me to be in danger of occurring in Levinas's position, although, as I said, I'm not deeply familiar with it.

PLR: Although you claimed to agree with Derrida's critique of Levinas, I think that you and Derrida are fundamentally at odds

---

25. Jacques Derrida (1978), *Writing and Difference*, trans. Alan Bass. Chicago: University of Chicago Press, pp. 79–153.

since you do believe in the possibility of genuine recognition that bridges difference.

JB: Yes.

PLR: We've arrived at the synthesis you achieved in *The Bonds of Love.* The de Beauvoir conference seems to have been an important catalyst that brought home in concrete fashion the thinking you had done theoretically. If I could try to summarize one of the arguments you make in the book, it is that the relation of paradox to attunement is analogous to that of polarity to domination. Paradox is the expression of an attuned relationship to the other, whereas polarity is the expression of a relationship of domination and subordination.

JB: Yes, except that I think I would use "recognition" instead of "attunement" since recognition is a more complex concept. One of the things I've worked on in the 10 years since *The Bonds of Love* is an elaboration of my developmental model. Lew Aron did something very helpful for me by pointing out that my concept of recognition is really one of intersubjectivity as a developmental achievement. In that light, I've been spelling out more precisely what those stages are. Attunement is the baseline form of recognition, but even with attunement at some point there is a confrontation with difference and lack of attunement.

PLR: You speak of "postoedipal complementarity" in the positive sense of a renewed gender fluidity. But ordinarily, when you use the word "complementarity," you use it pejoratively to mean the opposite of "mutuality."

JB: Yes.

PLR: Do you think that there might be a problem in using the same word in different senses?

JB: I do, but I have an intuitive feeling about things like this. The paradox of using the word differently at different moments highlights the fact that even though complementarity is opposed to mutuality, it has an indispensable function. First of all, our mental life cannot be freed of splitting because binary categories are fundamental to the way the mind works. As Ogden points out, if you don't have splitting and simply have fusion, it's psychotically disorganizing and terrifying.[26] So there has to be an initial process of splitting. Buddhists also think that's what mind does. That's why they think mind is a problem.

---

26. Thomas Ogden (1986), *The Matrix of the Mind.* Northvale, NJ: Aronson.

The point is to reach, in a more specific sense, a form of *gender complementarity*, in which complementarity gets *aufgehoben*.[27] It doesn't get *aufgehoben* into mutuality; it gets *aufgehoben* into the possibility of free movement between the opposites sufficient for them to become something else and for the binary terms to be partly subverted. I think that the only possible subversion of binary terms is this sufficiently rapid oscillation that creates something else. This something else, which I've been increasingly thinking of as thirdness, has to do with a space in which the fluidity of oscillation is such that the defensive quality of the binary fades into something much more like contrast. You still have light and dark, but their intermingling creates an entirely different sense of the values of lightness and darkness, and that's what happens in transitional space. Expanding the idea of transitionality into the idea of thirdness, I have argued that there is a nascent form of thirdness in the dyad. It doesn't rely on an intervening third term, which is what I've always criticized in Lacan.

PLR: I think you already worked this out in *The Bonds of Love*.

JB: Really? Do tell.

PLR: As you've said, you argue against Lacan and Juliet Mitchell that the mother–child relationship is not asocial.[28] So there's already a thirdness or what I would call potential space—since I don't think Winnicott ever speaks of "transitional space"—in the mother–child dyad. I think that insight is already present in *The Bonds of Love*.

JB: It is, but I wasn't able to elaborate it fully enough. In "Recognition and Destruction: An Outline of Intersubjectivity," which I wrote only a couple of years after *The Bonds of Love*, I showed how the dialogic process between the mother and child—or any adult and child—can contain this potential space, as Winnicott said.[29] Potential space *is* the third.

PLR: Right. But it doesn't have to be equated with the phallus.

JB: No, I think that's a major misconstrual. The insistence on the

---

27. *Aufgehoben*, a term from Hegelian dialectics, is ordinarily translated as "sublated" and refers to the way that, in a synthesis, the thesis and antithesis are simultaneously canceled, preserved, and raised to a higher level.

28. Benjamin, *The Bonds of Love*, pp. 93–95; and *Like Subjects, Love Objects*, p. 96.

29. Benjamin, *Like Subjects, Love Objects*, pp. 27–48.

phallus goes back to a category that I abandoned because it seemed too ideological, but that I used originally, of false differentiation. It's a defensive modality. The other idea in *The Bonds of Love* that pertains to this is an incipient notion of multiplicity. This idea has been developed further in the work that's been done by my closest feminist colleagues—Bassin, Dimen, Goldner, Harris.[30] What I said in *The Bonds of Love* is that we switch between the different positions of "I as female," "I as male," and "I as neutral" and that these positions can coexist. I said that the so-called narcissism of that preoedipal constellation is actually a strength rather than a weakness. One of the ways we are able to overcome splitting is by tolerating the simultaneity of different positions. Juliet Mitchell explicitly argued against Dimen, who took up the case for paradox and multiple positions. Mitchell said that experiencing opposite positions simultaneously is psychotic and intolerable.[31] I think that has it exactly backwards. What could she mean?

PLR: I think that her hard-core, Freudo-Lacanian allegiance is reflected in that assertion. It's striking how certain theorists who are widely considered feminists or radical—such as Kristeva and Mitchell—turn out to be retrograde in many of their assumptions.

JB: I'm not sure why that is. Since I was never a structuralist, I've always operated on a different level from them.

PLR: But your fondness for thinking in terms of binary oppositions and their sublation, which, of course, is Hegelian in one of its antecedents, is also structuralist.

JB: Well, it is and it isn't. Remember that in the 1960s and 1970s there was an entire controversy between the structuralists and the Hegelians. The structuralists repudiated Hegel. Althusser repudiates Hegel.

---

30. Donna Bassin (1997), "Beyond the He and She: Postoedipal Transcendence of Gender Polarities." *Journal of the American Psychoanalytic Association*, Suppl. 44:157–190; Muriel Dimen (1991), "Deconstructing Difference: Gender, Splitting, and Transitional Space." *Psychoanalytic Dialogues*, 1:335–352; Virginia Goldner (1991), "Toward a Critical Relational Theory of Gender." *Psychoanalytic Dialogues*, 1:249–272; Adrienne Harris (1991), "Gender as Contradiction: A Discussion of Freud's 'The Psychogenesis of a Case of Homosexuality in a Woman.'" *Psychoanalytic Dialogues*, 1:197–224.

31. Juliet Mitchell (1991), "Commentary on 'Deconstructing Difference: Gender, Splitting, and Transitional Space.'" *Psychoanalytic Dialogues*, 1:353–359.

PLR: He probably repudiated everybody. [laughs] Althusser was a structuralist Marxist, but I wouldn't call him a structuralist proper in the sense of Lévi-Strauss.

JB: The truth is, if we can diverge a little more, that it's only recently that I read the translation of Lacan's First Seminar and realized the connection between what I had arduously worked out about recognition and split complementarity and what Lacan was trying to say from the same Hegelian point of view.[32] But the Lacanians I've read never seem to highlight this strand in his thinking, which is the most astonishing thing to me. The whole story is there as far as I'm concerned, not exactly the way I would tell it, but the main points about what he terms the seesaw relationship—which I call complementarity or the fundamental do-or-done-to relationship—and how the Symbolic is a way of releasing oneself or the other from that.

PLR: The Symbolic takes one out of the symbolic equation, so to say.[33]

JB: Yes. The idea of intersubjectivity, which I'd always seen presented in a linguistic way by other people, is very clear here. Lacan argues that you can't simply view the other as an object of need, the way that object relations theorists do, because you will then remain locked in a dyad in which I drink your milk until you have nothing left to give, and at that point you can eat me. The implication of that is that there has to be maternal subjectivity.

PLR: What you report about the First Seminar seems to diverge from the Lacan of the *Écrits*.[34]

JB: Yes, that may be. I'm not saying that I agree with Lacan completely, but he is struggling with the same issues arising from the Hegelian problem of recognition that I had worked through. But the idea of the phallus as the third term excludes the possibility of convergence from my point of view.

PLR: But there's a dimension of Lacan that is very valuable in that respect. Hegel was not an influence on object relations theory or on ego psychology. Part of what is so rich about your work is your

---

32. *The Seminar of Jacques Lacan: Book I. Freud's Papers on Technique. 1953–1954*, ed. Jacques Alain-Miller, trans. John Forrester. New York: Norton, 1988.

33. Benjamin, *Like Subjects, Love Objects*, pp. 202–208.

34. Jacques Lacan (1966), *Écrits*. Paris: Seuil; see also *Écrits: A Selection*, trans. Alan Sheridan. New York: Norton, 1977.

grounding in philosophy as well as in developmental thinking—the synthesis of Hegel and Winnicott, so to say.

JB: Yes, because Winnicott and Hegel saw the world in an entirely different way, except that they didn't. It's an amazing discovery.

PLR: This raises an important question. If I could go back to the simple way I summed up one of your arguments in *The Bonds of Love*, but substitute recognition for attunement, we've got the structure of an analogy where recognition is to paradox as domination is to polarity.

JB: Yes. I like that a lot.

PLR: One of the crucial issues that arises is whether polarity or domination is an inherent condition or whether it should be regarded as a breakdown phenomenon that can be avoided if one has a good-enough experience.

JB: No, it can't. I've been influenced by thinkers such as Thomas Ogden and Michael Eigen, who consider the paranoid-schizoid position to be essential and valuable, even though it clearly needs to be counterbalanced.[35] I reject the view of Guntrip[36] or Kohut[37] that breakdown is avoidable, because this view leads to idealizations that have disastrous clinical effects. I always return to the idea that splitting is unavoidable. Clinically, this means that the patient has to enlist the analyst's subjectivity to play the opposing part in his or her own internal split. This is necessary because, in order to reveal parts of self and make visible traumatic experience, these splits have to be enacted dramatically.

So breakdown in the analytic situation—what Freud would call a repetition—is not to be seen primarily as an unfortunate coming apart but a necessary part of the process. Freud saw the side of this that had to do with patients, but not the side that had to do with analysts. It has taken almost a century for analysts to begin talking about their own experience, their part in such dramas. As I see it, what relational psychoanalysis has tried to do is to highlight the analyst's subjective experience of being part of a two-person dynamic in

---

35. Ogden, *The Matrix of the Mind*; Michael Eigen (1993), *The Electrified Tightrope*. Northvale, NJ: Aronson.

36. Harry Guntrip (1971), *Psychoanalytic Theory, Therapy and the Self*. London: Maresfield Library, 1985.

37. Heinz Kohut (1977), *The Restoraton of the Self*. Madison, CT: International Universities Press.

which each partner reveals and brings out aspects of the other. It is not that we reject the idea of a therapeutic, in which we provide the patient with understanding, with good-enough experiences that might have been lacking in the past; but that we think such experiences have to include sometimes living through, certainly understanding, more painful experiences, which may well be enacted in the analysis.

PLR: So you now accept the idea of a Lacanian split subject?

JB: Not exactly. It's not that the subject *is* split. The subject *does* the splitting. As I argue in *Shadow of the Other*, there's a profound difference.

PLR: Is there ever a time when the subject is not split?

JB: Yes. I think there is a time when the mind is not yet capable of splitting; that is a protection mechanism not yet available to the baby. That's why it's crucial to have early attunement. That ground of being provides the basis for True-Self experience because it's where you make a spontaneous gesture. But even having perfect early attunement doesn't guarantee that you won't go on to split. The emergence of splitting and the breakdown of recognition do not seem to me to be contingent phenomena. They are just as absolute as recognition itself.

PLR: In your work you emphasize Winnicott's concept of the discovery of externality through the object's survival of the subject's destructive attacks.

JB: Yes.

PLR: Another way for me to ask the same question is whether or not you think it inevitable that the object will not survive. Do all objects retaliate?

JB: That's a different order of question.

PLR: If we agree that the relation of domination and subordination is the result of the loss of recognition, then it's not inevitable.

JB: But for recognition to be really lost, there has to be more than one breakdown or one retaliation. If all goes well, a developing relationship will have cycles of breakdown and repair. For reasons I don't fully understand, my work is seen by some feminists as playing down the inevitability of breakdown and positing an idealized vision of harmonious, perfect reconciliation. For instance, Judith Butler argues that I see destruction as something that can be survived once and for all.[38] I suspect this misunderstanding comes about because there is such a difference visualizing breakdown in a clinical rather than a social context. In a clinical context, we certainly do posit repair of breakdown as a meaningful goal that we expect to achieve with a significant number of patients. There would be no point doing therapy if we didn't think it was possible to survive and ameliorate destructiveness.

Of course, it is not something we achieve once and for all. It really is an ongoing process, sometimes extremely daunting and desperate. But from the perspective of psychoanalysis, even very small shifts toward mutuality are meaningful and harbingers of possible change. Any session in which we feel there has been a little movement, a little understanding—for instance, a patient who is usually inhibited or self-blaming makes a dry observation about some habit of the analyst in which the analyst recognizes herself—a moment of shared laughter or recognition of pain, can qualify as a moment of overcoming breakdown. Recognition isn't a utopia or a panacea, but it is a psychic potential whose presence is felt even in our remarking on its absence. In *Shadow of the Other* I tried to elucidate why recognition is the superordinate concept. Even given the dialectic between recognition and breakdown, if breakdowns are repaired and recognition is restored, then recognition stays intact as a capacity.

PLR: Exactly. It's only a partial breakdown.

JB: But at another level of experience, recognition and negation—or recognition and breakdown—are equally intrinsic to mind.

PLR: I think there may be a slippage in your use of the term negation between something that is inevitable and something that is contingent. From my standpoint, in *Shadow of the Other* you're grappling with postmodernism in a much more theoretically engaged way than in *The Bonds of Love.*

JB: Yes. I wasn't really grappling with it in *The Bonds of Love.*

PLR: To a great extent, you are responding to the critiques of your work in the intervening decade. But my concern, coming from a position very similar to yours, is whether you haven't given away too much.

JB: Do you think so? I could have.

---

38. Judith Butler (2000), "Longing for Recognition: Commentary on the Work of Jessica Benjamin." *Studies in Gender and Sexuality,* 1:271–290.

PLR: For example, looking back at *The Bonds of Love*, you say, "Nor can any appeal to the acceptance of otherness afford to leave out the inevitable breakdown of recognition into domination."[39] If we accept your earlier model, domination is the result of the failure of the other to survive the destructive attack. But now you're saying that this must happen.

JB: Yes. I said that at the end of *The Bonds of Love* as well. The question is not whether there are breakdowns, but whether equilibrium can be restored. I think there have to be failures of survival. Every human being knows something about domination in his or her soul because of that.

PLR: But there's still a difference between relationships that are mutual and relationships based on domination.

JB: But even a relationship that is basically mutual, such as a really good analytic relationship, is going to have its moments of domination. This is precisely analogous to what I say about the idea of postoedipal complementarity. Complementarity remains as a structure. What changes that structure is that it moves into the third space and becomes something more complex that we can play with. The values of light and darkness or of good and bad still remain, as do those of recognition and negation; but what organizes them is something different. In *The Bonds of Love* I explicitly say that domination is present in any good erotic relationship, but it becomes part of the play. That's what I mean by the assertion that domination is inevitable.

PLR: But when you say that domination is incorporated into a relationship of play, that's very different from the structure of a sadomasochistic relationship in which precisely that element of play is lacking.

JB: Absolutely.

PLR: I think the danger is that a remark such as the one I read could be interpreted to mean that domination is inevitable because all relationships are basically sadomasochistic.

JB: That's only if you decontexualize it from the rest of my work. Even in that book I say that recognition is the superordinate concept and that, if you restore recognition after breakdown, you're still weighing in on the side of recognition.

---

39. Benjamin, *Shadow of the Other*, pp. 83–84.

PLR: Well, I hope so.

JB: My goal is to give away as much as possible to that position in order to show, as with recognition, that I can sustain maximum breakdown. I'm trying to sustain a maximum amount of attack on my point of view and still make it stand up.

PLR: I think that's extremely admirable. What I've tried to do is to look at your work as something that has evolved over time and to see that, even though there is great continuity in your thinking, some realignment has taken place largely through the influence of post-modernist critiques.

JB: You might see that as something else that had to be survived.

PLR: I'm all in favor of seeing things from different points of view, but it seems to me that there was a cohesiveness to your model in *The Bonds of Love* that has been somewhat attenuated in your more recent work. It's again a question of whether too much has been given away. Another key issue is that of identity.

JB: That's where I think I might give away too much. Not around recognition and breakdown.

PLR: But the two are linked. In Winnicott's view, there will inevitably be interruptions in the continuity of being, but it's not inevitable that the interruptions will reach a traumatic or catastrophic degree of intensity.[40]

JB: But it's a spectrum, not just a choice between being catastrophic or good enough. There are a lot of things in between that allow human beings to know something of pain. That's what's being brought into play around the concept of multiplicity.

PLR: That is extremely important, but I'm trying to take these points one at a time. We talked about the distinction between partial breakdown and full breakdown. Again, to set up an analogy, partial breakdown is to disruption as full breakdown is to rupture.

JB: Yes.

PLR: The question that then seems to me crucial is whether full breakdown or only partial breakdown is inevitable. I would certainly agree with you that partial breakdown, or disruption, is inevitable and indeed perhaps desirable.

---

40. Winnicott, "The Location of Cultural Experience." In *Playing and Reality*, p. 97.

JB: That's all I'm saying. It's both inevitable and desirable.

PLR: But would you also say that full breakdown, or rupture, is inevitable?

JB: Absolutely not.

PLR: So we agree about that too.

JB: But full breakdown and partial breakdown are similar enough in their emotional valence that I can understand something about full breakdown from being deeply in touch with my experience of partial breakdown.

PLR: Quite so. As a reader of *Shadow of the Other*, I would only say to you that it was not clear to me that you were continuing to maintain the distinction between partial and full breakdowns. When I read a statement such as "alienated forms of complementarity, based on idealization and repudiation created by splitting, are inevitable,"[41] it seems as though you're saying that full breakdown, and not partial breakdown, is inevitable.

JB: You're doing a very close reading of my work, and I appreciate it. But that sentence is not in contradiction to what I just said. I think it means that even partial breakdowns may give rise to alienated byproducts. Even people who don't have catastrophic experiences will understand something of, and participate to some extent in, these forms of idealization. One way this happens is through a process of mediation in which you are inducted into a culture whose symbolic forms express historically the experience of full breakdown. You may grow up as a contemporary Jewish person without experiencing cataclysmic breakdown in your personal life, yet your family is imbued with the culture of the Holocaust, from which you imbibe a victimological fantasy about the world and an idealization of the Jews. Breakdown experience is so profoundly embodied in cultural forms and so intergenerationally transmitted that the fact that a parent or a parent's parent or someone else had a breakdown experience becomes inescapable. Yet for a person to absorb that experience thus indirectly, there has to be some paranoid and idealizing strand. There has to be that potential for splitting. So I'm not sure whether the breakdown experience always has to lie within the individual.

PLR: It's probably desirable to leave some things unresolved, but, if I might refocus the same question around the issue of identity,

---

41. Benjamin, *Shadow of the Other*, p. 97.

it's clear in *Shadow of the Other* that you are offering a critique of identity.

JB: Yes.

PLR: You said a little while ago that that was an area where you felt you might have given away too much. I wanted to ask you about that and at the same time to raise a larger question about the role of biology in your work. You don't talk about biology in any of your books.

JB: I try to stay away from it.

PLR: Obviously, biology can be brought into discussions of gender, but it can also be brought into discussions of identity or human nature more generally. Although your work engages crucially with issues of gender, it moves beyond them to nongender-specific issues of recognition and domination. For simplicity's sake, we might leave out the biology of gender and just talk about the biology of human identity. At least in *The Bonds of Love*, where you write that the baby is "already a unique person with his or her own destiny. . . . Although dependent, the baby brings his own self, his own unique personality, to bear on [his and his mother's] common life,"[42] it seems to me that you're accepting the idea of temperament.

JB: Definitely.

PLR: Temperament, of course, refers to the genetic predispositions of an infant. Winnicott's title *The Maturational Processes and the Facilitating Environment* implies that there is something innate in the individual, beginning with conception, that has a biological basis. All that is required, at least in the earliest stages, is that the environment not impinge on the development of the organism, which unfolds according to a preprogramed biological schema. I would also maintain that some kind of species identity underlies the capacity for recognition between human beings, which we don't share with animals of other species.

JB: Oh, I don't know. I think we have some capacity to recognize dogs. [laughs]

PLR: But not intersubjectively. I'm simply trying to say that insofar as there is an essentialist strand in your work—with which I sympathize, though some might regard it as a limitation—the role of biology is crucial and underlies the processes of recognition.

---

42. Benjamin, *The Bonds of Love*, pp. 13–14.

JB: Yes, absolutely. The only problem I have is that by calling on biology you become implicated in the discursive matrix that has arisen around the issue of biology versus society. I don't use the term biology because I don't want to enter into that discursive matrix, not because I feel uncomfortable with acknowledging a certain essentialism. But where I part ways with the terms of essentialism most clearly is that I reject Carol Gilligan's brand of gender essentialism.[43]

PLR: Let's bracket gender and talk about essentialism in terms of the species.

JB: I have no quarrel with the idea that there are many universal attributes of the species, for example, that people can recognize facial gestures across cultures. All that has been documented. I told you that I believe the problem of recognizing the other is a universal problem.

PLR: So could you address the question of identity? If you think that, beginning at conception, there is a unique person with his or her own destiny, why don't you accept the concept of identity?

JB: Because identity implies cohesion, as if we weren't always dissociated or multiple. Where I might want to modify the critique of identity is that I think there's some persisting self that nonetheless struggles to hold or contain this multiplicity. But by calling it identity, it's too easily misunderstood in the present atmosphere. The other problem I have with the term identity is that it exists in relation to negation. Paradoxically, one term implies the other. The ego is negated in its identity by every impact of the other. For negation to occur, there has to be some notion of identity; but, at the same time, negation subverts identity. That dialectic is something I didn't feel philosophically prepared to work out, so it's a lacuna.

PLR: I think you can handle it. You've done the heavy lifting already. [JB laughs] But the way you use the word negation, both here and in your writing, is for me analogous to your use of the word breakdown. You say the impact of the other leads to a negation.

JB: Right.

PLR: But couldn't one say that the impact of the other leads to an affirmation? The one thing we can be sure of is that, if there is no impact of the other, there will be a radical negation.

---

43. Carol Gilligan (1982), *In a Different Voice: Psychological Theory and Women's Development.* Cambridge, MA: Harvard University Press.

JB: The encounter with the other is always a negation of myself as an absolute identity. In a Hegelian sense, the very dependency on the other for affirmation already gives the lie to our identity.

PLR: Only if we conceive of it as an all-or-nothing proposition.

JB: But that's what I think the term identity means.

PLR: I don't agree.

JB: Well, in an Eriksonian sense, identity means something quite different. The problem is to move from the terms of the Hegelian discussion of identity to a different framework. What I did was to use the term self for what you're calling this modified sense of identity. In doing that, it seemed to me that I wasn't simply giving in to political pressure, because the term self is just as much of an anathema to all the people who excoriate identity. I thought "self" was a broader and more useful concept; and, if we say that the subject is split, the self is what has to embrace all the conflicts and split-off parts.

PLR: It's helpful for me to have the terms clarified. You're using "identity" as it is defined in a Hegelian context. But when, in the passage I quoted from *The Bonds of Love*, you say that the baby is already "a unique person with his or her own destiny" who "brings his own self, his own unique personality," that to me is a notion of identity in a more Eriksonian sense. It's interesting, by the way, that you prefer to refer to what Stoller calls "core gender identity" as a "nominal gender identification."[44] Isn't gender identity in most cases something visceral and hard-wired that can't be easily discarded as one could change one's name?

JB: No, it's nominal because what you identify with is the name and not the content. The children who were given the dolls in the De Marneffe experiment would point to the wrong one and say it's the boy or the girl. What they are identified with is the name, and the name gradually becomes saturated with meaning, but to call it "core" implies that it already has a definitive content, which in many ways it doesn't. That's what allows for the multiplicity of positions. This is not to say that gender is not deeply identified with. As Fast says, subjectively you don't know right away what's considered to belong to boyness or girlness. You may have certain qualities with a biological or hormonal basis and others that are based in the way you've been treated—everybody's been calling you "big guy" since you were

---

44. Robert Stoller (1968), *Sex and Gender*. New York: Aronson; Benjamin, *Like Subjects, Love Objects*, p. 55.

two weeks old and you've been roughhousing with your father and all of that—but you don't know yet that that has to do with boyness. That's just your experience. The issue is, when does that all get hooked up? It doesn't happen right away. That's why I call it "nominal."

PLR: That's a very interesting analysis, and it seems to bring you close to Judith Butler because for her ultimately there's no sex but only gender. The linguistic or cultural register—what I understand you to mean by "nominal gender identitification"—is taken to determine gender, rather than there being a preexisting biological sex that leads, in most cases, to the consolidation of a core gender identity.

JB: I certainly wouldn't agree that biological sex leads to gender identity. That's simply unpsychoanalytic. But I'm not sure that I would agree with Butler either. We do have biological experience, but it doesn't get hooked up right away. One thing I should say about Stoller is that I don't think he was wedded to the idea of "core." People like to trash Stoller because he used concepts such as that of a core or imprinting, but he did that only because he didn't have the current infancy research at his disposal to talk about presymbolic functioning. But when my publisher sent Stoller a copy of *The Bonds of Love*, he wrote me a wonderful letter where he said that he agreed with everything I had written about gender identification. So I don't feel that his concepts have to be taken in a limited way.

This touches on the way I use the work of other people generally. I'm not interested in saying, "Oh, Stoller was wrong because he spoke of 'core gender identity.'" I'm much more interested in saying, "How can we use Stoller and what might he have meant if he'd had the chance to think his ideas through further?" I do that with everybody as far as I can. I do it partly because I find it so tedious and annoying when some people try to pin other people down and say, "Well, they said this, therefore that is now true of their thought," without considering the underlying intention of their work. Don't they understand that thinking isn't like that? Thinking is like the flow of the river. Yes, the river has certain definitions, but it moves with time.

PLR: Unfortunately, some people insist on affirming the correctness of their position.

JB: Those are the people I'm most likely to criticize because I don't see them as thinking.

PLR: You and I are very much akin in the way we aspire to work. But let's come back to identity and multiplicity. You reject the concept of identity in a Hegelian sense and argue that "the notion of splitting does not require that we posit a preexisting unity, or an ideal of unity to which splitting gives the lie."[45] My question arising from that has to do with the notion of continuity of being.

JB: Continuity of being is a different concept from unity.

PLR: Isn't it continuity that makes unity possible?

JB: Conceptually, they are different. They refer to the same phenomenon, but unity is a bad way of talking about that phenomenon and continuity is a good way of talking about it.

PLR: I'm not invested in the word unity, but you place a lot of emphasis on a critique of identity, which implies that you think it to be a mistaken concept rather than simply not the most useful way of talking about a genuinely existing phenomenon.

JB: As I've explained, I think that identity is a flawed, contradictory concept. But, if you take a concept such as unity and see people trashing it in a knee-jerk way that seems to miss the point, to my mind what you want to do is not necessarily to reclaim the concept. What you want to do is look at it in its dialectical connection to what they're opposing it to, which is splitting, and see the way in which it's being used as a straw man. Consequently, I'm not so interested in saying there really is such a thing as unity or in getting sucked into that ideological debate. What I am interested in is in saying there is a continuity of self, a history of self.

PLR: But what troubles me is that at times you seem to join with those who are attacking the concept. The same people who attack unity have no use for the idea of continuity either.

JB: I see nothing wrong with joining the criticisms to strengthen your own position. If you don't do this and simply try to defend your own concepts, you end up reaffirming the binary opposition, which inevitably puts you in an awkward position. For instance, Seyla Benhabib produced a version of self and autonomy and unity that got rid of all negativity and all breakdown.[46] She did the Habermasian thing. I see that route as problematic, and I don't want to take it.

---

45. Benjamin, *Shadow of the Other*, p. 89.

46. Seyla Benhabib (1992), *Situating the Self: Gender, Community and Postmodernism in Contemporary Ethics*. New York: Routledge, pp. 203–241.

PLR: I'm trying to articulate an unease I feel when reading your work that many other people might not feel. We're both caught up in the debates over postmodernism, and I'm trying to clarify your perspective on that position. In my view, it's certainly not a matter of discarding everything, but of trying to formulate a response that does justice to the critique and the challenge.

JB: That's exactly what Jane Flax does.[47] I'm not sure I can articulate for you right now why I don't do that, but for some reason it's very important for me not to do it that way.

PLR: Let me then ask you a question. It concerns your treatment of Judith Butler. You say that Butler "seems to posit an exclusion that has no opposing term, no *inclusion*."[48] You go so far as to refer to her lack of any concept of an inclusive self as the "main inconsistency" in her position.[49] I applaud your critique of Butler and think you've pinpointed a serious problem in her work. But I'm troubled by what seems to me a similar inconsistency in your own position, which is that you want to talk about difference without talking about identity.

JB: No, I talk about sameness and commonality. Commonality for me is the opposing term to difference. Commonality and difference refer to intersubjective relations. Now, identity is for me also an intersubjective concept that has to do with how I relate to the other. You want me to talk about identity as it pertains to the self, as an *intra*subjective concept. In this context, I tend to shy away from intrasubjective concepts altogether. But insofar as I do think about the self as intrasubjective, I think about it in terms of multiplicity and continuity. For me the opposing term to multiplicity is continuity.

PLR: But continuity is temporal, whereas multiplicity isn't. A moment ago you said that for you the opposing term to difference was either commonality or sameness.

JB: Yes, because difference is intersubjective.

PLR: That was helpful to me, although there is a book by Heidegger

---

47. Jane Flax (1990), *Thinking Fragments: Psychoanalysis, Feminism, and Postmodernism in the Contemporary West*. Berkeley: University of California Press.

48. Benjamin, *Shadow of the Other*, p. 102.

49. Benjamin, *Shadow of the Other*, p. 104.

entitled *Identity and Difference*,[50] and one could imagine a conceptual framework in which those were the polar terms. But you've clarified that you're opposing difference to sameness or commonality, which would in any case lead us back to a certain essentialism in the domain of intersubjective recognition. So maybe the term that we should use as the antithesis to unity or identity is not difference but multiplicity. At one point, you speak of "the importance of conceiving of a multiple rather than a unified self."[51] But what about conceiving of a flexible rather than a rigid self? Is the only choice between "multiple" and "unified"? Can't we have an identity that allows us to assume different positions and in that sense encompasses multiplicity?

JB: You can do that, but it's not something I chose to do because I bumped into too many other usages of the term identity that for me were problematic. Lew Aron has said something very like what you've just said in his discussion of gender multiplicity.[52] My aim is to use more transitive and dynamic terms.

PLR: I'm afraid you run the risk of sounding as though you're celebrating fragmentation.

JB: No, I don't sound as though I celebrate fragmentation.

PLR: You say that "the subject's agency and liberation derive from identity's very negativity, in the contradictions between its multifarious positions."[53]

JB: Where do I say that? [reads] "Attempting to get beyond the impasses proceeding from the deconstruction of the subject, such critics propose that the subject's agency and liberation derive from identity's very negativity, the contradictions between its multifarious positions."

PLR: Are you criticizing that view? It sounds to me as though you're agreeing with those who equate liberation with the negation of identity.

---

50. Martin Heidegger (1957), *Identity and Difference*, trans. Joan Stambaugh. New York: Harper Torchbooks, 1974.

51. Benjamin, *Shadow of the Other*, p. 105.

52. Lewis Aron (1995), "The Internalized Primal Scene." *Psychoanalytic Dialogues*, 5:195–237.

53. Benjamin, *Shadow of the Other*, p. 93.

JB: I'm not precisely criticizing that position, but I feel it's inadequate. In other words, I see some value to it, but I don't think it's good enough. What I haven't done is stopped to point out that this whole notion that liberation of self derives from the clash of positions has to presuppose that there's enough continuity for you to hold yourself together.

PLR: Exactly. That's all I'm asking for.

JB: Don't I quote Jane Flax saying that somewhere?

PLR: Unfortunately, I don't see her name in the index. This might be a good place to stop.

JB: Yes. You know, the one thing you didn't do, which I think you're going to regret later, is talk to me more about my clinical perspective.

PLR: I regret it already. Had we but world enough and time . . .

Peter J. Swales

Sovereign unto Myself

Peter L. Rudnytsky: I thought I might begin by quoting Janet Malcolm, who refers to you as "one of the world's leading authorities—perhaps *the* leading authority—on the early life of Freud and on the early history of psychoanalysis."[1] Obviously, I'm very interested in talking to you about how you developed your interest in Freud . . .

Peter J. Swales: Well, if that was true when she wrote it back in 1983, it's a lot more true today, I regret to say. Back then, there were only three or four or five of us who knew anything to speak of about 19th-century Freud history. And here we sit, nearly two decades later, and there are still only five or six persons who really know very much at all—about the *early* Sigmund Freud, at any rate.

PLR: You mentioned in a phone conversation we had that your view of Freud hasn't changed since it crystalized at an early stage of your thinking.

PJS: Absolutely. You could put it another way. My view of Freud antedates the first time I ever even heard of him. I still work with fundamental first principles that go back to when I was virtually an adolescent.

PLR: How does your view of Freud antedate your encounter with him?

PJS: When I was about 18, I became vaguely aware of the school of thought that emanated out of Nancy—meaning Liébeault and

---

1. Janet Malcolm (1984), *In the Freud Archives*. New York: Knopf, p. 91.

Bernheim.[2] Stereotypically it can be represented, I guess, by Bernheim's axiom, "*Tout est dans la suggestion.*"

PLR: How did you become aware of that school of thought?

PJS: I had intellectual interests in spite of what I was doing for a living. I was very actively interested in mysticism, psychology, philosophy, and history to an extent. Around the age of 17 or 18, I encountered the ideas of Gurdjiev.[3] In a manner of speaking, I had nothing to learn from Gurdjiev because I knew it all already. It was all so intuitively obvious to me. But he struck the right chord. It made consummate sense of my own existence—and comprehension of everything—up to the age of 18.

PLR: What was it about Gurdjiev's ideas that seemed intuitively true?

PJS: In this case, I speak about Gurdjiev as a psychologist and philosopher, and not as a cosmologist. Here I'm concerned only with Gurdjiev's diagnosis of mankind. You might say that Gurdjiev was a reluctant misanthrope, which is certainly what I am (given, of course, limitless exceptions for particular individuals). Axiomatic to Gurdjiev's *Weltanschauung* is that mankind is in a state of chronic somnambulism—that man's ordinary everyday state is one of unconsciousness. *That* is the true unconscious! Everything that ordinary man takes for his own convictions, beliefs, and opinions is actually only vicariously acquired. It's programmed through our cultural conditioning. Man actually has next to nothing of himself within him. To use Gurdjiev's terminology, men are all personality—or even *multiple* personalities—and have no essence to speak of. *That* they squandered during childhood. It's, again, axiomatic for Gurdjiev that simple people—rural people and peasants—live more in essence than they do in personality, as opposed to how it is in large urban centers. I didn't need Gurdjiev to tell me that.

And still within me even today there's just a country lad. I grew up literally on the fringe—almost even beyond the pale—in one of the last houses on the road of a small, provincial market town surrounded by the countryside and not so far from the ocean. Mind, in

2. See Henri F. Ellenberger (1970), *The Discovery of the Unconscious: The History and Evolution of Dynamic Psychiatry.* New York: Basic Books, pp. 85–89.

3. George Ivanovitch Gurdjiev (1872–1949), Armenian spiritualist and author. After the Russian Revolution, Gurdjiev settled in Fontainebleau, France, where he established the Institute for the Harmonious Development of Man (1922). Gurdjiev taught that ordinary people could attain higher awareness and take control of their lives.

the course of time I came to be hypnotized by the big city and its cultural trance—by its extended, remote influence of media, pop music, fashion, and the like. But even today I'm much more at home with simple country people than I am with big-city people. One of the tragedies or perversities in my own life is that I spend a big part of it orbiting in an environment like New York, which is not really my style. There's a contradiction here because I do float very well in New York, actually. It's a magnet and a hub for all aliens and exiles. And, existentially speaking, I've been an alien since the age of 12 or 13 and an exile for by now more than a quarter of a century.

PLR: How did you discover that you were an alien at that age?

PJS: Because I didn't believe in anything. For example, I grew up simultaneously in three religions—a Methodist chapel, a Protestant church, and a Roman Catholic church.

PLR: Were they connected with specific people in your life?

PJS: Two neighbors of ours, whom we called "uncle" and "aunt" though they weren't really, were devout chapel-goers and would take us to Sunday school and certain services. In the fullness of time, that meant that I went to their youth club. I also sang in a boys' choir in school, and almost all the concerts we gave were in chapels. At the same time, I was brought up formally as a member of the Church of Wales. For years and years I was a choir boy, served communion, and all that stuff. At the same time, however, my father, albeit that we were Protestants, became musical director of a Roman Catholic band. My two sisters and I—I'm a middle child, sandwiched—got press-ganged into this kids' band when I was about the age of nine. My education had been musical—piano and violin. So I just had to pick up a clarinet one day and start playing it.

PLR: And the musical saw?

PJS: That's a vestige of a decade of musical education that ultimately went off the rails. It's something that I was never taught but you might say I stole from my father. (Call it oedipal if you want!) Nobody needed to *teach* me to play that. I guess I learned that by osmosis.

PLR: So you had an upbringing in which you participated in various religious denominations, but at around 12 or 13 you realized that you didn't believe any of it?

PJS: No, well before that. By the time I was six or seven. And because I'm a baby-boomer, as they say—born in 1948—I grew up in the shadow of World War II. I was always intrigued by the matter of killing. My dear mother, invoking the Ten Commandments, would tell me that killing was wrong; but there was for me, from the age of six, this sheer discrepancy that under certain circumstances, just so long as the state condones it, it can be legitimate. I couldn't get to the bottom of that one.

PLR: Such as war or capital punishment?

PJS: Well, yes. If I have a private war in the sense of a vendetta against someone, give me a good reason why I shouldn't act on it. Not that I *wanted* to kill anybody. On the contrary, I wanted to be convinced why one *shouldn't* kill anybody! But it seemed to me that there had been enough louses in the world well worth the killing, beginning with Adolf Hitler. I grew up in a Britain that had only recently been involved in a bloodbath, so I only wanted someone to give me the correct reason why killing is wrong. At times it's licensed by society or the state or both. Modern history is, after all, largely a history of crime and warfare and killing. It's disgusting. Also, in the kind of place I grew up, people happily enough ate beef, pork, mutton, fowl, and fish. Why are we putting a special value on humankind?

PLR: So you're saying that from a very early age you were asking these fundamental questions and felt yourself to be an alien.

PJS: I was *tormented* by them. Also, people were psychologically transparent to me. So I couldn't help but be a little bit of a Machiavelli. I had to survive in a rather ruthless and brutal farming environment where people can be rough and aggressive and even malicious. I had a faculty of seeing through people, of mind-reading and anticipating several steps ahead, in a way that I had to be careful not to take advantage of. To me, people were fundamentally reactive, *ergo* predictable. I could guess that if I said *this*, it would evoke *that* reaction, and this was even borne out by experimentation. I would be astounded, and it used to scare me. I would worry a good deal about it.

PLR: Is there a particular occasion you can recall when you saw this power of yours in action?

PJS: Well, particularly in school. Funnily enough, Janet Malcolm, seeing as you've brought up her name, quotes me as saying that back in school I somehow had to get others to do my bidding for me.

PLR: You had to be second to the leader.[4]

---

4. Malcolm, *In the Freud Archives*, p. 117.

PJS: How that cashed out was protection. If I could render a dominant fellow beholden to me, I would be protected from external aggression. So I was virtually never bullied, because the others knew if they did that to *me*, so-and-so would come and smash their faces in. I was manipulating multiply. I was secure in the protection of the dominant guy, but it was also, of course, a bit of a manipulation against *him*. Talking about why I became an alien, something critical happened, which no doubt your typical vulgar Freudian would rush to use as a heuristic principle for my whole life. It was of major importance, but I think it would be banal and not do justice to all sorts of complexities to reduce everything to this one *Wendepunkt*— to this one turning point. But if you want, I'll tell you about it.

PLR: Please.

PJS: When I was 12 years old, living next door to me was an American kid, which was very unusual in those days. There were hardly any Americans in Britain. His father was one of the executives at an oil refinery they had recently built in nearby Milford Haven estuary. And that guy attached himself to me. I didn't particularly like it, but he appended himself to me because he had no other friends.

PLR: Was he your age?

PJS: Yes. His name was Billy Lockett. My best friend by then for five or six years had been another kid, Peter Biebrach. His father was a former German prisoner of war, imprisoned in my vicinity, who had then married a local girl. Peter Biebrach was a year younger than I and was an only child. We had air rifles, or what I think you call BB guns.

PLR: They fire pellets?

PJS: Yes. The Biebrachs had a very large chicken run behind their house in what had formerly been a mason's yard, used for making gravestones. So we would shoot off the rifles there. Now, I had serious qualms about pointing a gun at a bird, which my friend would do routinely. It plunged me into moral crisis. But one day there I was at home minding my own business, and a policeman turned up at the house. Now, this was terrible in a middle-class neighborhood in those days. The policeman said he wanted to speak to me and my parents. He then informed us that two windows in a hotel that overlooked the chicken run, called the Queen's Hotel, had been shot out. Three pellets had gone through one window, and one through another. He, the officer, had reason to believe that I was the culprit, along with Billy Lockett. I was deeply shocked, but retained my composure. So the inquiry proceeded, and at a certain point, the cop, who must have been struck by my ingenuousness in denying that I was the culprit—or, for that matter, that Billy Lockett could have been, to the best of my knowledge—asked me the following question: Did we ever use a fixed target on a particular wall? Now, I could see through the question and what it was that he was leading to: that the offense could be explained on the principle of charity by pellets that had regularly overshot a fixed target and gone through two windows.

In that moment I was confronted by a moral dilemma. In fact, we had never used a fixed target like this. But I could lie and say "Yes," because it was what he wanted to hear and it would have let me off. But what if it contradicted other testimony already given, or to be given, either by Peter Biebrach or even by Billy Lockett? I paused, and very rapidly it went through my head how different answers would ramify. Whereupon I said, "No. To tell you the truth, no." As far as my father was concerned, it was a foregone conclusion that I was guilty. Simply bringing a cop to the door was a pure enough disgrace. At a certain point, I said to the policeman, while he was wrapping it all up, "Pardon me, Officer, allow me please to ask you a question." "Yes." "You said that four pellets had been fired through these two windows?" "Yes, that's true." I said, "Well, then, in principle, surely the pellets would be retrievable?" "Oh, yes," he said, "I've got them right here in my pocket." (Only *now* he tells me!) I said, "Can I see those pellets?" Out he took four flattened brass objects. Brass. And I said, "I can tell you right away, I'm not the cuplrit. That exonerates me." "Why?" I said, "It's true that hypothetically my gun will fire that sort of pellets, but not reliably. Those are round balls. They only flatten out when they hit something solid. They're the kind of things that go in a BB rifle such as Peter Biebrach owns and his cousin Gwythyr Joyce uses. It's a repeater rifle that one reloads automatically—all the pellets are in the butt of the gun. Whereas my gun needs reloading by hand after every shot and properly fires only pellets that look like little hollowed-out caps. You can go and speak with Mr. Day at the toy shop in Bridge Street, and he will confirm to you I have never bought brass pellets, only these other lead or aluminum pellets."

To my disbelief, the cop wasn't at all interested, nor was my father! My father went the next day and paid for the windows, which absolutely appalled me. I can now understand where he was coming from, but at the time it totally pulled out the carpet from under me. The threat on the horizon was that Billy Lockett and I were going to get dragged before the Juvenile Court. Luckily, however, Billy Lockett

being an American and his father being an executive for Exxon—
Esso, as it was then called—well, this would have been complicated
in our little part of the world. Instead, one or two cops came to the
school, asked to see the headmaster, and talked about Billy Lockett
and Peter Swales. They learned that I routinely came top of the class.
The A-stream. There was an A, B, and C. I used to come within the
first three in the A-stream every year without even trying. In other
words, I had a good school report. So we didn't go to court. The matter was dropped, seeing as my father paid for the windows. The
immediate sequel was that Billy Lockett and I were both forbidden
to play either with each other or with Peter Biebrach. We never really
saw each other after that.

I became a trainspotter—as the English call it. Within a month I
had acquired an encyclopedic knowledge about the steam locomotives on British railways. I collected locomotive engine numbers and
used to go literally all over Britain in quest of, as it were, a very
lonely, exiled, and alien existence. I was existentially so profoundly
disillusioned with my world that I retreated into a hobby that, if you
want to use pathological language, you could say was obsessional.
Actually, it wasn't. It was an experience of pure love to be doing that.
It was a wonderful time in my life for about three years.

But here are two sequels, much more important. About 15 years
later I ran into Peter Biebrach in a pub. He'd had a few drinks.
Maybe I too had had a few drinks. We got to chatting. I asked him
about this episode. I worked around to it. I said, "Peter, you remember all that?" "Yeah," he said. I said, "Well, what was that all about?"
He said, "It was Gunth." Gunth was the nickname of his cousin,
Gwythyr Joyce. And in so many words he now conceded, "But I was
being pressured by him, in the spirit of family loyalty, not to betray
him, and to blame you and Billy Lockett." What a powerful vindica-
tion that was for me! By the way, I ran into him in the mid- or late
1970s, so I was surely by then already into my Freud work.

But here's the real punch line. Maybe a month or so after the incident itself, I had said to my dear mother, "You know, Mum, there's
no way I did that. Do *you* believe it?" And do you know what her
response was? She must have guessed that this was very disturbing
for me. She said, "You know, Peter, psychologists have proven that
people often do things and then suppress them into a part of their
mind, the unconscious, and they cannot recollect ever having done
such things." (Notice that she said "suppress," not "repress." That
wouldn't quite have been part of her vocabulary.) Well, I was gaga. I
was aghast. And I was dumbfounded. I said, "What? What a load of
baloney!" Because I knew and *owned* every moment of my own life.

Hypothetically, you could have asked me about a conversation I had had a year before, and I could have relived it and quoted it verbatim. I was so sovereign unto myself. I really had to ask myself, "Is it possible that there is something in me that acts without my own awareness? What a load of old cobblers!" Several years later I learned that during World War II my mother had read introductions to Freud, Jung, and Adler, and I even saw one or two such books in her bedroom on the shelf.

PLR: So your mother was trying to explain something charitably, but she still assumed it was true that you had done this, and that was unacceptable to you.

PJS: She just didn't know, I think.

PLR: But she didn't accept unqualifiedly your statement that you had not in fact done it.

PJS: I don't know.

PLR: Did you ever tell your father that, many years later, Peter Biebrach had acknowledged breaking the windows?

PJS: Yes. By then the whole business had lurked with me for years and years.

PLR: So you're saying that this experience was profoundly disillusioning for you?

PJS: It only *confirmed* my cynicism! It was corroboratory more than disillusioning. Do you realize that one of the imports of what I was telling you is that the cop was on the point of luring me into false memory syndrome? It was very profound for me at the time. Which road am I going to take? That was when I was still 12.

PLR: So what would be the clichéd Freudian interpretation of what happened?

PJS: Oh, Swales's entire life and work have been a reaction to that one event. The Freudians will always find a sow's ear in any silk purse. That's how they make a living. Let me tell you right now that my mother had what you call mental health problems. Within about 18 months, beginning when I was eight or nine through when I was 10, three times she went off to what we used to call a mental hospital in a town 30 miles away. She had electroshock and insulin-coma treatment. The first time she went for three months, virtually to the day. The second time, some six months later, she went for one month, virtually to the day. The third time, guess what? She went for just

24 hours. She came back home, and, though I was just a kid and she didn't confide very much at all to me about all this, she said, "There's no way those people are going to cure me. I'm going to cure myself. We're going to start a business." She revealed to me that she was going to start either a sewing shop or a music store. And she started a music store. It was completely mad. Thank God it was a music store! It took her about two years to finance the property and everything. So in 1961, when I was 12 coming up 13, we opened this music shop. Within a couple of years she had not only paid back every bit of the money she had borrowed to start the business, she had also made, for the time, a small fortune.

PLR: What work did your father do?

PJS: My father worked for the National Health Council reimbursing doctors, dentists, and pharmacists for their prescriptions and their services, and he kept on doing so till years later. By the end, he was Deputy Chief of the National Health Executive in Pembrokeshire, my native county. But all that time he had been a musician. He'd been in the Royal Marines Band, which is the élite musical corps in Britain, throughout the war years. He had had five years of war and had actually been there, at battle stations, at the sinkings of both the *Bismarck* and the *Scharnhorst*. He had one hell of a war, I can tell you. That was his university on the ocean, playing with the cream of the crop of professional musicians in that band and also in the dance-orchestra that he was delegated to direct.

PLR: What was his instrument?

PJS: He's a multi-instrumentalist. My father is by now Britain's most overqualified music teacher, with licentiates in eight or nine instruments across the board from classical guitar through violin to clarinet. It was a bane for me as a kid. I could see what my parents couldn't see. I wasn't particularly gifted musically. I'm a better consumer than I am a producer in music. I'm not inept, but I don't have that coordination of the fingers and so forth that you really need. I've a better *ear* than a lot of musicians. I was destined to become a piano tuner after my school career fell apart, and I actually registered in a piano-tuning college. But my father, all that time he was working for the National Health, had a dance band and a British Legion military band and private pupils and taught in schools. It's mind-boggling to me in retrospect. He was a brilliant breadwinner.

PLR: So your mother, after her third hospitalization . . .

PJS: So-called nervous breakdown.

PLR: Made a decision that the family would start a business, which became a music business.

PJS: That's right. Trading on my father's expertise.

PLR: So this was a store that sold instruments and sheet music and the lot?

PJS: And records. Everything. It became the biggest music store in Wales, probably even in most of Britain, except London, of course.

PLR: That's a fantastic story. We started by talking about how you had formed an image of Freud before you even discovered Freud.

PJS: [laughs] We did, didn't we?

PLR: I think I'm understanding that your decision to be honest at a crucial moment and to resist the false-memory temptation held out to you by the policeman was an experience that helped to form your attitude to psychoanalysis.

PJS: It's only a small part of the story, but it was quite decisive. Mind, what I had to tell you about my Mum is not in the least determinative or influential.

PLR: You mean about her breakdowns?

PJS: It's mind-boggling to me how insensate children can be about things. I didn't bat an eyelid about these three disappearances of my mother. To me it meant that I got to stay with my granny in Saundersfoot, a beach resort. It never had any impact. And nowadays I even feel guilty about that.

PLR: Was there a sense that your father's lack of belief in your account of what had happened and his paying for the windows even though you hadn't broken them meant that you had to prove something to him?

PJS: Let me be frank. My adolescent years vis-à-vis my father were very difficult—in fact, for me a bit of a nightmare. But perhaps also a bit of a nightmare for him, too. You see, my father had two wives— music *and* my mother. So he wasn't at home half the time. For that reason, things were difficult in the family. And we three children had a lot expected of us musically, so I at least was quite a disappointment. However, it has to be stressed, by contrast, that my father is actually a wonderful man, and I've got the highest respect for him. He's absolutely scrupulous, for a start. What he and I share in common—and it's profound—is that we're both autodidacts. Nobody ever really taught us anything. We taught ourselves, which to me is what education should be all about. And the problems we had are not necessarily to be imputed to my father's character so much as to the whole milieu. It was a difficult time, a difficult place. Both my parents have been nothing but good and indulgent to me since the day I left home. That's what it took, for me to go out there in the world and be independent. In principle, since the day of my 17th birthday, which was the day I fled home—and by extension, fled school—my relationship with them has been fine. We were always a very, very close family. My mother's been deceased for three years.

PLR: I'm sorry. Why don't you tell me a little bit about what your sisters have done? Where do they live and are they married?

PJS: I'd rather not. I wouldn't want to drag them into this. I'll only say that they inherited the family business and, as far as I can tell, do a fine job running it.

PLR: So they're still in Wales?

PJS: Yes. My older sister taught music for several years in an élite private school in London. She got her B.A. in music. My younger sister worked at a record store in central London for five years or so, then for the government for five years. But they then went back to Pembrokeshire and took over the family business. They shouldn't now have to suffer the burden of my mad life.

PLR: Absolutely not. So maybe we can pick up the thread of your story. You said you had become a trainspotter in the aftermath of this early experience of disillusionment in connection with the BB gun incident.

PJS: There must be a better word than "disillusionment." It was a purely existential crisis. I recollect that, for two years, any time the doorbell or the telephone rang, I was terrified that it was the cops. Sheer unmitigated anxiety! There were a couple of other false accusations, by the way.

PLR: I was going to ask whether there were any similar incidents that might have preceded that one.

PJS: There were three or four, none so serious as the one I told you about. However, I was not guilty of any of them. There were any number of other things that I *had* done and *was* guilty of.

PLR: Such as what?

PJS: Oh, trying to blow up the local gas works. [PLR laughs] I wasn't caught then. [PJS laughs] I was often involved with other kids in trying to derail trains and things like that. Mad!

PLR: Serious things.

PJS: Serious things. Kids can be demented. I wasn't caught for any of them. I was blamed, on the contrary, for three or four things I *hadn't* done. Setting a dog loose in a field of sheep was one of them. Or not stopping on my bicycle at a halt sign. Even my ultraconservative, bourgeoise older sister defended me on that one because she was my witness. There was this cop behind me in a car. I stopped for the halt sign but didn't put my feet down because if you're a good bike rider you don't have to. You can hold the bike in equilibrium for three seconds. The next thing I know, the cop goes to my house to file a complaint.

PLR: This was before the other incident?

PJS: Yes. It was when I was about nine. Pathetic!

PLR: So there was a series of these episodes. It reminds me of Rousseau's *Confessions*.

PJS: Oh, really? Persecution complex!

PLR: In the early books, he writes about one defining childhood incident when he was beaten for something he hadn't done, and then another when he blamed a theft he had committed on a servant girl. So he felt a combination of outrage at the false accusation and guilt at having let someone else take the punishment for something he had done.

PJS: What were you going to say about the trainspotting?

PLR: I was trying to resume the thread. As you described it, it seems that your interests shifted after the incident with the policeman and you became absorbed in learning about trains.

PJS: I grew up near the railroad. Steam locomotives were always wonderful, romantic objects for me. These were living creatures for me. So this was a species of zoology, comparative anatomy, and even embryology. I knew my steam locomotives, especially the Great Western ones. By the way, Britain stank in those years—the 1950s and early 1960s—of industry, of coal, of steam.

PLR: In the north of England?

PJS: Not just. Also in the south of Wales. Not where I come from, which is a national park on the ocean. But, if I traveled east, which

I did all the time as a trainspotter, all the grime and the soot, and the romance of it all . . . It's weird, isn't it?

PLR: Is a trainspotter someone who jumps trains and rides around?

PJS: Yes, but you take down the locomotive numbers. You go to the engine sheds. You buy a little guidebook that leads you to these locomotive roundhouses and you sneak in there. You're not really supposed to be there, although a lot of the train drivers were lovely blokes and would make you cups of tea, even give you a cigarette.

PLR: And so you jump the train and you ride around?

PJS: No, you don't jump. Not like a yardbird. You buy a special ticket that lasts a week, let's say, or a month, in the summer.

PLR: So it's not as though you're a hobo or anything of that sort?

PJS: Oh, no.

PLR: You're just traveling on the train with a ticket and hanging out with people?

PJS: And staying with relatives across the country. It wasn't very intelligible to most other people, but it was an academic study for me. I was encyclopedic. Most exciting about it was that it was an exploration of the central nervous system of the country with all the branches going off. Still today I study maps—railroad-maps or motor-maps—and make sense of the connections. That's where I'm at home. It's anatomy and physiology vis-à-vis the body politic.

PLR: I understand. So you were becoming an autodidact through the study of trains?

PJS: Well, I'm talking about how it was. I don't know how it is now. You mingle with other trainspotter kids, and you have instant relationships because all you do is talk engine numbers and engine names. It was brilliant. I loved it. Vis-à-vis my native milieu, mind, it was lonely, very lonely. But you're happy in your loneliness.

PLR: You were in your teens at that point?

PJS: I was 12, 13, 14. Even 15. The summer when I turned 15, literally at that moment I quit. I'd heard the Beatles and was more interested in girls.

PLR: So you became a girlspotter?

PJS: Yes. The activities were even combined for about six months. When I was trainspotting, I'd start chatting up girls on the train.

They'd write to me, and I'd never respond. [laughs] I was always embarrassed when my mother would hand me a letter written by some girl I'd met on the train.

PLR: That's lovely. Earlier you mentioned Gurdjiev and the idea of essence on one hand and personality on the other.

PJS: I think we should have to make it personalit*ies*, in the Latin sense of *personae*—masks or roles on the stage. People in life don't necessarily have any unifying principle. It's a question of degree. So that "Sybil"—as in Shirley Mason, the notorious multiple—is a conglomerate of personalities.[5] She's one person vis-à-vis her therapist, another vis-à-vis her roommate, another vis-à-vis her stepmother, another vis-à-vis her father, and so on. Each is for her a kind of dissociated hypnoid state. There's nothing unified about it. A person like me doesn't really belong in New York, because I generally speak and act from essence.

Before we turned on the tape we were talking about the stability in my marriage. That's because Julia and I don't live in an illusory world vis-à-vis one another or ourselves. I don't mean to sound arrogant or complacent. But this is the existential dilemma I have. We live in a consumer culture, and Julia and I are completely outside it. Here we are in the center of the cyclone, though it impinges on us very little. We must be among the last people in New York who actually cook, and we have banquets here for lots of people. I don't read newspapers as a rule. About twice a year I have an orgy, a binge, and I go out there. It's a bit like going into McDonalds and eating junk food when you're ravenously hungry. You gobble it down your throat, and then the next minute you want to vomit it. That's what happens to me with newspapers. I seldom watch television.

So I don't belong to the world in which psychoanalysis functions. I'm abstinent in terms of today's "culture" and am even puritanical about remaining so. I don't live in a societal structure that allows for an activity like psychoanalysis. To me it's as anomalous as it would be if you and I were living in a Greek village. Would you expect to find a psychoanalyst in the village? You might find a priest, and you might find a doctor. But the purchase of friendship? You don't pay a priest as a rule; you donate something to the collection. As for doctors, that's a different discussion. And I'm a Shavian on that one. What's Shaw's wonderful line? "All professions are a conspiracy against the layman." It's true. Journalists, accountants, attorneys, doctors, psychoanalysts. I don't want anything to do with all that.

---

5. Flora Rheta Schreiber (1973), *Sybil*. Chicago: Regnery.

PLR: Maybe we can jump ahead to London, where you had a famous period with the Rolling Stones.

PJS: No, infamous. [laughs] That was my university. That was my *alma mater*. I still think so today.

PLR: What did you major in?

PJS: Consumerism. I was a little anthropologist observing it all. That's a unique situation to be in. For me, boy, was it difficult! At 20, I found myself in at the deep end and didn't really know how to swim. But I've got nothing but good things to say about those guys.

PLR: How did you fall in with that bunch?

PJS: Jagger had learned about me through his secretary, who had checked me out as perhaps the right man for a particular job. He asked me if I'd come and work for the band as a promo man. I said, "Well, yeah, but Mick, you've got a problem. There's nothing to promote. Being a promo man's a full-time gig. You can't go out and promote one record a year." In 1968, the Stones had done just one album and one single, and the album hadn't even been issued because it featured a toilet seat on the cover and the record company wouldn't accept that.

PLR: But that was quite late. They had already become very big.

PJS: Yes, they were very well established by then—though, of course, they're still going today—but in the grip of a professional crisis. I wasn't even particularly a Stones fan. Or, rather, I was a reluctant Stones fan. I went to work for them because I'd had a chance to preview *Beggar's Banquet*. I thought, "Wow, that is superb! They've reinvented rock and roll. Suddenly it's mature. This ain't pop music any more. It's political. It's social. It's relevant." I don't think that about much of the junk since. But that's how I felt then. It was a brilliant moment, and I still think so today.

PLR: That was also the time of *Sergeant Pepper's*.

PJS: Yes. And I was right there, at the hub.

PLR: What were you doing just before that?

PJS: Working at another little record company in London.

PLR: And so Jagger's secretary contacted you and then you began working for the Stones for a period of time?

PJS: At first I said, "No, I'm not interested." The company I worked for was what you might call a family outfit, figuratively speaking. We were like one big family. I had not worked there long. I'd worked for two and a half years for EMI records, which was very stable, but I ventured to go work for this little company. But once I was there I saw I was on a sinking ship, and I didn't want to be a rodent. But, on the other hand, my self-preservation was at stake. I had to make a living. And so suddenly I got a phone call. At first I said no. She said, "Well, we can pay you more money." [laughs] I learned something then. That wasn't what I was asking for. That wasn't the issue. But finally, it became vivid enough to me, following an argument I'd had with Giorgio, my boss. He and a couple of friends of mine sat about one day much the worse for wear with whiskey slagging off— or badmouthing, as you say here—another artist friend of ours, Gary Farr, who I thought had terrific potential. They were totally mismanaging the situation. The internecine politics at the company were strangling everything. So I intervened in the discussion. I'd never done any such thing in my life. I walked in almost in tears, probably red in the face with fury, and said, "What do you people mean? If you keep on talking like that, what you're saying is precisely what's going to happen"—this on the model of a self-fulfilling prophecy. In that moment, I thought, "Uh-oh. Get out." But I earned their respect for that, by the way. I'd been "little Peter" before that. I'd never asserted my own voice with that independence of mind before.

PLR: So you decided to take the offer from the Rolling Stones?

PJS: I think what happened is I called up Jagger's secretary and said I was ready to consider changing my mind. So then I finally sat with Jagger in his house for a couple of hours. And around the same time I went with all the Rolling Stones, one of the last times the original five members were all together, to a Mothers of Invention concert.

PLR: Brian Jones was still alive?

PJS: Yes. I got to know Brian quite well in the course of the next nine months. He spoke pristine middle-class English. You never hear that these days. And yet he was a wreck. That was truly a disillusioning experience—if you want to use that word—to watch the decline and demise of Brian Jones. *That* was an education!

PLR: Was it drugs that did it?

PJS: Yes, in the strict sense of drugs, meaning vodka more than anything illicit.

PLR: Was it heroin too?

PJS: Oh, he would dabble in anything, I imagine. By the way, he was asthmatic. That was a liability. You can't do recreational drugs with impunity in quite the same way if you're asthmatic. He was always [inhales three times] with his machine. I think that's probably what killed him—that he drowned in the pool after inhaling. But just to see this guy, who had been so charismatic and so gifted, going to pieces—so bloated, a full-blown clinical paranoia, so much so that he couldn't tune his guitar in the same room with Keith Richards . . .

PLR: So it was directed at Keith, the lead guitarist, Brian being rhythm guitar?

PJS: No, actually, it had always been more the opposite, musically speaking. Keith was the great rhythm player. Brian's responsible for lots of those great licks and riffs in the lines. [Vocalizes the lead guitar part of "The Last Time."] Take "Little Red Rooster." Brian Jones is probably the first guy in Britain ever to play a bottleneck. [vocalizes.] He was a potential Clapton, believe it or not.

PLR: And then he played sitar, of course.

PJS: Anything. Recorders or saxophones or sitars. Put anything in front of Brian, and he could play it.

PLR: Was he the one you were closest to?

PJS: No, I was closest to Jagger and Charlie Watts. I never really got to know Keith Richards until about a month before I quit. But when I did get to know him, I thought, what a lovely, sweet guy. It's only through happenstance—including no doubt the fact that he was then rather strung out on lots of heavy stuff—that I didn't get to know Keith in the way I knew Charlie and Mick.

PLR: What were your impressions of them as individuals?

PJS: Admiration. I was 20 or 21 years old. They were between 25 and 30. They'd been going by then for five years and had seen the world. And come back again to tell the story. They had such chutzpah, such audacity, such spunk. They were undaunted, and I couldn't help but admire it. You could not intimidate them. That was for me quite awesome. This is the time when the cops were trying to weave a conspiracy. You know the guy who busted Lennon and got put away for planting drugs? Well, he with a vengeance was trying to get Jagger. There was a showdown one day on a London street.

PLR: Lennon was arrested in England, and that impeded his immigration to the United States?

PJS: Yes. But he had a good case to argue in the immigration court; the cop in question was later jailed in England for dealing drugs, or planting them, or giving false testimony, or whatever it was. That guy was a louse! I give you that just to instantiate the basic point that life with the Stones was tough. We were under attack. But they were unflinching. Mind, they were the band, and I was never over-familiar. I always retained a formality and a seriousness, because I was their employee. I never tried to fraternize. But, paradoxically, they would. They'd offer me a joint. Or Mick might say, "Peter, why don't you come around and we'll make a tape of *Nashville Skyline?*" I'd go round there, and he'd be very, very friendly to me in a big-brother kind of way. It was very difficult for me because I didn't want to transgress the bounds of what I understood had to be maintained in a professional relationship. Charlie insisted that I come down chauffeur-driven one day to his farm an hour and a half from London. "Right, Peter, I'm going to cook you breakfast!" [laughs] Smoked bacon and eggs and fried bread. It was delicious.

PLR: That sounds lovely.

PJS: It was lovely. And those were nice moments. But it always made me uneasy because I had seen too many disasters where people either overstayed their welcome or overstepped the mark, and I wasn't going to do that.

PLR: Do you still have any contacts with the band?

PJS: I had a letter a year ago from Jagger. I had produced a record with an Italian woman and we did "Gimme Shelter" on it. So I sent him a tape and got back a very nice reply. I had a letter a few years ago from Bill Wyman. I had read his biography of the Stones, which, as far as it goes, is definitive.[6] He had it ghost-written, but it's very good. I like the way that he does justice to Brian, as far as I know it to be true in a limited way. I came along late in respect of Brian. So I dropped Bill a note and got a very sweet letter inviting me to dinner at his restaurant, Sticky Fingers, in Knightsbridge.

PLR: You should take him up on it. Did you also know Ron Wood?

PJS: No, this was way before Ron Wood. I never wanted to know Ron Wood.

PLR: So when Brian died . . .

---

6. Bill Wyman (1997), *A Stone Alone: The Story of a Rock 'n' Roll Band*. New York: DaCapo.

PJS: Then Mick Taylor took over. I had a big role in Mick Taylor's arriving in the band because Mick had assigned me to find a new guitarist. Not only a new guitarist but a new bass player, as a matter of fact, but that's another story.

PLR: They thought Bill was going to leave?

PJS: No, at that time Jagger would have preferred Bill to leave and to get a nice, sexy, black bass player. There were reasons it didn't happen that had to do with the business relationship and the chemistry of the band. But at that time Mick was pretty fed up with Bill Wyman and wanted to reinvent the Stones. I had a nice rapport with Bill, but we all, not altogether justifiably, tended to regard him as just a passenger. We all were polite, even sycophantic, toward him, but we didn't really take seriously anything that he said.

PLR: "We" being the employees?

PJS: Yes. And the rest of the band, too. But I do regret that now because I think that Bill Wyman is salt of the earth. Lovely bloke. Now that I'm more mature, I can value a guy like that.

PLR: There's a certain stability there?

PJS: Yes. And he's also savvy and sussy—in the Cockney sense—about things. You can't easily hoodwink Bill Wyman. Not that I ever wanted to, but others might. All that time he was in a very quiet, private way observing, taking it all in, drawing his own conclusions. He understood his role in that band and the chemistry of it and didn't violate that. His role was to be submissive and compliant relative to Jagger and Richards. That was the beauty of that band. Charlie Watts was the stabilizing force, as a good drummer should be. (Same with Ringo in the Beatles.) Charlie was very dry, sardonic, sharp, witty. And again very astute. Jagger and he were quite close. Now Charlie was close with Bill, so it would have upset the boat to get rid of Bill. Also it couldn't easily be done because Rolling Stones Partnerships—the trading company under whose name we operated—needed four signatories to any check over £1,000. So it was a question of money. Okay, we can afford to get rid of Brian, but not two because we need four signatories on the check. Funny, isn't it? So that became a dead issue.

PLR: Did they get rid of Brian, or did he die before that happened?

PJS: In a big sense, Brian got rid of himself. He was finished, a liability. But, yes, they did get rid of him. They told him, "Sorry, Brian, you're fired." I had to break some of the bad news under the pretext that it wasn't possible to get him a visa for America to go on tour because of his drug busts. I remember he nearly broke down crying when I told him that. Why I should have been assigned to do that I don't know. It would have been the natural job for Jagger's secretary because she knew the woman at the visa office. I don't believe that actually he had been denied a visa, but it was a convenient ploy.

PLR: You were put in a position where you had to tell him?

PJS: I was instructed, "Well, Peter, that's your job." Something like that. [laughs] Many times I had to call Brian and say, "Brian, we've got a meeting on Thursday at two o'clock. Mick says everybody has to be there." "But Peter, I don't think I can be there." "Sorry, Brian, Mick's saying you've got to be there. You've *got* to." This was a veiled threat meaning: otherwise you're out of the band. Maybe I had to do that three of four times. I remember distinctly that this happened for a photo session for the cover of *Through the Past Darkly*. Also it was heavy stuff for a kid like me to have Jagger sharing confidences with me. "Peter, I want you to find a new bass player—preferably black—and a new guitarist who can double on keyboards." "What? Brian out of the band?" I couldn't believe it. But that was my job. Mind you, I didn't act on it, that time. About six weeks later Jagger came to me and said, "Well, what's up? What have you found?" "Mick, I don't know what to tell you. I think we're going to have to call up John Mayall." That was only meant to be a joke. Because Mayall had had Clapton, Peter Green, and so on. He was like a university for blues guitarists. And Jagger said to me, "Peter, that's a great idea! Shirley, get me John Mayall's phone number!" Probably he hadn't spoken to Mayall in four years. But that's how Mick Taylor came. This often happened between me and Jagger. Often I'd have a last-resort idea in desperation where I'd think, "Oh, God, what am I gonna do?"

PLR: So Mayall put him onto Mick Taylor?

PJS: Yes. Mick Taylor had played with Mayall.

PLR: So that worked out. Did you meet Julia around that time?

PJS: Oh, yes. Before that.

PLR: When did you meet her?

PJS: In the summer of 1967.

PLR: How did you meet?

PJS: I mentioned that I worked for a little family of a record company. My working for that company came about because I lived in a house with a rock group—one of those scenes of all the action between King's Road and Fulham Road during 1967–68. And Julia, being German, was befriended by the boss of the company, Giorgio Gomelski, who was a Swiss-Russian Jew. Julia's languages are French and German, and Giorgio's languages are French, German, Italian, and Russian. So they were friends. I met Julia through Giorgio, who was the manager of the rock group with whom I was living.

PLR: What was the name of the rock group?

PJS: The Ingoes. And some of Eric Burden's Animals lived in the same house too.

PLR: So let's take you to 1972. At a certain point you came to New York to work for Stonehill Publishing, was it?

PJS: Yes. This doesn't have too much to do with Freud, but we're getting there. [laughs]

PLR: Wasn't it at that point or shortly thereafter that you fell into *The Cocaine Papers*[7] project?

PJS: Yes. By the way, to go back to the Stones, I said I was there as an anthropologist studying consumerism, which is true in a sense. But the other thing of course is possession. That's what consumerism is all about. People don't read newspapers; they're *read by* the newspapers. People don't watch TV; the TV *consumes* them. It's demoniacal possession in modern guise. By extension, modern rock and roll music is a very highly sophisticated medium for inducing altered voodoo-trance states. It's no accident that African rhythms are at the basis of it. There's a lot more than that—English folk music, Irish folk music, and all kinds of other things too. It's an involving music, not an evolving music. Not like Indian ragas or something like that.

PLR: It's hypnotic.

PJS: Absolutely. Just walk into a disco—I love to do that—to see a modern Witches' Sabbath. A thousand people in a spell, acting in uniform motion more or less, in the grip of the beat. Now if I were to run into a psychoanalyst in a disco, I'd be impressed. I'd think, "Wow. He too must be interested in real psychology and real questions." Another major thing about the Rolling Stones is that it gave me a unique vantage point to observe just how suggestible and slovenly are the media. I could understand how a mass public—that is, consumers—

7. Robert Byck, ed. (1974), *The Cocaine Papers of Sigmund Freud.* New York: Stonehill.

are reactively motivated by the influence of the media. That was quite revelatory. Not that I hadn't anticipated it, but actually to witness it was amazing.

PLR: Did this perception that you had carry over into the world of psychoanalysis?

PJS: Absolutely. These are the fundamental first principles of Gurdjiev that I was talking about.

PLR: Could you elaborate on how those principles bear on the world of Freud studies?

PJS: As far as I'm concerned, psychoanalysis is a brilliant placebo. Just as long as you believe, it can be good for you. It's also a mode of indoctrination if you're suggestible enough to allow that to happen. But beyond that, psychoanalysis stands to me as *the* paranoid conspiracy theory *par excellence* of the 20th century. Freud has managed to convince an awful number of people over the course of the past century that there is a person living inside each of them about whom, however, they know nothing. But it—or he or she—does answer to Freudian principles! And it requires a trained Freudian psychoanalyst to decipher the code. So there's this conceit in respect to knowledge on the part of psychoanalysts. I don't think they really know anything at all. Freud and Kurt Eissler were the worst *Menschenkenner* who ever lived. [laughs] Psychoanalysts are just dreadful psychologists. But, on the placebo model, the only way psychoanalysis can operate is that the person who seeks help and is ready to pay for it—[gulps] God spare us!—*believes* that the analyst has some wisdom that he or she can impart. There's this confidence trick involved right there in the set and setting of psychoanalysis. In virtually all psychoanalysts' offices, there are going to be 24 volumes standing on the shelf, and you know what they are.

PLR: The *Oxford English Dictionary*?

PJS: [laughs loudly] No, commonly known as *S.E.* [laughs] There's likely to be either a photo or a statue of Freud. And there's a couch. If you submit and get into a supine posture, then this man or this woman's going to *do* things to you. [laughs] To me any discussion of the role of suggestion in psychoanalysis would have to begin before you even walk in the door. It has to do with cultural—and here's a neologism—mediatrogenesis. The cultural trance-state. The next stage is the setting. You're expected—not everywhere, but typically—to lie on the couch. The analyst will sit there, all composed, wise, and aloof. That's a second level of the locking in of suggestion. In this day and age, because everybody knows the word Freud and roughly what he's talking about, what the person delivers is under that influence. Even the word trauma is enough to set people going. They're going to start looking through their mind for traumatic events. Or if it's on a Jungian model, probably 90% of the people who show up for Jungian therapy already know about the collective unconscious . . .

PLR: Archetypes.

PJS: [laughs] Archetypes. Introversion and extroversion. Et cetera.

PLR: At the beginning of our conversation, you said that you were coming out of the School of Nancy. I think that had to do with your understanding of the role of suggestion in cultural experience and people's attitudes toward various stimuli.

PJS: Absolutely. I have a rubber stamp with which I often stamp my parcels. It says: "Back to Bernheim." To me the history of psychology went right off the rails with Sigmund Freud.

PLR: What about Charcot?

PJS: All right, if you want to get academic, the junction is prior to Freud with Charcot. Give me Bernheim, give me Delboeuf, give me William James, and I'm a happy man. Where I take a stand is that there is nothing really to be learned in psychology since William James's *Principles*.[8] There's no hard knowledge of any consequence to come out of it, as far as I'm concerned. That book is a masterpiece in the history of human thought, and it's very seldom read these days, which is a tragedy.

PLR: You've spoken of fundamental principles. It might be helpful if you would sum up the principles in James that you think we need to know about.

PJS: He doesn't pretend to knowledge. He's acerbic and skeptical. Read what he has to say about Fechner. His intelligence sings off the page. I'm a theoretical minimalist. Same with Bernheim. He's not really got much to tell you. Suggestion is everything.

PLR: So it's all the false things he *doesn't* believe that you like about him?

PJS: I'm not a student of James in the full-blown sense, and I don't doubt that he had some things to say that are nonsense. The Lowell

---

8. William James (1890), *The Principles of Psychology*, 2 vols. New York: Holt.

lectures of 1896 are for me the watershed. I don't read James for what comes after that. *The Principles of Psychology* was published in 1890, and there's a lovely little synopsis of it two years later.[9] Gurdjiev was well aware of the Nancy school. I came across the Nancy school at about the age of 18 because I was actively enough interested in Gurdjiev to follow up various allusions in his writings. By the age of 21 or 22, I had got myself a ticket to the Reading Room in the British Museum, and I would go there and check all these things out. I did research for a year or two on Gurdjiev-related subjects. For convenience, you might say that Gurdjiev takes what's axiomatic in Bernheim's teaching and uses it in the construction of a *Weltanschauung*. In Aristotle's sense, they are first principles for him. By the way, there are a couple of books that had quite a big impact on me in the mid-1970s.

PLR: Go ahead.

PJS: There are two books by William Sargant, *The Battle for the Mind* and *The Mind Possessed*.[10] He discusses trance states, voodoo, and indoctrination. In these books, he gives an embryonic revisionist reading of Freud's seduction theory that is utterly concordant with the current one, which reduces Freud's clinical claims to mere suggestive influence. The phenomenon of brainwashing has always been deeply fascinating to me, going right back to the religious things that we were talking about earlier.

PLR: The various Christian churches that you were exposed to?

PJS: Yes. I just thought that people were typically brainwashed according to the arbitrary factors of time and place and all the rest of it. That was the human condition. I used to look at one rather attractive woman in particular in my church—the Protestant church. She was obviously devout. I would think, "Well, yes, but if she'd been born in a Roman Catholic family, she'd not only be Roman Catholic but she wouldn't have the hostility toward Roman Catholicism that she has." Thought-experiments like that.

PLR: Montaigne says somewhere that he's a Catholic in the same way that he's a Frenchman. Because of the accident of his birth.

---

9. William James (1892), *Psychology*. New York: Holt.

10. William W. Sargant (1957), *Battle for the Mind: A Physiology of Conversion and Brainwashing*. Garden City, NY: Doubleday; (1974) *The Mind Possessed: A Physiology of Possession, Mysticism, and Faith Healing*. Philadelphia: Lippincott.

PJS: Exactly.

PLR: Are there other books that were influential on you at a certain stage?

PJS: One book that had a very big impact on me in the spring of 1975 was a little paperback of Thomas Szasz called *The Second Sin*.[11] It's not his best-known work by any means. It's composed of maybe 200 pithy statements.

PLR: Well, what is the second sin?

PJS: Speech! The acquisition of speech!

PLR: And the first?

PJS: I *hope* it's carnal knowledge. [both laugh] I should tell you that psychoanalysts are themselves all members of the oldest profession.

PLR: Some would say an impossible profession.

PJS: I wonder how prostitutes would feel about that.

PLR: Probably the same way. You've clarified the relationship of Gurdjiev's thought to the School of Nancy in terms of first principles. It seems that the role of culture, which expresses itself through consumerism, is to condition what Gurdjiev would call our personalities.

PJS: I can put it another way. What I like about William Burroughs[12] is that he reinvents the demonological world-view after enduring a decade of personal psychoanalysis. He starts out believing in demons and so on, then enters into analysis having about as many analysts as he spends years, and in the end comes right around to reinventing the demonological world-view in a very literal way.

PLR: Who were the analysts?

PJS: Herbert Wiggers, Eduardo Weiss, Kurt Eissler, Paul Federn, Lewis Wolberg, George Trevaskis, a woman whose name I can't remember, and René Spitz. There are also psychiatric consultations with David Rioch and someone at Payne Whitney whose name also escapes me at this moment. The merit of the demonological world-

---

11. Thomas S. Szasz (1973), *The Second Sin*. Garden City, NY: Anchor.

12. William S. Burroughs (1914–1997), American author, best known for *The Naked Lunch* (1959). His nightmarish and wildly humorous experimental novels, which portray his experiences of drug addiction, bisexuality, and the accidental murder of his second wife in 1951, influenced the Beat movement.

view is that it addresses the phenomenon of possession, as in hypnosis or trance states. In Freud's model, this gets revised as drive. But, going back to what you said about consumerism, yes, people consume, but *they are consumed*. There is *nothing left* of *themselves*. They are only a product of the way they're *shaped* by a consumer culture. Freud tells us in his obituary of Charcot that what he and Breuer are involved in is converting—in other words, transvaluing, to quote Nietzsche—the demonological world-view derived from the Middle Ages into modern psychological formulas.[13] But in doing that, they lose the essence of that world-view, which is precisely that people are *consumed* by the demons. They're *possessed*.

PLR: Doesn't the concept of the it or the unconscious also suggest that people are lived through by forces they don't control?

PJS: Let's credit that one to Groddeck![14] I think he's a wiser man than Freud on that one. It seems to me that in the long haul analysts are *agents* of consumer culture. They are exemplary members of the bourgeois state that feeds and yet steals away people's minds. My wife and I stay out of it as far as possible. We abstain from so very much of the world out there. Of course, we live a compromised existence. Yes, we travel on airplanes. Yes, I do drive a car. But I'm not mentally consumed by it. If I'm sitting on the subway in New York—which I seldom do since I prefer to walk—and look at people reading the newspapers or whatever they're doing, they are *absent*. If I'm in the subway, I'm very present; I'm very alert and observant. Living in a world like that locates you existentially in a very strange place because, except perhaps for all the cops and criminals who have to make it their business to stay alert, people are *consumed* all the time. *They're not there.* They're out to lunch. What they need to do for a start is to lead more multifacted lives. They should learn to put a roof on a house, or cook a meal, or make their own Christmas cards instead of buying them. It seems to me vital not to be a one-dimensional moron.

PLR: One thing that has struck me, both in your writing and in our conversation, is that you are, on one hand, a stringent critic of psychoanalysis, but, on the other, there is a sense in which what you are saying is not so removed from a psychoanalytic understanding of life.

---

13. Sigmund Freud (1893), "Charcot." *Standard Edition*, 3:22. London: Hogarth Press, 1962.

14. Georg Groddeck (1923), *The Book of the It*, trans. V. M. E. Collins. New York: Mentor Books, 1961.

I thought that when you were talking earlier about Gurdjiev you indicated there was some sense in which he had a concept of the unconscious. How would you distinguish Gurdjiev's unconscious from that of psychoanalysis?

PJS: Gurdjiev has no view of "an unconscious." What Gurdjiev diagnoses as the human condition is a *state of unconsciousness*. So consciousness has *gone missing*. There's *nothing there*. Personality, as opposed to essence, is being in the grips of a false persona—or several.

PLR: Could that be considered similar to Freud's concept of the ego?

PJS: No. It's a different structure of thought altogether. People who live in essence are generally more conscious.

PLR: So one strives for a state of enlightenment or being able to live in essence?

PJS: Well, you could put it like that. Let me emphasize that here I'm only concerned with Gurdjiev as a psychologist and to an extent as a philosopher, and therefore as a diagnostician. It's not as though I necessarily, in a literal way, buy into his construction of the cosmos and all the rest of it. He's a mystic. But I've always been a Gurdjievian and always will be.

PLR: You called Bernheim and James "theoretical minimalists." Is that true of Gurdjiev also?

PJS: I think the word theory is not apropos when we're talking about Gurdjiev, at least not in these areas. What he presents, as you'll find it vicariously transmitted in Ouspensky's book *In Search of the Miraculous*, is a whole picture of mankind and the modern world from the point of view of an ultimate misanthrope.[15] However, he is alarmed, horrified, and mortified that such should be the case because man is capable of so much better. So the Gurdjiev work, as it's called, is concerned in the first instance with setting right what's gone wrong. But then it offers the prospect of something more than that. Now, I had a teacher in the Gurdjiev work whom I still consider my teacher. In the Freudian system, she's the second of my two mothers. By the way, I'm even better off than Freud. I've got *three* mothers.

PLR: Who are they?

---

15. P. D. [Ouspensky] Ospenskii (1949), *In Search of the Miraculous: Fragments of an Unknown Teaching*. New York: Harcourt, Brace.

PJS: I've got my own mother, I've got my teacher, and I've got my wife Julia. My teacher was P. L. Travers, the author of *Mary Poppins*. I'm in the tradition of *Mary Poppins*.

PLR: Tell me about P. L. Travers.

PJS: Very soon after coming to New York, I joined a so-called Gurdjiev group on the Upper East Side in the summer of 1972. When I emigrated "on spec," as we say in Britain, in June of that year, I came armed with two or three testimonials to take to the Gurdjiev work here in order to be received into a group. So that is what I did just a few months later. Julia was to join me later because she was in New Mexico at the time. And that group of about 12 persons was conducted by a woman—dignified, aloof, elegant, and eloquent—who spoke with a sort of British-Irish-New Zealand accent. I had no idea who she was. She was just Mrs. Travers to me. But maybe eight or 10 weeks later, I learned that she was actually the author of *Mary Poppins*. The only thing is, I didn't really know who Mary Poppins was. While we had a group meeting one evening, down came the rain. It was pouring. She said to me, "Peter, you are a gentleman. Will you escort me to Third Avenue and put me in a taxi so I can go home to York Avenue?" I said, "Sure." I had an umbrella.

PLR: So did you have a cab ride with her?

PJS: No.

PLR: That's a joke. I'm thinking of your Geneva talk.[16]

PJS: Oh, I see what you mean! I like the joke, but I was never in a cab with her. We're talking about a woman of 70! [PLR laughs] I conducted Mrs. Travers over to Third Avenue, where the traffic goes one-way uptown, and hailed her a taxi. When I rejoined the group, which had convened in a café to organize breadmaking—we used to bake bread together, make quilts, and do all sorts of other things—they were joking that I had had the honor to escort Mary Poppins herself with an umbrella.

---

16. In *Jokes and Their Relation to the Unconscious*, Freud (1905) quotes an epigram from a Viennese jest-book: "A wife is like an umbrella. Sooner or later one takes a cab" (*Standard Edition*, 8:78). At a conference entitled "100 Years of Psychoanalysis," held in Geneva on September 17–18, 1993, Peter Swales presented a paper, "Did Freud Carry an Umbrella, or Did He Sometimes Take a Taxi?" in which he expounded his view that Freud had an affair with his sister-in-law, Minna Bernays, and contended that Freud's ardent advocacy of sexual freedom in his writings was consistent with this hypothesis.

PLR: Isn't that lovely!

PJS: I didn't know what the joke was because I didn't know anything about Mary Poppins. But later in life I've been called Mary Poppins, which I consider greatly flattering.

PLR: By people who didn't know of this connection?

PJS: Right. I have a tiny Fiat car in Britain that I drive all over Europe. That little car contains anything and everything that you would ever need, from a camping stove to saffron to Band-aids. Anything you want, I can make it come true out of that little car. So, in Italy, all my friends call me Mary Poppins because Mary Poppins has a bag that is bottomlessly full of whatever is needed.

PLR: That is terrific. So you have her umbrella and her carpet bag!

PJS: Mrs. Travers was very dear to me and died only maybe three days after my mother three years ago.

PLR: Two of your mothers, then.

PJS: Like that [snaps his fingers]! Within a week of one another, certainly. Julia and I were very close with Pamela Travers in the 1970s. So much so that she wanted us, because she adored Julia so much, to live with her in Chelsea in London, to where she had retired, and look after her. But I had other things to be doing with my life. What was very important for me back in 1972, though, was that in that group were a number of writers. I knew I was a natural writer, but I'd never written a word except advertising copy and jacket copy, at which, by the way, I was excellent—one of the best. Nobody had to teach me how to write. I taught myself by the age of 10. (I haven't learned anything, really, since I was about 10, even to this day.) But P. L. Travers was a writer. What most people don't know is that she was also a sort of poetess. Among her friends were George Russell ("A.E."), W. B. Yeats, Robert Frost. I have a cassette recording of her on *Desert Island Discs* in Britain in the late 70s where the only eight or ten things she requested were readings of poetry by such friends. It meant a lot to me that she demonstrated an active interest and concern in what I was doing with my life. It helped me conceive of myself as a possible writer. It was a huge step to take to think that I was going to write a book—on Freud. It was nothing like supportive therapy, just the existential matrix in which I was functioning. I was a bit like her son. But she had many other sons and many daughters.

PLR: This was in the framework of the Gurdjiev experience?

PJS: Oh, yes, exclusively so. She'd known Gurdjiev, and Ouspensky prior to that.

PLR: It seems that this is a kind of antipsychoanalysis for you. At least it's an alternative formative experience of a view of the world and a certain psychology that has truth to it from which you then could assess psychoanalysis.

PJS: A prior vantage point. Not that I had an agenda like that. I didn't know where it was going to go. But my comprehension of everything naturally was refracted through the kaleidiscope of the Gurdjiev experience. By the way, I never would have told you about P. L. Travers but for the fact that she died three years ago. She certainly didn't publicize and maybe didn't even indicate on the record that she had a whole other side to her life. I do cherish that relationship. After all, it's quite something to go from the Rolling Stones to P. L. Travers to Sigmund Freud.

PLR: It's a remarkable itinerary.

PJS: Not that that was the whole story. But she woke me up in a big way, which is what I needed at that time. I was a horrible specimen of humanity, at least by my own judgment. Not that anyone else would necessarily have thought so.

PLR: Janet Malcolm quotes you to the effect that you had a "spiritual crisis" about the way you treated your wife. You said: "In taking on Freud I was taking on the monster that existed in myself."[17]

PJS: [laughs] Did I say that? That's funny. I didn't know I was so eloquent.

PLR: Well, either you said it or she made it up.

PJS: No, no. I surely said it.

PLR: You didn't want to sue her about that, did you?

PJS: No way. I adore Janet Malcolm. [laughs]

PLR: I read Jeffrey Masson's *Final Analysis*, and it struck me that he was able to write the story of his involvement in the world of psychoanalysis without once mentioning the name of Peter Swales.[18]

---

17. Malcolm, *In the Freud Archives*, p. 118.

18. Jeffrey M. Masson (1990), *Final Analysis: The Making and Unmaking of a Psychoanalyst*. Reading, MA: Addison-Wesley.

PJS: That's what I would expect from him. He never did justice to history and never will. It's ironic how he allows himself to quote conversations that had happened 20 years ago as if he'd had a tape recorder working at the time, which is what he was suing Janet about. What that thing about my wife goes back to is that I came to this very Machiavellian city and was trying desperately to float. I was culturally dislocated. I was very taken in—I could almost substitute the word possessed—by a very close friend of mine, Jeff Steinberg, the originator of Stonehill Books. He was one of the few geniuses I ever knew but at the same time was a sheer and utter reprobate and lived outside the law in any number of respects— money, drugs, and the rest. But he was a lovely man. I learned a great deal from him, in a positive way and a negative way.

At that time, Julia and I had been living together for five years, and we got married to ensure I would get a green card but without even being sure that we wanted to be married. I was a kid, and I was pumping masculine hormones and was also very manipulative in a spontaneous way. I couldn't help it because things were too transparent to me. I didn't like the way that I was not being forthright with Julia. That's all. But I didn't have the ability to be forthright to myself. This came up actually in one of the P. L. Travers meetings. Not because of her but because of a guy there whom I won't name. At the superficial level, his observation was that I was manipulative vis-à-vis Julia; but at the deeper level—and it was obvious not just to me but to Julia—he had a sexual design upon my wife. I wasn't married at that point. I think he couldn't understand why I should have such a lovely woman in my life and he be bereft of a partner, and he resented me for that.

PLR: You and Julia were not yet married?

PJS: Not at that moment. We married in July 1974; this would have been 1973. I could read what his real motive was. But I didn't say anything. I let him attack me in that way, which was mean and not justified. But I let it pass. I even felt sorry for him. Part of the reason I could allow myself not to react was that I saw Pamela Travers's muscles flinch when he said that, because suddenly it got personal. It did set me thinking, and I had to concede something to it. *But I had already conceded it in front of the group!* I was as manipulative toward my mother! My father! Everybody! That was the only way I knew how to survive. I wasn't even particularly good at it. It would often backfire. There's a war going on in Kosovo. You have to mind-read the enemy. If you can't do that, you don't go to war. What I do is social archeology, decryption, and mind reading. Some people will say, "Who's the mind-reader now?" Because of the Fliess allegation against Freud: "The mind-reader reads into the other only his own thoughts."[19] But that's what doing history is, and that's what doing war is, and that's what doing business is, and that's what driving a car in traffic is all about. If any academics want to take issue with me on that, they'd better start learning something fast about the way the real world works. Otherwise they'll be a menace on the roads.

PLR: It sounds as though those meetings with Pamela Travers had something of the quality of a group therapy.

PJS: I knew you'd say that, but that's getting a sow's ear out of a silk purse. I don't have too much of a personal attitude to Freud, but there's one thing I can't easily forgive him. I don't really like him. Why? Because he's so self-obsessed. He's so precious unto himself. That's what psychoanalysis is all about. Every piece of trivia in your life is interpretable and thereby is ennobled and enshrined. And I don't like that.

PLR: Haven't you interpreted every little thing in Freud's life?

PJS: No, but to address first the point about this alleged group therapy, nothing gets like that in the Gurdjiev work. It's not like psychoanalysis at all.

PLR: There's no interpretation?

PJS: Fair enough. You can put it that way. But more than that, when you speak optimally, you're sovereign. You're not a neurotic wretch drowning in your own tears, nor are you obsessively attached to every piece of trivia in your own personal history. And it's certainly not about dependency.

PLR: When this other fellow made these statements about you, he wasn't speaking in a sovereign way. He was conflicted at that point.

PJS: You are the students or the pupils, and they're supposedly the teachers.

PLR: Who are "they"?

PJS: Mrs. Travers and whoever this might be that I'm talking about.

PLR: This was a leader of the group?

---

19. Letter of August 7, 1901. In *The Complete Letters of Sigmund Freud to Wilhelm Fliess, 1887–1904*, trans. & ed. Jeffrey M. Masson. Cambridge, MA: Harvard University Press, p. 447 (translation modified), 1985.

PJS: A deputy under Mrs. Travers. I didn't explain that. So when I say sovereign, I mean that you must be centered. That's the optimum. One important thing about the Gurdjiev work is that it's an anticult in that sense. Notwithstanding what I've said about autodidacticism, unless you can shut up and listen, you're not going to learn anything. As any of my friends will tell you, I'm the first to shut up and listen. I don't want to talk about myself, my life, my work. I want to learn.

PLR: This was one of Masson's defects.[20]

PJS: Absolutely. He can't learn because he's so glib and too busy doing the talking. He knows it all already, so how can he possibly learn? In the Gurdjiev work, you comply with the arrangement that these people have something to offer you. You don't have to be there. You can walk out.

PLR: How is that different from analysis?

PJS: First, psychoanalysis virtually entails a dependency—"transference." Second, the free-associative nature of psychoanalysis is out of place and unwelcome in that world. The more succinct and self-invested—in a noble sense—what you say is, the more it will be heard and even respected. Yours is a completely false analogy.

PLR: So what happens in a case such as this where the assistant leader directed personal observations at you?

PJS: He was out of line for a moment, that's all. The nice thing about it for me was that I didn't feel vindictive. I knew he had committed an awful *faux pas*. It's only a small moment. I'm trying to explain to you the context of the Janet Malcolm reference.

PLR: That comes back to the statement that you took on in Freud the monster that existed in yourself.

PJS: I was the monkey that is in me, not the human being I have the potential of being.

PLR: That sounds Buddhistic. Nina Coltart, an analyst who resigned from the British Psycho-Analytical Society and became a Buddhist, refers to Buddhist meditation as a sustained attempt at "getting behind the scrambling monkey of thought in order to stop it."[21]

---

20. Malcolm, *In the Freud Archives*, p. 105.

21. Anthony Molino, ed. (1997), *Freely Associated: Encounters in Psychoanalysis with Christopher Bollas, Joyce McDougall, Michael Eigen, Adam Phillips, Nina Coltart*. London: Free Association Books, p. 202.

PJS: That would be lot more congenial to me than psychoanalysis is, although I'm no Buddhist. Julia is. She's a private Buddhist, not a ritualistic Buddhist. I consider myself a mystic, very much so.

PLR: You're certainly a gnostic in your Freud scholarship.

PJS: I'm quite happy not to believe anything. I don't feel I know or believe in anything very much at all, and I'd rather it be that way, except, of course, in my particular areas of expertise. I *can* play a singing saw better than anybody—that's something I feel I know, for sure. But, for example, I'm completely a non-Darwinian—yet also a noncreationist. To me Darwinism just doesn't add up. The poverty of explanation simply doesn't do justice to the profundity of the wonders of nature. Every day I'm reminded of that and torment myself with the whole thing. But I'm not a creationist, as such. If you want to force me to answer, "Well, how are we here?" I do believe in authorship—that there's some conscious design there, but I don't know anything about it. (*Who* did it?) I wish I knew, but I don't.

PLR: Divine authorship of some kind?

PJS: I find the word divine a bit redundant, but something divine in a relative sense, compared with our own wretched intelligence. We can kill people in Kosovo and we can butcher animals, but we can't *create* one animal, not really. They nearly did it with steam locomotives—true alchemy—but not quite! [laughs]

PLR: They did it with Dolly in England.

PJS: I don't think there is any artificial intelligence of any worth, but that's another discussion.

PLR: I gather that your immersion in Freud scholarship began with your work with Robert Byck on *The Cocaine Papers*.

PJS: Yes.

PLR: Your perspective on Freud seems to me, as I said earlier, to combine stringent criticism with a certain grudging admiration.

PJS: I don't experience anything grudging about it.

PLR: You refer to him as "the most misunderstood person in all human history—albeit, perhaps, the most complex and fascinating."[22] I'm interested in the two-sidedness of your attitude to Freud.

---

22. Peter J. Swales (1982), "Freud, Minna Bernays, and the Conquest of Rome: New Light on the Origins of Psychoanalysis," *The New American Review* 1(2–3):1.

PJS: I don't see it as ambivalent or as discrepant. I'm ready not just to concede but to assert in a very forceful way that Freud has to be among the 10 most interesting specimens of modern humanity.

PLR: Your statement spoke of "all human history."

PJS: I'm inclined to stand by that. But Freud is fascinating in the same way that Machiavelli is fascinating. I need to be very careful of what I say here because an incontinent hermeneuticist could twist it to imply something that is not in my head. Adolf Hitler could hypothetically be the most interesting person in the century. But that doesn't necessarily mean anything good about him. In fact, he was a disgusting, loathesome louse. I only wish somebody had stomped on him by about 1937. He could nevertheless be a very interesting case of psychological study. I don't mean to smuggle in any adverse reflection on Freud. Freud is no Hitler.

PLR: Though Frederick Crews is willing to grant the comparison.

PJS: I can't speak for Fred Crews on that. I doubt very much he would say that.

PLR: There was the piece in *Lingua Franca* where he accepted the analogy.[23]

PJS: If he confined his statement to saying there was something totalitarian and fascistic about Freud, I think he'd have a good point. Given my knowledge of Fred Crews, I'd doubt very much that he'd go further than that, and I would wish that he hadn't. When I called Freud "the most complex and fascinating," I could have qualified it by saying "for me." I don't pretend to know about everybody. But I happen to have finished a paper about Giovanni Morelli, who to me in some ways is even more interesting than Freud.[24] If everything were equal in this world and my command of Italian were sufficient, which it's not, I'd rather be writing a biography of Morelli.

PLR: What interests you about Morelli?

PJS: He was three things. First, he was trained as a comparative anatomist in Germany where he was greatly influenced by Cuvier's ideas of geological unfolding; later he worked with Agassiz in Switzerland. Second, in addition to being a scientist, he was a politician.

---

23. Adam Begley (1994), "Terminating Analysis." *Lingua Franca*, 4:24–30.

24. Peter J. Swales, "The Piece of News That Never Was." Unpublished manuscript.

Thanks to him, the export of works of art deemed by the Italians to be national treasures became forbidden by law. Third, he is today best remembered as an art connoisseur. He specialized in detecting mere imitations and wrongful attributions. For example, he would look at pictures that had long been attributed uncritically to Botticelli. He would study the anatomy of the hands and the ears and little things like the halo or clouds. He would be able to demonstrate, in a way that is now by and large accredited, that these were the works of copyists or pupils and not the true originals. Those areas are of great personal resonance to me. I'd much rather be spending my life studying Morelli than Freud. But I couldn't make a career out of it! Another person is Ernst Haeckel. I would rather be writing about Haeckel just because he happens to interest me a lot. In fact, I have a whole library in 19th-century biology with all of Haeckel's works. That's for me a love prior to Freud—in the sense of subjective priorities, that is.

PLR: Since you mention Haeckel and 19th-century biology, that brings to mind Frank Sulloway. You've written that "the definitive intellectual biography of Freud will not be written, I venture to predict, from the limited standpoint of the history of science."[25] I wondered whether that was an implicit commentary on Sulloway's work.

PJS: Yes, it was, and Frank would agree with me. I got to know Frank around the very time his book was published, having read it in manuscript.

PLR: That was in 1979?

PJS: Yes. And one of the first things I did when I returned to America with a green card in 1980 after spending a few years back in Europe was to go up to Boston to see Frank Sulloway, whom I've come greatly to like and respect. I asked him, "Do you have any regrets? Did you commit any howlers?" He said, "I only wish I had put in a chapter on the humanistic influences on Freud." I said, "Absolutely. You can't claim to have written a *comprehensive* intellectual biography without having done that." But about 19th-century biology, I think Frank has got the wrong end of the stick there. His book is a watershed work. It's real scholarship. But he's made a blunder because he doesn't realize that Haeckel is more a *de facto* representative of 19th-century *romantic* biology than he is of Darwinian biology as such. Yes, Haeckel was indeed Darwin's foremost champion in Germany,

---

25. Peter J. Swales (1983), "Freud, Martha Bernays, and the Language of Flowers." Privately published, p. 14.

but he transformed Darwin's style of thought—he Teutonized it—
and quite radically so.

PLR: Along Lamarckian lines?

PJS: A little, but it has mainly to do with Goethe and morphology.
He converts Darwinism into more of a morphological science than it
can properly bear the burden of being. With his wonderful Celtic,
Anglo-Saxon intelligence, Darwin knew better than to start doing
these *Stammbäume*. It wasn't a sufficiently logical proof. He's more
epistemologically astute. But Haeckel is just intoxicated with showing morphological correspondences.

PLR: Between species and individual development?

PJS: Among various species and in terms of the gestation of an
embryo. He wants to construct great chains of being, to use Lovejoy's
term. He thinks these parallels actually *prove* the theory of natural
selection, but they don't. They simply beg all the big questions. Adolf
Grünbaum, a gentleman whom I adore and greatly respect for certain facets of his work on Freud, wrote a wonderful paper a decade
ago on thematic affinity in psychoanalysis and how it doesn't constitute a proof.[26] It exemplifies the fallacy of *post hoc, ergo propter
hoc*. "Thematic kinship" is Grünbaum's catchword for arguments
from morphological resemblance. What I wish he would do, if I may
put it like this, is to extrapolate that critique to a critique of
Darwinism, because the psychoanalysts do just what Haeckel did
and what Grünbaum explodes.

PLR: Did Darwin do that or only Haeckel?

PJS: Well, Darwin was more prudent and astute than certain of his
later followers, Haeckel among them. I love to *read* Darwin. I don't
agree with him, but he's an intelligence and so observant. People
would learn more about Freud if they reread Darwin, Haeckel,
Goethe, Feuerbach, Lessing, and Heine than they do by reading the
Standard Edition in English.

PLR: You seem to be saying that Sulloway, in his very learned work of
scholarship, didn't differentiate between Haeckel's revision of Darwin
and Darwin's original theory of evolution by natural selection.

---

26. Adolf Grünbaum (1989), "Why Thematic Kinships between Events Do
Not Attest Their Causal Linkage." In *An Intimate Relation: Studies in the
History and Philosophy of Science Presented to Robert E. Butts*, ed. James
Robert Brown & Jürgen Mittelstrass. Dordrecht: Kluwer, pp. 477–494.

PJS: Absolutely. Sulloway, like Ritvo and others, treats Freud as a Darwinian.[27] Properly, however, he should have treated him as a Haeckelian. I say "Haeckelian" and not "Hegelian" . . .

PLR: That's a crucial distinction!

PJS: Haeckel's real ancestry goes back not so much to Lamarck but to Goethe, the protocomparative anatomist and morphologist. That's the line of descent. It has less to do with ontogeny recapitulating phylogeny than with hermeneutics. Psychoanalysis is the bastard child of 19th-century morphological science. But even many modern medical historians don't know what that is because morphological science was never institutionalized in the German academic system in the way that most other subjects are. You're talking about the collaboration between Haeckel and the comparative anatomist Karl Gegenbauer in Jena 100 years ago.

PLR: By that you mean around 1900?

PJS: No, it goes from about 1860 through 1899.

PLR: Of course, Hegel had been in Jena too.

PJS: Yes. [laughs] That comes into it too, but it's out of my ken at the moment. This is very important, because it puts Freud back strictly into the tradition of *Naturphilosophie* and romantic biology, and not into the Darwinian system per se.

PLR: So there are Darwinian as well as Lamarckian or Haeckelian aspects of Freud, and Sulloway, by treating the biological contexts of Freud's work as an indivisible entity, did not differentiate sufficiently between these two traditions?

PJS: That's right. I don't like speaking *ad hominem*, but Frank's background is in Darwinian biology, and there aren't many people left today who know anything much more than that. But personally I would rather read Agassiz than I would a post-Darwinian biologist. I have on my shelf two or three works of Agassiz, because to me he is a profound intelligence.

PLR: He was a Lamarckian certainly.

PJS: Yes, and a disciple of Cuvier.

PLR: Your work on Freud has a deeper grounding in the humanities

---

27. Lucille B. Ritvo (1990), *Darwin's Influence on Freud: A Tale of Two Sciences*. New Haven, CT: Yale University Press.

than Sulloway's. You've emphasized Freud's relation to figures such as Jean Paul Richter, Carlyle, and Goethe.

PJS: My love affair there is with German culture of the 19th century, and that embraces Haeckel and even, by extension, Morelli. He trained in comparative anatomy with Ignatius Döllinger, a very important figure in the genesis of embryology. To me, Lorenz Oken is consummately interesting. He was the exemplary representative of nature philosophy and romantic biology. Morelli, then, was an Okenian, to coin a neologism.

PLR: Is that someone who wields a razor?

PJS: No. [laughs] No, Oken was competitive with Goethe for the theory of the vertebrate origins of the skull. Johannes Müller is also very interesting to me because he stands as intellectual grandfather to both Freud and Fliess. He was the teacher of Helmholtz, Dubois-Reymond, Brücke, Reichert, Wundt, and all the rest of them. Haeckel was virtually the last pupil of Johannes Müller. And it's Müller who reluctantly transvalues *Naturphilosophie* into a deterministic system.

PLR: That gets us from Goethe to Helmholtz.

PJS: You've got it! Actually, Müller was in correspondence with Goethe about hallucinations. This was about 1830. Goethe dies in 1832. It's Müller who ventures a more scientific method of doing research, as we understand it today. But it's Helmholtz, with his discovery of the reaction time of nerves, who proves to his very recalcitrant teacher that science can grapple even with matters involving the nervous system. If you want, it's all a bit oedipal.

PLR: That's fascinating. Jung's word association experiments also involve studies of reaction time.

PJS: Yes, exactly. They come down that very line of descent. Fliess was a student of Helmholtz, Reichert, and various other luminaries who were the pupils of Müller, as was Freud in Vienna with Dubois-Reymond and Brücke. But both Freud and Fliess shared a sort of scientific grandfather in the person of Haeckel, and he's an interesting case. Ostensibly, he was a resolute determinist and extreme monist. But you might say about Haeckel that he misunderstands himself, because he's actually an exponent of the pantheistic morphological approach of Oken or Goethe.

PLR: In a sense, the same could be said of Freud.

PJS: Yes. Fliess aside, Freud's closest intellectual precursor is Haeckel. I bring Fliess into it because he's even more radically a Haeckelian romantic than Freud is. But that's precisely the intellectual threshold shared by Freud and Fliess, and that's what Frank doesn't understand.

PLR: How is Fliess more radically Haeckelian than Freud?

PJS: For example, "All fear is a fear of death," according to Fliess.[28] He is, as it were, even more Freudian than Freud in venturing for the prototype—or the "imago," to use psychoanalytic parlance. Things are ontologically not what they seem to be, but, hermeneutically conceived, something prior in disguise. So, in the case in point, all anxiety is actually not anxiety, but the fear of death.

PLR: There's a latent content?

PJS: Yes, and this aspect of Freud is quintessentially Fliessian and, by extension, quintessentially Haeckelian. It has to do with embryology. They're always going to find an embryo and say that what is subsequent has its antecedent in this embryo. And there's an ontological reductivism built into it. A cigar is not really a cigar, it's a penis. Except, of course, when it's not. I take my stand on "once a cigar, always a cigar."[29] That ontological reductionism to me is nonsense.

PLR: You haven't allowed President Clinton's escapades to modify your views on that subject?

PJS: No, I was only waiting for the vulgarity of some journalist or psychoanalyst to draw the connection, just as you've disgraced yourself by doing in the last 30 seconds.

PLR: [laughs] Somebody had to do it.

PJS: I'll tell you a little anecdote. There was a time when I was closely involved with the book publisher Jeffrey Steinberg, and I barely knew the word Freud. We used to go out to the Hamptons every weekend during the summer for a couple of years to stay with his father and

---

28. Theodor Reik distilled Fliess's thought with these words at the November 15, 1911 meeting of the Vienna Psychoanalytic Society. See *Minutes of the Vienna Psychoanalytic Society*, Vol. 3, ed. Herman Nunberg & Ernst Federn, trans. M. Nunberg. New York: International Universities Press, 1974, p. 311.

29. Peter J. Swales (1995), "Once a Cigar, Always a Cigar." Review of *Why Freud Was Wrong: Sin, Science and Psychoanalysis* by Richard Webster, *Nature*, November 2, pp. 107–108.

stepmother. And, chronically, Jeffrey would run out of petrol. This might have happened three or four times. Maybe the fourth time, in the middle of the Long Island Expressway, I said, "Jeff, how could you do that? Why didn't you ask me to keep an eye on it?" He was humiliated. Can you guess his response? "But Peter, you've got to understand. It all goes back to my breast-feeding as a child. My mother obviously kept me at the breast too long." Notice that "obviously." This was an inference post hoc. "And so I go through life feeling I have this infinitude of fuel and that I'll never run out." I said, "*What?*" I'd never heard this kind of quasi-Freudian reasoning. Being a British kid brought up in a Celtic, Anglo-Saxon intellectual tradition, that was an anathema to me.

PLR: So how do you explain his running out of petrol?

PJS: Stupidity and inattentiveness and overindulgence in recreational drugs.

PLR: [laughs] That would cover it.

PJS: To me the real issue would be, how are we to solve this problem? If we go on through life like this . . .

PLR: I know you worked on Fliess for a long time and at one time were planning a Fliess biography.

PJS: Yes.

PLR: Is that a project you are still working on actively?

PJS: That's like a first love for me, too. I can only answer your question in a greater context. Aside from Freud's patients, Anna von Lieben ("Cäcilie M.") and Aurelia Kronich ("Katharina"), Fliess was the first project I devoted myself to in a comprehensive way.[30] I did research on him for a couple of years desultorily but determinedly, and I amassed, I reckon, almost as much material as Ernest Jones had at his disposal for his three volumes on Freud. Not so many extended correspondences, granted, but on that order of magnitude. This was from 1979 through 1982. Now, I had an obvious problem back then in completing a Fliess biography, namely, that Freud's

---

30. Peter J. Swales (1986), "Freud, His Teacher, and the Birth of Psychoanalysis." In *Freud: Appraisals and Reappraisals, Vol. 1*, ed. Paul E. Stepansky. Hillsdale, NJ: The Analytic Press, pp. 3–82; and Peter J. Swales (1988), "Freud, Katharina, and the First 'Wild Analysis.'" In *Freud: Appraisals and Reappraisals, Vol. 3*, ed. Paul E. Stepansky. Hillsdale, NJ: The Analytic Press, pp. 81–164.

letters to Fliess were not published in a complete form. It was always a quandary whether or not I should wait for them. I remind you that in Jerusalem and East Berlin I had discovered 10 or 11 unknown letters of Freud to Fliess. Obviously, knowing as much as I did about Fliess, I was poised to decipher any number of otherwise cryptic references in Freud's letters to him, even in what was published, let alone what wasn't published. This put me in what one would think was potentially a very strong negotiating position with Kurt Eissler to get access to all the then restricted letters because only I was competent to elucidate the references. So Eissler encouraged a contract between me and Masson—he put us together—whereby I would share all my information and what light that would shed on everything; and in exchange he, Masson, would give me the complete letters. More than once, in different letters, Masson undertook to do just that. It wasn't a legal contract, but I felt that no reputable scholar would dare to renege on such an agreement. Little did I imagine that Masson *would* renege on it. In a very Machiavellian way, he even embroiled Anna Freud so that, predictably, she would balk at my being given the complete letters. But in 1983, after all the acrimony with Masson, Eissler finally capitulated and said he would give me the letters from the Library of Congress.

So there I was, poised at last to write that book. I allocated five or six months to do it. But only then did Eissler learn that Ilse Grubrich-Simitis had gotten herself quietly appointed executrix by Anna Freud just before her death, and he had lost authority over that correspondence. So he couldn't give me the letters after all, after he had instructed the Library of Congress to do so. Eissler's motive had surely by then been that he wanted to spite Masson. I had been told by Eissler in writing that I would get these letters, and suddenly instead I received a letter informing me that it was all in the hands of Simitis and that I'd have to write to her. Well, I knew she wasn't going to let me have *anything*. But I sent off a nice, formal, polite letter of request and got back such a disgraceful abortion of a rationale for denying me these letters that it threw me right off track. I didn't know whether I should write the book anyway or whether I should wait for the better information that I hypothesized might exist in Freud's complete letters to Fliess.

Then, at last, Mark Paterson, a gentleman and an old friend of mine, interceded partly at the instigation of Sophie Freud and gave me a transcript of all the letters. They brought me *nothing*! I didn't learn *anything* about Fliess that I didn't already know. But by then it was September or October 1983, and I'd been in total crisis all that summer about not having the letters after I had been promised them.

The irony was that the letters needed me, but I didn't really need them! Later, after Masson's edition came out, it was reedited for German publication by Michael Schröter.[31] All kinds of information was illicitly leaked to Schröter by one or two former confidants of mine so that he could decipher otherwise cryptic references.

PLR: I take it you are referring to Gerhard Fichtner and Albrecht Hirschmüller. Had you by then collaborated with them on researching Freud's early patients?

PJS: On Katharina. On Anna Lieben we would have, but it didn't get off the ground in time before we had a schism, for which Masson was responsible.

PLR: How so?

PJS: He went to Tübingen and did damage. He slandered me. "I'm happy to cooperate with you," he said to Fichtner and Hirschmüller, "and to share with you all the resources of the Sigmund Freud Archives. All this restricted stuff that I have. Look!" And he opens this little briefcase and in there are originals of some two dozen letters of Freud to Minna Bernays. He's flying around Europe with them and showing them off. "I'm ready to share everything with you that I know, but not so long as you're involved with Peter Swales." "Why? What's the problem?"

PLR: What year was this?

PJS: August 1981. "It's got nothing to do with me. It's Anna Freud." "How do you mean?" "Well, Anna Freud's really upset because she's learned that Peter Swales is researching Freud's patients. She considers that a breach of confidentiality. And that he believes that her father slept with her Aunt Minna." But how do you think Anna Freud knew this about the Minna business? Only because Masson had been so malicious as to be sure to tell her. I'd not withheld it from Eissler and Masson when they confronted me about it. They had asked me in a very neutral way, "Do I believe *that*?" "Yes, I do."

PLR: This was at that famous brunch.[32]

PJS: Yes. So I told them straight. I wasn't going to lie about it.

---

31. Sigmund Freud (1986), *Briefe an Wilhelm Fliess 1887–1904*, ed. Michael Schröter & Jeffrey M. Masson, transcribed by Gerhard Fichtner. Frankfurt am Main: Fischer.

32. Malcolm, *In the Freud Archives*, pp. 104–105.

PLR: This was similar to your experience with the policeman.

PJS: [laughs] They were ready to listen to the wisdom pouring off my tongue. I knew 20 times more about Freud and Fliess, Freud and Minna, whatever you want, than Eissler and Masson knew. Now Masson, in August 1981, said to Fichtner in Tübingen that Anna Freud had said to him that, because Peter Swales believed such a thing about her father and her aunt, it was impossible to consider any reciprocal communication about all this restricted material unless they severed all contact with me. Furthermore, this situation would seriously jeopardize publication of the Freud-Binswanger correspondence, which had been entrusted to Fichtner. Masson was not just Projects Director of the Sigmund Freud Archives but had a position with Freud Copyrights, thanks to Masud Khan. Fichtner feared that Masson was going to torpedo his edition of the Binswanger letters. So Fichtner and Hirshmüller negotiated a deal with Masson, which they later confided to me. "Well," they said, "as far as we know, Peter hasn't done anything wrong, certainly not with us. We owe him a lot, and he owes us a lot. We've been in a collaboration, he's a great researcher, and he seems to know what he's talking about. We'll promise you not to share with him anything that we learn from you, but as far as our relationship with him goes and the things we want to publish together—Katharina to begin with—we'll hold things in abeyance and see how it goes. But maybe you're right."

I knew our relationship was untenable and doomed from that minute. Can you understand why? Because if they're privy to information that I don't know, it's not possible to communicate any more. In principle, we had pooled all our knowledge for research purposes. And you can't be doing research in collaboration with somebody in an unequal relationship. False understandings are inevitable and sometimes necessary preliminaries to arriving at the *right* understanding. Before you get to the right understanding of where some document might be or what happened to this family or whatever it is, you have to follow up many leads that later turn out to be false. And my concern was that they would judge any provisional false understandings that I might have arrived at by virtue of better information, which, however, they couldn't impart to me. So that relationship went out the window, much to my deep regret. Julia and I were really quite close with the families Fichtner and Hirschmüller.

PLR: Did anything happen to repair that after Masson was ousted?

PJS: No. Things got more and more acrimonious because Fichtner was by then under the thumb of Eissler. And Eissler had determined me to be a terrible person—paranoid, psychotic, hysterical, schizophrenic. Four different diagnoses. All those things he said about me on the record. In writing. I should have sued him. I was stupid not to. He should properly have had to forfeit his medical license.

PLR: He paid you quite a compliment.

PJS: By 1982 or so, Fichtner didn't dare come near me with a barge pole. He came to New York in late 1981, before going on to Masson in California, and found himself in the middle of all this Eissler/Masson/Swales acrimony. Fichtner would then illicitly impart to Masson and later to Schröter all sorts of materials deriving from my better knowledge. Otherwise they wouldn't have known who people were, et cetera. Then, in 1985, Schröter had the chutzpah to write to me asking whether he could use this, that, and the other from my work. This after I had been denied the letters by *his* sponsor, Grubrich-Simitis. I wrote back and told him in no uncertain terms what he could do. "You didn't let me have those letters or anything else. You represent the establishment that's tried to monopolize Freud studies and sabotage any independent research. And now you have the nerve to come to me asking me for the fruits of my labors."

PLR: Hadn't he been handed them already?

PJS: Well, yes, many things. But for some things he needed my permission, and he had got so many others wrong. For example, Fichtner had advised him of a long essay, which I've had by now for 20 years, by Fliess's son Conrad Charles about his father. It's an embryo for a biography. Fichtner allowed Schröter to see it, if he didn't actually give him a copy of the document. Conrad states something like, "My father often wrote for the *Neue freie Presse* and on that account knew Theodor Herzl well." Now, it's true that Fliess wrote for Vienna's *Neue freie Presse* more than once. Feuilletons about medical conferences and so on. It's also true that he knew Theodor Herzl rather well. But it's not true that he met Theodor Herzl in consequence of the *Neue freie Presse*. In fact, it's more likely to have been the other way around. To put an extreme construction on it, Herzl ended up working for the *Neue freie Presse* four or five years later partly as a result of social connections he had established through Fliess. It's little things like that. Schröter was taking everything at face value, but it needs some real research—it needs archeology—to figure these things out, and that's what I specialize in. So I thought to myself when Fliess's daughter Pauline gave me the document by Conrad, "Well, this is wonderful, but it needs research."

To link this up now, that threw me right off kilter in 1983. I couldn't finish the book right then as planned. And then, at the end of 1983 in *The New Yorker* and in 1984 as a book came Janet Malcolm's exposé of the Masson fiasco. That changed my life for a couple of years. Any number of hospitals and universities wanted me to come and lecture, and so on. Retreating from the high-profile aspects of that notoriety, I got a teaching assistantship and became a graduate student at Rutgers in philosophy in September 1984, and that occupied me for the next two-and-a-half or three years. So I simply couldn't think about Fliess. Then, in 1987 or 1988, when I started to prime myself to get back to it again, I realized that I hadn't really understood Fliess. Not that anybody else had either. To put it simply, I didn't know *where* he was coming from. I could tell you all about his life. On the basis of what I had accumulated, I could tell you what he was doing virtually every day from 1878, when he registered at university, right through 1900 and the end of the Freud relationship. But I couldn't understand intellectually what he was made of. To go back to our earlier conversation about romantic biology and nature philosophy, I didn't know about all that. I had to educate myself. Beginning about 1988, I spent two or three years exclusively concerned with Goethe and the whole history of morphology. Whereupon at last I understood Fliess's intellectual ancestry and, by extension, Freud's.

PLR: Of course, Sulloway's book had come out much earlier, so to some extent you must have been aware of that tradition.

PJS: No, all Frank has to tell us about is evolutionary biology, whereas all the morphology stuff is completely distinct. Were you ever present at a talk I've given called "Freud, Fliess, and the Skull on the Lido"?

PLR: No, but I've heard of it.

PJS: The skull on the Lido alludes to Goethe. It's in a dream of Freud's where he says it has to do with a remark made to him by Fliess.[33] What happened is that Goethe's manservant in the Jewish cemetery on the Lido opposite from Venice proper picked up a sheep's head, and allegedly, in that moment, Goethe conceived his vertebral theory of skull development. Later Oken made a rival claim that it was his discovery, and the two were in contention about it. Shades of Freud and Fliess! But that moment when Goethe picks up the skull

---

33. See Sigmund Freud (1901), *On Dreams. Standard Edition*, 5:664. London: Hogarth Press, 1953; and the October 4 addendum to the letter of October 3, 1897 in Masson, ed., *Freud–Fliess Letters*, p. 269.

is a nodal point in the history of science. So many strands go back to that. They cover areas that Frank doesn't know very much about, such as zoology, comparative anatomy, and embryology in the way that it was practiced in the early to mid-19th century.

PLR: You've mentioned "Freud, Fliess, and the Skull on the Lido" as well as your Fliess biography. You have a great deal of unpublished work with an underground reputation. I'm wondering about the status of the numerous projects that you've been working on for so many years.

PJS: I can pick up where I left off and cut to the chase. I worked on that Freud, Fliess, and morphology business, and it consumed me. When I do research, I actually go to Jena or I go to Venice and check these things out. I live it, with my wife, while I do it. But I didn't know how to combine the understanding that had emerged to me as per the skull on the Lido into the projected Fliess biography. It had gone from one extreme to the other. It could be a book in itself, along with my paper on "Freud, Professor Teufelsdröckh, and the Garden of Eden." But then, through the circumstance that part of the Freud Archives was opened up, I got diverted. I don't think it needs much apology if I tell you that then I got involved with Marilyn Monroe in a very deep way.

PLR: That would be enough to preoccupy anyone.

PJS: So I did her. [laughs] I got totally into that.

PLR: Has that work been published?

PJS: No. I'm coming to the punch line. That brought me into modern American culture and the reception of psychoanalysis. That I found interesting in a way I had never expected to. That in turn led me to William Burroughs, given the serendipitous discovery of a couple of case histories of his.

PLR: You mean in which he was featured as a patient?

PJS: Yes. By Federn and by a psychiatrist at Payne-Whitney.

PLR: The one whose name you couldn't remember earlier?

PJS: That's right. Lincoln Rahman. A hard name to remember. I have case histories by him, by Federn, and another by Wolberg. Burroughs was then still living. So I had the pleasure. What a gentleman! Look [shows a framed "Holiday Greetings" card on the wall]: "For Peter Swales—who put Freud in his place [signed:] William S. Burroughs." That was by now into the early and mid-90s.

PLR: Of course, you have published your work on the early case histories.

PJS: Yes, I'd done some of that. But you don't know anything about "Herr E."

PLR: Well, I know that his name was Oscar Fellner and that you have extensively researched his role in Freud's early history.

PJS: So in the last decade I did Marilyn and Burroughs and Fellner and a bit of work on Elisabeth von R. More recently, in the last six months, I've done "Sybil." But, in between, I've been involved in Freud work, including my "umbrella" talk in Geneva. The Fellner project was all-consuming—in fact, the most difficult project I've ever attempted. But because I at last succeeded in researching and identifying Freud's "Herr E.," it was very gratifying in the end. That I undertook in direct reaction to my mother's death in 1996, which is perhaps the most profound event in a man's life.

PLR: You could probably give me 2,467 reasons why.

PJS: Yes. [laughs] Insight such as this falls to one's lot only once in a lifetime! Fellner is perhaps *the* most interesting of all Freud's early cases. So all these things are in the bank. And what you don't know is that "The Piece of News That Never Was" is only a satellite paper of a bigger thing called "*In Statu Nascendi*: Freud, Minna Bernays, and the Creation of Herr *Aliquis*."[34] So this goes right back to where I started.

PLR: I'd like to ask you about something that links your work and mine. You have convincingly shown that the subject of the "*aliquis*" parapraxis is none other than Freud himself.[35]

PJS: You haven't read anything yet. That's what's in "*In Statu Nascendi*."

PLR: I think you've already established that beyond any doubt, just as Bernfeld demonstrated that Freud was the patient of "Screen Memories."[36] Your thesis of the affair with Minna Bernays is also

---

34. "The Piece of News That Never Was" has been reworked and expanded by Peter Swales into a manuscript retitled "Freud, Death, and Sexual Pleasures: On the Psychical Mechanism of Dr. Sigmund Freud."

35. Swales, "Freud, Minna Bernays, and the Conquest of Rome."

36. Siegfried Bernfeld (1946), "An Unknown Autobiographical Fragment by Freud." *American Imago*, 4:3–19.

very strongly argued, but one can set that aside and still accept without reservation your argument about Freud's role as the patient in the *"aliquis"* incident.

PJS: If you've got sexual problems of your own—if you've got an Oedipus complex—you might want to set the affair aside.

PLR: One thing I like about your work is that you actually show that Freud had an Oedipus complex.

PJS: [laughs] Iatrogenesis. Mediatrogenesis!

PLR: "Are you not the only true Freudian?"[37] What I wanted to suggest is that when Freud introduces his discussion of the *"aliquis"* incident, he says that he has "renewed the acquaintance of a young man of academic background" who is "not suffering from nervous illness."[38] It seems to me that that might be a covert reference back . . .

PJS: To me.

PLR: Absolutely. Well, I wasn't aware that you had an academic background. [PJS laughs] It's clear that you're not suffering from nervous illness. [PJS laughs] But it seems to me that Freud could be echoing his 1899 "Screen Memories" paper, where he characterizes himself as someone "who is not at all or only very slightly neurotic."[39]

PJS: Let me go back further, to the 1898 Signorelli paper, where he characterizes himself as "not neurotic," in so many words.[40]

PLR: Also, the profession of the patient in "Screen Memories" "lies in a very different field from psychology." This is echoed by the "academic background" of his disguise in *"aliquis"*. So we can trace a continuous thread of autobiographical writing in Freud. Maybe it's obvious, but I've never seen anyone say explicitly that the self-portrait in *"aliquis"* alludes back to "Screen Memories."

---

37. See Swales, "Freud, Katharina, and the First 'Wild Analysis,'" p. 154*n*45.

38. Sigmund Freud (1901), *The Psychopathology of Everyday Life*. *Standard Edition*, 6:8–9. London: Hogarth Press, 1960.

39. Sigmund Freud (1899), "Screen Memories." *Standard Edition*, 3:309. London: Hogarth Press, 1962.

40. In "The Psychical Mechanism of Forgetfulness," Freud (1898) averred that his repression of Signorelli's name was "compatible with an otherwise untroubled state of mental health." *Standard Edition*, 3:295. London: Hogarth Press, 1962.

PJS: I see what you mean. I think what we're talking about is impostorship. What you're calling "disguised autobiography," which I also use as a term, is ultimately impostorship. And that has a history right back to Jean Paul Richter. Part of the conceit and the spoof of reading Jean Paul Richter is, "Who is the author of this text?" It's the same with Morelli, Freud's hero, the art connoisseur, whom we talked about earlier. He wrote under a pseudonym "Ivan Lermolieff," which is a Russified anagram of his name Giovanni Morelli. He poses as a Russian art connoisseur inspecting the arts of Italy.

PLR: Not unlike "The Moses of Michelangelo."

PJS: Yes. Of course, that's where you'll find the one express reference to Morelli in those 24 volumes.[41] Impostorship is ingrained in 19th-century educated culture. It's always teasing there in the background.

PLR: Could we call it a process of fiction-making?

PJS: Yes, but I don't see any dividend in calling it that. That's axiomatic. People in comparative literature talk about "authorial intent." I have some first-hand experience with the psychology of authorship and impostorship, which goes back to when I started my work on Freud, when I used to write under a *nom de plume*.

PLR: You did?

PJS: Yes. And even before that. I would investigate consumerism by engendering bogus newspaper controversies in an anthropological experimental spirit. This was in my late teens and early 20s. I'd read an article in some newspaper and think, "That's a load of shit." I'd do an analysis in my head of the logic and the rhetoric and write a letter, not necessarily to advocate a point of view but just to deconstruct the article. Then the letter to the editor would get published in the paper under a *nom de plume*. I thought *noms de plume* were something awfully distinguished. So then, under a *different* name, I'd write a letter arguing against my original letter from an *opposite* point of view, saying, "Your correspondent is talking shit because . . . " [laughs] Then I'd write a letter against *that* one, and so on and so forth.

PLR: A truly dialectical imagination.

PJS: Just taking the piss, really. It started out in the musical papers. Totally fabricated controversies about the merits of Tamla-Motown, or whatever.

---

41. Sigmund Freud (1914), "The Moses of Michelangelo." *Standard Edition*, 13:222. London: Hogarth Press, 1955.

PLR: In the *New Musical Express?*

PJS: Yes, and *Disc* and *Music Echo* and *Record Mirror* and *Melody Maker*. By 1972, I was writing to the *Times* about a wooden bird dug up in an Egyptian tomb and whether it really flew or not. The aerodynamics of it and all that. [PLR laughs] I had some far-fetched pseudonyms such as Peter Wentworth and Pete Cropper (as in Steve Cropper of Booker T and the MGs). Because I used to like very much to read a French author called Henri de Monfried (with whom, by the way, I actually corresponded during the last year or two of his life), I converted my name into Joffre de Galles—Galles because Wales is *le pays de Galles* and because my name is Swales, although it's got nothing to do with Wales. There's a river in Yorkshire called the Swale. And my middle name is Joffre. I thought Joffre de Galles sounded elegant.

So I started doing my Freud research under the pseudonym Joffre de Galles, which I had used as a *nom de plume* in writing to newspapers. The reason for this was that Anna Freud had hit the roof in 1973 when she learned that Mark Paterson had authorized American publication of *The Cocaine Papers*, and so I feared I wouldn't get permission to quote passages extensively as "Peter J. Swales." I thought, what does it matter? A name is just a name. So for a few years I used this ludicrous pseudonym of Joffre de Galles, Joffre being my real name, and my father's name—there's the oedipal aspect for you. However, I became so serious about my work that I regretted what I had done and wanted to repossess my real name, to reown it. So one day I said, "No, I'm not Joffre de Galles any more. I'm Peter J. Swales. And I'm not writing under a pseudonym."

In the broader view, I had been in an existential crisis following on P. L. Travers. I didn't like myself and didn't want to own my own life or own up to the person I was. So I was ready to become a counterfeit and be a hack, that is, a prostitute. By writing something not under my own name, I could reinvent myself. But then, after all that, I had to go through the opposite process of reinventing *myself*. That was heavy. When I first started corresponding, for example, with Fichtner and Hirschmüller, or with Marianne Krüll or Josef Sajner— all of whom in due course became friends of mine—well, one day [laughs], I would turn up in Germany or in Czechoslovakia and announce, "Well, actually I'm not Joffre de Galles. My name is Peter." [laughs] Funny, now. To all of them I said, "I don't want to make any pretense about this." In fact, the pretense was in having been somebody else formerly. But I thought, "What's in a name?"

PLR: Very interesting.

PJS: So let me cut to the chase and say this. As you're fully aware, I've dabbled around, but in a very deep, intensive way each time, in any number of projects—from Fellner to Marilyn Monroe to William Burroughs to Sybil to *"aliquis"* and the rest in these many years. I haven't been wasting my time. By natural inclination, I'm a researcher. I'm not the best, but I'm damned good. I'd say Anthony Stadlen is the best researcher I know. That's my narcotic, and his too. I can't say no if I'm onto something. Writing, however, given my standards of perfection, requires a different discipline and a different sort of concentration. First, you stay at home. You don't travel; you write. You lock yourself up. And here I am, 50 years old, and it hasn't been congenial to me before now to give extended concentration to finishing Fliess, to writing up Fellner, et cetera. I was only too happy to do the research and compose the works as architectural constructions.

PLR: As lectures?

PJS: Well, yes, that way I keep myself in hand. I make the promise that I'm going to give a lecture. Okay, so I've got to deliver.

PLR: And the lecture is tape-recorded, so it's preserved.

PJS: Often, yes. Then I think, "Right, that's the embryo of what I'm going to write."

PLR: Coming back to the morphological principle.

PJS: [laughs] Yes. I write under intense pressure in the evening or two before I've got to give the lecture. It's mind-boggling to me. I can write a lecture that's as long as a little book in one evening if I've *got* to do it. I've been having too much fun to be able to go lock myself away and sit down and write in the way that I demand of myself. Those 15 pages there [points to a manuscript of "The Piece of News That Never Was"] have gone through 10 or 12 rewrites at least. And I won't use a computer. I'm not going to be possessed by a screen. So it's a martyrdom for me to write anything. I hate it. But I love *having* done so.

PLR: Writing is hell, but having written is bliss.

PJS: Yes. I went through all the birth pangs yesterday morning. I celebrated and got really drunk last night and didn't go to bed until seven in the morning. And there's not a word of it I'd want to change, in principle. Because, when I've written, there's nothing arbitrary about it. It's not like *Tristram Shandy* where you can go on and on. No, no. It's classically conceived in its architecture and its structure.

PLR: More like *Tom Jones.*

PJS: No, more like Aristotle.

PLR: Well, *Tom Jones* is a very Aristotelian work.

PJS: I thought you meant the Welsh singer! [laughs loudly]

PLR: No, I meant the Fielding novel. It's not unusual.

PJS: I don't read novels, but Julia's given me a detailed report on *Tom Jones*. Julia's my reader for fiction. I can't read fiction because I can't dream other people's dreams. I can't suspend my disbelief. But Julia reads novels and then tells me what they're about, and I look at the pages, but by then within the analytic structure of "Freud read this page." So now I'm 50, and I'm a smoker. And I like my wine, and I like my food, and I like my travel, and all that. But what I've got to do is devote myself to writing. No more research. What I've got to do now is sit down and construct all these different works. I've got all this capital in the bank, and I've got to cash it out. I can, for example, put together my Anna Lieben and my Katharina with the one on Fellner, with another I have on Anna O. that I never published, with another that I have with Richard Skues and Anthony Stadlen on Elisabeth von R., and another on Emma Eckstein that no one knows anything about. I assume I'm going to hit the grave when I'm 60. So I've got 10 years to write, but I mustn't do any more research. That is what I'm best at—social archeology, decryption, and mind reading. But I've got to stop it. One watershed moment for me was Peter Gay's 1988 biography and the glowing reception accorded it by critics and consumers.

PLR: You published a review of it in the *Los Angeles Times.*[42]

PJS: I tried in that review to be as charitable as I could, but to me it's an appalling book. Inasmuch as it has come to represent the received view on Freud, my work is virtually unintelligible to people, and I don't like casting pearls before swine.

PLR: How would you sum up your critical view of the Gay biography?

PJS: That's the problem. How can you sum up a book that is so utterly vacuous? There's nothing positive to be said about it. It goes beyond the fact that it's littered with banalities and errors.

---

42. Peter J. Swales (1988), "Protecting Freud's Image from Sigmund." Review of *Freud: A Life for Our Times* by Peter Gay, in *Los Angeles Times Book Review*, May 8, pp. 1, 13.

328 ◆ Peter J. Swales

PLR: Can you enumerate a few specific ones?

PJS: Well, for example, that Charcot was a psychiatrist and that from Charcot Freud learned how to cure people with hypnosis. Somebody who really thinks that that is the case shouldn't be doing work in the history of psychoanalysis. Gay's former graduate student Mark Micale should have been the man to set him right on all that.

PLR: While we're on the subject, I wanted to ask you about the alleged contemporary review of *The Interpretation of Dreams* that Gay published in *Harper's*.[43] You've had the dubious honor of exposing the flaws or engineering the downfalls of some eminent people with whom you've crossed swords, Masson being the prime example.

PJS: Was he ever eminent?

PLR: He certainly had a highly visible position—what Milton in *Paradise Lost* would call a "bad eminence." I wondered about your reflections on that *Harper's* episode as well as on Gay's Freud biography.

PJS: Gay staked his authority as Sterling Professor of History at Yale on the authenticity of that document in the very manner that he published it. I think it speaks to the squalor of the bourgeoissified cultural climate we live in that in the end he was able to get away with special pleading to assert his innocence.

PLR: To claim it was a spoof, in other words?

PJS: Yes. It still boggles my mind that he could *lie* his way out of it. This is the free expression of my opinion. How he didn't lose his authority, his credibility, his accreditation is to this day mind-boggling not just to me but to my friends, of whom there are many. I have many enemies—Peter Gay being one of them—but I have many friends, and they're in total solidarity with me on that.

PLR: Specifically, what did he lie about?

PJS: Lie number one is the very publication of the document with all the scholarly apparatus that he used to embellish his claims as to its ontological status. The other lies were in terms of the way he defended himself. Possibly that's arguable, but to me what he said was internally contradictory.[44]

43. Peter Gay (1981), "Mind Reading." *Harper's Magazine*, September: 83–86.

44. Peter J. Swales (1990), "Reading Freud." Letter to the Editor, *Times Literary Supplement*, August 3–9, p. 823.

PLR: There's no doubt in your mind that he wanted the piece to be perceived as an authentic review of *The Interpretation of Dreams?*

PJS: Otherwise it wouldn't have floated. It doesn't float as a piece of literature.

PLR: Didn't it appear in a series of articles that was intended to bring forward contemporary reviews of important historical and scientific works?

PJS: That's a very important point. Subsequent to his being exposed, Gay would trade on the claim of the editor of *Harper's*, Lewis Lapham—two partners in crime—that the very name of the column, "Revisions," indicated that anything that had appeared therein was not to be taken too seriously. This claim, by the way, assumes that every person who ever read *Harper's* was a subscriber and would read every issue. That's where the contextual argument hinges—on the notion that over time you would know it. But what about the casual purchaser? In any case, the whole argument is a nonstarter because the central fact of the matter is that Henry Cohen, Frank Sulloway, and I retrieved every single article that appeared in that column, none of which, apart from Gay's, was anything less than straightforward. In fact, the rubric "Revisions" was a hallmark that vouched for its very authenticity! The very opposite of what Lapham claimed.

PLR: If you hadn't exposed the spuriousness of the review, isn't it likely that it would have passed into the public record?

PJS: It had passed into the record, and not just because I quoted it but other persons had too. What Gay doesn't tell us is that E. James Lieberman, the biographer of Otto Rank down in Washington and a lovely bloke, within a year or so of the article's publication had congratulated Gay on his great discovery. Whereupon Gay turned on him and said words to the effect, "What do you mean? Only an idiot would believe that that's anything but a joke."

PLR: That was before you had pointed it out?

PJS: Oh, yes. Years before.

PLR: In a sense, couldn't Gay point to that conversation in his own defense by saying that he had never intended it to be taken seriously?

PJS: No, because he had already been found out by a former student of his in California, David James Fisher. He had written to Gay asking for a copy of the German original, whereupon Gay wrote back in an insulting way to the effect, "What do you mean? It's obviously a

joke." At best, Gay didn't realize that serious people would be mis-
led, and that this would go into the record. That speaks for his utter
irresponsibility as a historian. At worst, he wrongly anticipated that
no one would ever see through the deception.

PLR: That could be, but don't his reactions also suggest the possibility that he had assumed that people would take it as a spoof and had
been surprised that it wasn't recognized as such?

PJS: No, it doesn't work that way. The review's authenticity had to
be believed for the article to get read in the first place. And then at
the end there's no punch line. Let me confess something to you. In
1983, I sat with Janet Malcolm over the course of five months being
interviewed for what became *In the Freud Archives*. It was intense.
I met with her for five hours every Wednesday. During the course of
conversation, I made the point—and this was apropos of Frank
Sulloway's book—that there was any amount of research still to be
done. You could go out and find all sorts of stuff, as had Frank. And
she queried it with a "Like what?" So I said something to her to the
effect of, "Well, 18 months ago, Peter Gay, a historian up at Yale, discovered this amazing review of *The Interpretation of Dreams* that
came out just nine months after the book's appearance and published
it in *Harper's Magazine*." And she said, "Oh, really?" I typically don't
read newspapers and magazines, but in 1981 the Masson business
had spilled out in *The New York Times*.

PLR: Thanks to you, in no small measure.

PJS: In 1981, I had gone to a news store and glanced through the
magazines. I would never ordinarily have looked at *Harper's*. So I
mentioned this to Janet Malcolm, and she said, "Oh, that's curious."
I said, "I'll give you a copy if you want." "Oh, would you?" I gave her
a copy a week or two later. She took one look at it and said to me,
"But, Peter, how do you know that this is real?" I said, "What? How
do you mean?" "How can you be sure it's authentic, that it's a real
discovery?" "Janet, historians don't just go making up items to publish and putting them into the record. The whole field would disin-
tegrate if that's what they did. It says here that Peter Gay is Sterling
Professor of History at Yale. I don't know anything much about him,
except that I have his book *Freud, Jews, and Other Germans*.[45] Look,
he gives the bibliographical citation: *Grazer medizinische
Vierteljahresschrift*, Bd. 18, Nummer 3, Juli 1900, Seiten 139–48."

---

45. Peter Gay (1978), *Freud, Jews, and Other Germans: Masters and Victims
in Modern Culture*. New York: Oxford University Press.

"Did you check for it?" "It's funny you ask. I did. In the Institute for the History of Medicine in Vienna. But I couldn't find it. But that doesn't mean too much when you do history. Often things just aren't *there.*" So Janet pressed me, "But then how do you know it's real?"

PLR: So she scented it from the beginning?

PJS: Wait. By then I started to take offense because I'm the most studious and scrupulous of researchers in checking out sources. Imagine the burden and the expense if Janet Malcolm had to verify every citation she'd ever looked at. Scholarship and science would grind to a halt. I thought, "I don't get it. There's something I don't understand." I could have gone to my library and put 100 articles on the table that have documentation in them. And this wasn't even a bibliographical citation of a specific fact. It was a whole item. I was bewildered and dropped the whole thing. I don't know if you want to apply a Freudian model of repression to this, but I forgot that conversation. That's why I laid out for you the context of meeting with her every Wednesday for five hours in the course of five months.

PLR: So this had come up in the course of lengthy conversations about all sorts of things?

PJS: And it was a blur. I didn't recollect anything about this. The hook that I could grab onto to retrieve the memory ultimately was the fact that I had made a copy and brought it to her. To repeat, I had got from Janet, "But how do you know it's real?" That was spring of 1983. In 1984 or 1985, I got a letter from Janet saying that her friend Peter Gay—that was news—had been commissioned to write a short biography of Freud, and she had told him about my work. He would like to get my papers. Would I kindly oblige? So I did. I sent Gay the papers. I said, "I'll leave it to you, but if you want to send me a contribution I'd appreciate it because I don't have Xerox facilities."

In 1985, I was having tea with Janet. At that time I'd pop around and chat with her every now and again. Suddenly we heard the front door open downstairs. Somebody had put a key in the lock and come in. I thought, "Oh, it's Gardiner," Janet's husband. He would come in during our talks, and she'd make him a boiled egg. Instead somebody else walked up the stairs, and Janet got really uncomfortable and embarrassed. She said, "Oh, Peter, this is Peter Gay. Let me introduce you. Do you remember?" Of course I remembered. Now that's my one real meeting with Peter Gay. I've had one or two other brief encounters.

PLR: He had a key to her place?

PJS: Yes, because he was staying as her guest. That's how close they were. But she never let on to me about that. She is the consummate journalist!

PLR: When did you expose the *Harper's* piece?

PJS: Four years later.

PLR: In 1989?

PJS: Yes. So Peter Gay came in, sat at the table, and started asking me questions about Freud and Fliess. But, as he was asking me these questions, I thought, "He's not interested in listening to the answer. He thinks he knows it all already. This is a formality he's going through. Well, that's all right. I don't care." Now, fast forward four years to the controversy.

PLR: Where did you publish your exposé?

PJS: It didn't work like that. I was writing to him reqesting the German original of the review he had discovered, but he wouldn't answer. Rosemarie Sand, in the end, just by virtue of who she is, made him come clean and confess. He couldn't obfuscate any longer. I guess that he knew that Rosemarie is very close with Adolf Grünbaum. Rosemarie is one of my closest friends, in a manner of speaking. Significantly, Rosemarie worked for the embryonic CIA, smuggling rocket scientists out of Germany for the Americans. Espionage is my speciality too, so Rosemarie and I understand each other very well. Rosemarie took up the cudgels to write to Gay and got the letter of confession: "I must confess to you, although there is nothing to confess, that the whole thing was a hoax." Later I learned, through an intermediary, that Han Israëls, then a Gay-groupie, was saying that I had known all along that the document was a fake and had conceived in a very Machiavellian way a whole conspiracy to damage him.

PLR: Obviously, your conversation with Janet Malcolm shows that you didn't.

PJS: But here's the point. I thought, "What's the kernel of truth in this paranoia?"[46] What Israëls was saying was so wacky that I began to take it seriously. By then the whole thing had been unfolding for about six months. I suddenly went into a kind of altered state because I had pressing in my mind this recollection of having given Janet a Xerox copy of the review. I had to plunge back into the depths of my mind to dredge up what the circumstances were. The whole scenario

46. See Freud, *The Psychopathology of Everyday Life. Standard Edition*, 6:255–256.

then came back to me, and I could reconstruct what had happened with virtually 100% accuracy. As I said to you, I'd come back from Europe and Masson's name was all over the place. "That's right [snaps his fingers], I went into that bookstore," and it all swam back into my memory. Then I realized that Janet had had the better knowledge that it was a fake, but she didn't dare tell me. She was torn between the two Peters in her life. She didn't want to be disloyal to him, and yet, almost against the grain, she really liked me so much.

PLR: That comes through in her profile.

PJS: I'm happy you say that because that tells me you're a beatnik and not a bourgeois.

PLR: It's clear that she admires you greatly.

PJS: Go and tell that to some of the people who have read that book. Even Fred Crews thinks that Janet Malcolm is trying to make a fool of me. It's true and it's not true. She speaks out of both sides of her mouth. She's a consummate journalist. In the end, she alone is going to come out smelling better than roses.

PLR: So her only reason for questioning the authenticity of this document was that she knew from Peter Gay that it was not genuine.

PJS: That should by now be obvious. But I never brought it up with her. I think she's closer with Gay's wife than she is with him, but, whatever the case, she has a long-standing relationship with him. On the other hand, my relationship with her is totally spontaneous and against the grain. She's actually a bourgeoise/journalist/housewife/mother, but there's something beatnik about me and Julia that she admires.

PLR: I think she respects your intellect and your imagination.

PJS: I don't consider myself foremost a writer. Writing to me is only a means to the end of expressing what I feel a need to say and put into print. But I'll grant that I'm actually a very good and an unusual writer because I'm writing in an 18th- or a 19th-century classical style, not a modern style at all. Janet, like P. L. Travers, could see the truth of that. She first called me up on New Year's Day 1983 because she was impressed by my writing. She said, "Where did you ever learn to write like that? I've just read your paper, and I can't believe it." She had got it, and many of my polemical letters about Masson, out of Kurt Eissler's files, of course with his permission.

PLR: "Freud, Minna Bernays, and the Conquest of Rome?"

PJS: Yes. In manuscript. She called me with that excitement, and I appreciated that. The standard I uphold in anything I write—and judge me as deluded as you want—is education. I've never put into print a word I'd retract. It's lucid, it's honest, and its deeply considered. It's very judicious.

PLR: Janet Malcolm pays you a great compliment on your paper about Minna Bernays. She says it is "immensely satisfying as a piece of intellectual work; there are no loose ends, all the pieces fit."[47]

PJS: That it's virtually irrefutable, but . . .

PLR: I wanted to ask you about the "but." She goes on: "If Freud had had the misfortune to fall in love with his wife's sister, *and* to make her pregnant, *and* to have to get her an abortion, is it probable, psychologically speaking, that he would have sat down a few months later and cheerfully worked these miserable and sordid events into his clever and lighthearted Aliquis analysis." How do you answer her argument about the psychological improbability of Freud's having gone public about something so deeply compromising, if in fact it happened at all?

PJS: This is Kant vis-à-vis David Hume. It's a flight into a priori constructions in reaction to skeptical empiricism. What does she know about psychology? What does any shrink in this city know about psychology? They don't understand this man Freud. No inference that derives from his presumptive character—from the received wisdom, that is—is ultimately tenable in discussing Freud. I'm very careful never to proceed inductively. It's provable that Freud lied—once, twice, three, four, five, six times. But I never use that as an instrument for an argument. It's a permissible conclusion of an argument that he has lied, but just because he lied six times or 20 times or 100 times, that doesn't prove that he lied the 101st time. This is why in courts of law somebody's past record is not admissible into evidence when guilt or innocence is adjudicated—it comes only into the sentencing phase in the event of a conviction. On the other hand, the obverse of that is the circular appeal to Freud's integrity that we find in Ernest Jones and so many others, which is then invoked to vouch for everything he has to say.

PLR: Malcolm doesn't appeal to integrity but to plausibility. Why would Freud have published the analysis?

PJS: We're getting to issues of character. My response to that is that

---

47. Malcolm, *In the Freud Archives*, p. 124.

Freud is not your typical or usual character. How could he be? He's the man who invented psychoanalysis. What we have here is a Nietzsche *redivivus*. Freud is at that moment, within a week of Nietzsche's death, on August 25, 1900, reinventing himself as Nietzsche. And he is an "aristocratic radical," in Georg Brandes's construction of Nietzsche's philosophy. Why does Freud say to Putnam in 1915, "I stand for an infinitely freer sexual life, though I myself have made very little use of it. Only inasmuch as I felt myself entitled to define the limits of what is permissible in this area"?[48]

PLR: That's very profound.

PJS: This is what *"In Statu Nascendi"* is all about. That paper is Part 2 of my analysis of *"aliquis"*, written 18 years later. I spent three or four months last spring writing this. It's a greatly expanded version of a talk I gave at Payne Whitney informed not only by further research work of my own but also by critical research work by Anthony Stadlen and Richard Skues, who has found the smoking gun. It proves that Mr. Aliquis can be none other than Freud himself.

PLR: What is the smoking gun?

PJS: In the middle of my original paper from the summer of 1982, "Freud, Minna Bernays, and the Conquest of Rome," I throw out a speculation. Let me say in a general way that some people's speculations are worth more than those of others.

PLR: If they know where to prospect.

PJS: You've got it. It depends on how much they know. I mention that the blood-miracle of St. Januarius in Naples was scheduled to liquify on September 19, as it does every year. But I'm addressing the question of why Freud has the miracle in his head at this time. Why? It's the one association I can't explain in this paper. I say [reads]: "We must wonder, then, if Freud happened to read about the famous Roman Catholic blood-miracle around this time, perhaps in a newspaper, causing him spontaneously to associate it with the symbolically congruous matter of menstruation."[49] And Richard Skues has come up with the very item I predicted might exist—a book review by Georg Brandes in the *Neue freie Presse*, September 23, 1900. All about the blood of St. Januarius with its liquefaction mentioned right there in the text.

---

48. Ernst L. Freud, ed. (1960), *The Letters of Sigmund Freud*, trans. Tania & James Stern. New York: Basic Books, p. 308 (translation modified).

49. Swales, "Freud, Minna Bernays, and the Conquest of Rome," p. 12.

PLR: That's marvelous.

PJS: So that is the smoking gun. Everything hinges on that. The whole *"aliquis"* analysis starts from the end. You begin with the fact that Freud reads this in the paper, and then you can see that the associations actually go backward. They're a post hoc reconstruction. Now, apropos of your Janet Malcolm point, I would say that Janet in all good faith was under the influence of the received wisdom, à la Peter Gay and others, although he hadn't published his biography yet. As far as I'm concerned, that establishment view of Freud is a form of dogmatism. All persons such as I are depicted by the opposition as Freud-bashers.

PLR: Frederick Crews proclaims his own identity as a Freud-basher in the afterword to *The Memory Wars*.[50]

PJS: But in a facetious way.

PLR: I think he means it. You're in a different category.

PJS: I'm a non-Freudian. The so-called Freud-bashers are, after all, only the counterpart of Freud-launderers.

PLR: Exactly. Or Freudolators. Unlike Crews, I hope you and I would agree that we want to escape that double bind. As you've written, "The image of Freud as disinterested investigator and a man of sterling integrity served the function of authenticating and legitimizing the whole psychoanalytic enterprise, not only scientifically but also ethically."[51] I think that's a very important observation and that people such as I, who still work within a psychoanalytic framework, need to take into account all the instances of distortion or what I would call fiction-making in Freud's work. These range from his concealment of his identity as the subject of "Screen Memories" or the *"aliquis"* parapraxis to more serious deceptions such as his misdating of the cocaine paper and the illness of his daughter Mathilde in the Irma dream, which, as Robert Wilcocks has argued, impugn his scientific integrity.[52]

PJS: No, that's completely outrageous. He's doing Freud a great injustice about the Mathilde business.

50. Frederick Crews (1995), *The Memory Wars: Freud's Legacy in Dispute*. New York: New York Review of Books.

51. Peter J. Swales (1997), "Freud, Filthy Lucre, and Undue Influence." *Review of Existential Psychology and Psychiatry*, 23:130.

52. Robert Wilcocks (1994), *Maelzel's Chess Player: Sigmund Freud and the Rhetoric of Deceit*. Lanham, MD: Rowman & Littlefield, pp. 227–280.

PLR: I thought Wilcocks had shown that, whereas Freud asserts that Mathilde's diphtheria occurred two years before the Irma dream took place, it actually occurred not in 1893 but in 1897, that is, two years *after* the dream but two years before he wrote it up. Are you saying that Wilcocks makes a mistake in this case?

PJS: It's worse than a mistake because I gave him an opportunity to correct his own lapsus. It really upsets me. If you're going to be a Freud-basher, at least do it impeccably. You don't take cheap hits. Wilcocks wrote to me about precisely that before his book was published. Freud writes in the Irma dream apropos of what he saw in her throat [reads]: "The white patch reminded me of diphtheritis and so of Irma's friend, but also of a serious illness of my eldest daughter's almost two years earlier and of the fright I had had in those anxious days."[53] For a start, he doesn't actually say that his daughter had diphtheritis, only "a serious illness." We're in July 1895. What's almost two years earlier?

PLR: August–September 1893.

PJS: You've got it. So we go back to August–September 1893 and look at the Fliess correspondence. Wilcocks is seriously mistaken in supposing that these letters are a complete record of Freud's correspondence with Fliess. You've only got to study the book to realize there are chunks missing. For example, September 1894 through Christmas 1894. Where are those letters? They're gone, assuming Freud and Fliess were in correspondence. When Fliess was in Vienna, they didn't correspond. Also, the Masson-Schröter edition is very deficient.

PLR: What are the specific problems with their edition?

PJS: One is that, unlike the McGuire edition of the Jung letters, you don't learn when Fliess and Freud meet. You've got to know that because there are allusions to recent conversations that otherwise seem like non sequiturs. And to be able to piece together their meetings, you have to be able to do research on Fliess's life and be a bit of an archeologist—for example, looking at cure lists at various spas where you find that Freud and Fliess were present at the same time. Now, it's obvious contextually that there was a meeting between Freud and Fliess in early September of 1893 in Reichenau. It goes undocumented, although you can see from the antecedents that they're hoping to meet. Fliess visited Vienna and Reichenau *circa* late August–early September 1893. That can be established. There's no letter until September 14, then there's a letter on September 29.

---

53. Freud, *The Interpretation of Dreams. Standard Edition*, 4:111.

In that letter, Freud mentions—to rely here on Masson's abominable translation—that "shortly after our epidemic of throat infections, there were several light cases of scarlet fever in Reichenau."[54] It's obvious that something has happened, and it's only an accident of fate that we don't have full documentation about it because it was spoken and not written. With throat infections in those days, the first thing a father and mother were going to worry about is diphtheria. I am actually named, by the way, after my father's younger brother Peter, who died at age 14 or 15 from diphtheria. So I know all about diphtheria and the misery it wreaked across Europe.

PLR: So the fact that Mathilde suffered from diphtheria in 1897, which is what Wilcocks seizes on, is irrelevant to the Irma dream.

PJS: It's neither here nor there. Freud is talking about an epidemic of throat infections and scarlet fever in 1893. The two are medically related. He *feared* she had contracted diphtheria.

PLR: That information is very helpful to me because I had accepted Wilcocks's argument as establishing an example of deception on Freud's part that goes beyond his disguised use of his personal experience in various writings.

PJS: When Freud reports information in his case histories and his dream analyses, he is on the whole not inaccurate. I don't know of many fabrications in Freud.

PLR: What are those you know about?

PJS: This paper I've just written, "The Piece of News That Never Was," alleges that Freud fabricated the story in his Signorelli interpretation that one of his male patients committed suicide on account of an incurable sexual disorder in summer of 1898.[55] I have my reasons for exploding that claim as a pure fabrication, just as the claim that he had run into some fellow, Mr. Aliquis as I call him, is a fabrication. Both are in *The Psychopathology of Everyday Life.* But generally Freud was not a fabricator. His sins are more at the hermeneutic level.

---

54. Masson, ed., *Freud–Fliess Letters*, p. 56.

55. See Freud, "The Psychical Mechanism of Forgetfulness" (*Standard Edition*, 3:294), where he states that his forgetting of "Signorelli" occurred after he "had received a certain piece of news" but does not specify what it was; and *The Psychopathology of Everyday Life*, where he reports that it concerned a patient who "had put an end to his life on account of an incurable sexual disorder" (*Standard Edition*, 6:3).

PLR: If we want to assess Freud's ethical conduct, I think it's important to differentiate between autobiographical fictions and outright lies, such as I thought he had perpetrated in the case of the Irma dream, where his statement about Mathilde's illness follows immediately after the reference to the first cocaine paper, which he misdated by a year.[56] That is clearly an effort to cover his tracks after having advocated that cocaine be administered by subcutaneous injections and the ensuing death of Fleischl.

PJS: That's the worst lie.

PLR: Absolutely. The misdating of Mathilde's illness struck me as the capstone of that type of indictment. It's helpful to know that that is not the case, because in my own thinking I would place the use of his own experience in disguised or fictional form, where in a sense he's protecting his own confidentiality as one might permit an analyst to do with any patient, in a different category from more serious ethical breaches such as his attempted burial of the paper where he recommends subcutaneous injections of cocaine.

PJS: Get ready for Ilse Grubrich-Simitis's attempt to whitewash the Fleischl business. In her book *Back to Freud's Texts*, where she so agitatedly opposes the historicization of psychoanalysis, she wants us to go back to the *Gesammelte Werke* and read them as one might have read the Ten Commandments on Moses' tablets.[57] But you can't understand what Freud is saying unless you have enough contextual history. In a more recent essay on *Studies on Hysteria*, she bends over backward in a consummate *arc de cercle* not to cite any of the follow-up research, beginning with Ellenberger, who discovered the original case history of Anna O. and showed how discrepant it was with the published version, through to Hirschmüller and Swales.[58]

---

56. In *The Interpretation of Dreams* Freud wrote that he "had been the first to recommend the use of cocaine, in 1885" (*Standard Edition*, 4:111). In a footnote, James Strachey points out that the paper in question, "On Cocaine," was actually published in 1884, but he dismisses this inaccuracy as a "misprint."

57. Ilse Grubrich-Simitis (1996), *Back to Freud's Texts: Making Silent Documents Speak*, trans. Philip Slotkin. New Haven, CT: Yale University Press, pp. 8–10.

58. Ilse Grubrich-Simitis (1997), *Early Freud and Late Freud: Reading Anew "Studies on Hysteria" and "Moses and Monotheism."* London: Routledge, pp. 15–52. For the revisionist scholarship, see Henri F. Ellenberger (1972), "The Story of Anna O.: A Critical Review with New Data," *Journal of the*

PLR: We can dismiss that as Freudolatry. Would you say that the refusal to acknowledge that Anna O. wasn't cured is a further example of deception on Freud's part?

PJS: Freud and Breuer's book of 1895, whether they like it or not, gives us a historical panorama of turn-of-the century Vienna. It's located in time and place with real people. So if scholars illuminate the milieu in which *Studies on Hysteria* had its genesis, it's got to be relevant to a centennial evaluation. But not for Grubrich-Simitis, because history for her means the relativization of Freud's putatively universal truths.

PLR: I find it curious that Wilcocks didn't want to profit from your ability to rectify his mistake; I thought his book was lively and witty and I learned a lot from it.

PJS: That obstinacy was really egregious. He wrote me on this very matter of the Mathilde business, and I tried to set him right. But he didn't want to hear it and was ready to build interpretation after interpretation to salvage what was the linchpin of his book. Corresponding with him became acrimonious because he wouldn't address the points it took me three minutes to lay out for you. Give Freud the benefit of the doubt! It's the principle of charity. There's very powerful historical material documenting that Freud had serious ground for worry about his daughter two years before the Irma dream.

PLR: So that is exploded. The larger point is the degree to which the image of Freud "as disinterested investigator and a man of sterling integrity" underpins the psychoanalytic enterprise. I share your insistence that we have to be fair to Freud and even extend the principle of charity if possible, but also to take full account of the various distortions in his work.

PJS: Absolutely. But that's not in *Freud's* interest; that's in the interest of scholarship and honesty in the discourse. If we're going to impeach Freud, let's do it without getting dirt on our hands. Just six months ago I had occasion to be very depressed by a friend of mine who had written something about Freud informed by work of mine that I had cause to take great objection to. We know that in the end

---

History of the Behavioral Sciences, 8:267–279; Albrecht Hirschmüller (1978), *The Life and Work of Josef Breuer: Physiology and Psychoanalysis*. New York: New York University Press, 1989; and, most recently, Mikkel Borch-Jacobsen (1996), *Remembering Anna O.: A Century of Mystification*, trans. Kirby Olson. New York: Routledge.

Freud lobbied for his professorship. This person I'm talking about considers this to be evidence of Freud's sleaze and that he had gotten his professorship dishonestly. Wait a minute! Freud, just for his work on infantile paralysis that he delivered to Nothnagel, deserved that professorship there and then. Furthermore, I personally don't doubt Freud's allegations that he was being denied a professorship on account of anti-Semitism, though that claim is not easy to document. Now, if I were in that position and somebody were discriminating against me just because I'm Welsh or not Roman Catholic or not Jewish, I would consider it legitimate to lobby behind the scenes. It's what any of us would do. We'd seek a counterinfluence. I would never hold something like that against him.

PLR: He had his goldfish to help him out.

PJS: Yes, he had his goldfish.[59] She's the one who did the work. But good luck to him on that! I don't hold that against him, except perhaps insofar as he had to exploit a patient.

PLR: I think that assessment shows an attempt to be balanced and fairminded in your own work that speaks very well of you.

PJS: I don't set out to be "balanced." My objective is to follow the facts wherever they may lead. My pledge as of 25 years ago has been to tell it as it really was to the best of my ability. But fairness is very important to me. I don't play chess or Monopoly wanting to win by cheating. The game wouldn't be worth the candle. It's not a game any more if you're going to cheat to win. You have to be utterly scrupulous.

PLR: You've said that as a physician Freud "inadvertently caused the death of at least one, and maybe more, of his patients."[60] How many such cases were there?

PJS: That's a problematic question because I know about things that aren't in the public domain. For example, Oscar Rie's brother Kurt committed suicide while in treatment with Freud about 1904. Norbert, Rie's nephew and the brother of Marianne Kris and

---

59. Freud referred to Baroness Marie Ferstel, a wealthy patient whose donation of a painting to a gallery controlled by the Minister of Education clinched his appointment to a professorship, by this unflattering epithet. See letters of September 27, 1899 and March 11, 1902 in Masson, ed., *Freud–Fliess Letters*, pp. 375, 456; and Swales, "Freud, Filthy Lucre, and Undue Influence."

60. Peter J. Swales (1982), "Freud, Fliess, and Fratricide: The Role of Fliess in Freud's Conception of Paranoia." In *Sigmund Freud: Critical Assessments*, Vol. 1, ed. Laurence Spurling. London: Routledge, 1989, p. 323.

Margarethe Nunberg, implied that there was some kind of connection there.

PLR: An early version of the Tausk episode?[61]

PJS: I don't know the circumstances well enough. Freud did have to deal with a few suicides. The most interesting one is Eduard Silberstein's first wife. Do you know how Freud came to live in Berggasse 19?

PLR: No, I don't.

PJS: This is purely interpretive. It's not the facts of history, but the way they speak to me. A few months earlier Silberstein's wife had come floating out the window two or three stories above Freud's office in the House of Atonement, the Sühnehaus. Do you think the neighbors liked having a neurologist whose patients did that sort of thing? You'll find a very sanitized version of the story in Walter Boehlich's introduction to the Silberstein letters, but the facts are a lot more sinister than he allows.[62] There's a history of suicide in Freud's practice.

PLR: I was also thinking of instances of misdiagnosis, patients who died as a result of some medical error on Freud's part.

PJS: That's a different story. I think that we misunderstand Freud and Breuer's notions about hysteria. In a way, hysteria is a completely superfluous category. Freud wasn't endeavoring to treat real illness in the medical sense.

PLR: But when he didn't recognize real illness for what it was and called it hysteria, that oversight could have fatal consequences. That's the thesis of Richard Webster's book. He emphasizes the lack of a medical basis for the diagnosis of hysteria and cites the case of an adolescent girl with appendicitis who died as a result.[63] Is that one of the examples you had in mind?

PJS: A protocase of a patient for whose death Freud considered himself culpable, which appears in the Irma dream, is Mathilde

---

61. On Freud's role in the 1919 suicide of his follower Viktor Tausk, see Paul Roazen (1969), *Brother Animal: The Story of Freud and Tausk*. New York: Knopf.

62. *The Letters of Sigmund Freud to Eduard Silberstein, 1871–1881* (1990), ed. Walter Boehlich, trans. Arnold J. Pomerans. Cambridge, MA: Harvard University Press, pp. xiv–xv.

63. Richard Webster (1995), *Why Freud Was Wrong: Sin, Science, and Psychoanalysis*. New York: Basic Books, pp. 142–143.

Schleicher, for whom he overprescribed sulphonal. Hirschmüller's done the scholarship on that.[64]

PLR: That case is linked to Fleischl, who died as a result of Freud's recommending the injection of cocaine.

PJS: That needs to be set in a broader context. Even Breuer was reckless in prescribing morphine, as was Fliess with cocaine.

PLR: Anna O.'s addiction to morphine is never mentioned in the published case history.

PJS: Nor chloral hydrate. What you've got is a predominantly male medical establishment whose clientele was utterly submissive. They believed that these physicians knew what they were talking about and that everything was scientific and exact. But sometimes things went drastically wrong. It happened to Fliess, Breuer, and Freud. Probably every doctor, even in this day and age, fears malpractice suits because accidents and blunders are part of everyday life. Unfortunately, it only needs a Masson to come along and put the worst construction on such mishaps. Believe me, Fliess is nutty, but you can't doubt his good faith, whereas Masson would paint him as a sadist, as if he were being malicious.[65] The same with Freud. I don't think Freud wanted to kill off Mathilde Schleicher or the adolescent woman.

PLR: Or even poor Fleischl.

PJS: Though I think there was something quasihomosexual about the Fleischl business.

PLR: Do you think Freud wanted to kill off Fliess?

PJS: I've been accused of alleging that Freud had a plot to kill Fliess. That's not what I say. I document, first, that Fliess believed that. Second, I can grant, giving Fliess some benefit of the doubt here, that Freud could have had fantasies about that.

PLR: The kernel of truth in Fliess's paranoia?

PJS: Absolutely. I also think Freud had some fantasies about killing off his wife! But that's a different story.

---

64. Albrecht Hirschmüller, ed. (1990), Sigmund Freud, *Casi clinici 9: Mathilde/Nina R., 1889–1893*. Torino: Boringhieri.

65. J. Moussaieff Masson & T. C. Masson (1978), "Buried Memories on the Acropolis: Freud's Response to Mysticism and Anti-Semitism." *International Journal of Psycho-Analysis*, 59:199–208.

PLR: So there's no clear distinction between males and females in that regard?

PJS: The drug victims you mean?

PLR: You said there was a homosexual dimension to Freud's feelings for Fleischl. But he could have had a similar fusion of erotic and aggressive impulses with regard to women.

PJS: Fleischl is a special case because of his relation to Freud. Freud wanted to emulate Fleischl. Fleischl was everything that Freud wasn't. He was of the German-Jewish nobility—Fleischl von Marxow. Freud had the fantasy of sharing Martha with him.[66]

PLR: I think we should bring this conversation to a close. Are there any concluding reflections you'd like to share on everything we've discussed, which in some ways only scratches the surface [PJS laughs] of the subject of Freud and psychoanalysis? It seems to me that your work makes two major contributions. The first is to historical scholarship by identifying and contextualizing Freud's patients and his milieu in such a way that we can never read his early work in the same way again.

PJS: Much more than you know, because I've only published 10% of it.

PLR: Second, you've presented a vision of Freud involving interpretations and conclusions that reflect your skepticism about the notions of the unconscious and repression.

PJS: It is true that certain things are axiomatic to the way I look at Freud, but they belong to common psychology. For example, you will hardly find the word "vanity" in the *Standard Edition*. It's got no currency or value in psychoanalysis.

PLR: You could call it narcissism.

PJS: To me they're totally different. Narcissism loses the bibical sense of *omnia vanitas*. Vanity is not just narcissistic; it's also empty within.

PLR: The same could be said of narcissism.

PJS: This goes back to what we discussed hours ago about presumptions to knowledge. It's true that I regard Freud as a man of boundless ambition. My view is completely ulterior to Jones's view of Freud. Jones denies that Freud was ambitious, apart from his desire to travel or collect antiquities. It took Erich Fromm, whom I

---

66. Swales, "Freud, Martha Bernays, and the Language of Flowers," p. 48.

regard as one of the more profound psychoanalysts, to restore the balance in *Sigmund Freud's Mission*, which is a virtual rejoinder to Ernest Jones's biography.[67] How can you deny that Freud was ambitious?

PLR: This, again, is Webster's thesis.

PJS: Fromm is very perceptive about Freud's marriage and relations to women. I could read 50 psychoanalytic books and find nothing in them, but *Sigmund Freud's Mission* is a lovely little book. It was also evident to Thomas Szasz that Freud was a man of maniacal ambition.[68] The same is true of Ernest Becker, whose *The Denial of Death* also influenced me quite a lot when I read it in 1975.[69] That book was very important in helping me see that aspect of Freud.

PLR: He was one of the first to bring out the importance of Rank.

PJS: Absolutely. Rank merits a lot of interest, as do Ferenczi and others. I only wish somebody would tell us more about Stekel. He's my favorite. Mad! It's a first principle for me that Freud was a man of boundless ambition. By extension, he was a man of incredible vanity. He was very sophisticated in his ways of masking that and being humble, but that's Machiavellian and a posture. He was self-obsessed!

PLR: He wanted to live out the myth of the hero.

PJS: Absolutely. He was so precious unto himself that every moment of his life had to go down in history. It's an amazing thing about history that with *Sartor Resartus* Thomas Carlyle wrote Freud's biography 150 years before Ernest Jones got around to doing it,[70] before Freud was even born, in the person of Professor Diogenes Teufelsdröckh—devil's shit!

PLR: And you had already formulated your understanding of Freud before you ever heard of him.

PJS: Yes, Carlyle and I are two of a kind. I love Thomas Carlyle.

PLR: Let it be said.

PJS: *Satis. Sufficit.*

---

67. Erich Fromm (1959), *Sigmund Freud's Mission: An Analysis of His Personality and Influence*. New York: Harper Brothers.

68. Thomas Szasz (1976), *Karl Kraus and the Soul-Doctors: A Pioneer Critic and His Criticism of Psychiatry and Psychoanalysis*. Baton Rouge: Louisiana State University Press, p. 58.

69. Ernest Becker (1973), *The Denial of Death*. New York: Free Press.

70. Thomas Carlyle (1836), *Sartor Resartus*. London: Dent, 1975.

Index

Transference; Unconscious;
Winnicott, D. W.
Freud, Sophie, 318
Frink, Horace, 113
Fromm, Erich, 104, 108, 344–345
Fromm–Reichmann, Frieda, 112
Frost, Robert, 303

G

Galles, Joffre de (Peter J. Swales),
325
Gattel, Felix, 206
Gay, Peter, 327–332, 336
Gegenbauer, Karl, 312
Gender identification, 84, 88,
98–99, 245–246, 256–258,
266–269, 272
see also Vagina
*General Introduction to
Psychoanalysis* (Freud), 211
Ghent, Emmanuel, 247–248, 251
Gillespie, William, 36
Gilligan, Carol, 267n
Glover, Edward, 65
Goethe, Johann Wolfgang von, 128,
196–198, 311–313, 320
Goldberg, Susan, 225n
Goldfarb, William, 28
Goldner, Virginia, 258n
Gomelski, Giorgio, 290, 295
Goodheart, Eugene, 100n
Gorer, Geoffrey, 4n
Gould, Stephen Jay, 136, 178
Greenberg, Jay R., 110n, 116–117n
Grillparzer, Franz, 112
Groddeck, Georg, 300n
Grosskurth, Phyllis, 137
Group therapy, 306
Grubrich–Simitis, Ilse, 316, 319,
339n–340
Grünbaum, Adolf, 181n–182, 311n,
332
Guntrip, Harry, 54, 70, 260n
Gurdjiev, George Ivanovich, 288,
296, 298–299, 301–307
see also Unconscious

H

Habermas, Jürgen, 128, 270
Haeckel, Ernst, 139n, 147, 150,
198, 205, 227, 310–314
Hamilton, William, 141n
Harlow, Harry, 40, 86
Harries, Karsten, 102
Harris, Adrienne, 250, 258n
Harris, Armstrong, 74, 76
Hartmann, Heinz, 223n, 225
Harvard University, 99, 138, 140, 180
Hegel, G. W. F., 205, 237, 253, 255,
257n–260, 268, 270, 312
Heidegger, Martin, 271–272n
Heine, Heinrich, 311
Helmholtz, Hermann von, 39, 195,
313
Hermeneutics, 115, 117, 121, 126,
133, 171, 184–186, 189, 191,
199, 225–226, 309, 312, 314, 338
Herzl, Theodor, 319
Hirschmüller, Albrecht, 317–318,
325, 339–340n, 343
Hitler, Adolf, 64, 241, 278, 309
Hoffer, Hedwig, 73
Holmes, Jeremy, 27n
Holocaust, 123, 265
Holt, Robert R., 28n, 104
Holzman, Philip, 180
Home, H. J., 74n–76
Homosexuality, 79, 84, 160, 178,
206, 239, 245, 252, 344
Horney, Karen, 245
Hume, David, 334
Hunter, Virginia, xi$n$
Huxley, Julian, 40
Hypothesis testing, scientific
model of, 36–37, 93, 96,
144–145, 171, 175, 181,
184–186, 188–193, 198
Hysteria, 172, 342

I

Identity:
critique of, 247, 264–272, 288
politics, 253–254